Strategic Communication in Business and the Professions

Strategic Communication in Business and the Professions

DAN O'HAIR
Texas Tech University

GUSTAV W. FRIEDRICH
University of Oklahoma

HOUGHTON MIFFLIN COMPANY ❑ *Boston*

Toronto ❑ *Dallas* ❑ *Geneva, Illinois* ❑ *Palo Alto* ❑ *Princeton*

Sponsoring Editor: Margaret Seawell
Associate Project Editor: Susan Yanchus
Design Coordinator: Martha Drury
Production Coordinator: Frances Sharperson
Manufacturing Coordinator: Sharon Pearson
Marketing Manager: Karen Natale

Text and photo credits begin on page A-32

Printed in the U.S.A.

Library of Congress Catalog Number: 91-71969

ISBN 0-395-5139-4

ABCDEFGHIJ-D-987654321

Contents

Part 1   *An Introduction to Communication in Organizations*   *1*

Preface

*B*usiness and professional communication presents unique challenges to employees in an era of increasing competition, diversity in the work force, and technology-mediated communication. With these factors in mind, we set out to write a book that would be comprehensive enough to include all the basic communication contexts students will face after graduation but at the same time present material in a way that captures the dynamics of the contemporary work environment.

Our task presented us with a paradox: how can we discuss contemporary communication issues without limiting our relevance to the future needs of students? The solution was not long in coming. To maintain its relevance and vitality, the book must incorporate a framework that gives structure to the study of all communication contexts and that withstands the test of time by its ability to adapt to innovation.

The strategic approach introduced in this book ensures that the essential elements and skills in any communication setting can be easily understood, remembered, and used by students. By recognizing basic similarities in all forms of communication, the text aids students in applying their skills to any communication situation they encounter.

The Model of Strategic Communication

The model of strategic communication comprises four dimensions that are essential to effective communication. *Goal setting*, the first dimension, is frequently overlooked by communicators except in situations they believe to be of exceptional importance; yet, as this text argues, any communication has a greater chance of succeeding when the participants identify clear and specific objectives.

Situational knowledge, the second dimension of strategic communication, stresses the importance of knowing beforehand the context and audience of the communication. This knowledge allows communicators to anticipate and prepare for successful interaction.

Strategic communication also includes *communication competence* — learning and implementing effective and appropriate communication skills. Skills are at the heart of strategic communication, and the student can build a strong understanding of both how and why they should be used in the many discussion questions and activities provided throughout the text.

The fourth dimension of strategic communication is *anxiety management*. Inevitably, despite thorough preparation and skill development, communication situations have the power to evoke anxiety, although not all forms of communication elicit the same type or level of anxiety in all communicators. Therefore, we introduce possible causes of and resources for handling anxiety in each of the communication contexts covered in the text.

Plan of the Book

Strategic Communication is divided into five parts. Part 1 introduces the major issues of business and professional communication — organizational and communication theory, strategic communication, and management theory — while emphasizing that successful communication depends on the commitment to shared meaning between communicators. Part 2 focuses on basic communication skills — listening, verbal, and nonverbal skills — stressing the importance of encoding, decoding, and interacting. Part 3 begins our exploration of communication contexts with three chapters on the basics of interpersonal, or one-to-one, communication. Part 4 shows the changes and adaptations that occur in a group communication context, the specific challenges of problem-solving meetings, and methods of negotiation and conflict management. Finally, Part 5 presents a thorough examination of presentational speaking, including basic principles, specific advice for informative and persuasive presentations, and a discussion of special presentational formats, such as televised speaking. The Appendix addresses the emerging communication issues raised by diversity in the workplace and provides the reader with a basis for thinking about how cultural differences affect business communication.

Special Features

We believe that the increasing demands of the workplace reinforce the role of communication skills as the foundation of successful professional development. Therefore, each chapter includes numerous activities and discussion questions that can be done either alone or in a group. Self-checks and evaluations throughout the text (whose "write-on" format encourages the reader to complete them) help students to identify their own skill levels in order to improve. In addition, many chapters contain a special "Interact!" feature that introduces a communication problem or simulates a communication event for readers to analyze and work through.

Concepts are explained in a variety of ways. Contemporary and relevant examples add interest and draw connections to the real world. "Focus on Corporate Communication" features in many chapters show the application of concepts to actual companies and organizations. And learning objectives and chapter summaries help the reader to identify and focus on the important topics in each chapter. The book provides thorough coverage of the emerging key topics in business communication: presentational speaking, critical thinking, listening, and conflict management.

Supplementary Materials

The Instructor's Resource Manual, written by Kelly McNeilis, a teaching assistant at The Ohio State University, provides a range of teaching aids and activities unequaled in the field of business communication. We hope that both experienced and beginning instructors will find the manual a useful tool and source of ideas for their courses. The manual includes test questions for every chapter as well.

A set of transparencies corresponding to illustrations in the text aids instructors in their lectures. A video demonstrating a variety of communication skills and settings is also available.

Acknowledgments

The end of a project brings a realization of the effort and support from so many people necessary to reach that point. The scope and depth of this book comes in part from our colleagues who reviewed the work in progress and who provided insight, criticism, suggestions, and enthusiasm. We would like to thank Ruth D. Anderson, North Carolina State University; Pat Brett of Emory University School of Business Administration; C. William Colburn, University of Michigan Alumni Center; J. Daniel Joyce, Houston Community College; Harold J. Kinzer, University of Utah; William G. Kirkwood, East Tennessee State University; Douglas J. Pederson, Pennsylvania State University; Tony J. Rodriguez, Sr., Cerritos College; Robert A. Stewart, Texas Tech University; and Sally Webb, University of Wisconsin.

In addition, we would like to acknowledge the enormous contribution of Karl Krayer, Training Specialist, Dr. Pepper/Seven Up Company, who provided a "real-world" perspective on the manuscript and contributed many of the activities presented in the chapters. We are also indebted to William H. "Skip" Boyer of Best Western International, Robbie Neely of Pacific Bell, Adrian Rhodes of the United Negro College Fund, Debbie Morgan of Warner-Lambert, Kevin O'Connor of Hewlett-Packard, Maureen Martin of Ben & Jerry's, and Bud Good of the American Red Cross for their help in preparing the organizational profiles included in the book.

Of course, the writing of a book like this cannot occur without family support. Long hours of sitting in front of a computer screen or chasing down material at the library sometimes replaced family opportunities. Mary John, Rena, Erica, Bruce, and Jonathon were more than generous in allowing us the extra time to share our ideas on strategic communication. This book is dedicated to them.

D. O.
G. W. F.

An Introduction to Communication in Organizations

Part 1 provides an overview of communication in business and professional settings. It explains the role of communication in achieving organizational goals and the challenges posed by the new communication technology, the diversification of the work force, and the globalization of the marketplace.

❑ Chapter 1 covers the basic communication process and major theories in organizational communication.

❑ Chapter 2 introduces the model of strategic communication — a four-part process of setting goals, gathering situational knowledge, building communication competence, and managing anxiety.

❑ Chapter 3 reviews basic management theory and provides an approach to developing leadership skills.

Communication in Organizations

OBJECTIVES

After working through this chapter, you will be able to:

1. Identify the major challenges the information age presents to business communication

2. Describe the components of the interactive communication process

3. Give a brief summary of theories of organizational communication

4. Explain the differences between classical and humanistic theories of organizational communication

5. Name the four elements of strategic communication

Like a multifaceted city skyline, organizational communication comprises many independent yet interdependent systems and individuals. And, in the same way that civil engineers work to increase the quality of urban life, communications scholars work to understand and improve the effectiveness of communication in organizations. Knowledge of their findings — communication skills and theory — is a valuable asset as you prepare for your career. Oral presentations and report briefings, interviews, small group communication, listening, and leadership are just a few of the communication activities you will perform in the "real world."

Studies of Fortune 500 executives have uncovered the value, and continuing necessity, of effective communication to business success.[1] Without exception, these executives have reported that communication, especially oral skills, is a key component of success in the business world. Interestingly, these executives have indicated that university courses (rather than in-house training or input from outside consultants) provide the best oral communication training. Furthermore, executives who hire college graduates believe that oral communication skills will become even more important for career success.

The burgeoning importance of communication skills grows out of one feature of the present age: the amount of information that must be transmitted, consumed, analyzed, returned, or discarded. Because of this focus, the "information age" is considerably different from the industrial age of years past — this age is less certain, more volatile, and more communication based. One way to study this contrast further is to look at the distinctions between the industrial age and the information age made by William Ruch and summarized in Table 1-1.[2]

TABLE 1-1
Ruch's Distinctions Between the Industrial and the Information Ages

Industrial Age	Information Age
Human knowledge doubles every ten years.	Human knowledge doubles every year.
Information is shared worldwide by delayed transmission.	Information is instantaneously shared worldwide by satellites.
Managerial control is based on supervising people.	Managerial control is based on giving people feedback.
Information is acquired as needed.	Information is central to operation.
Manager acts as a decison maker.	Manager functions as an information processor.

SOURCE: Based on W. V. Ruch, *International Handbook of Corporate Communication* (Jefferson, N.C.: McFarland, 1989).

Communication skills take on new significance when routine tasks incorporate high technology. Here, a supermarket manager receives a faxed order from a customer.

This shift in the value and volume of knowledge in the marketplace means that different criteria determine business success. The companies that succeed in the information age are those that integrate new technologies without alienating employees, handle information more efficiently so that they are not swamped by data, and actively seek to enhance their communication through technology. None of this can be accomplished unless employees from the president to the shipping clerk know how to communicate effectively.

Indeed, communication skills are central to promoting excellence now and in the coming years.[3] These skills have six main components.

1. *Creative insight* is the ability to ask the right questions. Although asking tough questions is not the most pleasant task, such inquiries are necessary if a business is to deal with a dynamic work force and economy.

2. *Sensitivity* means a business practices the Golden Rule with its workers. Every employee is integrated into the scheme of things and is made to feel that she or he can personally make a difference.

3. *Vision* means being able to create the future. Leaders of organizations must have a clear picture of where their organizations are going in turbulent times.

4. *Versatility* is the capacity for anticipating change. Without versatility, neither the company nor the employee can understand and adapt to unexpected goals or issues.

5. *Focus* is required to implement change. Because change is a fact of life in today's world, those who can quickly and easily embrace and effect change have an advantage.

6. *Patience* allows businesses and people to live in the long term. Implementing necessary change may take time, and those who can remain patient during delays have the best chance of success.

According to leaders of many companies, the information age is not on the way — it is already here. Chief executive officers (CEOs) of major organizations have accepted that the information age is here to stay, and many have already encouraged a corporate culture that accepts and benefits from new information technology. To these leaders, the next challenge is the *globalization* or worldwide scope of the marketplace made possible by new communication technologies as well as by international political events. As former Citibank chairman Walter B. Wriston remarked:

> Unquestionably, globalization is a large part of the new age. . . . From the manager's viewpoint, [globalization of business] means suddenly waking up with a guy you've never heard of from a country you're not too sure where it is, who's eating lunch in your hometown. That's new. And it requires new skills in managers — it means that leaders must have a wide enough span, a broad enough vision to understand the world and operate in it. . . . To be successful, managers must be able to work with people who don't speak their language, who may not share their value systems, but who have the talent, the business needs.[4]

And CEO Reuben Mark of Colgate-Palmolive, whose company gets 64 percent of its revenues from outside the United States, said:

> Partnerships of all kinds will be the thrust of the Nineties and beyond: increasingly strategic interdependencies between companies, governments, people. . . . We have all kinds of programs to identify and reward our most productive employees. Believe me, it is far more difficult to engineer that kind of encouragement consistently worldwide than you would ever expect. . . . It's easy to make videotapes about the company's strategy and vision. What's tough is to make sure they're showing the tapes in the plant in Turkey.[5]

Of course, many companies, particularly small ones, are not capable of building global markets or maintaining an international network of employees. But the effects of globalization can still be seen in these companies in the general diversification occurring in the workplace. Even if a company does not have representatives in Brazil or Rumania, it is highly likely that some of its employees are speaking English as a second language, following a wide variety of cultural norms, or having different benefits or scheduling needs than the "traditional" worker. James Houghton, CEO of Corning, explained that "companies simply can't prosper in a diverse, multicultural world unless they reflect that diversity to some degree. . . . As companies reflect more cultural diversity, they will become more tolerant, more willing to use differences, rather than sameness, as criteria for individual success within the organization."[6]

In this way, a *global attitude* — that is, one that recognizes the value of diversity — can be a source of innovation and adaptation to change in any organizational setting. One of the best ways to develop this attitude is through organizational communication.

The Interactive Communication Process

Communication in a business or professional setting draws on the fundamental skills and concepts of communication used in social contexts, although the differences must be carefully considered. The essence of communication in all contexts is that people exchange messages in the service of accomplishing goals and objectives. Because people bring different goals, backgrounds, styles, habits, and preferences to the process, truly effective communication is interactive. This means each person taking part in the communication listens and responds to the others. As you read the following description of the communication process, notice how each of its elements contributes to making communication interactive.

Message

Messages are the content of communication with others — the ideas people wish to share. Messages may be expressed verbally, which includes messages expressed in spoken (oral) or written form, or nonverbally. Verbal messages use words and sentences to express ideas. Nonverbal messages, which can be equally meaningful, use gestures, postures, facial expressions, and even clothing. Interactive communicators are open to this broad range of messages and pay careful attention to their intended meanings.

Source

Sometimes referred to as the *sender,* the source is the person who creates a message. The source determines what type of message is to be sent and the best way to go about sending it. When deciding how and what to send, a sender practicing interactive communication takes into account the needs of those who will be receiving the message.

Encoding

Encoding refers to the physical process of organizing elements of the message for transmission to the receivers. In verbal communication, encoding is the act of choosing and vocalizing words or sounds; in nonverbal communication, it means choosing clothing, acting out gestures, smiling, or nodding, among others. Interactive communicators consider all possibilities for improving the accuracy and meaning of the messages they intend to send — for example, they may consider adding visual aids and friendly gestures to spoken messages to make them more readable and accessible.

Channel

The channel is the path a message takes once it is encoded by a source. When people talk with each other, they are using the air as the channel. If you work in an organization with a computer network, for instance, you may choose electronic mail as the channel for a message to your co-workers. Other channels include memos, phone conversations, telegrams, and even tele- and video-conferencing.

Receiver

The destination of the message is the receiver. Receivers include *all* persons who pick up the message, regardless of whether they were the sender's intended targets. As you are aware, some receivers get messages inadvertently. Such "sidestream listening" can create problems. Imagine a situation in which two managers casually trade semiconfidential information while waiting outside their supervisor's office — not realizing that a third person waiting to see the supervisor is a sharp-eared representative of a competing company.

New communication technology increases the chance that unintended receivers will pick up messages. Just a few examples include leaving memos at the copy machine or at a computer printer, receiving electronic mail meant for someone else, or even having computer files broken into by "hackers."

Decoding

As the counterpart of encoding, decoding is the process that receivers go through to make sense of the message they receive. Decoding is influenced by many factors, including cultural background, listening abilities, and attitudes toward the source or channel. For example, while direct eye contact and a steady gaze are considered signs of honesty and trustworthiness in the United States, they signal lack of respect and even personal affront in many Asian cultures. The head nod, which is used almost universally to mean "yes," will be decoded as "no" in Greece and Bulgaria.

Feedback

Feedback is any response, verbal or nonverbal, a receiver makes to a message. Most senders seek feedback during the communication process because it shows the sender if the message has been understood correctly. Feedback can take the form of a verbal or nonverbal response, a written memo, a phone call, or an organized forum such as a status meeting or quality circle. Feedback can even occur involuntarily. For example, you may receive a message that makes you particularly upset, but you are determined not to respond. Nevertheless, you grit your teeth, clench your fists, or blush. All of these reactions constitute feedback.

Noise

Noise is anything that interferes with the communication process. The common definition of noise is distracting sounds that prevent people from hearing or making themselves heard. But noise is a more encompassing phenomenon than this description suggests. It includes psychological distractions such as nervousness or tension, emotional distractions such as extreme happiness or sadness, and even physiological distractions such as fatigue or illness. All of these affect the quality of the message sent and received. Noise can occur at any point in the communication process.

Shared Meaning

Figure 1-1 illustrates the communication process we have just described. Notice the term *shared meaning* in the center of the illustration. Shared meaning is the mutual understanding that results when the sender and all intended receivers interpret the message in the same way. Even though sources and receivers nearly always try to share meaning with one another,

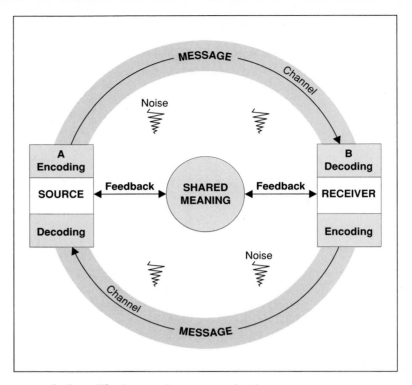

FIGURE 1-1   The interactive communication process

they do not necessarily succeed in doing so. There are degrees, or stages, of shared meaning attained in this process.

Point A represents the first opportunity for shared meaning. At this point, the source has just encoded a message intended for the receiver, and the receiver is aware that a message is being sent. This is shared meaning at its lowest level — the sender has simply caught the attention of the receiver.

Point B represents a potentially higher degree of shared meaning. At this point, the receiver is in the process of decoding the message and making sense of it. Notice we qualify Point B as a "potentially" higher degree of shared meaning. In an unsuccessful communication, the receiver may decode the message incorrectly — that is, in a manner inconsistent with the sender's original meaning. The receiver may assume a wave means "Hello" when in fact the sender means "Go away; I'm too busy to talk now!" Or the receiver may take a memo on the company's new sick leave policy that states, "Employees' absenteeism records will be reviewed to better structure their health care benefits" to mean that absences will be punished by a loss of benefits when the sender is actually trying to increase health care coverage by assessing the needs of the employees as a group. The receiver responds by giving feedback to the sender. The feedback message indicates whether shared meaning was attained in the communication.

Communication is not an either/or concept; rather, varying degrees of communication are possible depending on how the message is treated at each point. If you think about it, a great deal of communication occurs without the full benefit of shared meaning, but enough information is exchanged between sources and receivers so they can function together in a minimal fashion. For example, imagine that you and your supervisor are in a crowded and noisy elevator. Your supervisor tells you the location, time, and agenda for an upcoming meeting, but because you can barely hear, you exit the elevator certain only of the location and time. You know enough to be able to get to the meeting, but your supervisor intended for you to know what was going to be discussed so that you could prepare some notes. Shared meaning was not fully achieved: even though the meeting was held, it did not accomplish all that the supervisor had planned it to.

Business and professional communicators are wise to strive for shared meaning, yet there are many obstacles to achieving it. We introduce these to show the shortcomings of typical communication styles.

Reasons for Communication Failure

A number of experts have suggested reasons communication fails. One approach was taken by Osmo Wiio, who likened communication to Murphy's Law — "If communication can fail, it will." "If you are sure that communication cannot fail, it necessarily will fail." "There is always someone who knows better than you what you meant by your message."[7] This pessimism is founded on the innumerable potential communication problems in organizations. The following are some of the more common causes of communication failure.

Inadequate Information

Managers and employees frequently complain that they do not receive enough information to do their jobs effectively. In some cases, upper management provides too little information when issuing orders. In other cases, information may be provided, but it is not the right type. Managers often assume that employees have the same background and knowledge as themselves (or do not consider these factors at all) and expect employees to accomplish goals that they do not fully understand. One manager we know intentionally withholds information from his subordinates because he feels that they would just become confused by "too much information." He is actually working at cross-purposes with his employees because they usually have to get that information from other sources.

Information Overload

The technology of the information age has for the first time made it possible for employees at all levels of an organization to be overwhelmed by too much information. In an effort to ensure that people get enough information (especially in situations where they are not sure what is useful), managers often overcompensate and send employees more information than necessary. To be safe, they send their employees so much information that much of it winds up being ignored.

Poor-Quality Information

Information may be readily available to employees but may be of little use because of its poor quality. When a planner asks an engineer for a quick report on the progress of a construction project and receives a lengthy, disorganized, jargon-filled description of bedrock at the construction site, neither person is benefiting from the communication. Other examples of poor-quality information include dated, erroneous, misleading, overemphasized, and disorganized information.

Poor Timing

Having the right amount of information at the wrong time does little good. Sales reports, marketing figures, or consumer trends are of little value to decision makers if the information arrives too late to be used — for example, in a planning meeting or a marketing campaign. Similarly, if information arrives too early, the receiver may set it aside for later use but then forget that he or she has it. Information timing is just as important as information quantity or quality.

Lack of Feedback/Follow-Up

Frequently, a sender forwards a message with the expectation that the receiver will respond with feedback or a follow-up message. If the receiver does not recognize that a response is requested or does not bother to reply to the message, the sender is forced to waste time waiting for a follow-up or sending a second message asking for feedback. In either case, time and effort are wasted. In one instance we are familiar with, Jill called Charlie to inform him about the next budget meeting. As Charlie was not in, his secretary took the message about the meeting. "Tell him to let me know" was the last thing Jill said to the secretary. Charlie did not respond, so Jill did not schedule Charlie's report for the meeting. When Charlie showed up expecting to make his report, both he and Jill were angry, blaming each other for the feedback error.

Problems with Channels

The communication channels that carry organizational messages can include face-to-face conversation, telephones, public speeches, memos, and letters. Problems can occur when senders use the wrong channels to convey information. For example, using a phone call to notify an employee that she or he is not going to get a raise is inappropriate because the issue is personal and sensitive. A better channel would be face-to-face contact. Likewise, contacting ten people separately about a new telephone policy is an inefficient use of time and resources when these ten people can be informed collectively in a meeting.

Incompetent Communication

Some organizational members do not possess the communication skills necessary to be effective in today's professional world. For instance, a multimedia presentation will be ineffective if the presenter does not know how to use the equipment, experiences technical difficulties, or has tried to liven up a dull topic merely by adding flashy graphics rather than improving the content of the presentation. People who attend meetings unprepared just waste others' time. People with poor listening skills frustrate those who have to repeat information for them. Those who make inappropriate grammatical or vocabulary choices embarrass themselves and those around them. Incompetent communicators hurt the organization they represent.

Ineffective Goal Setting

One of the most important skills in effective communication is setting appropriate goals. When goals are set too low, the communicator wastes the opportunity to influence, motivate, or inform the audience effectively. When goals are too high, the communicator becomes disappointed or disillusioned because the audience fails to grasp the message or simply dismisses what she or he says. Can you think of some examples of ineffective goals you have encountered?

Communication Anxiety

When communication situations cause a person to feel nervous, stressed, or apprehensive, the effectiveness of his or her efforts is at risk. Anxiety can hamper the ability to think, talk, gesture, and even listen. In the face of such anxiety, the communicator must be able to cope effectively enough to succeed in the communication. Not all communication situations cause anxiety in people, however; each person reacts differently to communication settings. To minimize such anxiety in yourself, recognize those situations in which you experience anxiety, and use the techniques described in this book to control your nervousness.

When all these communication failures occur in social situations, at worst the communicators wind up confused, embarrassed, or annoyed. But when communication fails within a business organization, the results can be much worse — inefficiency, loss of morale, decreased productivity. The specter of such negative results highlights the importance of studying organization communication, particularly when it is possible to do so before one joins an organization.

Studying Organizational Communication

Organizational communication is the exchange of oral, nonverbal, and written messages within (and across the boundaries of) a system of interrelated and interdependent people working to accomplish common tasks and goals. This broad definition encompasses much of the activity that occurs at work — it includes such tasks as alerting workers to production goals, scheduling meetings within and between departments, planning how the company will communicate with its customers and respond to their messages, and producing in-house informational material about policies and goals. A narrower definition would exclude many of these messages and would therefore deemphasize the fundamental importance of communication in organizations. It is well known that a good understanding of facts can help you perform better on a test, a good understanding of political issues can help you to be a better citizen, and a good understanding of other people can help you to improve your personal relationships. In the same way, a good understanding of organizational communication provides you with options when faced with tasks that need to be accomplished efficiently and effectively. When you understand how an organizational context affects communication you will be in a much better position to achieve the goals you have set for yourself.

Nevertheless, communicating in organizations is not an easy task. Obstacles to effective communication are always present. Assumptions about other people can be wrong ("I thought you were going to cover the southeastern sales territory this month!"), and closed communication channels can inhibit the exchange of messages ("I only want to hear good news about

In her job as Plant Communicator for Caterpillar Corporation's Mossville, Illinois, plant, Angela Azzaretti writes speeches for top management, publishes the plant newsletter, and produces videotapes for employees and managers.

sales figures!"). Even reluctance to receive new ideas and information from people inside and outside the organization can be detrimental to its goals.

Many theories have been advanced to explain how organizations work, what relationship exists between management and labor, and what function, if any, communication performs in the working of an organization. These theories have had significant, and in some cases continuing, influences on organizational practices. Note, however, that none addresses the unique challenges of the information age.

Classical Theory

The classical school of thought includes older theories that emphasize a high degree of structure, rules, and control. Included in this category are Taylor's scientific management theory, Weber's bureaucracy theory, and Fayol's administrative management theory. Although developed near the turn of the century, many of the principles of classical theory are still in use.

Scientific management. Frederick Taylor published *Scientific Management* in 1911 and revolutionized the way managers thought about work in general and employees in particular.[8] Taylor was an engineer who was convinced that work activity could be observed, analyzed, and restructured to produce additional output. Although a number of textbooks have claimed that Taylor considered workers lazy, shiftless, and uncreative, he had a great deal of respect for workers. He was one of the first advocates of systematic training and development to improve workers' proficiency in their duties. He also encouraged organizations to match workers' abilities with the duties and responsibilities of their jobs. According to Taylor, four principles promote good management: the development of a true science of work, the scientific selection of the worker, the scientific education and development of the worker, and friendly cooperation between management and labor. From these principles grew a philosophy that advocates the following goals:

◆ Science, not rule of thumb, should be stressed.

◆ Harmony, not discord, should be encouraged.

◆ Cooperation, not individualism, should be advocated.

◆ Maximum output should be valued in place of restricted output.

◆ The development of each person to his or her greatest efficiency and prosperity should be a priority.

Bureaucracy.   Max Weber, who is generally known as the father of the study of bureaucracy, was born in nineteenth-century Germany. Strong structures of authority and control were common features of German life at the time, and not surprisingly, in looking at groups and organizations, Weber turned his attention to authority structures. He proposed three types: charismatic, traditional, and rational-legal.[9] In Weber's classifications, charismatic authority results from the personal qualities (expertise, knowledge, vision, values) of a leader. Traditional authority results from the recognition of and adherence to power produced by history, succession, or norms. Rational-legal authority grows out of rules, policies, procedures, laws, or other legalistic avenues of conferring power.

This last authority is the basis for bureaucracy (Weber is best known for this aspect of his theory). Government agencies, large corporations, even the university you are now attending, are good examples of bureaucracies. A bureaucratic structure enables organizations to define very clearly what behavior in employees is acceptable and expected. Bureaucratic authority structures concentrate a great deal of power at the top of a hierarchy, with successive, or lower, levels getting their power from upper layers. In Figure 1-2, a typical hierarchical chart depicts how each succeeding layer is dependent on and subservient to the previous level of authority. Bureaucracies adhere to formalized rules and policies they put in place for themselves, and communication goes by the book. Workers cannot skip levels

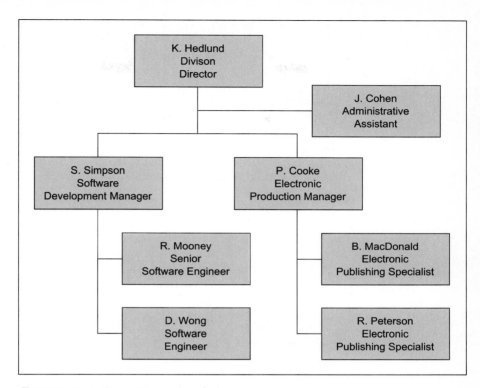

FIGURE 1-2   Hierarchical chart

of authority when sending messages to superiors or inferiors — the message must pass through each layer on its journey to the receiver.

Communication in a bureaucracy is highly routinized. Procedures, probably written ones, regulate the process of oral and written communication. For example, one organization we are familiar with specifies that during the period of time for annual employee evaluations, each supervisor must notify each subordinate in writing and in person ten days in advance of the evaluation meeting. The evaluation itself is conducted in person, with a written follow-up. Both the supervisor and the subordinate must sign a statement that stipulates that the procedure was followed according to company policy.

Administrative theory. Administrative theory, or *administrative management* as it is often called, focuses on the duties and responsibilities of managers in the organization. Henri Fayol, a French social scientist, laid the foundations of administrative theory. Like Weber, Fayol believed in a strong hierarchical structure, and like Taylor, he believed that the responsibility of those at the lower end of the hierarchy (workers) was technical expertise and nothing more. Management performed organizational and administrative duties. Impartiality, objectivity, and a highly structured approach to tasks and relationships within the organization were preferred.

Strengths and weaknesses of classical theory.   Gareth Morgan has suggested that classical theory describes an organization that functions like a machine.[10] Machines perform repetitive tasks in specific and unchanging ways that are determined by their structures and are totally subservient to the people operating them. Morgan elaborated characteristics for identifying those organizations in which the classical theory of management is appropriate. These characteristics include the following:

When there is a straightforward task to perform
When the environment is stable enough to ensure that the products produced will be appropriate ones
When the same product is produced time and again
When precision is at a premium
When the human "machine" parts are compliant and behave as they have been designed to do

As you read the list, think of organizations you have worked for. Do any of them match these characteristics? It would not be surprising if your response is "no." The changing nature of the American work force in the twentieth century — larger numbers of college graduates, white-collar workers, and larger business organizations — has contributed to a diminished popularity of classical theory, and few contemporary organizations rely strictly on its principles. Its views now seem overly mechanical and impersonal, unsuited to the developing consciousness of workers as human beings with needs rather than faceless, impersonal "parts" of a business machine.

Humanistic Theory

A school of thought known as humanistic theory gained popularity on response to classical theory's overly mechanistic approach. It focused on the needs of labor rather than the structure of management.

Human relations theory.   In the late 1920s and early 1930s a number of studies on productivity were conducted at the Western Electric Hawthorne plant in Cicero, Illinois, under the leadership of Elton Mayo, a Harvard professor.[11] One of the first studies examined the effect of lighting in the workplace on workers' productivity.

As experimenters increased the lighting in the Hawthorne plant, productivity increased. Productivity increased each time illumination was increased. The engineers at the plant were delighted but puzzled because the control group (which did not get increased lighting) also increased its productivity at about the same rate as the experimental group. Furthermore, when the experimenters *reduced* the illumination for the experimental group, productivity *continued* to increase.

The researchers concluded that increases in productivity were not the result of changes in lighting; rather, the special attention being paid to the workers during the study enhanced their productivity. The researchers proved that technical factors were not the only influence on work efficiency; human factors affected the work of employees as well. According to Mayo, "Social study should begin with careful observation of what may be described as communication: this is, the capacity of an individual to communicate his feelings and ideas to another, the capacity of groups to communicate effectively and intimately with each other. This problem is, beyond all reasonable doubt, the outstanding defect that civilization is facing today."[12] Mayo's most important finding, which stood in stark contrast to classical theory, was that informal groups and camaraderie among workers; supervisors' demonstrated interest, encouragement, praise, and recognition; and the ability to form relationships on the job were more effective than economic incentives in increasing workers' productivity and morale.

Human resources approach. Human relations theory came under criticism for focusing too narrowly on workers' happiness and for not taking into account that happy workers might also be unproductive. A reevaluation of human relations began, based on one of the most influential motivational theory books yet written: *The Human Side of Enterprise* by Douglas McGregor.[13] This book struck an area of compromise between classical theory and human relations theory: that workers will be more productive not only if they are happy but if they are given the proper working conditions.

McGregor proposed two theories of motivation that have become part of everyday language in business, government, and even academia: theory X and theory Y. Theory X holds that workers are unproductive, unmotivated, and must be coerced through constant supervision to perform their tasks. Theory Y suggests that workers are creative and motivated persons who do not require coercion except in rare circumstances and when given the chance can perform exceedingly well. These theories have prompted a great deal of debate between supporters of their competing viewpoints (see Table 1-2).

McGregor's theory X–theory Y concept continues to influence organizational theory even though it is not fully understood. The contrasting characteristics seem to stem in part from human nature and consequently are difficult to dismiss as the creation of an academic with no real-life business experience. As a number of managers told us, "Some people are theory Xers who have to be watched and supervised carefully; others are theory Yers who you can just leave alone." Of course, the same distinction can be applied to managers and supervisors. Think for a moment of organizations that you are familiar with that fit a theory X profile. Were the

TABLE 1-2
Contrasting Viewpoints: Theory X and Theory Y

Theory X	Theory Y
1. Workers have an inherent dislike of work and will seek to avoid it if possible.	1. Activities and tasks at work are as natural as those at rest or play.
2. Most workers have to be coerced, forced, controlled, directed, and threatened to put out adequate effort on the job.	2. Control and coercion are not methods for obtaining adequate effort. Workers can and will exercise self-control to accomplish organizational objectives.
3. The average person prefers to be directed, likes to avoid responsibility, lacks motivation, and desires job security above all else.	3. The most significant reward for a worker is satisfying ego or self-actualization needs. The result of personal effort can be reward enough.
	4. Under the right conditions, the average worker may even seek responsibility.
	5. The ability to creatively and imaginatively solve organizational problems is widely distributed in the population. Creativity is not a managerial monopoly.
	6. The potential of the average worker is underdeveloped.

employees lazy and unmotivated, causing management to constantly coerce and control them? Or were employees unmotivated because management did not trust them? What about theory Y organizations? Were the managers trusting, openminded, and nurturing with workers, thereby causing them to be self-reliant and independent, or did the workers first demonstrate self-initiative, persistence, and reliability, and thus lead management to think of employees more humanistically?

Systems Theory

The debate about organizations did not end with theories X and Y. Both classical and humanistic theories finally revealed a common shortcoming: neither brought the environment into considerations of organizational effectiveness. The response to this lack, systems theory, added a third element, the environment, to an equation that previously had contained only two: management and labor.

Systems theory draws heavily from the work conducted in botany by Ludwig von Bertalanfy, which suggests that organizations are comparable to living organisms and have needs, desires, faults, shortcomings, and other features characteristic of living creatures.[14] Most importantly, the parts of the organization and the parts of an organism are related in a similar way. If one part of an organism breaks down (for example, when you catch a cold), the rest of the system is directly affected (through fatigue, achiness, fever).

Organizational members rely on one another to accomplish goals and tasks. Rarely can one member assume total responsibility for an organizational objective. If one person on an organizational team is absent or fails to do her or his share of the work, the entire team suffers. In systems theory, this concept of relatedness is termed *interdependency*.

The notion of interdependency gives rise to a second concept: *synergy*. This is the phenomenon whereby the combined and integrated talents, energies, abilities, and knowledge of organizational members are greater than the sum of the isolated efforts of individuals. In other words, people who work in systems can learn from each other and be more creative because of their interactions with each other.

Of course, from these two concepts comes a third: *environment*. It includes the political, economic, and social characteristics of society that affect the way an organization operates. Classical theory did not recognize environment as a factor in workers' effectiveness. Even humanistic theories did not emphasize the strong influence that the environment has on the organization. Figure 1-3 illustrates the relationship of these concepts in systems theory.

Consider the example of the fast-food industry. Several years ago few fast-food restaurants offered chicken sandwiches as menu choices because customers apparently were satisfied with burgers and fries. Along came the "health" movement, and people began to demand healthier and less fattening choices at fast-food restaurants. Fast-food companies that ignored the demands of those health-conscious customers stood to lose a lot of business, and so it is hardly surprising that today nearly all fast-food outlets offer (and strongly promote the health benefits of) salads, low-fat foods, and all-natural ingredients.

Open and closed systems.   Organizations that attempt to respond to customer desires and needs are faced with a number of critical issues. What is the competition doing? What will suppliers be able to provide? What shape will the economy be in next year or the year after? Where can capital be raised? In terms of systems theory, responses to these issues are developed in either *open* or *closed* systems.

Open systems are those that allow free movement of energy, informa-

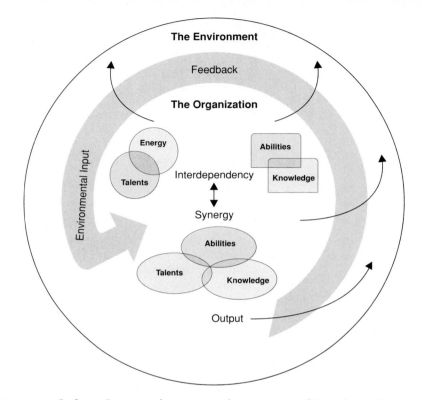

FIGURE 1-3   *Systems theory uses the concepts of interdependency, synergy, and environment to explain organizational behavior.*

tion, ideas, data, people, and so on across organizational boundaries. *Closed* systems deliberately shut themselves off from the outside environment. You can imagine the problems closed systems face in contemporary business as markets expand and become more open and as competition intensifies. The old Chrysler Corporation is frequently used as the quintessential example of a closed system.

Chrysler automobiles were always known for their large size, gas guzzling, and "planned obsolescence." When the oil embargo hit the United States in 1973, gasoline shortages caused long waiting lines and exorbitant prices. Although their big cars no longer suited customers' needs, Chrysler executives were reluctant to allow new ideas, information, or plans to cross the organization's boundaries. They felt either that the gas shortage was going to be short-lived or that consumers would continue to buy large cars in spite of the shortage. They were wrong. As a result, Chrysler almost went bankrupt — it took a $1.2 billion bailout from the federal government and an openminded new leader, Lee Iacocca, to turn things around.

Now Chrysler is an open system with fresh ideas about how to compete and make the best use of technology. According to Iacocca, "You have to understand processing as well as design, comprehend exchange rates and how the world ticks. Our kids have to learn that if they want to compete."[15]

Open systems can take a variety of forms. Organizations may develop work groups that invite expert outsiders to discuss cutting-edge technology or representatives of several different departments to discuss new ideas for cooperation. They may encourage outside speakers at their meetings, hold open houses, or sponsor joint fund-raising activities with the community.

Open systems encourage employees to take college courses, obtain advanced degrees, participate in special workshops outside the organizations, volunteer in the community, or even collaborate with persons outside the organization. Not only does this new knowledge help the organization by providing additional expertise and ideas; it improves morale among the work force.

Culture

Although systems theory went far in explaining the dynamics of organizational communication and the reasons why some businesses are able to adapt to environmental change faster than others, unanswered questions remained. One of the most significant was "Why would a communication system that is highly successful at one company be a failure at another?" The answer was provided in part by one of the more recent organizational theories, *culture*.

As defined by Ralph Kilmann, organizational culture is "the social or normative glue that holds an organization together. It consists of values and beliefs that some groups or organizational members come to share."[16] Two best-selling books in the early 1980s — Terrance Deal and Allan Kennedy's *Corporate Culture: The Rights and Rituals of Corporate Life* and Thomas Peters and Robert Waterman's *In Search of Excellence* — drew public attention to organizational or corporate culture.[17] According to these theorists, the following components are elements of an organizational culture:

Values: the goals, ideals, and philosophies that an organization holds important.

Rites and rituals: the activities and performances that illuminate the important issues of the organization

Heroes: the noteworthy organizational members who have achieved success in advocating the culture of the organization

Communications: the informal network that carries messages about work and social topics

Norms: the task, social, and personal norms, standards, or ways of doing things in an organization

FOCUS on Corporate Communication

BEST WESTERN INTERNATIONAL, INC.

*B*est Western hotels may be familiar to you as vacation destinations, meeting sites, or stopovers during long trips. You will probably be surprised to know that, unlike other franchised or corporate-owned lodging organizations, each of the more than three thousand Best Western hotels is independently owned and operated. As a result, the organizational culture has a unique feel to it — an extended family in which each "relative" has an equal and experienced voice.

Older "members," as hotel owners are called, have a very personal investment in Best Western as the company reaches its forty-fifth anniversary in 1991. Many remember the earliest meetings and have built the traditions that form the organizational culture today. The company produced a booklet, *40 Years of Moving On,* to commemorate its fortieth anniversary in 1986. In preparation for a half-century celebration in 1996, employees are encouraged to locate and collect Best Western memorabilia, such as old travel guides, correspondence, and postcards that will be put on display.

The corporate culture at Best Western is also strongly influenced by its democratic, nonprofit structure. It is reinforced through monthly directors' meetings, an annual series of seven regional meetings, and an annual international convention. At these events, members develop programs and policies that apply to all levels of management in the organization. Although an official written code of ethics is not in place, values and expectations are clearly understood and upheld because of the strong sense of equality and interdependence in the organization.

Communication plays a central role in the Best Western organization, the logical result of its corporate culture and service-industry orientation. Staff employees (at the corporate headquarters in Phoenix, Arizona) have access to both traditional and electronic bulletin boards, staff meetings, memos, and a "Breakfast with the Boss" session with the president and CEO. Hotel owners have additional communication support in the forms of a biweekly newspaper, a computer bulletin board, regular face-to-face meetings with staff, and special publications (e.g., manuals and newsletters on specific topics). An active and effective grapevine also links members, despite the large distances between many hotels.

Personal communication skills are critical to the organization. Internal publications, produced by the corporate communications department, usually contain features and articles

Stories, myths, and legends: the retold experiences that function as important events in the history of the organization

Climate: the feeling or general attitude formed by the way members interact with one another and with persons outside the organization (customers, suppliers, vendors)

devoted to a variety of communication issues as well as suggestions for improving communication in areas from supply transportation to reservations. One recent newsletter article discussed methods for easing the anxiety of public speaking, and another discussed clarifying personal values and increasing self-awareness.

The organization's education and training department sponsors seminars and classes that often touch on communication issues as well. One recently introduced seminar for reservation agents who handle group and international bookings focuses on effective communication skills — including listening, questioning, and persuasion — to increase employees' awareness of customers' needs and boost their confidence in themselves and the organization.

Best Western is also increasing employees' confidence through communication technology. Sales updates and "news of the day" messages are given when employees log on to their computer terminals. New technology affects communication in other ways as well. The computerized reservations system increases the speed at which jobs are performed and the skills necessary to perform them. Best Western takes care to focus on the people — the "liveware" — between the hardware and software used in the reservations system. The organization has a very personal approach to business and emphasizes personal communication and service in addition to high-tech applications.

One communications challenge to Best Western results from its international scope and the variety of jobs within the organization. The company's demographics show employees from approximately forty different countries, ranging in age from seventeen to seventy. Some are new to the industry; others are fourth-generation hoteliers. The Best Western in Sun City, Arizona, recently began a drive to recruit senior citizens from the large retirement community surrounding Sun City. The inn runs ads specifically stating that senior citizens are welcome to apply and is investigating the possibility of computerizing and adding technical training programs for its older employees.

Communications at Best Western is an interesting and often challenging combination of the traditional and the innovative. While seeking to take full advantage of the ever-changing technology of communications, staff members strive to maintain the personal touch and feel of "family" that is at the heart of the organization. While technology will allow service to improve with speed, the goal of Best Western is never to allow it to overshadow the relationship of one person serving another.

Culture provides a portrait of the actions, norms, motives, and philosophies that an organization values. In a sense, an analysis of culture is an attempt to understand how organization members feel about themselves as a whole. *Shared meaning, shared understanding,* and *shared sense making* are all different ways of describing that culture. In talking about culture, we are really talking about a process of reality construction that allows people to see and understand particular events, actions, objects, or situations in distinctive ways. These patterns of understanding also provide a basis for making behavior sensible and meaningful.[18] Knowledge of an organization's culture provides members with a sense of purpose. They come to realize their importance in the organization.

A Model for Communication in the Information Age

So far we have discussed a wide range of organizational philosophies or theories, which at the time of their development seemed very reasonable and rational ways of organizing workers and activities. Scientific management, bureaucracy, administrative management, human relations, human resources, systems theory, and especially organizational culture contain elements that are quite useful for organizations today. But we offer a new approach to understanding these elements that incorporates skills specifically designed to help you succeed in today's information-rich environment — strategic communication.

The information age demands that communication be planned carefully because there are so many new options to consider in the creation and transmission of messages. To succeed in this age, you will have to know how to integrate technology with communication skills and how to communicate with people who have diverse backgrounds and a wide range of goals and expectations. Most importantly, in making the most of your business career, you will want to present yourself as a competent communicator because your communication skills will be your best selling point in job interviews, sales meetings, and company presentations. To do this, you will be wise to communicate *strategically*. This approach, which we have developed and applied in both the classroom and the real world, is designed to maximize the opportunities for communication you will encounter now and after graduation.

Strategic communication means achieving your potential in four areas:

1. Goal setting — each communication situation can be approached as a goal-setting activity. You will be more likely to succeed in your communication if you set clear and challenging goals for yourself.

2. Situational knowledge — this refers to the information you have (or can collect) about the requirements for successful communication in a particular context. You greatly improve your chances of successful communication if you know what is appropriate and expected of you.

3. Communication competence — when you plan communication strategically, you choose a number of factors, such as type of message,

type of channel, style of delivery, that demonstrate your understanding of the organization's values and needs. Communication competence also entails adapting correctly to situational demands. You learn to make these choices consistently and correctly.

4. Control of anxiety — job interviews, meetings with superiors, and group problem-solving meetings are a few of the many situations that may cause anxiety on the job. Control of anxiety is a critical element in effective and strategic communication. You can learn to keep your nervousness at a "threshold of anxiety" that energizes your communication without destroying its effectiveness. As Figure 1-4 illustrates, these four components provide a base for developing communication skill within the context of the dynamic business environment.

Information

Strategic Communication

• Goal setting

• Situational knowledge

• Communication competence

• Controlling anxiety

Globalization

Organizational growth and change

*FIGURE **1-4***   *Strategic communication helps employees adapt and respond to the changing business environment by ensuring that they attend to fundamentals.*

Plan of the Book

Because we are taking a strategic perspective throughout this text, we show you the advantages of the model of strategic communication whenever we can. Some chapters are more conducive to various aspects of the model than are other chapters. For example, anxiety management is one of the most important elements in our discussion of public speaking and presentational communication.

The strategic model is a sound approach to business and professional communication, especially in today's turbulent environment. We know that it will enhance your ability to communicate so that you maximize your ability to share meanings with other communicators. The information age, globalization, and the organizational context influence the creation of shared meaning and affect the choices that communicators in organizational settings must make. If communicators engage in the strategic communication process based on an assessment of these factors, they are in a much better position to share meaning with other communicators.

Discussion

1. How can communication help an organization to achieve its goals?

2. What implications do the information age and globalization have for organizational communication?

3. How is the communication process affected by an organizational context?

4. What is *shared meaning?*

5. Which of the causes of communication failure discussed in the chapter have you experienced? What were the results, and how would you avoid repeating the situation in the future?

6. What are the major differences among classical theory, humanistic theory, and systems theory in organizations?

7. What elements make up an organization's culture?

Activities

1. This chapter lists eight aspects of the communication process. Select *one* element that was a particularly important barrier in one of your recent communication transactions. Describe the role that barrier played in the transaction to the members of your small discussion group.

2. Labor and management unrest has been prevalent since the formation of labor unions in the late nineteenth century. Explain how the con-

cept of "shared meaning" has been particularly relevant in the communication efforts between these groups.

3. Using your own school, work, or volunteer experience, explain how you believe effective communicators:
   a. Obtain adequate information to do their jobs
   b. Avoid information overload
   c. Receive and send information in a timely manner
   d. Set goals effectively
   e. Manage communication apprehension

4. What merits accrue to organizations that adhere to principles of classical management theory versus humanistic theory? Choose an organization you are familiar with or that you would like to find out more about. Research the company's organizational structure by reading articles in business journals, newspapers, or even interviewing an employee. Prepare a brief report on the organization, making sure to explain how its structure developed, and its strengths and weaknesses as you see them. Be ready to present your report to the class.

5. Many people have maintained that communication and culture are linked such that a change in one effects a change in the other. Write a brief essay in which you explain whether you believe this link exists. Be sure to give an example.

Notes

1. J. C. Bennet and R. J. Olney, "Executive Priorities for Effective Communication in an Information Age," *Journal of Business Communication* 23 (1986), 13–22; V. S. DiSalvo and J. K. Larsen, "A Contingency Approach to Communication Skill Importance: The Impact of Occupation, Direction, and Position," *Journal of Business Communication* 24 (1987), 3–22.

2. W. V. Ruch, *International Handbook of Corporate Communication* (Jefferson, N.C.: McFarland, 1989).

3. P. Drucker, *Management: Tasks, Responsibilities, and Practices* (New York: Harper & Row, 1974).

4. W. B. Wriston, "The State of American Management," *Harvard Business Review* (January-February 1990), 80–81.

5. In "Today's Leaders Look to Tomorrow," *Fortune*, March 26, 1990, p. 32.

6. Ibid., p. 56.

7. O. Wiio, *Wiio's Laws — And Some Others* (Espoo, Finland: Welin-Göös, 1978).

8. F. Taylor, *The Principles of Scientific Management* (New York: Harper Brothers, 1911).

9. M. Weber, *The Theory of Social and Economic Organizations* (New York: Free Press, 1947).

10. G. Morgan, *Images of Organizations* (Newbury Park, Calif.: Sage, 1986).

11. E. Mayo, *The Human Problems of an Industrial Civilization* (New York: Macmillan, 1933).

12. E. Mayo, *The Social Problems of an Industrial Civilization* (Andover, Mass.: Andover Press, 1945), p. 22.

13. D. McGregor, *The Human Side of Enterprise* (New York: McGraw-Hill, 1960).

14. L. von Bertalanfy, *General Systems Theory: Foundations, Development, and Applications* (New York: Braziller, 1960).

15. In "Today's Leaders," p. 31.

16. R. H. Kilmann, *Managing Beyond the Quick Fix* (San Francisco: Jossey-Bass, 1989).

17. T. Deal and A. Kennedy, *Corporate Culture: The Rights and Rituals of Corporate Life* (Reading, Mass.: Addison-Wesley, 1982); T. Peters and R. Waterman, *In Search of Excellence: Lessons from America's Best-Run Companies* (New York: Warner Books, 1982).

18. Morgan, *Images of Organizations.*

Chapter 2

*T*he Model of Strategic Communication

OBJECTIVES

After working through this chapter, you will be able to:

1. Recognize the importance of strategic organizational communication

2. Understand how values and ethics influence communication activity

3. Set goals that are appropriate and effective

4. Use situational knowledge to enhance your communication

5. Demonstrate communication competence by choosing the proper message, form of exchange, and channel

6. Understand the causes of communication anxiety and how to deal with it

Over the years, many businesspeople, communications theorists, and teachers have advocated approaches to business communication similar to our model of strategic communication. You will recognize elements of our model in the theories discussed in Chapter 1. These approaches, though much talked about and even partially implemented in the workplace, have not had the broad impact expected of them. The main reason for their limited success has to do with a concept mentioned earlier: environment. The environment of American business was relatively stable and insulated up through the 1970s; companies were more homogeneous and tended to focus on domestic markets. There was no pressing need for American businesses to adopt the flexible and open communication systems described in Chapter 1.

Such insularity is no longer possible. Radical changes have occurred in the past two decades, among these increasing competition and diversity (globalization) and increasing dependence on technology and access to information (the "information age"). As a result, there are new demands on managers' time as organizations try to become more competitive by holding down costs without cutting back on products and services, work is being redefined as all types of descriptions become increasingly complex and require knowledge of new technologies and information systems, and the computerization of the workplace allows employees to have quick access to information that even a decade ago was not available to top management and planners.[1] This competitive environment demands a new approach to on-the-job communication that provides efficiency (communication is not wasted for lack of planning) and flexibility (people at all levels are encouraged and included in communication).

Strategic communication is effective because it helps you to pinpoint the areas in which you excel and those in which you need to improve. In this chapter, we use the model to illustrate strategic communication in the organizational context. In each of the remaining units, the four components of strategic communication — goal setting, situational knowledge, communication competence, and anxiety management — are the basis for understanding and improving your skills for interpersonal, group, and public communication. As we develop the model of strategic communication in each unit, you are introduced to practical and straightforward methods for setting and achieving communication goals in a number of contexts. Before we begin our discussion of the model, however, we introduce the framework within which it functions: organizational values and ethics.

The Organizational Framework: Values and Ethics

One of the key elements in any communication activity is the values of the organization. Values are the principles and ideas that people or even organizations strongly believe in and consider important. When people are in doubt about decisions, they frequently rely on deep-seated values to help them to make the right choice. In organizations, such reliance on shared values makes setting goals easier in the face of the competing ideas, desires, and objectives of individual employees.

Values

Just how are shared values established in an organization? The process is difficult because values are fundamental and enduring and because each person has a particular personal value system. Despite these drawbacks, an organization has several choices when it comes to establishing values. Upper management can organize focus groups, small groups of seven to twelve employees who meet to derive a list of values they believe are vital to the organization. These lists are circulated among all the focus groups for review and analysis. A committee studies the values generated by the focus groups and arrives at a composite set that can be voted on by organizational members.

Values can also be derived through members' responses to questionnaires about their values. Questionnaires provide quantitative data about issues of importance to employees and about the values they uphold. Another way to establish values is through the work of organizational consultants. One of their many tasks is to interview key employees to determine their value systems. Consultants can play an important role as objective outsiders in assessing which values are common among members as well as which values promote the mission of the organization.

Organizational values vary depending on the nature of the business or profession. Listed below are some values commonly found in a large number of organizations.

Primacy of the customer	Fair treatment
Honesty and integrity	Innovative thinking
Respect for other workers	Quality service
Importance of every person	Creativity
Maintenance of high professional standards	Reliance on ethical standards

Communication Ethics

So far we have focused our discussion on business and professional values in general. This gives us an excellent base to work from in discussing the ethics of business and professional communication. As we have stated earlier, everyone in the organization is responsible for ethics, and this is certainly the case for communication. William Howell provided a general suggestion for ethical communicators by recommending that they have a "well developed sense of social responsibility."[2] The following guidelines come in handy when uncertainty arises about ethical communication behavior.[3] Before you consider these, read the following case as an example of ethical communication in businesses. Determine how many of the guidelines apply to this case.

> Kent had been with his company for twenty-seven years and was disturbed to learn that he was being demoted, with a decrease in pay, because his company was merging with another company and his position was being eliminated as a result. Kent was angry but could not quit because he was too old to get a similar job elsewhere. Kent began to take two-hour lunches; help himself to office supplies he did not need; and talk incessantly with co-workers about how unfairly the company was treating him. When asked to relay information to others, he always delayed until the information was virtually useless and would actually change the tone or intent of the message if included. Prior to the merger, Kent was one of the company's most trusted and loyal employees.

Ethical Guidelines

1. Maintain candor. Candor refers to truthfulness, honesty, and frankness in your communication with other people. Although revealing everything you know about a situation may not always be appropriate — for instance, showing your entire hand to adversaries during intense and sensitive negotiations will only compromise your position — it is usually wise and ethical to be as open and frank about information as possible. Others will take note and mirror your behavior, creating openness throughout the organization.

2. Keep messages accurate. When you are relaying information from one source to another, communicate the original message as accurately as possible. Ethical communicators do not take liberties with the messages they pass on.

3. Avoid deception. Ethical communicators are always vigilant in their quest to avoid deception — the fabrication, intentional distortion, or withholding of information — in their communication.

4. Maintain consistent behavior. One of the most prevalent, yet noticeable, areas of unethical behavior is communicating one thing and doing another. You must always monitor your behavior to ensure that it matches what you say to others.

5. Keep confidences. When someone tells you something and expects you not to divulge that information to others, a sacred trust has been placed on you. Even if you then tell someone else and make her or him promise not to tell others, you cannot really expect that person to

take you seriously. More often than not, the original information gets back to the source, and undermines the confidence placed in you.

6. Ensure timeliness of communication. As we mentioned in an earlier section, the timing of messages can be critical. When you delay sending messages so that others do not fully benefit, they can (rightly) assume that you have acted unethically. Ethical communication requires that you determine when messages can best achieve the most good for the most people.

7. Confront unethical behavior. To maintain a consistent ethical viewpoint, you must confront unethical behavior when you observe it. Public indictment of unethical persons may not be necessary, but it is important that such people understand that your own tolerance for unethical behavior is low.

8. Cultivate empathic listening. By lending a sensitive and empathic ear to those who are troubled by their own or other's unethical behavior, you can better understand and help to solve the problems associated with these acts. After all, many unethical acts are the result of circumstances that co-workers feel are beyond their control.

The Advantage of Ethics

Although many experts believe that it is difficult to expect substantial progress in the area of business ethics given the present state of affairs, we are not so pessimistic. For one thing, more and more students are being exposed to the issues of ethical behavior in organizations. For another, once employees realize the advantages of ethical behavior, substantial progress is likely to be made in this area. So what are the advantages of ethics in the professional world? And if there are advantages, why do so many people ignore ethics? Answers to these questions are not entirely obvious, nor are they simple.

One of the advantages of ethics in the workplace is long-term integrity. Although compromises on ethics may yield short-term benefits, over the long haul each of these acts is eventually found out and contributes to a dishonorable, unscrupulous, and unprincipled professional atmosphere. Such an atmosphere perpetuates the myth that the only way to get ahead is by engaging in unethical behavior. When ethics are openly practiced in the workplace, everyone sees the limitations of disreputable activities and recognizes that the only profitable course of action is an ethical one.

Competent people are more likely to search for organizations that maintain high ethical standards. They know that ethical practices are the only sure way to succeed in life. When competent people migrate toward ethical firms, everyone benefits because both competence and ethics are perpetuated. Indeed, it is quite easy to make the argument that competence and ethics go hand in hand. Those who understand how to succeed know that unethical behavior leads only to covert and clandestine activities that are time consuming and unprofitable. Ethical firms therefore enjoy the advantage of employing more competent professionals.

Employee commitment is likely to be higher in ethical businesses. (Surveys have reported that all employees want to work for organizations with high ethical standards.[4]) Employee commitment yields a number of benefits, including higher employee morale, less turnover, greater productivity, and enhanced creativity. When leaders maintain high ethical standards, they can use their power for the good of the organization and its employees. We provide a more detailed discussion of leadership ethics in Chapter 3.

Goal Setting for Organizational Communication

Once you feel knowledgeable about the organization's values and ethics, you will be able to work on appropriate goals for your communication. It is not enough simply to set positive-sounding goals ("I hope my department does better this quarter"). Research reveals that goals must be set with particular criteria in mind. In situations in which you must communicate to achieve objectives, it is usually best to set specific, rather than vague, goals. Specific goals enable communicators to map out the conditions that must be met for the goals to be reached.[5] In addition, organizations have found that when high goals, instead of low ones, are set, performance is usually better. Therefore, setting specific and high goals is in your best interest when you anticipate a communication encounter. Consider the following example:

> Charlene Perkins, head of distribution at Popular Ice Company, made an appointment to discuss budget problems with her boss, Harold Danzak. Charlene planned to ask Harold for an increase in operating funds because the distribution department was having a tough time making ends meet. Charlene and Harold occasionally bowled on the same team and went to the same church, so Charlene felt pretty comfortable about the meeting. She did not plan out what she was going to say because she felt sure that Harold would see the situation her way.
>
> When Charlene arrived at Harold's office, she was kept waiting for almost thirty minutes. When Harold finally saw her, he told Charlene that he had to catch a plane for Detroit in twenty minutes. He looked at Charlene and said, "This is the worst year for budgets I have ever seen. Every department seems to need more funds to operate and I don't have much to give. I can help only the departments that really show a need." Charlene swallowed hard because she had planned to use the hour-long meeting to secure money from Harold on the basis of their friendship.

Charlene had come into the meeting with no data, hard facts, or specific goals. She did not even have a figure in mind for her budget increase request. She left the meeting with Harold encouraging her to keep up the hard work. Unfortunately, Charlene left without any increase in her operating budget.

Charlene's experience shows the importance of specific goals. They are valuable because they take set conditions into account and identify targets for communication. Specific goals allow a communicator to plan her or his actions and behaviors in advance of the communication encounter. Charlene should have set specific goals such as "I will present four points each with supporting material." "I will prioritize my points so that if we run out of time, the most important ones will be covered." "I will show how our department is in greatest need of extra funds." "I will ask for a 20 percent budget increase, in hopes that Harold will actually give me 15 percent." By setting specific and high goals, Charlene would have been in a better position for handling such a difficult situation.

Nevertheless, sometimes flexible goals are a better alternative. The business and professional world is often uncertain, and setting highly specific goals may lead you to an inflexible position or give you an unfavorable reputation as a rigid or difficult person. Communicators must plan for some flexibility when the environment is uncertain so that they have some room to maneuver. In general, however, set goals in as many instances as possible, even if they have to be less specific than you would like.

The Goal-Setting Process

Once you have recognized its importance, goal setting in business communication is not much different from setting goals for other aspects of performance. You can achieve effective goal setting by using the following steps:[6]

1. *Identify the problem.* As a first step toward goal setting, specify as exactly as possible what is to be accomplished from the communication event: the job, assignment, or responsibility to be completed. Whether you are giving a persuasive presentation, being interviewed for employment, or just talking with your boss, specific goals ensure that your performance will be effective.

2. *Map out a strategy.* Determine the level of performance necessary to achieve the desired goal, and create an evaluation measure that will tell you if you have reached that level. This measure may be as sim-

ple as an informal check list that points out specific items necessary to success, or it may be a complex and sophisticated formal evaluation form that measures your level of performance in a variety of categories.

3. *Set a performance goal.* We have argued previously that high goals are preferable to low goals because low goals may keep you from realizing your full communication potential. But in setting your goals, you must realize your capacities and limitations. You may not be able to "give the best public speech in the world," so stating that as a goal is not productive. But it is a good idea to push yourself beyond what you honestly feel would be your best performance. We predict that you will reach that goal more often than you think!

4. *Identify the resources necessary to achieve the goal.* Time, equipment, money, favors, encouragement, and moral support are just a few of the resources you may need to achieve your goals. Anticipating your resource needs will strengthen the plans and actions you take later, and planning how you will use resources can make your goals more real and concrete.

5. *Recognize contingencies that may arise.* Contingencies are events, obstacles, or circumstances that prevent you from reaching your goal. If you keep in mind Wiio's Law ("If communication can fail, it will"), you will anticipate potential problems such as equipment failure (for example, overhead and slide projector failures), hostile people, cramped spaces, time constraints, and even illness or fatigue. If you devise your goals so that a large number of potential obstacles can be removed or mitigated, you will have a better shot at achieving the performance level you desire.

6. *Obtain feedback.* Recall from Chapter 1 that feedback clarifies messages and verifies shared meaning. Feedback also makes goal setting more effective because it indicates when and where you may need to adjust your direction or methods so that you are achieving your best.

   Feedback can also provide encouragement. If you receive feedback messages that support your goals and your progress toward them, you are more likely to reach those goals and set higher ones in the future.[7] Furthermore, the higher and more specific your goals are, the more feedback you need. In essence, the process reinforces itself: setting higher goals leads to better effort and elevated performance; learning of success through feedback encourages still higher goals in the future.

As you design goals, consider *when* you intend to receive feedback. You can plan to receive periodic feedback about ongoing communication events through regular group meetings or surveys. Or if you have to make the same presentation at several occasions, getting feedback after each event through formal question-and-answer sessions or informal mingling with the audience can help you improve your next presentation. The following example illustrates the goal-setting process.

> Kevin Burd was elected chairperson of the program committee of the chapter of the Preprofessionals Club at the local junior college. His responsibility was lining up speakers for each month's meeting. He immediately identified his duties as getting speakers committed well in advance of the meeting (#1). He knew that he had to contact a variety of people to suit the varied interests of the club membership, that the speakers must be well respected in their fields, and that they would have to be willing to participate on an assigned date (#2). He set the following as performance goals (#3): speakers are to be known to the membership, they must have ten years' relevant experience in their field, they possess effective speaking skills, and they are willing to answer questions and socialize with the members after the presentation. Kevin then developed a game plan for attracting the best speakers (#4). First, he listed all those people he personally knew who fit his speaker profile. Next, for names of qualified speakers, he contacted the chamber of commerce, the speaker's bureau on campus, all the professional associations in town, and his relatives who were businesspersons in the community. Next, he submitted the names to other committee members for their advice and feedback. Finally, he contracted with the campus media center to provide all the visual aids needed for the speakers. Kevin then listed all the things he thought might go wrong (#5). He made sure that he called the speakers one week before and then again one day before the presentation to ensure that they were still committed. Next, he made sure that the equipment (slide projectors, extension cords, VCRs, etc.) had replacement parts in case something failed. He also arrived early for each presentation to ensure that the room temperature was appropriate, that the refreshments had arrived, that the chairs were set up, and that ample lighting was available. Finally, Kevin devised an evaluation sheet that he submitted to each member after the speaker left to determine how he or she felt about the speaker, topic, visual aids, and other details that were relevant to his job as program chair (#6). In this way, he was able to gauge his performance and improve on each month's meeting.

Benefits of Goal Setting

The primary benefit of effective goal setting is higher performance level, but it is not the only one.[8] Goals help to direct attention and action during communication because they give you a target to shoot for. During communication you can become easily confused if you do not have a specific goal toward which to direct yourself.

Goals are useful in mobilizing the effort you need to perform at peak levels. Setting goals makes you aware of the mental, emotional, and physical energy you will need for the communication task and encourages you to conserve and mobilize energy carefully.

Goals can prolong your efforts over time and help you persist. Lacking strong goals, you may feel the temptation to quit your effort when you meet with an obstacle or other interference, and you may be easily distracted from your mission. Goals hold you to specific results within specific time periods. Goals aid you in developing relevant and innovative strategies. When you have set important goals, you will be surprised at how ingenious and innovative you can be in devising communication strategies to reach those goals.

Situational Knowledge: The Context of Organizational Communication

The second component of the model of strategic communication is situational knowledge. This term refers to the information or facts you use in devising an effective communication strategy. In an organizational context, situational knowledge also refers to employees' awareness of the communication issues involved in their jobs. To communicate strategically, you must be familiar with both the structure and the character of your organization. This familiarity places your goals within the context of your organization. In later chapters, we will show you how to gather situational knowledge for specific purposes such as developing work relationships, preparing for meetings, and giving presentations. The fundamental concept, however, remains the same: You can increase your communication effectiveness by gathering a thorough knowledge of the person or people with whom you are communicating.

Organizational Structure

Each organization's ability to respond to challenges depends on its structure. *Structure* is an organization's physical, procedural, and patterned methods of conducting business. *Physical structure* is the actual environment where the organization is located. Some organizations may occupy several floors in a large office building; others may have branch offices, the result of which is that employees are physically spread out. Departments within an organization may be contained in one location or split among several locations. The physical structure of an organization has a strong effect on its communication style. For example, college academic departments that concentrate their faculty members on one floor facilitate more frequent communication patterns than do those that scatter faculty out over several floors or even buildings. Faculty members who are remotely located from their colleagues can feel isolated and lonely.

Procedural structure encompasses the formal policies that regulate the behavior of employees. For example, company policy may require subordinates to approach their immediate supervisor about a problem before contacting anyone at a higher level of authority. Procedural structure usually affects on-the-job communication by limiting it. A policy at many universities requires that travel requests first be made at the department level, which then forwards the request to the dean, who sends them to the vice president, who then approves them and sends them to the budget office. The budget office then issues a check for the travel, which must be recorded by the bursor's office.

Patterned structure refers to regular informal methods of communication among employees. The grapevine is an example of a patterned structure. It carries a great deal of information to organizational members and is generally thought to be fairly accurate. Another example of a patterned structure is the informal protocol used in group meetings. Some organizations may have unwritten rules that regulate who talks to whom and when in a business meeting. Interrupting someone else in a meeting may be taboo in one organization but encouraged in another. Whereas physical and procedural structures may be readily obvious to a new employee, understanding of the patterned structure requires time on the job, experience, and maybe a friend who is willing to clue in the newcomer. Figure 2-1 shows the relationship among these three types of structures.

Another way to understand structure is to look at the hierarchy, or pyramid of authority, a business maintains. *Tall* organizations have a large number of hierarchical positions. Banks are notorious for tall structures. At the top of the hierarchy is the board of directors, followed by a chief executive office (CEO), president, executive vice-presidents (VPs), senior VPs, VPs, associate VPs, assistant VPs, cashiers, assistant cashiers, tellers, and finally bookkeepers. The chain of command in tall organizations usually requires that a subordinate who wants to suggest any sort of change to top management must first communicate with his boss, who will talk to her boss, who will contact his boss, and so on. In extreme instances, a message can take weeks or even months to make its way up the chain.

Flat organizations have few rigid hierarchical levels. They try to place a large number of employees at the same level without ranking jobs as "above" or "below" others in the organization. The chain of command is generally quite short in flat organizations, which allows a more rapid movement of messages throughout the organization. The modern trend in business is toward reducing the middle-level hierarchy. Figure 2-2 compares a "tall" organization with a "flat" organization.

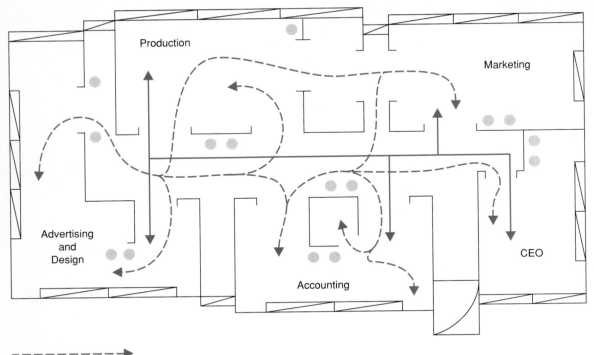

Informal lines of communication
(patterned structure)

Formal lines of communication
(procedural structure)

FIGURE 2-1   *Within the physical layout of the organization, managers'*
needs to restrict and regulate the flow of information result in procedural
structures; employees' communication needs and interests promote patterned
structures.

Organizational and Environmental Uncertainty

Knowledge of organizational structure, though important, is not enough
information on which to base strategic communication. Observing the various structures of your organization, you may find conflicting policies,
confusing patterns of communication, or even a chain of command that has
many branches of authority rather than one. Researchers use many terms
to describe conflicting information and knowledge within organizations.
Such terms as *uncertainty* and *ambiguity* are commonly used to signify
the difficulties of objectively assessing situational knowledge. Uncertainty

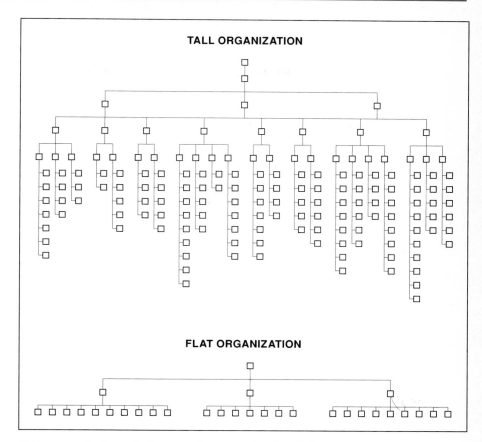

FIGURE 2-2   *Tall versus flat organizational chart*

arises when communicators do not have enough information; ambiguity
refers to information that, though available, is vague, ill-defined, and confusing. It is frequently the case in ambiguous situations that more information only adds to the confusion experienced by communicators, a condition referred to as *information overload.*

Reducing Uncertainty

We have discussed how organizations are becoming more information
based. As information increases, the human ability to assimilate, interpret,
and effectively utilize this raw data stays the same or perhaps even decreases (because of fear of information overload or failure), which intensifies
uncertainty. How can this problem be resolved? Many methods of reducing
uncertainty and ambiguity are used in business and the professions. We

have chosen to group these into two categories: organizational learning and on-the-job training.

Organizational learning.   To communicate effectively, people in business have traditionally thought it best to know everything about an organization and its environment. Although it is true that employees who monitor the organization and environment for data and information are in a better position to make informed decisions about communication, the demands of the information age have altered how such monitoring takes place. There is simply too much information for it to be analyzed piece by piece.

According to Irving Janis and Leon Mann, trying to do so leads to information overload. The drawbacks of information overload include defensive avoidance (delaying decisons unduly), overreaction (making decisions impulsively to escape the anxious state), and hypervigilance (obsessively collecting more and more information instead of making a decision).[9] Clearly, both new employees and workers dealing with large amounts of information for the first time need methods for learning about the organization without being overwhelmed.

There are several ways to accomplish this goal.[10] Employees can engage in *adaptive learning* to better understand how goals, policies, procedures, and other people's actions conform to the dynamics of the workplace. Adaptation is a survival skill in today's organizations. When employees see routines, policies, or goals altered to suit the organization, they are made aware of its important and definitive characteristics.

Employees can learn about the organization by *understanding organizational values* and assumptions. Recall from the preceding discussion that values are deep-seated beliefs and philosophies that guide organizations and people. Knowing and embracing organizational values clarify employees' awareness of how and why organizations make the decisions they do.

Developing specific knowledge of the organization is another way to avoid information overload. Employees can cultivate awareness of the norms, policies, procedures, politics, and accepted behaviors that govern their workplace. A communication strategy benefits from knowledge about what rules and boundaries are in place; otherwise, the strategy can result in errors or violations of policy.

Employees also learn by *observing successes and failures*. Essentially, they can learn a great deal about what works in an organization and what does not by assembling a track record of how they succeed and fail.

On-the-job training.   As a new employee, one of the first opportunities you will have to learn about your organization is likely to be an orientation program designed to introduce you to the company. Frederic Jablin termed the initial period of employment "assimilation."[11] New workers coming into

On-the-job training can be a rich source of organizational knowledge and values while reinforcing basic job skills. Job Corps trainees learn railroad management as part of their programs.

the organization are expected to assimilate the philosophies and operations of the workplace.

Employee orientation programs can do this by providing important information about how the company operates, the chain of command, the relationships among departments within the company, and a number of other issues. Assimilation can occur through formal training programs or through informal meetings with an immediate supervisor, handbooks, or conversations with co-workers. As Jablin put it, the "breaking in" period is a crucial process because during this time employees learn how to deal with the various relationships in the organization. Once they have mastered the various bits of knowledge about the company and the job, a "metamorphosis" occurs — they become functioning members of the organization. By this time, their situational knowledge has reached a relatively high level.

Employees continue to increase their situational knowledge by finding out about and participating in such activities as performance appraisal interviews, career development activities such as seminars and workshops, and annual business meetings. Even the informal grapevine provides a forum by which members can gain knowledge of the organization. It is to every employee's benefit to take advantage of ongoing training and educational opportunities, even when he or she is no longer new to the company.

Politics

Knowledge of an organization is incomplete without awareness of the organization as a political entity. All organizations qualify as political systems because they organize and distribute power, resources, and rewards in pursuit of specific goals. When you collect situational knowledge on an organization, it is important to consider the political climate that it maintains. Peter Frost described organizational politics as the embodiment of the exercise of power.

> "[Organizational politics] is represented in the strategies and tactics actors use to get their way in the day-to-day, ongoing, present-time functioning of organization — it is power in action. . . . It is difficult, for example, to imagine innovation and change, management or conflict, or "thinkering" with the system taking place in organizations in the absence of political activity. . . . Organizational politics in such instances becomes necessary when old alignments in the organization . . . no longer function, so that new alignments are needed that are not accommodated or anticipated by existing structures, systems, and practices."[12]

This definition emphasizes the role politics plays in shaping people's behavior in the workplace.

Politics can be viewed from two perspectives: negative/destructive behaviors that should be avoided or important aspects of communication that must be accounted for in a strategic communication plan. Although frequently used in a negative sense, politics is not necessarily disastrous. For example, in your years in school, you may have found yourself in a situation in which you needed the support of faculty, alumni, parents, or administrators to achieve a goal you strongly believed in. Building cooperation among different groups and influencing peoples' opinions to support worthwhile goals or causes are political actions. You may have little choice about whether to use politics, simply because business communication requires it. Even small details such as dressing appropriately and treating co-workers politely can be considered politics. The following political strategies are frequently employed in the workplace:[13]

◆ Selecting criteria that favor your position

◆ Using outside experts to support your position

◆ Controlling the agenda of a meeting so that only items of interest to you appear

◆ Building coalitions of "friendly" people
◆ Trading favors
◆ Adhering to policies thought desirable by powerful people
◆ Being sensitive to dress
◆ Appearing to be successful at tasks

Other political strategies include:

◆ Associating with the "right" people
◆ Appearing at official functions and meetings
◆ Assuming seating positions at group meetings that display power
◆ Making meaningless concessions to obtain compliance

If you decide to use any of these strategies, consider the ethical consequences of your communication. One way to do this is by posing questions such as the following about the potential results of the decision you intend to make.[14]

1. Who may be affected by my decision/action?
2. What is my responsibility to these parties?
3. Will my decision/action violate any commitments to these parties?
4. What may be the negative consequences of my action?
5. Will people be better or worse off in the long run?
6. What is my motivation or intent in making this decision?
7. Would I be comfortable with my decision becoming company policy for others to use?
8. Will my decision/action stand the test of time?

It is wise to take stock of the political atmosphere in the organization and determine how your own political communication style fits in. This type of situational knowledge will be valuable as you try to infuence others in accomplishing your goals, as the following example indicates.

Teresa is a recent graduate of Brugle College and has taken a job with a merchandising firm in a neighboring state. She is bright and generally perceptive when it comes to figuring out what other people are up to. Teresa was a bit shy at first but over time has made good friends of just about everyone. She prides herself on this accomplishment. She also has little trouble recognizing who has "real" power in the company and can therefore help to advance her career. She initially steered clear of the two political factions in the organization but managed to stay on amicable terms with members of both. It was not until the two factions disagreed over whether to begin a paper recycling program that Teresa decided to affiliate with the side supporting the program. She believed recycling to be an important project and felt that in the long run, the company's interests would be better served by the pro-recycling faction.

Communication Climate

As we have indicated, situational knowledge also includes information on an organization's character. Climate is one aspect of character. Scott Poole and Robert McPhee argued that climate is a function of the interactions and social processes that occur in the workplace and that climate may change depending on the development and redevelopment of organizational communication systems.[15] Thus, although climate may be a relatively stable quality, it is nevertheless subject to modification.

According to Charles Redding, the ideal communication climate consists of the following five dimensions:[16]

Supportiveness: superiors, subordinates, and co-workers provide psychological and physical support to one another.
Participative decision making: workers have opportunities to formulate decisions that affect them directly.
Trust, confidence, and credibility: the workplace is characterized by integrity.
Openness and candor: free, honest, and open communication abounds.
High performance goals: established goals reach beyond average performance.

The ability of an organization to achieve an "ideal" climate depends on the knowledge it has of its own shortcomings. Recognition of this gap between the actual and the ideal is the first step in establishing a desired climate. Of these five dimensions, openness is a particularly critical influence on climate.

Openness.   Rogers pointed out that openness is a receiver-oriented concept: it focuses on being receptive and responsive to information from others.[17] An open organization promotes communicative responsiveness among people at different levels of authority and responsibility. Being receptive and responsive to messages shows others that you are interested in what they have to say. You can encourage openness in several ways. Ask questions that demonstrate a desire to communicate with other organizational members; they will probably appreciate your efforts and respond positively to you. Show genuine interest in discussions with others. (We discuss specific listening skills that can be used for this purpose in Chapter 4.) Respond to others' communication actively. Feedback is one of the most important indications of an open organizational climate. Rogers has developed a communication openness measure that gives thirteen characteristics of an open organization.

1. Supervisors ask for suggestions.
2. Supervisors act on criticism.
3. Supervisors listen to complaints.
4. People ask for supervisors' opinions.
5. Supervisors follow up on people's opinions.
6. Supervisors suggest new ideas.
7. People ask co-workers for suggestions.
8. Supervisors listen to bad news.
9. People listen to new ideas from co-workers.
10. Supervisors listen to new ideas.
11. Supervisors follow up on suggestions.
12. Supervisors ask for personal opinions.
13. People listen to supervisors' suggestions.

In your experiences, how many of the organizations you have associated with had these characteristics? Often it is difficult to be receptive and responsive to people whom you do not like, trust, or respect. But openness, even if initially forced, can yield positive results.

The potential advantages of communication openness have been described by researchers studying organizational communication. Included among these advantages are improved organizational performance, enhanced job satisfaction, improved role clarity (understanding what your duties are), and increased information adequacy (having the right amount of information for your job).[18] Open communication also has advantages, such as encouraging conscientious, openminded, task oriented, and innovative people to interact with and positively influence others. People respect those who are receptive and responsive to communication and can learn from their success in the organization.

Strategic ambiguity. A completely open communication climate may seem ideal, but it may turn out to be unrealistic given the complexity of communication in most organizations. Indeed, some types of information are best communicated in vague and nonspecific ways. Such *strategic ambiguity,* as Eric Eisenberg has made clear, is appropriate for topics that cannot be discussed in an open fashion.[19] When a person has to decide

FOCUS on Corporate Communication

PACIFIC BELL

*T*he complex and changing environment of the telecommunications industry reflects the nature of communication at Pacific Bell. In addition to employee and customer needs, the organization must address the demands of government regulators, legislators, consumer activists, the media, and community organizations. It must also adapt to continual technological advancement, increasing population and service loads, and stepped-up competition resulting from recently overhauled regulatory requirements. These demands have acted as a force for change in both the corporate culture and the role of communication at Pacific Bell.

Pacific Bell's corporate communications department has three major arms. Headquarters, which employs about one hundred people, is based in San Francisco, California. The headquarters staff provides employee communication, media relations at the statewide and national levels, customer information, executive speeches, consumer relations, and corporate television services. The second outlet is a network of ten field offices employing about eighty people, who concentrate on local community relations and public affairs. A separate holding company, Pacific Telesis, handles government relations, shareowner relations, and national media relations on financial, investor, and federal matters. Pacific Telesis also provides some communication

and executive support services for subsidiaries other than Pacific Bell.

This multifaceted structure illustrates the goal of corporate communication at Pacific Bell: to act as the intersecting point between corporate goals and stakeholders' (which include customers, employees, government, shareowners, media, and communities) issues and to work out a balance when interests are in conflict. Nevertheless, the structure of communications also shows a potential for problems — the system may not provide enough upward communication from the employees and customers.

To meet the challenges of the competitive marketplace it now faces, Pacific Bell is working to change its corporate culture. A key component of that change is how employees communicate with one another. The organization had traditionally employed a one-way, top-down style that relied heavily on formal media, but it is evolving into an interactive, highly individual culture.

A number of channels have been introduced to make the change possible. One of the most important is the "communications round table," which includes thirty managers responsible for improving two-way communication within their departments. Because most of these managers did not have prior formal communication training, part of the round-table meeting time is spent developing interactive communication skills under the guidance of the Director of Communication Strategies. Formulating a "communicator's cookbook" (a series of goals and ideals for two-way communication), working on personal communication plans for the business units, and discussing issues raised by increased two-way communication are all methods of learning by doing for the round-table members. The director also provides support for their questions and problems during regular work hours.

These managers help others in their departments to react effectively to downward communication in the organization by, for example, putting news in perspective and providing background information. They also help to plan communication for maximum employee involvement in solving business problems. This "proactive" communication includes starting recognition and reward programs, encouraging employee suggestion plans, managing local newsletters, setting up departmentwide communication over voice mail, and arranging executive forums.

Managers are not the only people responsible for creating a more open and interactive environment at Pacific Bell. Commitment to interactive communication exists at all levels of the company. For example, in addition to local executive forums in which division heads respond to their employees' questions and concerns, the president of the organization holds an open forum in a different city each month. At these forums, employees have the opportunity to hear about company strategies and goals and are free to ask about anything on their minds. People are also encouraged to send letters and commentary for publication in the company newsletter, whose title was recently changed from *Update* to *Connections* to emphasize the importance of sharing information and open communication.

Within the corporate communications department, jobs are being reoriented to allow employees greater freedom and personal control. As communicators begin looking at issues more broadly, their strategic thinking skills become a high priority. In the past, one "communications planner" would design an overall plan for addressing a communication issue and then assign parts of the plan (articles, speeches, or other tasks) to various specialists. Increasingly, people at all levels of the department "own" their issues. They analyze, determine the appropriate communication techniques and tools with which to address issues, and design the supporting communication. Because of this, the ability to analyze all sides of an issue, to think strategically, is one of the foremost skills required of employees in communications at Pacific Bell.

Top-notch verbal and written skills are a must for any communicator, but in the corporate world, negotiating skills and the ability to relate well with peers and senior management are just as important. Analytic skills and strategic thinking are increasingly important as the job of balancing stakeholders' needs and corporate goals becomes more challenging.

between openness and ambiguity, a contingency approach, according to Eisenberg, is the best method for doing so.

A *contingency approach* means taking into account factors such as the need for personal privacy and the desire to maintain objectivity before communicating. For example, some employees may feel uncomfortable discussing organizational politics. Others may not appreciate communication about the personal problems of co-workers.

Eisenberg identified specific situations that may require strategic ambiguity rather than communication openness. Bargaining and negotiation settings may not lend themselves to a totally open communication atmosphere. Negotiators who are too open may "give away the farm" if they reveal all their bargaining strategies. Crisis situations may require that information traveling up or down the hierarchy be communicated less specifically. Full disclosure of the details of a crisis may ignite an overload of counterproductive emotions that can hurt the organization's ability to take action.

Think about your work experiences. Were there times when information was withheld from you or others for similar reasons? Did you agree with the decision at the time? Such examples suggest that although communication openness is an intrinsically valuable standard, situations may arise in which strategic ambiguity is a better option. If faced with such a choice, use your goals, organizational values, and situational knowledge to guide your decision.

The Benefits of Situational Knowledge

Situational knowledge is a significant component of our model of organizational communication for several reasons. First, knowledge about the organization helps employees to achieve personal and organizational goals. Knowing who to communicate with and how enhances the acceptability of their ideas. Second, knowledge of the organization's reward system gives employees a better idea of what is valued and considered a priority. One of the biggest problems employees face is lack of information about the significance of their contributions to the organization. This can be minimized when organizational knowledge is high. Third, situational knowledge allows for better coordination among members of a department or between departments. Recognition and understanding of the relative relationships among various people and units can save time and effort. Fourth, situational knowledge allows for greater employee development. When employees recognize the different paths to enhancing their careers, they are in better positions to perform those roles that can lead to promotions. Employees who know that they can grow, develop, and mature with an organization are much more likely to be loyal and to remain with the company.

Communication Competence

Communication competence, the third component of our model, means the ability to communicate appropriately *and* effectively with other people. Communication strategies can be effective without being appropriate. Consider the following example.

> Trudy arrived at the monthly staff meeting with one goal: to persuade John, the division manager, to approve her request to attend a conference out of state. As the meeting progressed, she repeatedly brought up the subject until John finally remarked, "Although travel requests are not an issue we have on the agenda today, I will give tentative approval just so we can all concentrate on the problems at hand. In the future I expect personal requests to be presented at least one week before the staff meeting so we can plan time to discuss them.

Trudy may have been effective because she accomplished her goal, but she was inappropriate because she did not handle the situation properly and hurt her chances to gain John's cooperation in the future. To ensure effective and appropriate communication, consider three factors: the message content, whether it is internal or external, and the appropriate channel.

Messages

As you learned in Chapter 1, messages are the ideas you wish to communicate. Messages may be instructive, informative, persuasive, humorous, complimentary, or even critical. Regardless of the form, the message must be effective and appropriate to be competent. The following are general suggestions for ensuring that your messages are proficient:

1. Be specific: include as many details and definite facts as possible to prevent vagueness.
2. Be accurate: ensure that what you are communicating is as authentic and reliable as possible.
3. Be honest: do not give in to temptations to use data, facts, and relationships in less than forthright ways just to make your case.
4. Be logical: messages are most easily understood when they follow a logical, rational, and sequential path.
5. Be complete: check your potential message to ensure that you have provided all the information the receiver requires.
6. Be succinct: be as brief or concise as possible. No one in the professional world has time for unnecessarily long messages.

7. Include time frames: all receivers need to know the time frames you have in mind for acting on your message. Give a specific indication in your message when you need action.

8. Be relevant: make sure that the only people getting your message are those who need or want it. Sending messages to just anyone wastes time all around.

9. Use the proper rate: especially for oral messages, ensure that your messages are not sent too rapidly or too slowly. Receivers sometimes refuse to handle such messages.

10. Be timely: ensure that when sending messages, you have sent them in a timely fashion. Messages that arrive too early or too late are not as effective.

11. Ask for feedback: elicit information from receivers about their feelings about and reactions to your message.

Internal Communication

Internal communication refers to messages sent and received within the organizational boundaries of the company. Formal internal communication can include policy statements from the president, changes in operating procedures, and instructions from superiors. Less formal patterns include patterns of address. For example, workers at IBM are addressed as "Mrs.," "Miss," "Mr.," or "Ms." in keeping with the formal atmosphere of the organization, although no specific policy requires this behavior. Not every organization communicates the same way. Think of the communication patterns you have encountered in your work or school experience. Would you consider them to be formal or informal?

Messages can be exchanged in three directions: downward, upward, and horizontally. There are specific reasons for communicating in these three directions, and how a communicator does so depends on his or her needs at the time.

Downward communication. Downward communication refers to messages from superiors or subordinates. Daniel Katz and Robert Kahn identified five types of downward communication in organizations.[20] *Job instructions* are messages that specify how to conduct tasks on the job ("Always submit budget requests two months in advance"). *Job rationales* are messages that explain why tasks must be performed and how these tasks relate to other activities of the organization ("We require advance notice so that we can plan ahead"). *Procedures and practices* are those messages that inform organizational members about the organization's responsibilities, obligations, and privileges ("According to the procedures

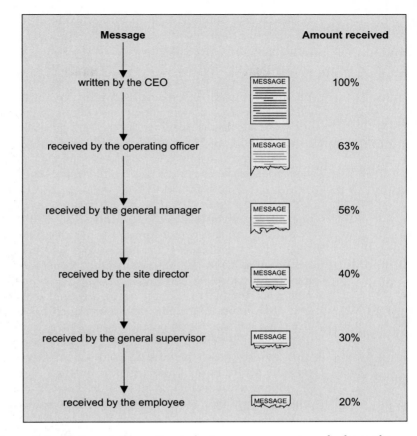

Message		Amount received
written by the CEO	MESSAGE	100%
received by the operating officer	MESSAGE	63%
received by the general manager	MESSAGE	56%
received by the site director	MESSAGE	40%
received by the general supervisor	MESSAGE	30%
received by the employee	MESSAGE	20%

FIGURE 2-3   Information is lost as a message travels down the organizational chain of command.   Reprinted by permission of the publisher, from Managing by Design, *by Ray Killian © 1968 ANACOM, a division of American Management Association, New York. all rights reserved.*

manual, we follow affirmative action guidelines to the letter"). *Feedback* is made up of messages that inform employees of their performance in the organization ("I am happy to note that your last project was a real success"). *Indoctrination of goals* comprises messages that teach employees the mission, goals, and objectives of the organization ("As you can see from our shared values list, we feel that customer service is our number one job").

Although very common and often necessary to ensure that employees can do their jobs, downward communication can generate its share of troubles. One problem results from the chain of command. Typically, a message originates near or at the top of an organization (for example, the president's office) and is sent down the chain person by person. This *serial communication* negatively affects the accuracy of the message. Think of the "gossip" game that you played as a child, in which one person whispers a message to another, who in turn whispers it to the next person, and so on. By the time the message reaches the last person in the chain, it is usually quite different from the original message. Figure 2-3 shows the percentage of information lost in each transfer.

The same effect can occur in a message that must travel down a long chain of command, especially if it is circulated through more than one channel. When practicing downward communication, you are wise to imagine yourself as the receiver. Does the message make sense to you? Is it effective without being disrespectful? A carefully considered message can forestall many of the more common communication failures. Asking these questions of all your messages can help prevent miscommunication.

Upward communication.   Upward communication is made up of messages from subordinates to superiors. Katz and Kahn, again, were instructive in revealing types of upward communication. These include messages that reflect employee performance and job-related problems ("Jorge, we continue to have trouble getting the proper notice for shipping dates"); messages that reveal information about fellow employees ("Freda and Elizabeth are unable to participate in the fund-raising campaign"); messages that communicate attitudes and understandings about organizational practices and policies ("It is becoming obvious that most line employees do not appreciate the new work schedule"); and messages that report on the activities and tasks associated with goal accomplishment ("I am glad to report that the McKendrick project is now finished").

There are several advantages to upward communication.[21] It shows superiors whether their ideas, plans, and policies are being accepted by subordinates. It gives subordinates an opportunity to participate actively in the decision-making process and thus satisfies their need to feel valued. Talking to superiors can release the tension or stress subordinates may feel in coping with their jobs. Often, people simply need someone to listen so they can feel good about what they are doing. Finally, upward communication can alert superiors to impending problems from which they may be isolated. Nevertheless, upward communication tends to be "rosy" because lower-level organization members rarely want to send bad news to their supervisors.

Horizontal communication.   Messages exchanged at the same hierarchical level in an organization constitute horizontal communication. Thomas Daniels and Barry Spiker identified several functions of horizontal communication.[22] It facilitates problem solving ("Why don't we get together over lunch to hammer out the details?"). It allows information sharing across different work groups ("Send that information over computer network to the Dayton office"). It promotes task coordination between departments or teams ("I am glad that the public relations and advertising departments are exchanging information on the Sierra project"). It enhances morale ("It helps to know that other units experience similar types of frustrations"). And it affords a means for resolving conflicts ("When we are able to get together, we have an easier time seeing each other's point of view").

The frequency and effectiveness of horizontal communication depend on the structure of the organization. Some organizations, particularly tall ones or those in traditionally conservative fields such as banking, may rely primarily on vertical (especially downward) communication; horizontal communication is rare or used only for social reasons. Flat organizations frequently use horizontal communication because it is appropriate to their structures. Companies in highly innovative or creative fields use it because they need flexibility.

Despite its benefits, horizontal communication does have drawbacks. Daniels and Spiker suggested three reasons for these problems: territoriality, specialization, and lack of motivation. In the case of territoriality, people or departments may feel that communicating with others will prematurely reveal ideas and plans and thus reduce their overall impact. Some employees may also feel that interacting with others gives away hard-earned territory or privileges. Or jealousy and envy may prevent effective horizontal communication.

Specialization occurs as members of departments work together on projects and develop certain frames of reference, mindsets, and jargon specific to their responsibilities. Lacking this knowledge, people outside the departments (even if they are at the same level in the organization) have a difficult time understanding or appreciating such specialized communication.

Some employees may not understand the importance of lateral communication and may simply avoid it because they lack the motivation to do otherwise. Attitudes such as "If you want something done right, do it yourself" and "Why cooperate with the other departments if we have to share the credit?" demonstrate cynicism about horizontal communication.

Informal networks. In addition to direction, messages often travel along paths (channels) outside officially specified channels. These informal networks, which are often equated with the grapevine, are frequently used as a substitute for downward, upward, or more formal horizontal communication. Messages exchanged in the hallway, in the coffee room, at parties, or in restaurants are examples of informal communication. Figure 2-4 shows the nature of message exchange in a grapevine.

It is often argued that informal communication occurs in organizations because insufficient opportunities exist for formal communication. Although some people believe that informal communication must be minimized or controlled, Gerald Goldhaber summarized much of the research in the area and reported the following results:[23]

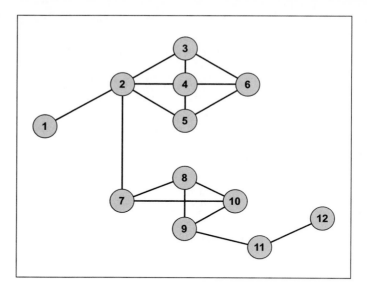

FIGURE 2-4   *Communication in the grapevine tends to be informal yet efficient and diffuse yet effective.*

The grapevine is fast.
The grapevine is generally accurate.
The grapevine carries much information.
The grapevine gives an indication of employee attitudes and
   sentiment.
The grapevine is a common channel for rumors.
The grapevine travels by clusters.

The grapevine is generally a highly effective communication system, especially if formal paths of communication are overburdened. For example, one manager in a paper manufacturing firm became so frustrated with the delay in getting information disseminated to other workers that he used Friday afternoon socials to provide them with the needed information.

External Communication

External communication refers to messages exchanged between the organization and its environment. Although many of the messages that are sent to and received from the environment are anticipated, even perfunctory (e.g., newsletters, annual reports, advertising, good-will speeches, corporate sponsorship of nonprofit events), many of these messages are exchanged in an effort to reduce environmental uncertainty. These messages can also enable workers to understand how the environment affects the internal efficiency of the organization.

Listening carefully to customers' needs, being receptive to new ideas or information emanating from competitors, learning new techniques from new employees, and employing expert consultants are some ways organizations can "listen" to their environments so as to reduce uncertainty. To a large extent, such activity is compatible with our discussion of situational knowledge; as employees gain additional information about the environment, they build on their knowledge of the overall situation.

Public relations departments are usually charged with reducing environmental uncertainty by sending messages into the environment. A public relations department does this by sending out press releases that show the company in a favorable light, promoting community relations, participating in fund-raising activities, and working with other organizations on a common problem or issue. As a result, the company's mission and values become clearer to environmental actors, and there is less uncertainty all around. James Kouzes and Barry Posner made a very compelling case for paying attention to external communication:

> We can understand how some work groups and organizations become myopic and unimaginative. It isn't that people themselves are dull or slow-witted. It is that they have become too familiar with their routines and too isolated from outside influences. To infuse ideas into an organization, a leader needs to shake it up periodically. Whatever the technique, the leader must be on the alert for hardening of the communication arteries.[24]

Channels

Choosing the appropriate channel for your messages is critical to communication competence. Recall that channels are the media that carry messages to receivers. Channels include conversations, speeches, interviews, memos, letters, phone calls, and even computer and satellite networks. A channel's characteristics, especially its richness, determine its viability in a particular message exchange.

Channel richness. Channel richness refers to the ability of a communication channel (such as a telephone call) to handle information or convey the meaning contained in a message.[25] Some channels are best for certain messages, whereas other channels may be inappropriate for those same messages. Whether a channel or medium is high or low in richness depends on four conditions: the capacity to transmit immediate feedback from the receiver; the ability to communicate multiple communication cues, such as facial expressions, body language, appearance, and dress; the extent to which the message can be shaped or tailored to a specific situation; and language variety, or the ability to use a wide range of word choices. If you think about these criteria, it becomes clear that the richest channels are face-to-face meetings with few language restrictions. The least rich channels are undirected written memos (such as flyers addressed to "occupant"). Figure 2-5 illustrates the range of channel richness. As you can observe from the figure, if you start at the top where the richest channel is located and move down, each sequential channel is less able to satisfy the criteria we just listed.

Which channels are most effective for sending messages differ from one organization to another. Some organizations are "memo happy" — communication is defined as an 8½″ × 11″ page that begins with "To:." Other organizations emphasize videos that update employees on the current state of affairs. The increasing use of electronic mail (E-mail) demonstrates its popularity as a quick and moderately rich channel.

Selecting the proper channel.   Competent communication involves choosing the appropriate channel for the message. Given the effort you have put into the message so far — setting a goal, collecting situational knowledge, formulating an effective message — your work will be wasted if you use an ineffective channel, such as interoffice mail, rather than hand delivery, for an important report on a competitor's product. Research has shown that managers prefer the richest media: face-to-face meetings and telephones.[26]

As a rule of thumb, rich media are best when the message is designed for specific people, when time is important, when immediate feedback is necessary, when the situation is stressful, when the message is vague or difficult to understand, and when personal information is to be conveyed. Less rich media are most useful when routine information, orders or policy is to be transmitted; when large numbers of people have to be reached at once; when immediate feedback is unnecessary; and when formal communication is more appropriate (public presentations at an awards banquet).[27]

Choosing the proper channel for communication is not an easy task, but the following guidelines can be helpful when evaluating your options.[28] Consider *speed:* oral and electronic channels are the fastest means of communicating with others in the organization. When *accuracy* is at a premium, written, and to a lesser extent electronic, means are the preferred channels of communication. *Feedback* can be obtained by any of the three channels. Oral communication, especially when conducted face to face, provides a great deal of immediate feedback, not only about the content of the message but also about the emotional level of the communicator. Written channels are less likely to obtain spontaneous feedback.

Some messages are not appropriate or effective for everyone in the organization or even in a work group. Highly sensitive or confidential messages may need to be directed at only some people. Therefore, *selectivity* in the use of channels must be practiced. Oral communication channels

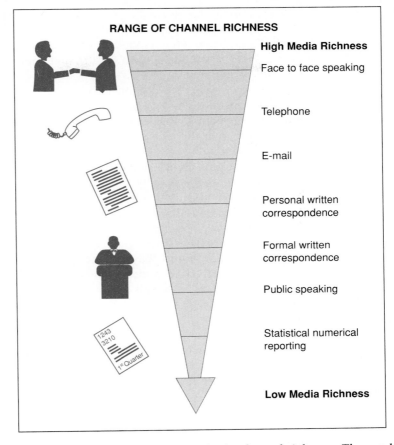

RANGE OF CHANNEL RICHNESS

High Media Richness

Face to face speaking

Telephone

E-mail

Personal written correspondence

Formal written correspondence

Public speaking

Statistical numerical reporting

Low Media Richness

FIGURE 2-5   Wide variations exist in channel richness. The sender considers the goal of the message and characteristics of the intended receiver (or receivers) to determine the most appropriate channel.

are effective for sensitive messages, although private memos may be used as well.

Appropriateness is another consideration. Some channels of communication simply are not as appropriate for some messages as others. Communicating companywide policy changes through an oral channel exclusively is inappropriate, as is communicating the termination of an employee on a bulletin board. Some issues are sticky and require a special channel for conveying that information.

A number of *cost* issues arise in the selection of a communication channel. For an organization with branch or remote facilities, it is easy but expensive to talk to other employees about day-to-day affairs. The advent of the facsimile (fax) machine makes written communication convenient but costly. Nevertheless, employee cost must also be kept in mind: constructing a memo could take fifteen minutes to write, type, print, copy, and distribute to someone. A telephone used for the same purpose saves some portion of that fifteen minutes.

Accountability, the responsibility a receiver has for responding to a message, includes not only providing feedback to the sender of the message but also responding to the instruction, information, directive, request, or other purpose of the message. Written channels are usually more likely to gain accountability for the purpose of the message.

Not all channels are equally acceptable forms of communication to all people. *Acceptance* usually depends on the person. For example, some people despise memos, while others feel oral channels are too informal. If you are concerned about the impact of your message, ask yourself, What medium does my target prefer?

Researchers have investigated the effectiveness of channels for different messages. According to Wayne Pace, who did a synopsis of studies in this area, the most effective modes of communication are (in rank order) presenting information in both oral and written channels, presenting information to a group orally, presenting information to each member of the group in written form, posting the information on a bulletin board, and making no presentation of the information in either oral or written form (allowing informal channels to pick up the slack).[29] Because human beings have a tendency to be attracted to multimedia stimuli, it stands to reason that information presented in oral and written channels is most effective.

Anxiety Management

Anxiety management refers to a communicator's ability to control the nervousness, anxiety, fears, stress, and worries associated with a communication event. There are many reasons communication events cause people to get anxious. Sometimes people are most anxious before communicating because they have spent so much energy anticipating what they will have to do. Others are more anxious while they are communicating. Still others worry and fret over their communication performance after the fact. In any case, one thing is certain: each person's method of handling the anxiety associated with communication episodes is unique.

Because stress or anxiety all too often prevents a communicator from doing her or his best, managing communication anxiety is an essential ingredient in developing effective communication strategies. Such management requires knowing the causes and effects of communication anxiety and knowing how to treat it.

Causes of Communication Anxiety

For many years, researchers have tried to identify the causes of communication anxiety. The best conclusion that can be drawn from their studies is that multiple factors are responsible for the fears and worries that people have about communicating. Some of the most common factors include:[30]

> Novelty: people are more anxious in new communication situations.
> Formality: communication situations that require prescribed actions and behaviors and allow little deviation from those norms frequently cause anxiety.
> Subordinate status: being in a subordinate position often causes people to feel intimidated and ill at ease.
> Conspicuousness: communication situations that put people at the center of others' attention (such as public speaking) can be uncomfortable.
> Lack of skill: a lack of the communication skills necessary to be effective in some situations can induce anxiety.
> Past experiences: failure in certain communication situations (such as job interviews) may cause anxiety about future encounters.
> Evaluation: knowing that communication skills are being assessed can cause a person anxiety, especially if there is a lot at stake in the assessment.

Inappropriate communication load is another frequent cause of stress and anxiety on the job. Communication load, as defined by Richard Farace, Peter Monge, and Hamish Russell, is "the rate and complexity of communication inputs to an individual."[31] Rate is determined by the number of communication demands (requests, orders, memos, telephone calls, etc.) on the receiver. Complexity refers to the number of decisions the receiver must make about the information. In other words, a person's communication load is a function of how much information she or he must deal with, coupled with how difficult it is to do so.

The important issue at this point in our discussion is the *relativity of load*. Relative load depends on the receiver's processing capability, which varies for different receivers. One person may experience more load than someone else given the same information and conditions. Anxiety can be caused by both communication overload and communication underload.

Communication overload.   Communication overload occurs when the amount of information received exceeds an employee's or department's ability to process that information. You have probably heard people complain about overload on the job; they are probably being bombarded by information that they cannot process in the allotted time. Communication overload can be a serious concern in organizations because of the problems associated with this phenomenon.

Productivity may fall when people or units are unable to process the information they receive. A bottleneck of information may occur at that point. Communication overload severely taxes physical, psychological, and emotional energies. Fatigue, alertness, anxiety, and confusion may appear as specific symptoms of overload. As a general rule, the best method of coping with overload is to reduce the information input until such time that an optimal balance between input and processing abilities is possible.

Communication underload.   Underload, in contrast to overload, refers to the underutilized processing capacity of a unit or person that results when too little information is received from the system or environment. Some jobs are made up of routine, simple, monotonous, highly predictable tasks that require very little mental effort. Most employees experiencing underload suffer from many of the same symptoms associated with communication overload, and it is often overqualified employees who feel these effects most strongly.

In particular, underload can cause tension, anxiety, psychological confusion, and a decline in self-identity.[32] The problem is that the person is not stimulated enough in his or her normal duties. What can be done about underload? Again, as a general remedy, workers have filled the void created by a lack of information by daydreaming, talking to others, or even creating new tasks for themselves.

Knowing the causes of communication anxiety is a first step toward managing the stress and fears that may be associated with communication situations. At this point, take out a piece of paper and list the causes of communication anxiety that most affect you. Think about these as we continue our discussion.

Effects of Communication Anxiety

Communication anxiety takes its toll on the occupational, professional, and vocational interests of some people. Research has demonstrated a number of negative effects resulting from the uncontrolled anxiety associated with communication.[33] People who are afraid to communicate may be negatively perceived by others. Co-workers and bosses may see those who refuse to communicate as uncooperative and may not trust these people with important tasks. Or communication anxiety may cause people to appear incompetent in their communication performance (pausing, stuttering, making poor eye contact, etc.). It has also been the case that people who suffer from a high degree of communication anxiety are unassertive and shy compared to people who do not experience such anxiety.

These negative perceptions result in many unfavorable effects for anxious communicators. They have fewer leadership opportunities; they are less likely to be chosen for leadership positions and take less initiative in attempting to gain leadership roles. Anxious communicators are also perceived as less attractive because communication skills are deemed an important social function in occupation settings. As a result, anxious communicators are granted fewer job interviews, receive lower pay and fewer promotions, enjoy less job satisfaction, and do not retain their jobs as long as communicators who are less anxious. It is no wonder that people who experience high degrees of communication anxiety seek out occupations with lower communication demands (accountants, farmers, construction workers).

Communication Anxiety Management

You may think that we have painted a very dreary picture for those who experience some degree of communication anxiety. Actually, most people are anxious in at least some situations. As you look back at the causes of communication anxiety, you may feel that only one or two of these apply to you, or you may identify with many of them. Controlling anxiety means understanding where you stand and how you feel about the stressfulness of a communication situation. When you listed the causes of anxiety, you learned what may be producing nervousness in certain situations. Another way of identifying anxiety is by recognizing which communication situations are most stressful for you. Take a look at the situations on page 66 and rate their relative stressfulness for you.

As you look over your ratings, you will probably notice that some situations elicit a greater degree of stress than others. It is perfectly natural to be "situationally" anxious. These are the circumstances that you have to work on to become an effective communicator. You can do so by learning to focus your nervous energy and thereby maximize your communication effectiveness. Keep your responses to this self-check in mind as we discuss the phenomenon of communication anxiety throughout this book and suggest methods to assess and control it in a variety of business contexts including interviews, meetings, and presentations.

Summary

The model of strategic communication described in this chapter presents a practical perspective on organizational theory. It also offers tools for dealing with the effects on business of globalization and the dependence on information. Goal setting, the first aspect of the model, enables the communicator to plan the most effective campaign or tactics for continued organizational success. The second aspect, situational knowledge, allows

COMMUNICATION APPREHENSION CHECK

On a scale of 1 to 10 (with 10 being the highest level of stress and 1 being the lowest), rate your degree of stress for the following communication situations.

1. _____ interviewing for a job
2. _____ leading a group
3. _____ arguing with your boss
4. _____ asking friends for a charitable donation
5. _____ disagreeing with a co-worker
6. _____ speaking up in a hostile group
7. _____ telling jokes or funny stories at a bull session
8. _____ making an excuse for a mistake
9. _____ giving a media interview
10. _____ challenging someone's point of view
11. _____ presenting a report to your boss's boss
12. _____ giving a brief report to co-workers
13. _____ conversing with a new acquaintance
14. _____ persuading a co-worker
15. _____ giving a formal presentation to strangers
16. _____ answering questions
17. _____ refusing to grant a request
18. _____ explaining your actions
19. _____ demonstrating leadership skills
20. _____ denying responsibility for a misunderstanding

for greater flexibility in assessing, selecting, and evaluating the messages that are exchanged within the organization and with the environment. Such knowledge also reduces uncertainty and helps the communicator to know when strategic ambiguity is appropriate. Communication competence, the third aspect, enhances the ability to achieve goals in the context of differing communication networks, allowing greater opportunity for improved productivity. Anxiety management focuses on maintaining those elements of organizational communication that are essential for establishing and maintaining the highest level of performance possible.

Discussion

1. How are shared values established in an organization? In your opinion, which of the techniques would be most effective, and why?

2. What are some advantages of ethical behavior in organizations?

3. Why are specific communication goals more useful than general goals? How does goal setting improve organizational communication?

4. Discuss several of the methods for collecting situational knowledge presented in the chapter. Which would be more effective for large organizations? For small organizations?

5. What is organizational politics? How can you evaluate the integrity of "political" actions and communications?

6. Why is downward communication in organizations sometimes problematic? What does the balance of downward, upward, and horizontal communication reveal about an organization's structure, climate, and culture?

7. Discuss the criteria for choosing an appropriate channel. In the following situations, which criteria would be most important?
   a. Scheduling a performance review
   b. Doing a performance review
   c. Demonstrating a new product to sales managers
   d. Announcing a new benefits policy

8. What are some causes of communication anxiety in organizations?

Activities

1. Select any major organization you wish to research. Through an examination of its propaganda, pamphlets, shareholder statements, and recent media coverage or through interviews with executives and other employees, explain what you believe its values are.

2. Explain from your own experience whether you think ethical communication makes businesses and organizations stronger.

3. Imagine you are a department manager in a large electronics store. Use the six steps in goal setting, and design a proper goal for the communication behavior of a new salesperson. Document each step. What changes or improvements might you expect in the salesperson's performance as a result of these goals?

4. Modern trends demonstrate that organizations are flattening their hierarchies by eliminating the jobs of many middle-level managers. How do you believe this has affected communication in these organizations?

5. Share with your class an example of when you communicated horizontally (to a co-worker) instead of vertically (to your boss) on a job you held recently. Why did you make the decision to communicate in the direction that you did?

Notes

1. J. Case, "The Open-Book Managers," *INC.* (September 1990), 107–108.
2. W. S. Howell, *The Empathic Communicator* (Belmont, Calif.: Wadsworth, 1982), p. 192.
3. S. P. Golen, C. Powers, and M. A. Titkemeyer, "Ethics," in S. P. Golen (ed.), *Methods of Teaching Selected Topics in Business Communication* (Urbana, Ill.: Association for Business Communication, 1986), pp. 3–8.
4. C. M. Kelly, *The Destructive Achiever* (Reading, Mass.: Addison-Wesley, 1988), pp. 196–197.
5. E. A. Locke, D. Chah, S. Harrison, and N. Lustgarten, "Separating the Effects of Goal Specificity from Goal Level," *Organizational Behavior and Human Decision Making* 43 (1989), 270–287.
6. E. A. Locke, K. N. Shaw, L. M. Saari, and G. P. Latham, "Goal Setting and Task Performance: 1969–1980," *Psychological Bulletin* 90 (1981), 125–152.
7. Locke et al., "Separating the Effects"; Locke et al., "Goal Setting."
8. Ibid.
9. A. Etzioni, "Humble Decision Making," *Harvard Business Review* (July-August 1989), 123; I. Janis and L. Mann, *Decision Making: A Psychological Analysis of Conflict, Choice, and Commitment* (New York: Free Press, 1977).
10. P. Shrivesta in R. L. Daft and G. P. Huber, "How Organizations Learn: A Communication Framework," *Research in the Sociology of Organizations* 5 (1987), 1–36.
11. F. Jablin, "Organizational Communication: An Assimilation Approach," in M. Rolof and C. Berger (eds.), *Social Cognition and Communication* (Newbury Park, Calif.: Sage, 1982), pp. 255–286.
12. P. Frost, "Power, Politics, and Influence," in F. Jablin, L. Putnam, K. Roberts, and L. Porter (eds.), *Handbook of Organizational Communication* (Newbury Park, Calif.: Sage, 1987), p. 518.
13. Ibid.
14. R. E. Reidenbach and D. P. Robin, *Ethics and Profits* (Englewood Cliffs, N.J.: Prentice-Hall, 1989).
15. S. Poole and R. McPhee, "A Structural Theory of Organizational Climate," in L. Putnam and M. Pacanowsky (eds.), *Organizational Communication: An Interpretive Approach* (Newbury Park, Calif.: Sage, 1983), pp. 195–219.
16. C. Redding, *Communication within the Organization: An Interpretive Review of Theory and Research* (New York: Industrial Communication Council, 1972).
17. D. Rogers, "The Development of a Measure of Perceived Communication Openness," *Journal of Business Communication* 24 (1987), 53–61.
18. Ibid.
19. E. Eisenberg and M. Witten, "Reconsidering Openness in Organizational Communication," *Academy of Management Review* 12 (1987), 418–426.
20. D. Katz and R. Kahn, *The Social Psychology of Organizations* (New York: John Wiley and Sons, 1966).
21. J. Koehler and G. Huber, "Effects of Upward Communication on Managerial Decision Making" (Paper presented at the annual meeting of the International Communication Association, New Orleans, 1974).
22. T. Daniels and B. Spiker, *Perspectives on Organizational Communication* (Dubuque, Iowa: William C. Brown, 1987).

23. G. Goldhaber, *Organizational Communication* (Dubuque, Iowa: William C. Brown, 1990).

24. J. Kouzes and B. Posner, *The Leadership Challenge: How to Get Extraordinary Things Done in Organizations* (San Francisco: Jossey-Bass, 1987), p. 58.

25. R. L. Daft and R. H. Lengel, "Organizational Information Requirements, Media Richness, and Structural Design," *Management Science* 32 (1986), 554–571; R. L. Daft and G. P. Huber, "How Organizations Learn: A Communication Framework," *Research in the Sociology of Organizations* 5 (1987), 1–36; G. P. Huber and R. L. Daft, "The Information Environments of Organizations," in Jablin et al. (eds.), *Handbook of Organizational Communication,* pp. 130–164.

26. Daft and Lengel, "Organizational Information."

27. Daft and Huber, "How Organizations Learn."

28. This section is adapted from D. A. Level and W. P. Galle, *Business Communicator: Theory and Practice* (Dallas: Business Publications, 1980); A. J. Melcher and R. Beller, "Toward a Theory of Organization Communication: Considerations in Channel Selection," *Academy of Management Journal* 10 (1967), 39–52.

29. W. Pace, *Organizational Communication: Foundations for Human Resource Development* (Englewood Cliffs, N.J.: Prentice-Hall, 1983).

30. A. H. Buss, *Self-Consciousness and Social Anxiety* (San Francisco: W. H. Freeman, 1980); J. Daly and J. L. Hailey, "Putting the Situation into Writing Research: Situational Parameters of Writing Apprehension as Disposition and State," in R. E. Beach and L. Bridwell (eds.), *New Directions in Composition Research* (New York: Guilford, 1984), pp. 259–273.

31. R. Farace, P. Monge, and H. Russell, *Communicating and Organizing* (Reading, Mass.: Addison-Wesley, 1977), p. 100.

32. C. Stohl and C. Redding, "Messages and Message Exchange Processes," in Jablin et al. (eds.), *Handbook of Organizational Communication,* pp. 451–502.

33. V. P. Richmond and J. C. McCroskey, *Communication: Apprehension, Avoidance, and Effectiveness* (Scottsdale, Ariz.: Gorsuch, Scarisbrick, 1985).

Chapter 3

*L*eadership and Management Strategies

OBJECTIVES

After working through this chapter, you will be able to:

1. Identify the functions leaders perform and the skills they need

2. Understand the major theories of management

3. Explain the concept of strategic leadership

4. Develop goal-setting skills based on vision and values

5. Collect knowledge about yourself and the organization's leadership needs

6. Demonstrate leadership competence by empowering others

7. Manage leadership anxieties through optimism, persistence, passion, and acceptance of responsibility for failure

Our overview of the information age and globalization trends illustrates that successful organizations adapt to new environmental conditions by helping employees and managers to take on new roles. When you enter the work force, you will probably be expected to assume a variety of complex roles. If you are in management, you may be expected to act as a generalist who coordinates the technical, human, operational, and creative functions of your organization. If you are in research, design, or other production-related jobs, you may be expected to use new technologies and communicate effectively with a diverse set of co-workers. Added to these will be increasing competition and demands for economy. To meet challenges at work, you will want to apply the skills you are learning now in new and creative ways. Regardless of your position in the organization, it will help you to know and apply leadership skills in the performance of your duties.

One way to develop leadership skills is to adopt an outside-in perspective on your organization. This means focusing on the technological forces outside the organization and assessing its strengths and weaknesses from the perspective of outside stakeholders, such as customers, the competition, and even the government. It means creating a wider, more universal view of your organization's role in the environment.

To do so requires *vision*. According to David Campbell of the Center for Creative Leadership, "The best visionaries aren't necessarily those who can predict the shape of the 21st century. Rather, they are people who can draw a conceptual road map from where the organization is now to some imagined future and say, 'This is how we get there.'"[1] This sort of leadership has few, if any, mystical qualities — it is a practical and strategic approach designed to meet the specific challenges of the information age. Leadership can be learned, and it can be adapted to solve problems.

That is what this chapter is all about: understanding and developing leadership skills. We first review the skills and functions traditionally associated with management and leadership. Then we give a brief overview of management theory. Finally, we introduce an approach to leadership based on the communication that includes skills, attitudes, and techniques to help you succeed professionally, academically, and personally.

What Does a Leader Do?

The terms *leadership* and *management* are often used interchangeably, which sometimes leads to confusion about the actual delegation of responsibilities in organizations. Leadership and management are complementary concepts that emphasize slightly different mindsets and courses of action but are based on the same fundamental skills. Let us begin with some of the behaviors, skills, and functions generally associated with both management and leadership before moving on to a more theoretical perspective on the two concepts.

Managerial and Leadership Functions

Management generally has four functions: planning, organizing, motivating, and controlling.[2] *Planning* comprises setting goals and outlining steps to achieve those goals. *Organizing* is the process of accumulating and coordinating the human and capital resources necessary to undertake the plan. *Motivating* requires generating commitment and support for the plan. *Controlling* means using authority and power to ensure that the plan succeeds.

All these functions are important to organizational success, but the degree to which each is emphasized depends on the circumstances. For instance, the planning function may be more important in industries that experience a great deal of change or innovation. Controlling may be used less in businesses where creativity is at a premium. Organizing may not be as important in routine labor operations such as assembly lines, where motivating may be the most important function.

To some extent, these functions are important to you as a student as well. You are already developing the ability to plan your time, organize study or research materials, and motivate yourself to finish your work. You may or may not be in a position to "control" others. But consider experiences you may have had on sports teams, in previous jobs, or at other activities in which you were in a position to direct a group of people toward a goal. You may be surprised at how many potential leadership situations you have encountered. You can prepare yourself for leadership responsibilities now by identifying those opportunities and actively seeking to incorporate leadership functions in your daily routines.

Managerial and Leadership Skills

Technical, human, and conceptual abilities are important to managers' work.[3] *Technical skills* include the ability to use data, information, innovations, and techniques in your work. As a new employee, you may be given special training in technical areas, such as seminars in using the company's computer software. Often you may be expected to learn technical skills on your own. One of the best ways to do this is to observe an expert or someone with a lot of experience. Asking questions is another way to gain technical information and at the same time show your enthusiasm for learning.

Human skills entail the ability to work with people in accomplishing goals. Regardless of your position in an organization, you are called on to understand your co-workers' needs and motivations and recognize their strengths and weaknesses. In your past work experience, have you found yourself more, or less, productive when working with a person whose strengths and weaknesses differed from your own? What types of people did you work best with? Developing leadership ability starts with being able to figure out which people will work well together. To make these decisions, you must know how to gauge others' abilities objectively and draw on your past experience.

Conceptual skills refer to the ability to see your job in its relationship to the entire organization as well as recognize how the organization interacts with its environment. A good way to begin developing these conceptual skills is to think critically about how organizations in which you are currently a member interact with the environment. For example, think about the relationship your school has with the town or city in which it is located. How could the relationship be improved? In particular, what could students do to encourage the improvement? Students at one school we are familiar with hold a biyearly "Neighborhood Day," in which they help to clean up the campus and surrounding neighborhood, volunteer to make minor repairs to neighbors' houses, or run errands for neighbors who are elderly or invalid. Such activities can promote leadership skills.

Future-Oriented Skills

The ability to handle the information age is a vital leadership skill. Gareth Morgan suggested that as information becomes the most important good, service, and commodity in the global and national economy, the ability to obtain, assimilate, analyze, and communicate this information will be critical to organizational success. According to Morgan:

> New modes of electronic communication will increase the amount of data available in decision making, creating the problem of information overload. Managers will have to learn to overcome the paralysis, or clouding of issues, that can result from having too much information and develop "information management mindsets" that allow them to sort the wheat from the chaff. Skills in the design of information systems, data management, and data analysis and interpretation will become increasingly important. Managers will also have to be more computer literate and learn to dialogue electronically — with both people and data — with a high degree of skill.[4]

As a new employee, you may indeed be faced with a technological dilemma. If you are a recent graduate, you may be expected to know more about new communication and information technology than long-time employees because your employers consider you a member of the "computer generation." If you have been out of school or the work force for some time, you may find that you are still expected to know about the latest in technology, regardless of your experience.

Managers increasingly are expected to be familiar with a variety of computer skills. In this case, a manager tracks data and compares sets of budget figures for later discussion.

Be sure to do your best to prepare for the technological demands of the workplace. Learning word processing and computer programming and even getting familiar with presentation equipment through classes like this one are invaluable ways of making yourself as effective as possible. If, despite your best efforts to prepare, you find yourself in need of additional skills training, consider workshops or classes that benefit you and others in the company as well. In this way, you can demonstrate forward-thinking leadership skills.

In addition to future-oriented skills, managers must communicate well. Communication is more than sending clear messages — it is listening as well. Listening skills are necessary for responding to and understanding employees' needs, motivations, and intentions. Communication also entails giving and acknowledging feedback about actions or decisions made in the workplace.

Although most managers practice the skills and functions described here, the way in which they do so can vary widely. Just as organizations develop different structures and patterns of communication to achieve goals, managers use a variety of different techniques to motivate and reward employees. In the next section, we introduce you to some important theories of management that describe these techniques.

Management Theory

A number of researchers have proposed theories about how management is accomplished in organizations. The earliest of these, Rensis Likert and the team of Robert Blake and Jane Mouton, based their work on the ideas of Douglas McGregor, whose theory X/theory Y description of organizational communication we discussed in Chapter 1. Later theorists advanced more complex and dynamic theories in response to changes in the structure and goals of business organizations and their employees. We briefly introduce you to the most widely known of these: Robert House, Victor Vroom and Philip Yetton, and Karl Kuhnert and Philip Lewis.

Likert's Systems of Management

Rensis Likert described management in terms of whether managers focused on tasks or on relationships with their employees; he assumed that more emphasis on one meant less emphasis on the other.[5] His thinking can be illustrated by a continuum bounded by task orientation at one end and relationship orientation at the other (Figure 3-1). He proposed four systems that characterize common management styles.

System 1.   A system 1 style of management is task oriented, with a highly structured authoritarian focus. System 1 managers trust subordinates very little and do not involve them in the decision-making process. Subordinates work in a climate of intimidation and fear. Communication takes place only through the downward chain of command.

System 2.   A system 2 style of management is task oriented but maintains a less authoritarian control of the organization or unit. Managers are condescending to subordinates and, although not as strict, continue to demonstrate distrust of subordinates. Some decision making is allowed at lower levels, but organizational problems are resolved at the top of the organization. Although most of the communication from managers follows the chain of command, some interaction is carried out directly between upper management and lower level subordinates.

System 3.   System 3 managers openly place confidence and trust in subordinates. Managers "control" subordinates through negotiation and communication. Decision making is allowed at lower levels, especially in areas that directly affect those workers. Communication flows relatively freely both up and down the organizational hierarchy.

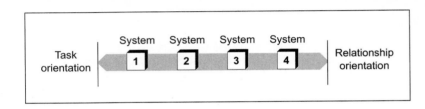

FIGURE 3-1   *Likert's management continuum*

System 4.   System 4 managers concentrate on the relationships between superiors and subordinates. They promote confidence and trust in workers and encourage decision making at all levels of the organization. Fear, threat, and intimidation are not used; workers' motivation results from their participation in goal setting. Free and open message exchange occurs among superiors, subordinates, and peers.

Notice that these systems are quite similar to the classical and humanistic schools of organizational theory that we examined in Chapter 1. For example, systems 1 and 2 correspond to the assumptions of Taylor's scientific management and Weber's theory of bureaucracy; systems 3 and 4 reflect more concern for the worker's personal growth and satisfaction, a tenet of the theories of the human relations and human resources schools of thought.

Blake and Mouton's Managerial Grid Theory

Robert Blake and Jane Mouton pictured management as a grid composed of two juxtaposed factors — concern for people and concern for production.[6] The grid allows an observer to compare the relative importance of these two factors to management by assigning a numerical value from one to nine to each and then plotting the resulting point. Unlike Likert's conception of management, Blake and Mouton's model shows that managers can be concerned with both tasks and relationships (or concerned with neither tasks nor relationships!).

Concern for people manifests in a leader's regard for her or his workers, particularly the concern that subordinates are being treated well by the organization. Concern for production refers to the manager's emphasis on achieving goals and objectives of the organization. Although a very large number of combinations can be made from the two factors, Blake and Mouton proposed five major managerial styles. Figure 3-2 provides a brief explanation of each of these.

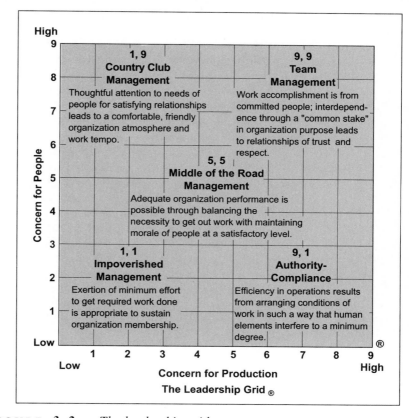

FIGURE 3-2   *The leadership grid*   *Source:* R. Blake and A. McCanse, *Leadership Dilemmas — Grid Solutions* (Houston: Gulf Publishing Co., 1991), p. 29. ©1991 Scientific Methods, Inc. Reproduced by permission of the owners.

House's Path-Goal Model

Robert House proposed a model of leadership in which managers set precise goals and make the paths to these goals easier to follow.[7] Successful path-goal management depends on the presence of clearly defined goals. When goals and paths are simple and clear, employees need less active supervision to achieve them. Ambiguous goals or complex paths require more from the manager in terms of directions, guidance, and motivation. Path-goal managers provide opportunities for employees to learn and grow on the job by allowing them to direct themselves. In both cases, consideration from the leader can be worthwhile.

Vroom and Yetton's Leader-Participation Model

Victor Vroom and Philip Yetton's research focused on the degree of followers' participation in the decision-making process.[8] According to their model of leader-participation, five options describe how subordinates can be involved in the decision-making process. These options range from no participation at all to full participation. Table 3-1 displays how each of the five levels of leader-participation differs. As the table shows, decision making can range from authoritarian (levels 1 and 2) to democratic (levels 4 and 5). Level 3 represents moderate follower involvement.

The leader-participation model is important for two reasons. It can describe leaders who choose one level of participation consistently and whose subordinates have come to expect that level of participation in decision making. It also shows that flexibility exists among decision-making styles. Sometimes more participation by employees is appropriate; at other times less participation is needed. Some situations may not involve employees directly, so no participation is necessary. In emergency conditions, decisions may be made without participation by employees for reasons of time constraints. Of course, when the decision has long-term implications for co-workers, they should be fully involved in the decision-making process. People are more likely to accept decisions when they have had a hand in making them.

TABLE 3-1
Vroom-Yetton Leader-Participation Model

Level	Follower Participation	Decision Process
1	None	Leader only
2	Leader gathers information from followers	Leader only
3	Leader obtains ideas and suggestions from selected followers	Leader only
4	Leader shares problem with followers as a group and collectively obtains ideas and suggestions from them	Leader only
5	Leader shares problem with the group	Joint decision making of leader and group of followers

Kuhnert and Lewis's Transactional Leadership Theory

Transactional leadership, a recent theory proposed by Karl Kuhnert and Philip Lewis, describes relationships between superior and subordinate that are based on exchanges for mutual gain. According to this theory, managers offer subordinates things they want, such as higher salaries, time off, or benefits, to obtain certain things in return, such as extra work on special projects, overtime, and loyalty to the manager. A *transaction* occurs in which each party gives one thing in exchange for something else.[9]

Transactional management works only if each party has something the other wants. What happens, however, if managers cannot offer anything followers value? For example, in times of financial hardship, managers may be unable to provide bonuses for extra work, yet the work still has to be done. In such a situation, the manager must find other alternatives, such as promises of raises when times improve or public approval or recognition, to offer workers. For this management to be effective, both parties have to realize the mutual dependence of their relationship.

Transformational Leadership

Kuhnert and Lewis identified a second type of leadership known as transformational leadership. In contrast to transactional leadership, the idea of transformational leadership focuses on reaching goals through appeals to deep-seated values among organizational members.[10] The transformation process begins when the manager communicates her or his values to employees. As employees reach agreement on a set of organizational values, they elevate one another to new heights of inspiration, motivation, and morality.

Transformational leaders do more than just communicate their values to followers; their behavior reinforces the values they represent. According to Kuhnert and Lewis, successful transformational leaders possess self-confidence, a dynamic personality, strong convictions, the ability to communicate goals, a facility for image building, and a talent for motivating others.

Notice that these qualities are not used in an exchange process — transformational leaders do not view followers as bargaining chips, as is the case in some forms of transactional management. Transformational leaders communicate well and thus inspire others by their own example to achieve excellence in the workplace, with the goal of emphasizing workers' growth and development.

Transformational leadership is important because it is value based. As you recall from the last chapter, identifying and promoting values are keys to organizational success. Transformational leaders view workers as willing participants in a value-conversion process that makes the entire organization stronger.

Leadership versus Management

Although leadership is a skill that may or may not be part of a person's management style or needs, most management positions offer the opportunity to demonstrate leadership ability. Consider the following example:

> Mike and John are both managers in a video production company. Mike is in charge of accounts receivable and John is a marketing manager. The company has recently created a new job, director of human resources, and plans to promote a current employee to the position soon. Mike and John are top candidates. Upper management wants the chosen candidate to demonstrate exceptional leadership skills because the job is an important and highly visible component of the company's new program to recruit more women and minorities to management positions.
>
> Mike is a superb technician. His department has a flawless record, and he has been very loyal to the company, even turning down competing job offers. But Mike tends to do things the way they have always been done; his personal motto is "Why fix what isn't broken?" John, however, is quite vocal in his recommendations for change in his unit and focuses more on "what should be instead of what is." He has an effective track record in his department, although he is not overly concerned about the day-to-day details of the job. Upper management selects John for the new position, and Mike is outraged that someone like John is chosen ahead of him.

If you were upper management, what would you tell Mike? In this situation, upper management chose John's creativity over Mike's dependability. The high profile of the job, as well as the program's newness and forward-thinking focus, made John the better choice. Mike's skills, although recognized and valued, were not as appropriate for the job.

In your career, you will find that some promotions are made on the basis of creativity, personality, or other "intangible" qualities; other promotions are based on demonstrated talent and dedication. The job, not the candidates themselves, often determines whether a "leader" or a "manager" is needed.

There is no shortage of definitions for leadership. Table 3-2 compares several views on leadership.[11]

These definitions offer similar descriptions of leadership. They agree that leadership is a process and that leaders are influential in achieving important goals. After considering these definitions and our own leadership experiences, we have defined leadership as *the process of influencing subordinates, superiors, and peers toward the attainment of goals by using*

TABLE 3-2
Varying Views on Leadership

Theorist	Leadership Definitions
Terry	Leadership is the activity of influencing people to strive willingly for group objectives.
Tannebaum, Weschler, and Massarik	Leadership is the interpersonal influence exercised in a situation and directed, through the communication process, toward the attainment of a specialized goal.
Koontz and O'Donnell	Leadership is influencing people to follow in the achievement of a common goal.
Kotter	Leadership refers to the process of moving a group of people in some direction through non-coercive means; it also refers to people who are in roles where leadership is expected.

strategic communication methods. Strategic communication methods encompass values, vision, goal identification, future-oriented thinking, and other important behaviors that enable adaptation to the challenges of the information age.

With determination and practice, anyone can improve the communication skills vital to effective leadership. As you work through the following sections, remember that leadership is not reserved for the wealthy or the well connected — people are not necessarily born with leadership skills. Also remember that leadership must permeate all levels of an organization, not just exist at the top.

The model of strategic communication provides the direction for our discussion of leadership skills. The skills are divided into four major components: goal setting, situational knowledge, communication competence, and anxiety management. Attending to each of these areas can ensure that you have covered all the bases necessary for developing leadership ability.

Goal Setting: Managing the Present and the Future

In Chapter 2, we stressed the need for goal setting in any communication situation. Leadership is no different. Leaders must be forward thinkers and doers. To set goals for yourself as well as for an organization, consider three factors: shared values, visions, and management of change.

Shared Values

One of the most widely discussed aspects of leadership is the importance of the values leaders hold. A leader's identification and promotion of values are critical to organizational success because values provide all members of the organization with a sense of guidance as they perform their daily tasks. Without shared values, a leader is unlikely to be successful. The following example is helpful in beginning our discussion on shared values.

> Chita, Ming, and Sallie are entry-level unit management trainees at HighTech, Inc. During their orientation sessions, the personnel director stressed the shared values of the organization. Chita was impressed with these values but was struck even more that the company believed in them enough to actively promote them to new employees.
>
> Chita decided to follow the personnel director's example and made up a laminated handout of the values to distribute to each of her subordinates. She held three meetings to discuss the values, and her subordinates were eager to embrace these values as their own, especially after suggesting two more that were specific to their unit.
>
> Ming and Sallie were also impressed with the values of the company but made no obvious attempt to instill the values in unit members. Indeed, Sallie's and Ming's behavior sometimes contradicted those values. After a while, other managers began to notice that Chita's unit was showing impressive increases in customer satisfaction and operating efficiency and decreases in absenteeism.
>
> At HighTech's annual awards luncheon, Chita was asked how her unit had been so successful. She distributed copies of the laminated sheet of values to everyone in the room and stated, "The single best action I took last year was believing in this company's values and having my people believe in them too. Once people know, understand, and believe in the company's values, you really don't have to do much more. They will know what to do." Chita's understanding of the importance of shared values paid off.

How do leaders ensure that values are shared by organizational members? Three approaches can help leaders promote shared values among their co-workers.[12] These are *clarity*, *consensus*, and *intensity*.

Clarity.   Good leaders try to ensure that values are clear to all. Asking people how they feel about the organization's stated values is one way to evaluate how clear they are. Workers' impressions of, and reactions to, stated values reveal the depth of their understanding of those values. An effective leader often acts as a cheerleader for the organization's values, articulating them frequently in clear and concise language. Once values are clear to workers, they can internalize them and even adapt them to specific work situations.

Consensus. Having a consensus about values means that people not only understand the stated values but also share them. Leaders and those who aspire to leadership can do a great deal to gain consensus about values by setting an example. When followers see a leader acting on the stated values of an organization, they are assured those values play an important part in the organization's success.

Leaders can use values to assess the work of others. If an employee excels on a project, the leader can point out ways in which his or her work promotes the values of the organization. Consider work experiences you have had. Did managers consistently relate the importance of organizational values? Did they respond to suggestions from subordinates only after lengthy complaints? If you were in a management position, how were you expected to treat your co-workers?

Intensity. Employees in companies with high levels of intensity about shared values frequently discuss them in regular conversation.[13] Intensity means that employees connect emotionally to the company's values, live up to them, and demonstrate more than a passing interest in keeping them alive. Leaders can then reinforce intensity by showing strong commitment themselves.

The significance of shared values. James Kouzes and Barry Posner studied the merits of shared values among a number of different organizations. Their research surveyed more than 2,300 employees across the United States. They found that organizations with strong shared values enjoyed a number of benefits, including high levels of company loyalty, strong norms about working hard and caring, strong feelings of personal effectiveness, consensus about key organizational goals, and reduced levels of job stress and tension.[14]

Shared values also promote ethical behavior at work. The ethical differences of a culturally diverse work force can be transcended by a coherent set of ethics for the organization as a whole. Indeed, the organization's ethical standards may be better suited to resolve differences than members' specific codes of ethics are.

Visions

The visions that leaders have for their department, unit, or organization are based on shared values. According to Bennis and Nanus,

> A leader must first have developed a mental image of a possible and desirable future state of the organization. This image, which we call a vision, may be as vague as a dream or as precise as a goal or mission

FOCUS on Corporate Communication

UNITED NEGRO COLLEGE FUND

Strong leadership, progressive business strategies, and dynamic communication among college presidents, corporate leaders, volunteers, and donors are at the heart of the United Negro College Fund's (UNCF) history of successful fund-raising. The organization, which includes about two hundred forty-five paid staff and over thirty thousand volunteers, has raised hundreds of millions of dollars for private, historically black colleges. Since 1972 alone, more than $550 million has been raised under the leadership of Christopher F. Edley, who retired in 1990 after an eighteen-year tenure as president and chief executive office. Edley's successor, former Congressman William Gray of Pennsylvania, has pledged to build on Edley's achievements.

Many of those in executive management positions are people who have been with the organization for many years. The UNCF nurtures and retains bright, creative individuals who move up through the organizational ranks to provide a continuity of leadership and vision. For example, the chief operating officer has been the second in command at the organization for more than a decade, having moved up from a previous position in middle management.

The UNCF demonstrates strong leadership in several important ways. Individual leaders like Edley are a major factor in generating contributions during fund drives. One outstanding example is the success of Campaign 2000, the UNCF's capital campaign to raise $250 million, which has already generated a $50 million challenge grant from publisher Walter H. Annenberg and some $37 million in additional funding.

Two governing bodies, the Board of Directors and the Institutional Members, carry out complementary leadership functions in setting and implementing policy. The Board of Directors includes leaders of business and industry who are committed to education and the UNCF's goals. The board is responsible for business functions such as hiring (and firing) the executive management, managing property, distributing funds, and making policy.

The Institutional Members (presidents of member institutions) have authority in matters relating to education, such as tracking new government legislation, identifying programs to receive special funding, and determining the formula by which the Board of Directors is to distribute funds. In addition, the member presidents make all nominations to the Board of Directors. Together, these two boards, with the able assistance of staff, take care of the UNCF's many ties to the business, academic, and legislative communities.

Committees (also made up of member college presidents and corporate board members) provide another source of leadership. They focus on major issues of importance to the organization, such as budget and investment, strategic planning, review of fund-raising policies, and government relations. In the area of communication, a public information task force monitors the messages communicated to the public, advises ad agencies and other suppliers on maintaining continuity in the UNCF's image, ensures that all affiliated institutions are treated equally in communication, and makes suggestions for future campaigns.

Opinion leaders, such as Michael Jordan, Michael Jackson, George and Barbara Bush, Whitney Houston, Oprah Winfrey, Janet Jackson, Paul Simon, and Robert Woodruff, create positive publicity through their gifts to the UNCF and encourage the general public to give what it can. And the award-winning Ad Council-sponsored campaign, "A mind is a terrible thing to waste," has been an ongoing success in increasing public awareness of the UNCF and its goals. This campaign utilizes television, radio, billboards, and consumer and business print ads to convey vital messages about UNCF's mission, and the slogan is one of the most widely recognized in America.

The leadership structure and style of UNCF reflect the relaxed but efficient corporate culture within the organization itself. The UNCF, despite its nonprofit status, is run like a business — under Edley's leadership, a well-defined management style and long-term fund-raising strategies were put in place to ensure the organization's continued success in years ahead. In addition, the UNCF attracts many young, creative, ambitious people who stay with the organization because it gives them the opportunity to develop a wide variety of skills and tackle multiple responsibilities — and rewards those who do.

Leaders and employees at all levels of the organization emphasize oral communication in both identifying challenges and deciding how to resolve them. Informal and formal discussions and meetings are the source of many solutions and ideas. Nevertheless, field staff employees and volunteers located in thirty area offices receive additional support from the national staff in the form of an in-house newsletter, "INFOCUS," and a magazine, *A Mind Is,* which highlights the achievements of graduates from the UNCF's member schools. The organization also makes use of computers for communicating, desktop publishing, and accounting.

People at the UNCF see their work as a source of challenge and enrichment, and they are working to provide the best in education and leadership opportunities to Black Americans. The talent and resources mobilized by the organization make those opportunities a reality.

statement. The critical point is that vision articulates a view of a realistic, credible, attractive future for the organization, a condition that is better in some important ways than what now exists.[15]

Developing visions.   One of the key aspects of vision is originality — seeing new goals and new ways to reach those goals. Developing original ideas is not automatic or easy. It helps to be always looking out for alternatives as well as getting inspiration from your own experiences.

Managers practice creativity in a specific context and with a specific focus. For example, Martha, a marketing manager, believed that her department could increase its profits by offering its market research service to outside clients for a subscription fee. She knew demand for the service existed because her department had received many requests from outsiders to use the marketing statistics it had gathered. She also knew that the department would have to provide at least three different services to subscribers to make a profit because in her experience, demand for specific kinds of data usually fluctuated during the course of a year.

Although she was not sure how to approach potential subscribers or how to bill for the service, she knew that Randy Carson, an administrative executive, would be able to give her some suggestions. His experience plus her interest in developing new ideas helped Martha to create a realistic and worthwhile vision for her department.

Clarifying visions.   Just as values must have clarity, so too must visions be readily understood by those who are expected to act on them. A vision must be presented so that others can see the potential benefits of acting on it. Followers of a vision know that they are contributing to its fulfillment in a large or small way. Employees often need to feel that the tangible results of a vision will benefit not only themselves but the organization in which they work.

The most effective visions are described in language that others can understand. This may be one of the hardest parts of being a leader, not only because it is difficult to choose the correct words to fully describe a vision but also because articulating a vision makes it less of a personal dream.

One way to test the clarity of your vision is write it out in as much detail as possible. After you complete this process, ask someone you know to read it back and explain what you wrote. If the friend has difficulty, rewrite the vision using different language and writing styles. Repeat this process until your friend's understanding of the vision corresponds to yours.

Acting on visions.   Developing a vision can be a major challenge, but the process of leadership does not stop there. Leaders must make a conscious effort to behave in ways that reflect the vision.

Vision may also require occasional adjustment. When problems occur, workers and leaders are wise to remain flexible and strive to modify and improve the original vision. A vision need not be scrapped the moment an obstacle appears; visions are general images of the future that can be achieved with the understanding that different approaches often lead to the same destination. If a vision becomes a rigid pattern of behavior instead of an inspirational challenge, it may do more harm than good.

Benefits of visions.   Many people face an ongoing problem of keeping up with the various maintenance activities their jobs require. Routine phone calls and visitors, meetings, and paperwork take time. So too do unexpected crises that must be taken care of immediately. One manager had taped an eloquent summary of her company's goals to her desktop — and then found she usually could not read them because she had so much paperwork on her desk!

The organization as a whole can benefit from a clearly articulated vision. Vision can be used to prioritize daily activities, guide decisions about what project to handle first, and remind managers to delegate some activities to others who are dedicated to the same vision.

Management of Change

Articulating a vision almost always entails changing the status quo for an as-yet-untested alternative. To set goals for the future, astute leaders anticipate and manage change effectively.

There will always be resistance to change. Some people like the status quo. Others may fear that change will affect them adversely. Still others resist change because the effects of change are unpredictable. Leaders become agents of change by making and publicizing decisions that support the plan for change.

Strategic change.   Managing change in an organization requires a strategy based on several steps. The first step is to anticipate problems, which are most likely to occur when a vision is implemented. A backup plan can help avoid potential problems. For example, confusion can result when people perceive the vision differently. This difficulty can be avoided when employees have written implementation details for reference.

The second step is to focus the organization on the vision. Day-to-day obstacles frequently discourage dedication to the original vision. After evaluating the obstacles, the leader can either modify the vision or solve the problems.

As the third step, leaders and employees alike look at results rather than processes. This step enables everyone to consider alternative approaches to tasks.

The fourth step entails considering the long-term effects of change. Long-range thinking concentrates on the innumerable benefits of change, thereby showing that change is not simply the result of the leader's personal whim.

The last step is to build a strong, supportive network of people committed to the process of change. John Kotter suggested that several members of this network must be in key positions of power, maintain strong working relationships with one another, and be highly motivated to accomplish tasks related to the change.[16]

Once a leader has made change agents out of influential people in the organization, they can motivate others to recognize the value of change and embrace it with enthusiasm. Leaders cannot manage change alone. They must empower others to advocate productive change at all levels of the work force. Such grass-roots participation is the most effective way of implementing change.

Situational Knowledge: The Foundation of Strategic Leadership

Goal setting is enhanced by situational knowledge, or the information a leader needs to effectively manage a situation. This knowledge includes information about the organization and its employees as well as knowledge about the self. The more a leader discovers about his or her abilities, weaknesses, and personal style, the better prepared that leader is to take charge effectively and appropriately.

Knowledge About Self

How well defined is your self-concept? Most people think they have a very accurate self-awareness. We are not so sure. We have met a number of people who believed they had skills in certain areas when they did not. Joke telling is a classic example of this problem. Think about the last time someone you knew told a joke and it went over like a lead zeppelin. Some people can tell very funny jokes; other people just think they can. Still others know they cannot but ignore that knowledge and blunder into social embarrassment time after time. Like everyone else, leaders are not perfect. They have shortcomings and weaknesses that challenge their ability to lead. Effective leaders first inventory their imperfections and then successfully minimize them to gain others' support.

Your opinion of yourself, or self-concept, is important to the development of leadership skills. Leaders should have a healthy view of themselves — not that leaders should be self-righteous, self-promoting egotists — they should know their strengths and weaknesses. Complete the following self-evaluation to check your awareness of your own characteristics.

How many 3s, 4s, and 5s did you have? These are areas that can use improvement. Look for those areas where you placed 7s, 8s, 9s, and 10s.

LEADERSHIP SELF-CONCEPT EVALUATION

Rate yourself on a scale of 1 to 10 in each of the listed areas, with 1 being weakest and 10 being strongest.

_3_	physical attractiveness	_8_	intelligence
_3_	sexual attractiveness	_7_	creativity
_9_	persistence	_7_	ambition
_5_	confidence	_9_	education
_9_	empathy	_9_	openmindedness
_10_	strong values	_5_	tolerance for ambiguity
_10_	sense of humor	_6_	loyalty
_6_	good interpersonal skills	_6_	dedication
_5_	cleverness	_6_	intuition
_8_	imagination	_7_	resourcefulness
_8_	challengeability	_8_	trustworthiness
_5_	high self-esteem	_7_	likeableness
_8_	motivation	_7_	adaptability

Are these areas where you have been told you excel or even been recognized for your talents? These are areas worth promoting and emphasizing.

Another method of self-evaluation is to assess your views on current issues that affect you. You may think that you have opinions on certain issues, but until you actually write them down or articulate them, they may be surprisingly vague. Try this exercise: select an issue that you are familiar with, and review your knowledge and opinions about it. It can be a personal issue such as your feelings about a relationship, a political issue such as gun control or environmental protection, or a social issue such as welfare or health insurance. Draw a line down the middle of a piece of paper. On the left side write the heading "Things I Feel Very Strongly About." On the right side of the page write the heading "Things I Am Unsure About."

Honestly assess the strength of your combined personal opinion and knowledge of the issue as you write in statements on each side of the page. You may be surprised at the number of items you have listed on the right-hand side of the page. It is always a good idea to take stock of yourself and gauge your point of view. It is not always an easy task, but knowing yourself can help you to perform better in all areas of your work as well as to develop leadership ability.

Avoiding hubris.   Hubris is another word for excessive pride — a belief in personal invincibility and omnipotence. Successful leaders sometimes develop hubris and have a tendency to believe that they are able (and permitted) to do anything, including illegal or unethical actions.

In many ways, success builds self-confidence. But when you are successful, you are smart to consider the organization, its vision, and others' contributions to your successes so as to avoid becoming hubristic. In school and in your career, consider keeping a journal of your achievements in which you also note others who received or deserved credit for these accomplishments. You can refer back to these cooperative accomplishments when you feel tempted to see only yourself as responsible for success. Chances are, if you give others the credit they deserve, they will reciprocate.

Organizational Knowledge

Astute leaders recognize all the tasks involved in the organization's operation, although they are unlikely to know the specifics of every single job description. Only by recognizing both the big picture and the fine print are leaders able to coordinate all the factors required for achieving goals.

Tom Peters and Robert Waterman suggested that managers learned about the business by "wandering around."[17] Others have talked about "hands-on management." Such phrases suggest that effective leadership is both active and interactive and depends in part on leaders taking interest in others' contributions to the organization. They also suggest that the best leaders may be people who began modestly and worked their way up from the lower levels of the company. Such people bring years of real and practical experience to leadership decisions.

Organizational knowledge goes beyond the internal structure and functions of the company. Leaders and workers must also be receptive to the environment to know what the competition is doing, what the customers want, what the national economy is doing, and how the global market is performing. Knowledge of this nature is acquired only by continual learning.

Continual learning.   Leaders analyze and learn from the past, present, and future, a skill known as *continual learning*. It can be practiced regardless of a person's position in the organization. There are three components to continual learning: anticipation (expecting events rather than simply reacting to them), learning and listening, and participation.

One of the prime sources of continual learning is also one of the most unpleasant: failure. You and most people probably view failure as something to avoid. Nevertheless, leadership experts stress the importance of taking risks and learning from failure. Effective leaders have failed, but they are noteworthy in their ability to learn from failure and use it to strengthen their leadership ability. It is often said that if employees do not fail every now and then, they are not trying hard enough. Leaders may feel that they are not taking risks or being creative enough.

You can become more comfortable with risk (and demonstrate your leadership potential) by developing a response plan to turn failures into learning experiences. Formulating such a plan entails performing four tasks — review, assess, predict, and resolve.

Immediately after a failure has occurred, *review* the chain of events leading to the failure by yourself or with those involved. Determine the point at which reality deviated from the ideal. Next, *assess* the deviation: Was the problem minor? Major? Were there several problems? Did the problem result from lack of preparation, incorrect information, conflicts between workers, or some other factor? Use the assessment to *predict* the likelihood of such a problem occurring again. Was it a one-in-a-million situation? Or is the problem likely to recur next week? Finally, *resolve* how to handle such a situation in the future based on your analysis of the first three factors. Consider the following example.

> David Wildon is responsible for supplying data charts to an account manager whose projects are generally behind schedule. David had noticed that the spreadsheet program for preparing the charts had recently caused some errors in the account figures but assumed that taking care of the problem was not his responsibility. One month, the data provided by the manager did not match the results produced by the spreadsheet, so David decided to use estimates to save time and get the project finished. The manager, running late as usual, did not check the finished chart before sending it to his boss for the annual planning meeting. The next day, he stormed into David's office demanding to know how the mistakes got into the chart and threatening that David would get both of them fired.

In this situation, David and his boss can make several resolutions to avoid such a failure in the future. The boss can resolve to keep his projects on schedule. David can resolve to alert those responsible for maintaining the software if he notices a problem with it. David and his boss can resolve to go over the completed charts together to make sure that they are free of error. Such resolutions can reduce the likelihood of failure in the future as well as the stress resulting from fear of failure. Implementing plans for learning from failure can be an important step in developing leadership ability.

Communication Competence: Demonstrating Leadership Skills

What are the communication skills necessary for leadership, and how can you begin to develop them now? The critical elements of communication are building trust, promoting understanding, and empowering others. *Trust* results from a strong commitment to ethical behavior within the organization's system of values. *Understanding* others means listening, using clear and respectful language, and relying on appropriate techniques for behavior control. *Empowerment* means allowing people the opportunity to think and act for themselves within the guidelines of the shared values and vision of the organization. The benefits of trust, understanding, and empowerment include greater creativity and productivity as workers take initiatives to succeed without the direct control or coercion of managers or leaders.

Trust

Trust, the first of the critical leadership skills, is the faith and confidence that workers place in the organization's leaders. Leaders do not receive trust automatically; it must be earned and re-earned.

Trust is also a two-way street. For followers to have trust in their leaders, leaders must first demonstrate that they have trust in their followers. The concept of mutual trust is important. Managers or supervisors who trust employees with additional or important responsibilities often win respect for their insight into the employees' abilities. Followers then begin to trust managers in other areas ("Well, if she trusted me with the ABC project, she must know what she's doing; I trust her judgment"). Over time, leaders and workers can build a mutual store of trust that can be tapped to achieve important goals.

Another characteristic of trust is its often limited durability. Building trust can be a long and slow process, but it often takes only one or two betrayals for many followers to lose faith in a leader they may have trusted for years. Trust is one of the most important ingredients in leadership, yet it is one of the most tenuous.

The relationship between trust and ethical behavior.   In Chapter 2, we discussed the importance of communication ethics. Trust in organizations begins with leaders setting appropriate role models for ethical behavior. Employees may be discouraged from ethical behavior if they see their leaders performing unethical acts.

Ethical behavior is based on the values that have been espoused by the organization. Values can be directly stated — for example, in a code that says, "We value honesty and integrity as a way of doing business." Ethical standards can also be communicated indirectly — for example, by leaders choosing to uphold ethical standards such as honesty and equality instead of pursuing questionable courses of action that may be more profitable.

Defining ethical behavior.   Managers and executives are constantly watched by employees for cues to guide their actions. It is imperative that managers demonstrate ethical behaviors for employees to emulate. According to Kenneth Andrews, "The personal values and ethical aspirations of the company's leaders, though probably not specifically stated, are implicit in all strategic decisions. They show through the choices management makes and reveal themselves as the company goes about its business. That is why this communication should be deliberate and purposeful rather than random."[18]

Defining a code of ethics is one of the most difficult aspects of leadership. All employees have personal systems of ethics that they have cultivated over the years, and these are their first reference in a questionable situation. Ethics are largely determined by culture, and so it is difficult, if not impossible, to formulate a universal set of ethics.

If ethics are determined by the culture in which they are found, how can leaders modify them to work in an organization made up of people from diverse backgrounds? It helps to consider the essence of ethics codes, which is their role in strengthening and promoting the values of social, familial, or organizational culture.[19] Behaviors that weaken cultural values are considered unethical.

But if cultural values shift in response to changing societal or economic factors, must the code of ethics shift as well? Presumably, the answer is yes. That is why codes of ethics are not only culturally bound but are also context or situation sensitive. Although a grand set of rules by which to communicate in the business world would be helpful, such a code would ultimately fall short in specific circumstances.

Managers may ask, "If ethical behavior means different things in different situations, how do I know for sure that my own actions are proper?" This question is best answered by consulting experts in business ethics. Their experience and research have generated a number of guidelines that can help a person to determine if her or his behaviors fall in line with ethical principles.[20]

Ethical Leadership Principles

Always be truthful
Obey the law
Demonstrate trust in other people
Act consistently when dealing with others
Remove corrupting influences from the workplace
Look for the good in others
Review the organization's code of ethics often
Openly celebrate the organization's values
Listen to others with an empathic ear
Demonstrate genuine concern for others
Call attention to unethical behavior
Reduce ambiguity about self
Give credit where it is due

Publicize instances of high ethical behavior
Provide incentives for promoting high ethical behavior
Watch for signs of slippage

These recommendations promote the ideal of "the most good for the most people." A code of ethics need not be viewed as an obstacle to organizational productivity and success; on the contrary, many of the preceding suggestions can be used to create a highly positive and open organizational culture that is committed to success.

Sustaining trust.   Once leaders and employees have achieved a state of mutual trust, they still have to work at maintaining that trust. According to Bennis, there are four keys for sustaining trust: constancy, congruity, reliability, and integrity.[21] *Constancy* is the ability to stay on course, to remain focused on the vision and goals regardless of setbacks. Followers respect and trust leaders who stay calm and undistracted in the face of adversity. *Congruity* is the parallel between what a leader says and what she or he does. Leaders' actions and behavior should match their statements, goals, and views. *Reliability* means that leaders support employees and co-workers in times of need, whether personal, organizational, or professional. *Integrity* is the keeping of promises and commitments coupled with the refusal to make promises that compromise the well-being of co-workers and the organization. Employees may not like all of a leader's decisions, but they will trust a leader who clearly upholds their interests and keeps her or his word.

Problems with mistrust.   As you can imagine, there are a number of complications associated with mistrust. People generally will not give their best effort to someone they do not trust. Furthermore, when leaders are mistrusted, the whole organizational climate may suffer withholding of information, distortion of facts, rampant suspiciousness, low levels of information exchange, deception, closemindedness, low morale, and poor interpersonal relations.[22]

Trust is an essential component of leadership. Without it, leaders fail; with it, leaders have a chance to make a real difference in how the organization prospers. Most of the characteristics, elements, and qualities of strategic leadership discussed in this chapter can be actualized only if trust is established between leaders and followers.

Understanding

Understanding, the second critical communication skill, begins with attending to what employees are saying. Listening promotes understanding because it shows that leaders think highly of employees' input and take their comments seriously. Asking for advice, gathering opinions, and soliciting suggestions from followers are ways in which leaders can demonstrate their openness to listening. Van Fleet provided some helpful suggestions to leaders for asking advice from followers:[23]

◆ Include co-workers in discussions of problems and issues.
◆ Encourage individual thinking.
◆ Make it easy for subordinates to communicate their ideas to you.
◆ Follow through on these ideas.
◆ Reward those who give advice.

When employees can see that their advice is valued, they are more likely to give it. This is just one example of how effective listening helps to accomplish the goals of the organization.

Language. The capacity for understanding includes a conscious and respectful relationship to language. Effective leaders' language has been studied, and the conclusions are quite interesting. In his study of U.S. presidents' language, Rod Hart identified four major categories of commonly used words or phrases.[24] The first category, *realistic* words, includes tangible and concrete words that reflect reality. "Budget," "profit," and "overhead" are realistic terms that have specific and practical meanings in business.

The second category is *optimistic* words. Employees need positive projections about their organization. Words expressing hope, promise, and encouragement can increase feelings of job satisfaction and security. "Rosy," "bright," and "reassuring" are examples of such words.

Activity words make up the third category. These words describe specific actions that must be taken to realize goals. Words such as "expand," "mobilize," and "support" are a few examples. Activity words provide motivation for achieving the organization's vision.

The final category of leadership words conveys *certainty*. Employees generally appreciate statements of belief in the organization's vision and values. Words that convey certainty include "assurance," "conviction," and "confidence."

Inclusion of words from the four categories can produce the most successful communication. Think about the language choices of your professors, elected officials, students, or co-workers. What types of words do they use most?

Communication styles. Like language choices, communication styles vary according to the form of leadership and its intention. Hines described several styles:[25]

Tell: the leader makes decisions and tells followers how to carry them out.

Persuade: the leader unilaterally makes decisions but attempts to persuade followers to accept them.

Consult: the leader asks for input on decisions, followers provide different options, and the leader chooses from among these alternatives in making the decisions.

Join: the leader brings employees together and participates in the decision-making process as an equal group member.

Give: the leader provides group members with all necessary information and asks them to make the decision on their own; the leader agrees to abide by any decision reached.

Which of the above styles do you feel most comfortable with? Does your answer depend on the situation?

Once you have identified your natural or usual style(s) of communication, make a conscious effort to adopt an alternative style for a set period of time, such as a day. Observe how others treat you. Does the alternative style seem to work for you?

Behavior alteration techniques.   Another way to categorize the understanding component of communication strategies used by leaders is to identify the behavior alteration techniques, or BATs, that they use frequently. BATs describe a range of potential communication strategies. Employees react variously to different techniques. Table 3-3 shows the range of BATS available to leaders when they want to influence subordinates.[26]

Some of these techniques are domineering and authoritarian. Legitimate–personal authority, legitimate–higher authority, and punishment from source are examples of authoritarian techniques. Others, such as altruism and positive personal relationship, are more democratic.

In one study, Patricia Kearney and her colleagues discovered that subordinates perceived their supervisors to use most frequently a combination of authoritarian and democratic techniques as communication strategies.[27] Kearney also found that subordinates were least satisfied with their bosses when they used authoritarian or disciplinarian techniques.

Techniques Commonly Used	Techniques Least Liked
expert	punishment from source
self-esteem	referent-model
reward from behavior	legitimate-higher authority
legitimate-higher authority	punishment from behavior
personal responsibility	personal relationship-negative
	legitimate-personal authority

Table 3-3
Behavior Alteration Techniques

Technique	Example
1. Reward from behavior	You will enjoy it. It will benefit you to do it.
2. Reward from others	Others will respect and like you if you do as I say.
3. Punishment from source	I will make your life miserable if you don't comply.
4. Referent-model	This is the way I do it. People you respect do it.
5. Legitimate–higher authority	It is a rule; you have to do it. I was told to do it, so you have to do it.
6. Guilt	Others will be harmed if you do not do it.
7. Reward from source	I will give you a raise if you do it.
8. Normative rules	Everyone else does it.
9. Personal responsibility	It is your obligation to do it.
10. Expert	I have a lot of experience in these matters, so believe me; do it like I said.
11. Punishment from behavior	You will be hurt if you do not do it.
12. Self-esteem	You are the best person for the job. No one else could do it.
13. Debt	You owe me this one.
14. Personal relationship (negative)	I will lose respect for you if you don't do it.
15. Altruism	It will help others if you do it.
16. Personal relationship (positive)	I will think better of you if you do it.
17. Duty	Your department needs your help.
18. Legitimate–personal authority	You don't have any choice. Just do it.

You can see from the foregoing discussion that leaders have the choice of directing the actions of subordinates without resorting to authoritative measures. Subordinates will appreciate the respect displayed through positive communication strategies.

Empowerment

Empowerment, the third critical skill, means entrusting people with the authority to act independently. Empowerment can promote creativity, cooperation, and inspiration among employees. Although managers may resist the idea because they fear losing control of their employees, allowing employees to be independent increases their effectiveness. But employee empowerment can be realized only through effective leadership communication skills, such as reduction of status differences and team building.

Reduction of status differences.   Effective leaders are generally perceived to be of higher status than followers. Their higher status allows them to assume responsibility for making important decisions. At the same time, however, large status differences between leaders and followers can have a debilitating effect on morale, efficiency, and productivity. Leaders who concentrate on building such differences encounter these problems. A workable balance occurs when employees understand that leaders are senior partners working with employees to achieve goals.

Leaders can reduce existing status differences by being considerate. Consideration for employees includes showing warmth, asking for opinions, showing concern for employee welfare, giving credit where credit is due, and being open to suggestions. One example of considerate leadership can be found at Preston Trucking, which uses an employee suggestion program to increase job satisfaction and productivity. In 1988, employees submitted 4,412 suggestions for money-making ideas that were estimated to be worth more than $1.3 million to the company. In 1989, management's goal was to receive 5,800, or one from every employee.[28]

Leaders can also be less directive in their communication. Earlier we discussed research on BATS and concluded that employees respond more favorably to and are more likely to accept positive communication. Getting cooperation and productivity through positive communication reduces the perception of a leader "cracking the whip" over employees and results in a more enthusiastic climate.

Team building.   Team building empowers people because it enables work to be accomplished with less direction from the management level. Team building contains two related elements: involvement and integration.

Involvement, or getting people working in activities other than their daily tasks, gives employees a sense of importance in the organization. Involvement in special activities such as quality circles (see Chapter 9 for more on quality circles), goal-setting sessions, professional development workshops, and organizational surveys all can give employees a sense of involvement.

Integration, or bringing people together so that their varied talents and

Preparing and serving a large gourmet dinner calls for exceptional team work and communication. Here, chefs huddle to receive instructions from their leader.

skills can be complementary and mutually supportive, gives employees a sense of cooperation. Just as sports teams integrate members' talents to win contests, employees can appreciate each other's skills when they successfully complete a project together. Teams can be especially gratifying because working with others can make each employee perform even better than she or he would alone.

Anxiety Management

Managing anxiety is an important part of leadership. You may have heard people make remarks such as "He could really be a successful person, but he is afraid of failing," or "She has all the skills, but she is afraid of success." Leaders experience anxiety just as everyone else does. The nature of the fear may be different for each person, but it is present for all leaders at some time or another. Effective managers and leaders control their anxieties and do not let them become overwhelming. Following are some of the methods leaders use to overcome the anxieties of their jobs.

Optimism

Effective leaders remain optimistic even in the face of adversity. Those with an optimistic attitude consider setbacks a challenge. They try to prove their optimism by overcoming setbacks and proving pessimistic people wrong. Strong personal self-confidence and self-awareness, which we discussed earlier in the chapter, form the basis for an optimistic attitude.

Persistence

Leaders also overcome anxieties by being persistent in their actions and behavior in spite of pessimism and short-term setbacks. Persistence involves dedication to the vision of the organization in spite of tense situations, ominous events, or failures. All these have the potential to cause great anxiety among employees and managers alike, but persistence can diminish fear of these events. Persistence, or "hardiness," helps people to "take the stress of life in stride. When they encounter a stressful event — whether positive or negative — (1) they consider it interesting, (2) they feel that they can influence the outcome, and (3) they see it as an opportunity for development."[29]

Passion

Passion reduces the anxiety that leaders face. Enthusiastic commitment helps managers to set aside their doubts and worries and concentrate on the important issues. Employees have more confidence in managers who demonstrate commitment to the shared values of the organization, and their support helps to lessen the anxieties leaders may have.

Accepting Responsibility for Failure

To accomplish goals, leaders must take risks. Some of these risks result in mistakes and failure. Leaders have an obligation to own up to their mistakes and take the blame for failure. Employees know that management is fallible, and their trust in the organization's leadership will suffer if they observe managers blaming subordinates for their own mistakes.[30]

Once you have decided that you will admit your mistakes, you will be less anxious about what you do. Think about it. One of the most stressful activities is speculating on the possible outcomes of your actions. You can decrease your anxiety, if only a little, by resolving to accept what happens and to be honest about it. You can believe in your integrity no matter what else happens. You will have more respect for yourself if you admit mistakes instead of trying to blame them on someone or something else.

Summary

Management and leadership, although not the same conceptually, do share several functions — planning, organizing, motivating, and controlling — and do require similar technical, human, cognitive, and future-oriented skills. These functions and skills are all made more effective by astute and practiced communication.

How management is conducted and what makes for good management are subjects of research and debate. Likert's systems of management, Blake and Mouton's managerial grid theory, House's path-goal model, Vroom and Yetton's leader-participation model, and Kuhnert and Lewis's transactional and leadership theory provide a broad perspective on the variety of management found in organizations.

Strategic leadership skills can benefit anyone who needs to communicate with a group or win support for an idea. These skills are not the exclusive property of executives; they can benefit everyday communications. The four components of the model of strategic communication can show any communicator how to address the major aspects of personal leadership development.

Goal setting includes developing and promoting shared values and visions and managing change. Situational knowledge encompasses obtaining information about the organization and self. Communication competence means demonstrating organizational ethics, promoting understanding in decision making, and learning effective communication strategies for the purpose of empowering others. Anxiety often accompanies the risks of leadership communication and can be counteracted by optimism, persistence, passion, and acceptance of responsibility for mistakes.

The material in this chapter has implications even for people who clearly recognize that they are not interested in leadership. All organizations need a good staff, and leadership skills can be a tremendous help to people even if their interest is solely in the daily activities of an organization.

Discussion

1. What are the major skills and functions of managers? How are they affected by the contemporary business environment?

2. Compare the management theories of Likert, Blake and Mouton, House, Vroom and Yetton, and Kuhnert and Lewis. Can you identify

some basic similarities in these approaches? Which would you prefer as an employee? As a manager?

3. What is the relationship between leadership and management?

4. How can a strong value system improve the quality of leadership in an organization?

5. What can managers and employees do to learn from communication failure? Discuss the four-step process of continual learning and its role in the development of organizational knowledge.

6. What is empowerment? How can effective communication result in the empowerment of employees?

7. What are some methods for handling leadership anxiety?

Activities

1. For each of Blake and Mouton's five management styles, explain the communication behavior you believe would be exhibited in a business or professional organization.

2. Use the leadership/management styles and descriptions from this chapter to classify each of the following corporate leaders:
   a. Lee Iacocca, Chrysler
   b. Michael Eisner, Disney
   c. Wayne Calloway, Pepsico
   d. John Sculley, Apple
   e. Thomas Kearns, Xerox
   Explain why you made the decisions that you did.

3. Find a copy of President Ronald Reagan's address to the nation after the space shuttle *Challenger* exploded on January 28, 1986. Analyze that speech according to Hart's four categories of effective leaders' language.

Notes

1. David Campbell in W. Keichell, "A Hard Look at Executive Vision," *Fortune*, October 23, 1989, p. 207.
2. P. Hersey and K. Blanchard, *Management of Organizational Behavior: Utilizing Human Resources* (Englewood Cliffs, N.J.: Prentice-Hall, 1982).
3. Ibid.
4. G. Morgan, *Riding the Waves of Change* (San Francisco: Jossey-Bass, 1988), p. 11.
5. R. Likert, *New Patterns of Management* (New York: McGraw-Hill, 1961).
6. R. Blake and J. Mouton, "Managerial Facades," *Advanced Management Journal* 31 (July 1966), 30–37.

7. R. House and T. Mitchell, "Path-Goal Theory of Leadership," *Journal of Contemporary Business* (Autumn 1974), 81–97.

8. V. Vroom and P. Yetton, *Leadership and Decision-Making* (Pittsburgh: University of Pittsburgh Press, 1973).

9. K. Kuhnert and P. Lewis, "Transactional and Transformational Leadership: A Constructive/Developmental Analysis." *Academy of Management Review* 12 (1987), 648–657.

10. J. M. Burns, *Leadership* (New York: Harper & Row, 1978); J. Kouzes and B. Posner, *The Leadership Challenge* (San Francisco: Jossey-Bass, 1987).

11. G. Terry, *Principles of Management*, 3rd ed. (Homewood, Ill.: Richard D. Irwin, 1960); R. Tannenbaum, I. Weschler, and F. Massarik, *Leadership and Organization: A Behavioral Science Approach* (New York: McGraw-Hill, 1959); H. Koontz and C. O'Donnell, *Principles of Management*, 2nd ed. (New York: McGraw-Hill, 1959); J. Kotter, *The Leadership Factor* (New York: Free Press, 1988).

12. Kouzes and Posner, *The Leadership Challenge*, p. 336.

13. Ibid., p. 196.

14. B. Z. Posner, J. M. Kouzes, and W. H. Schmidt, "Shared Values Make a Difference: An Empirical Test of Corporate Culture," *Human Resource Management* 3 (1985), 293–310.

15. W. Bennis and B. Nanus, *Leaders: The Strategies for Taking Charge* (New York: Harper & Row, 1985), p. 89.

16. J. Kotter, *The Leadership Factor* (New York: Free Press, 1988).

17. T. Peters and R. Waterman, *In Search of Excellence: Lessons from America's Best Run Companies* (New York: Warner Books, 1982).

18. K. R. Andrews, "Ethics in Practice," *Harvard Business Review* (September-October 1989), 103.

19. W. S. Howell, *The Empathic Communicator* (Belmont, Calif.: Wadsworth, 1982); S. P. Golen, C. Powers, and M. A. Titkemeyer, "Ethics," in S. P. Golen (ed.), *Methods of Teaching Selected Topics in Business Communication* (Urbana, Ill.: Association for Business Communication, 1986), pp. 3–8.

20. S. Kerr, "Integrity in Effective Leadership," and R. Harrison, "Quality of Service: A New Frontier for Integrity in Organizations," in S. Shrivastva (ed.), *Executive Integrity: The Search for High Human Values in Organizational Life* (San Francisco: Jossey-Bass, 1988), pp. 122–139, 45–67; C. C. Walton, *The Moral Manager* (Cambridge, Mass.: Ballinger, 1988).

21. W. Bennis, *On Becoming a Leader* (Reading, Mass: Addison-Wesley, 1989).

22. Kouzes and Posner, *The Leadership Challenge*.

23. J. K. Van Fleet, *The 22 Biggest Mistakes Managers Make and How to Correct Them* (West Nyack, N.Y.: Parker, 1982), p. 147.

24. R. Hart, *Verbal Style and the Presidency* (Orlando, Fla.: Academic Press, 1984).

25. G. Hines, "Management of Leadership Styles," in A. Dale Timpe (ed.), *Leadership* (New York: Kend, 1987), pp. 105–111.

26. V. Richmond, L. Davis, K. Saylor, and J. McCroskey, "Power Strategies in Organizations: Communication Techniques and Messages," *Human Communication Research* 11 (1984), 85–108.

27. P. Kearney, T. Plax, V. Richmond, and J. McCroskey, "Power in the Classroom III: Teacher Communication Techniques and Messages," *Communication Education* 34 (1985), 19–28.

28. A. Farnham, "The Trust Gap," *Fortune*, December 4, 1989, p. 70.
29. Kouzes and Posner, *The Leadership Challenge*, p. 67.
30. Van Fleet, *The 22 Biggest Mistakes*.

Basic Communication Skills

Part 2 introduces the fundamentals of successful communication — listening, verbal, and nonverbal skills. These chapters discuss how each contributes to successful interaction and how to avoid communication breakdowns. Numerous self-tests and evaluation activities can help to identify areas for improvement.

- ❑ Chapter 4 explains the role of perception in listening and teaches interactive listening skills.

- ❑ Chapter 5 discusses the relationship between verbal and nonverbal communication and suggests ways to create effective messages.

*L*istening
Skills

OBJECTIVES

After working through this chapter, you will be able to:

1. Understand the importance of listening in business and the professions

2. Differentiate between listening and hearing

3. Identify the problems caused by ineffective listening

4. Recognize how perception shapes listening

5. Use interactive listening skills to enhance strategic communication

6. Gain control of your listening and eliminate receiver apprehension

7. Know how to evaluate the success of your listening

Listening is the most frequently used communication skill. Researchers have estimated that typical employees spend as much as fifty percent of their workday communicating; about forty-five percent of this time is spent listening. Communications consultant Germaine Knapp contended that "effective listening can be used to help persuade, motivate, improve productivity, boost morale, obtain cooperation, sell, teach, inform, or achieve other goals."[1]

Yet most people take listening for granted. This lack of attention to the significance of listening is heightened by the popular belief that technology will be able to solve most, if not all, problems in the workplace. As we emphasize throughout this book, society's increasing dependence on the use of technology makes basic communication skills — listening, verbal skills, and nonverbal skills — *more critical* in business than ever before. According to one business professor, "Technology has led us to impose tighter time frames on ourselves, to reduce standards and fundamentals, to be information-obese, and to substitute technology for basic skills and problem solving. . . . Because information is available, we consume it indiscriminately without thinking through whether we need it."[2]

Your listening ability is particularly susceptible to indiscriminate overloading because you are constantly exposed to aural input — from televisions, radios, peers, professors, supervisors, and more. It is more difficult to filter out and analyze important information than ever before and easier to get distracted and lose concentration.

Hearing versus Listening

You have been using your sense of hearing longer than you are able to remember. Even before you were born, you were able to hear sounds generated outside your mother's body. Sound waves can penetrate the skin and tissue layers of a pregnant woman and reach the hearing mechanism of the fetus. As the ninth month of pregnancy approaches, many obstetricians suggest that to familiarize unborn babies with the sound of their parents' voices, the parents talk directly to the babies.

Nevertheless, there is a critical difference between the sensory process of hearing and the skill of listening we address in this chapter. *Hearing* is an automatic process in which sound waves stimulate nerve impulses to the brain. *Listening* is a voluntary process that goes beyond simply reacting to sounds and includes understanding, analyzing, evaluating, and responding.[3]

Listening also requires concentration, which means holding a key idea in your mind while considering alternative or conflicting concepts. Effective listening entails synthesizing new information with what you already know.[4] You may have heard people refer to others' "short attention span," "lack of consideration," or "weak concentration." All these remarks boil down to the same message: "That person does not listen well." Both now and after graduation, you will need strong listening skills, and others will expect you to have them. By reading this chapter, you can learn why effective listening is indispensable in organizations. You can also understand how listening fits into the total human communication process — that is, you can comprehend the interactional nature of communication. You can acquire skills and techniques to help you to become a more effective listener.

We cannot guarantee you that this chapter will solve all of your personal problems, make the rest of your college years a smashing success, and get you the job of your dreams. We cannot even guarantee that it will make you a perfect listener. But we can assure you that more effective listening skills will improve your chances for personal and professional success and allow you to avoid the pitfalls associated with poor listening.

Listening in Your Career

Many people assume that competence and excellence in a career must be demonstrated through speaking — showing others what the speaker knows and how well she or he can articulate it. In many cases, however, excellence can be demonstrated through effective listening as well. In organizational settings, the managers who are perceived as most competent are those who know their employees well and are sensitive to their ideas and concerns. These managers are also rated as the best listeners in the organization.

Benefits of Good Listening

At this point in your life, your primary "career" is as a student, although you may be working as well. You may or may not know exactly what field you want to pursue after graduation, but you will find that effective listening is a critical skill in becoming successful. Research has shown that listening is the most important skill for entry-level professionals in business.[5] Furthermore, some researchers estimate that approximately forty-five percent of a businessperson's salary is earned listening, and that percentage increases as a person rises in his or her career.[6]

Many people earn a great deal of their income by listening. Physicians, therapists, and attorneys must listen carefully to patients and clients to provide desired services effectively. In other jobs, listening can save lives. For example, police officers assigned to work on 911 (emergency) hotlines use their listening skills to identify and respond to emergencies as they occur. According to an officer in the Division of Training and Education, Boston Police Department, 911 officers are required to take a forty-hour training course that emphasizes skills such as listening for key information (for example, specific descriptions of people or locations), using silence to calm upset callers, and focusing listening concentration to make up for the

Interactive listening is critical to understanding others' needs and discussing possible solutions to problems. A day care worker and her supervisor hold a conference during nap-time.

lack of visual cues inherent in phone communication. This training yields more and better quality information even from highly disturbed callers as well as enabling officers to use new technology, such as computerized response programs, to supplement their listening skills.[7] Strong listening skills are essential in many other fields as well.

Good listening is universally expected by others. Even though human behavior is difficult to characterize, it is certain that most people are very ego involved when they talk. That is to say, when you decide to speak, you usually feel you have something valuable to say, and you expect others to listen. When others speak, they expect you to listen.

Problems with Ineffective Listening

Trouble arises when you do not listen carefully to others. Comments such as "You need to pay closer attention to directions," "Concentrate on what you are doing," and "I don't think you understand what I'm saying" are good indications that your listening skills can use improvement. Failing to listen effectively can produce some embarrassing moments, like the time a business traveler sleepily boarded the red-eye flight to (she thought) Oakland, California, and landed hours later in Auckland, New Zealand. There are three areas in which poor listening can cause trouble in your career.

Poor listeners are perceived as less intelligent.   When other people perceive that someone is not listening carefully, their first reaction is that this person is unable to process the information. This is especially true when poor listening becomes a habit. Others become wary of a poor listener's ability to handle even the simplest amount of information, and the results can be quite negative.

Poor listening is costly.   One of the greatest costs of ineffective listening is wasted time. Repeating information is time consuming and causes problems if the task at hand requires a quick response. Repeating messages also consumes effort and energy that can be put to better use. If you are experiencing fatigue or are enduring stressful conditions, an ineffective listening partner compounds your problems. Wasted effort resulting from poor listening is a significant cost in a world that already drains people's cognitive, physical, and emotional resources.

Poor listening can cost money too. Misinterpretation, failure to hear information correctly, and physical or mental distractions are listening problems that cost businesses money. For example, if you are traveling and fail to hear your flight number being called, you lose time and money if you have to take a later flight. When you book hotel rooms, if you are not listening carefully to the reservation clerk when she or he mentions that your company is eligible for a corporate rate, you cost your company money.

Poor listening limits your chances for success.   Most people's careers are characterized by steps toward a particular ultimate goal. Effective listening is necessary in the journey toward this goal. Promotions, recognitions, salary increases, and awards are possible only after employees have demonstrated their competence in critical areas, and performance appraisals are often based on criteria directly related to effective listening abilities. Even now, while you are in school, you can achieve more success by improving your listening skills. Concentrating on what others are saying before you ask a question can prevent you from repeating the same question someone else has already asked. Being open to new information allows you to make creative connections while learning.

Listening enables you to take advantage of opportunities and avoid potential problems. Those professionals who maintain only average listening abilities will probably achieve only average success in their careers. Those people with exceptional career success will tell you that they consider listening a critical element in their strategic climb up the career ladder. An example of corporate commitment to listening is Unisys Corporation, which has been a leader in promoting listening among its employees. This organization is so convinced of the importance of listening on the job that over 20,000 employees have formal training in listening.[8]

The Role of Perception

You may have heard the old adage "You have to know where you are before you can go anywhere." To improve listening skills, you need an idea of your listening framework — your perceptions. Perception is the process of creating meaning based on experience. In other words, your understanding of events depends on your accumulation of sensory knowledge about people, objects, and events.

People have different perceptions because their backgrounds vary. Someone can make the statement "The sky is blue," and your perception of that message will be different from the rest of your classmates, even though all of you hear the same words. You may think, "Yes it is blue, but it looked like that yesterday morning and it rained in the afternoon." The person who sits beside you in class may interpret the statement as, "Yes it is blue, but cloudless skies are pretty dull." Another classmate may not perceive any meaning at all and think, "So what? What does a blue sky have to do with making a buck?" The sender's intended meaning could have corresponded to either of the first two interpretations, or it might have been altogether different such as that he or she delights in the color blue. Take a moment to look at Figure 4-1. Do you see two profiles, or do you see a goblet? Your perceptual framework determines what you initially see in the figure.

If every person who receives a message perceives it somewhat differently, consider what happens when a message is sent in a business environment. The message is likely to be received by a large number of people from a wide range of backgrounds and with very different organizational experiences. A message such as "Because of a drop in business, some personnel cuts in some key areas may occur in the near future" can become the center of controversy and insecurity among employees because it is vague and thus even more likely to be interpreted in myriad ways. Therefore, it is extremely important to assess your perceptual framework and the possible perceptions of others when communicating. The first step in doing so is understanding the factors that influence perception.

Factors Influencing Perception

Reception and attention are important factors in perception. *Reception* refers to the physical process of hearing aural and seeing visual stimuli. Not only are words and sounds available signals for listening, but nonverbal cues also act as part of this process, as we discuss in Chapter 5. Reception can influence perception in several ways. First, the condition of your hearing and sight determines to some degree the amount and type of message you receive. For example, if your hearing is impaired for some reason, you

FIGURE 4-1 *What do you see? Depending on your own perceptions, your first impression may be of a vase, candle holder, or goblet. Or, you might see two faces staring at each other.*

are likely to miss messages and thus have inaccurate perceptions of communication.

Second, selective and focused *attention* to the message is crucial for accurate perception to occur. Goss has suggested three principles that comprise the listener's attention process:[9]

1. The number of stimuli to which a person can attend at one time is very limited.

2. Some stimuli go unnoticed or are attended to only in an unconscious way.

3. The amount of attention a person gives to a stimulus varies according to the difficulty of the task at hand.

These principles point out that many variables, both external and internal, affect the listening process. We now discuss one of the most important of these variables, perceptual assessment.

Assessing Your Perceptions

Although perception is often blamed for communication problems, it is a necessary element in making sense of the world. Your perceptions act as a category system that helps you to understand messages. If you were unable to categorize messages according to your supply of knowledge and experience, every message would be difficult to understand. It would be like having to relearn the concept of reading every time you opened a book.

Problems with perception occur when your interpretation of people or events is distorted by negative or erroneous impressions or category systems. In extreme cases, perception is replaced by *prejudice*, preconceived negative judgments or opinions formed without a basis in reality. For example, you may have difficulty communicating with a member of the legal profession because you have been raised to believe that lawyers are corrupt and untrustworthy. Instead of facilitating communication, prejudice acts as a barrier to effective and open exchange. Therefore, the first skill necessary for interactive listening is the ability to diagnose your own listening behavior. The following personal listening profile shows you "where you are" and can help you to plan specific improvement strategies. Think carefully about each statement before responding. Only honest and well-considered answers will allow you to learn about yourself.

The personal listening profile helps you to see how you understand your own listening preferences in specific circumstances. For example, if you rated statements four and seven with a "5," it may indicate that you are uncomfortable with nonpersonal communication — that is, communication mediated by technology. You can then cultivate awareness of this perception and make a conscious effort to overcome your hesitation so that you can gain more benefit from such communication. Of course, this profile is not completely comprehensive. People often mistake their ability levels, and you may find that particular situations that influence your perceptions have not been included. But thinking about these issues is a good way to identify others and can be the first step toward improving your listening.

A second step in understanding your perceptions is discovering your listening priorities. Listening priorities can vary quite a bit among people and situations. Some people set their listening priorities highest for situations involving close interpersonal relationships (family, relatives, close friends, co-workers), while others may reserve listening priorities for more social situations (socializing at the office, talking to neighbors and acquaintances). Still others may focus their listening priorities on occupational or professional matters (listening to reports, superiors, subordinates, peers, briefings). If you perceive the listening situation to be important, you are more likely to be open and willing to engage in interactive listening.

Finally, it is a good idea to consider how emotionally charged words affect your perceptions of people and ideas. You may hold very strong opinions about certain words or subjects, such as *conservative*, *liberal*, *AIDS*, *chemical weapons*, or *taxes*. Your opinions are likely to be accompanied by strong emotional energy that derives from your experiences or knowledge of those issues, the way you have been brought up, or the environment you are living in. Emotion is a positive quality because it

PERSONAL LISTENING PROFILE

Rate each statement according to the following scale: (5) Always true for me; (4) Frequently true for me; (3) Sometimes true for me; (2) Rarely true for me; (1) Never true for me.

1. ____*2* Listening to public speeches is boring.

2. ____*3* Listening to someone talk on the radio is very entertaining.

3. ____*4* It is easy to concentrate when others talk about their problems.

4. ____*2* Listening to my supervisor over the telephone is more difficult than talking to him or her in person.

5. ____*5* Listening to several people talk at once in a group discussion is very distracting.

6. ____*3* Listening to small talk is an enjoyable activity.

7. ____*2* Listening to videotaped instructional or training materials bothers me.

8. ____*2* Listening to critically important information makes me nervous.

9. ____*3* Listening to people in authority is exciting.

10. ____*3* I avoid listening to people I do not like.

11. ____*4* I am often distracted if I must listen for a long time.

12. ____*3* It is easy to concentrate on what others are saying if they gesture with their hands.

13. ____*3* I enjoy listening to others talk about themselves.

14. ____*1* I feel uncomfortable when listening to technical information.

15. ____*2* I look forward to the opportunity to listen to people argue skillfully about a controversial topic.

Look back over the responses you gave. Add your score for numbers 1, 4, 5, 7, 8, 10, 11, 14. Call the total "Score A." Add your score for numbers 2, 3, 6, 9, 12, 13, 15. Call this total "Score B." Subtract Score A from Score B. If the resulting total is between twenty-five and thirty-five, you see yourself as a very competent listener. If you scored between twelve and twenty-four, you see yourself as an average listener. If you scored between negative fifteen and eleven, you see yourself as a below average listener, and if you scored negative sixteen or below, you perceive yourself as a poor listener.

reflects the strength of your beliefs. But it can also be a barrier to listening if you focus on the charged words instead of the message and fail to process information objectively. You may stop listening to the speaker entirely to prepare a defense of your position on the issue. To listen effectively, you are wise to recognize others' point of view and actively control your emotions.

Assessing Others' Perceptions

Empathy is identification with and understanding of others' feelings. Sympathy is the act of sharing the feelings of another person. Sympathy and empathy are important elements of perception. By attempting to feel the same way as a speaker (empathize with her or him), you can better understand the message. Furthermore, by demonstrating that you understand a speaker's feelings (sympathize with him or her), you can enhance the shared meaning of the communicated message. Consider the following propositions:

◆ Understanding a speaker's feelings allows insight into her or his motivations.

◆ Recognizing the emotional state of other communicators provides knowledge about their communication strategies.

◆ Demonstrating sympathy to speakers allows them to communicate more efficiently.

◆ Demonstrating sympathy in listening situations provides speakers with knowledge of your motivations and intentions.

Not all situations call for an obvious display of sympathy or empathy from the listener. Nevertheless, many situations do. It stands to reason that empathy allows more accurate perception because a lack of knowledge about a speaker's feeling inhibits the listener's ability to carefully analyze the message.

Strategies for uncovering a speaker's feelings include questioning techniques ("Are you feeling all right?" "Is there anything you want to discuss with me?") and reflective tactics. The latter are a special type of empathic strategy in which the listener asks empathic questions, such as "Are you angry because of what George said about your department in front of the regional manager?" (reflective leading question), or "Why do you get so upset when the quarterly reports are due?" (probing question). Even closed questions are useful as reflective techniques: "Are you excited because we get more time off or because we get overtime pay?"

Keep in mind, however, that it may not be appropriate in all situations to use these techniques because some speakers do not wish to share their feelings. The most important part of empathy is true concern for others and respect for their communication.

Goal Setting for Interactive Listening

As with all important communication activities, such as speaking up in meetings, talking to co-workers, or interviewing, preparation for listening allows you to do the best job you can. You can prepare for listening situations by accomplishing several tasks. These include setting goals, building motivation, and generating energy. For example, attending a meeting or presentation can be more profitable if you identify specific objectives ("I will learn at least five new things at this meeting"), build motivation for the event ("I know that the things I learn will benefit me later"), and generate sufficient energy to be alert ("I will conserve my physical and mental energy for the meeting"). Let us examine each of these steps individually.

Identify Objectives

Three questions are worthy of consideration in goal setting: What must I get out of this listening situation? What would I like to get out of this situation? What should the other persons get out of my listening to them? As you answer these questions, keep in mind that goals should identify basic objectives, such as getting background information needed to perform at an adequate level. Comprehensive goals also identify additional rewards that might be reaped from the listening situation, such as learning about how you and your actions affect larger processes in the organization or how the speaker feels about the subject of the conversation. Goals for listening situations, as with all communication goals, must be specific, difficult enough to provide satisfaction on achievement, and realistically obtainable based on the resources and abilities available to you.

Consideration for the other person or people in the listening situation is another important goal. Consciously remind yourself to keep an open mind, respond honestly, and concentrate fully on what is being said. It is a great advantage to those who are speaking or talking to know whether you are comprehending the communication.

Build Motivation

Setting difficult but achievable goals can certainly produce motivation for some people. Important situations or important people often motivate people to listen as well. But what about daily, routine listening — how can you improve your motivation in the typical exchanges that make up the bulk of your communication?

Try to get a sense of what type of listening is called for. There are four types: for information, for enjoyment, for evaluation, and for feelings. Some people make more of an effort to listen in situations in which information is disseminated than in situations that speak to feelings. Others are more interested in being effective listeners when evaluation comes into play than when enjoyment is the point. Knowing more about your listening style helps to improve your motivation. In the following box, indicate where your listening priorities lie.

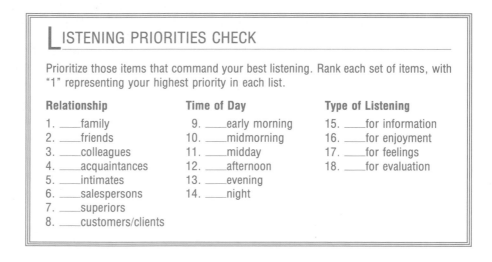

L ISTENING PRIORITIES CHECK

Prioritize those items that command your best listening. Rank each set of items, with "1" representing your highest priority in each list.

Relationship	Time of Day	Type of Listening
1. ___family	9. ___early morning	15. ___for information
2. ___friends	10. ___midmorning	16. ___for enjoyment
3. ___colleagues	11. ___midday	17. ___for feelings
4. ___acquaintances	12. ___afternoon	18. ___for evaluation
5. ___intimates	13. ___evening	
6. ___salespersons	14. ___night	
7. ___superiors		
8. ___customers/clients		

This exercise allows you to critically compare listening priorities. What did you learn about yourself? Were you surprised at some of the rankings that you made? Are there some changes that you might want to make in your listening efforts based on this self-examination?

There are several methods for building motivation for listening situations. *Recognize* the tangible *rewards* of the listening situation. *Understand* that most listening situations have some *usefulness*. *Recognize* that some listening situations offer *delayed benefits*. *Become adept* at knowing which listening situations to *avoid*. *Use goal setting* as a game to *create interest* in the message. *Use self-competition* (determination to improve yourself) as a tool for progressively *building listening motivation*. *Realize* that poor motivation will *cost* you time, effort, and money in the long run.

Generate Energy

Some communication situations demand more energy than others — consider the difference between listening to a fellow student talk about the success of a project the two of you worked on together and listening to a group of people you do not know very well talk about their plans for the summer. You may be surprised to realize that the hidden benefits of the second situation far outweigh those of the first. Whereas you already know about the successful project (after all, you worked on it too), you have the opportunity to learn quite a bit about the possibilities for summer jobs from listening to the group conversation. The key is to energize yourself and make the most of the situation.

Two types of energy make up listening — physical and mental. Physical energy is required to listen effectively. Fatigue can have a surprisingly strong effect on listening ability, yet many people do not take this factor into account, particularly students for whom late nights and inadequate sleep are a fact of life. Fatigue dulls the senses and can lower your ability to process information. If you are tired, sick, stressed, or otherwise incapacitated, the following advice can help you to make the most of the situation.

1.   Indicate to the source of the message your physical condition and ask for consideration.

2.   Muster stored energy for the listening situation (deep breathing, muscle tension/relaxation, avoidance of physically stressful activities ahead of time).

3.   Avoid those listening situations for which you simply cannot build any energy; it is better to postpone such situations than not listen well.

The level of a person's mental energy also shapes the listening process. Many people put less mental energy into activities at the end of the day, either because they are tired or because they are beginning to think of other things — what to do after work or after class. Worries, anxiety, or apprehension over work-related or personal matters are other common causes of low mental energy.

Of course, it is very difficult (and sometimes impossible) to put such concerns aside to prepare for a listening situation, but it nevertheless helps to put your worries in perspective. If there is nothing you can do about the worrisome situation at the moment, accept that fact, resolve to tackle the matter at another time, and stop worrying about it.

Situational Knowledge: Preparing for Interactive Listening

As you recall from Chapter 2, situational knowledge refers to information that is useful for recognizing and understanding the variables operating in communication situations. Taking situational details into account as much as possible enables you as a listener to prepare effectively for the communication encounter. Following are a number of situational parameters that can govern listening effectiveness.

Speaker's Communication Style

The speaker's communication style may call for the application of special listening considerations. Some people have a tendency to talk rapidly, gesticulate broadly, or otherwise distract you from the message. Others show no expressiveness or talk slowly; this style may leave you second-guessing the meaning of the message because you have insufficient cues to guide your interpretation and a lot of time to question the meaning of the words.

Unusual dialects or accents may also cause listening difficulties. One of the best ways to overcome this obstacle is to familiarize yourself with new speech patterns. You can do this by *listening more carefully,* talking less, and concentrating harder when communicating with someone who has a dialect or accent. Do not focus on your own comprehension difficulties; listen instead for the speaker's ideas, the content of the message. Identify common speech patterns (for example, many native Spanish speakers pronounce "bit" as "beet," many people from the northern United States pronounce "hair" as "here," and so on), and become comfortable with them.

Do not hesitate to ask the speaker to repeat what she or he said or to slow down. You will both benefit from such requests, particularly if they are phrased in a polite, confident voice. The worst response is to decide you simply cannot comprehend the speaker and so should not bother trying.

Environmental Distractions

The communication setting may contain a variety of distractions to effective listening. Noise, the presence of others, or even listening on someone else's "turf" can have an impact on your capacity for listening. Try to move the communication even to a setting with less noise or other distractions, if possible. If this is not possible, make the best of the setting. For example, if you are in a crowded room, see if you can find a relatively quiet corner; if you are in an unfamiliar office, visualize a more comfortable setting. Although setting is a situational parameter that is often difficult to adjust, both you and the speaker will benefit from making it as comfortable as possible.

Emotional Distractions

As we mentioned in our earlier discussion of perception, the emotions of the communicators are a determining factor in any listening situation. Emotionally aroused people often react to communication situations differently from people who are calm. If you are negatively aroused, you may not listen effectively, which compounds the problems you already have. Speakers who are emotionally charged may mislead you into thinking that they are passionate about the topic when something else is bothering them.

When you listen to a highly emotional speaker, focus on the content of the message rather than on the delivery. Control your impulse to argue until you have heard the complete message. As you listen, evaluate the strengths and weaknesses of the speaker's position by summarizing the main points of the argument in your head. Doing so will help you to remain calm (much like forcing yourself to count to ten before losing your temper) and will also help you to respond effectively when the time comes.

Physical Condition of Communicators

Fatigue, illness, or stress can negatively influence your ability to listen. Earlier we discussed physical and mental energy and gave some guidelines on how to increase your energy level for communication. If the speaker appears to be tired or is having difficulty talking for some reason, increase your concentration accordingly. Effective listening is never a passive activity.

Message Content

The message itself plays an important role in listening. Most people are more motivated to listen effectively if the consequences of the communication are important. Formal situations, such as presentations, lectures, or interviews, usually require more systematic listening, with more precise comprehension of the speaker's language.[10]

If the situation is informal, however, or if the topic is not particularly meaningful to you (for example, a colleague tells you about a report unrelated to your area), you may be tempted to minimize listening effort. Nevertheless, keep in mind that it is impossible to predict all the outcomes of a listening situation, so it is a good idea to make the most of every listening opportunity. That colleague's report may contain information you will find useful at a future date.

Small talk, social conversation, and personal self-disclosures usually do not require the same type of listening skills as does content that is highly technical, vague, controversial, or innovative. By considering the content of the message, listeners can better anticipate the conditions of the listening situation.

Communication Competence: Interactive Listening

Interactive listening is an ongoing, complex, and dynamic process. Our own work in listening training has convinced us that the maximum rewards from listening result from strategic planning, assessments of self and others, and feedback and verbal encouragement. Interactive listening is not only an auditory skill; you listen best if you listen with all your available senses. Elements of verbal and nonverbal behavior can help you to process maximum amounts of information in a listening context.

Becoming more interactive as a listener consists of reducing the amount of time you spend talking, using questions to become more aware as a listener and to help others, and using the strategic aspects of nonverbal behavior. These skills, along with the listening competence skills you learned earlier in the chapter, will be invaluable in improving your listening.

Reduce Talk

It is difficult to listen when you are talking. People often feel that what they have to say is the critical component of any conversation, and thus they feel compelled to provide a play-by-play commentary on every event and idea that occurs to them. People with reputations as good listeners are admired, and their primary skill is the ability to remain quiet!

As a strategy, silence works in many communication situations. People frequently elaborate or provide additional information if their conversational partner is silent. Consider the following situation.

> Clarissa knew that George had recently had an important meeting with the district manager of the software division in which they both worked. She overheard two co-workers, John and Peter, pestering George with questions about the meeting. George's responses were evasive; he seemed uncomfortable with their aggressive questioning and gave them very little information. Clarissa and George were not particularly good friends, but she decided that if she approached him in a nonthreatening way and allowed him to talk, she might find out what went on at the meeting. When George referred to the meeting in a later conversation with Clarissa, she was strategically silent and did not prompt him for information. This seemed to put him at ease, and they were soon discussing the goings on of the meeting. George had wanted to talk to someone about the meeting, but he was uneasy and distrustful of people who seemed to care more about their questions than his answers. He wanted to talk to someone who would really listen.

Use Questioning Techniques

Interactive listening entails more than simply receiving a message — it requires listeners to respond at critical points in the communication process. Questioning techniques are one type of response that can improve listening by making speakers more efficient. When listeners and speakers are more aligned on the topic, meaning, consequences, and language use, listening effectiveness improves immensely. Strategic questions that improve the speaking/listening process consist of closed, open, probing, and leading questions. Each of these question types is used for different purposes depending on the listening situation. Table 4-1 describes questioning techniques.

Questioning techniques are especially useful in guiding a speaker to a point in the conversation that is necessary to accomplish a goal. Speakers can get off the track, mislead, provide aimless and useless information, or even deceive listeners. To avoid conditions of listening that may reduce your chances of achieving your goals, use these questioning techniques.

Use Nonverbal Behavior

Earlier in this chapter we showed how important it is to correctly interpret a speaker's nonverbal cues so as to receive the optimum amount of information in the message. The same is true in reverse: *giving* the speaker nonverbal cues to show that you are comprehending (or not comprehending) the message. It is inherently important to listen when someone speaks to you (and we certainly hope that you agree by now), but perhaps even more important is that the other person *perceives* that you are listening. The use of head nods, forward leans, gestures, "uh-huh's," smiles, and so forth are vital. It is a shame to be listening if the other cannot see that you are.

Understanding, agreement, empathy, and emotional responses can be displayed effectively through nonverbal cues. For example, frowning generally indicates disagreement or misunderstanding. Nodding can connote agreement or comprehension. Shrugs can communicate lack of interest or

TABLE 4-1
Techniques for Questioning

Type	Purpose	Example
Closed	Obtain a short, specific response.	"Do you mean this fiscal year or last fiscal year?"
Open	Allow freedom and choice in the response.	"What is your attitude on cost accounting?"
Probing	Encourage the speaker to elaborate on the topic (by using why-type questions).	"Why do you feel that way?"
Leading	Imply expected response in question.	"Are you saying that our computer system needs to be upgraded?"

Read my fingers . . . listening is enhanced by nonverbal behavior such as gestures and facial expressions. In performance, musicians must attend to these cues as well as listening to their own and each other's playing.

ambiguity. No response at all can convey a lack of awareness. To get a sense of how nonverbal behavior facilitates interactive involvement, take a look at Table 4-2.

Of course, other behaviors function to regulate the interactive nature of listening. We discuss these at length in the next chapter. Because nonverbal communication is crucial to speakers, you are wise to recognize how your nonverbal behavior affects communication in particular situations.

Dismantle the Three D's

Competent listening also involves dismantling the barriers to your own reception of the message. The most common listening problems are *di*straction, *di*sorientation, and *de*fensiveness. Fighting boredom is another important skill for competent listening — communication is not inherently boring; it is tiresome if *you* fail to see its importance to you or to a project you are involved with. Several strategies, such as listening for ideas, "plan-

TABLE 4-2
Nonverbal Behavior and Interactive Listening

Behavior	Function
Eye gaze, eye contact	Facilitate other's conversation
Gestures (open palm, motioning)	Encourage additional information
Paralanguage (increase volume, pitch)	Encourages clarification
Proxemics (giving people more space)	Makes people more comfortable
Tactile (pats on the back, shoulder)	Provides confidence builder
Body orientation (face person directly)	Provides sense of importance
Nodding, shaking head	Give information about feelings

ning to report," and taking notes, can help you combat the three D's and boredom and make your listening pay great dividends.

Distraction, disorientation, and defensiveness severely inhibit the listening process. Distractions move the focus of attention away from the message. Disorientation is a breakdown in the mental and emotional processes that assign meaning to the message. Defensiveness produces biased judgment about messages because of overly emotional feelings about certain issues or people. Table 4-3 gives a more complete picture of the three D's. One way to avoid the three D's is to listen for ideas by asking questions of yourself as you listen. Ask yourself if the speaker's points are logical, if you agree or disagree, if what is being said corresponds to or contradicts your own experience. In this way you can keep yourself focused on the content of the message and at the same time put the message in the context of what you already know.

Another method for competent listening is taking notes. You can take notes in two ways: writing down the highlights of what is being said or identifying the organizational pattern used by the speaker. For example, many people organize their ideas into lists, arrange events in chronological order, identify a problem and then a solution, or present one point of view and then an opposing position.[11] Listen for cues such as "The three causes of increased productivity are . . . ," "Since 1987, several important events have occurred," or "Absenteeism is increasing; we can survey the employees to find out why." If you hear a cue, get ready to take down that important information. Remember that other people are impressed by the care and effort demonstrated when a listener takes notes.[12]

TABLE 4-3
The Three D's

Problem	Components	Consequences
Distraction	Mental	Missing needed information
	Environmental	Appearing uninterested
Disorientation	Confusion	Appearing dazed, flustered
	Boredom	Seeming apathetic
	Self-reflecting	Appearing self-centered
Defensiveness	Disliking the speaker	Making biased judgments
	Resenting the situation	Reducing alternatives

Avoid Boredom

You are able to process information at about 500 words per minute, but the average rate of speech is only 150 words per minute.[13] Inevitably, there are going to be instances when you are acutely aware of this difference — you will be bored. In many other listening situations, without realizing it, you are tuning in and out of effective listening simply because the information is coming in much more slowly than you are processing it. These situations are probably the most dangerous kinds because you may not even be aware of your boredom. Here are some tips for determining your boredom level for most listening situations.

> Finding yourself in another world
> Being easily distracted
> Having to have information repeated
> Watching the clock
> Planning other activities
> Thinking about yourself
> Wondering about the speaker's attire
> Grooming or preening yourself
> Reducing eye contact
> Fiddling with objects or clothing

To reduce your boredom, make the situation a contest in which you challenge yourself to retain all of the important information. By more carefully monitoring your boredom level, you will have a greater opportunity to increase your interest level in the spoken message and improve your chances for more effective and strategic listening. Following are some suggestions for minimizing your boredom in listening situations:

Set goals for obtaining information in a listening situation.
Remember the costs associated with missed information.
Focus on the content of the message.
Relate this information to your current knowledge base.
Identify the main points of the message and memorize them.
Recognize that distractions cannot be handled until after the current
    listening situation is over.

Make the Most of Listening Opportunities

When we talk about making the most of a listening opportunity, we are referring to improving both the situation and your own skills. You can improve the setting of a communication by moving office furniture to listen better, ensuring that your seat at a luncheon faces the speaker, or getting a central seat in a group or committee meeting.

Controlling yourself is an important skill in listening. If you hold strong opinions about a point that others are discussing, you may feel the urge to jump into the conversation prematurely, without invitation or planning. Patiently waiting until a speaker finishes allows you to know the other side of the issue better and gives you time to formulate just the right rebuttal. Table 4-4 gives you further clues for maximizing the benefits of communication encounters.

Anxiety Management

You may be wondering why anyone would be anxious in listening situations. But if you think carefully about it, you will recognize that some situations evoke some anxiety. Having to listen to a boss's reprimand, listening to others brag about themselves, listening to highly technical information, listening to criticism, or even listening to bad news are just a few of the circumstances that can cause anxiety. A small amount of anxiety or apprehension may actually stimulate and motivate your listening, but too much anxiety is harmful.

The problems associated with listening anxiety are numerous. Anxiety during the listening process can be distracting and can lead to forgetfulness, disorganization of information, distortions of data, and other cognitive shortcomings. Anxiety hampers your ability to process information and ideas in an efficient manner.

The following scale will help you to determine your level of "receiver apprehension" (listening anxiety). This scale is similar to the personal listening profile, but it focuses on listening anxieties rather than listening preferences and habits. As a result, your score will have a different meaning from your personal listening profile score.

RECEIVER APPREHENSION CHECK

Answer the following questions according to whether you strongly agree (1), agree (2), are undecided (3), disagree (4), or strongly disagree (5).

1. ___1___ I have no fear of being a listener as a member of an audience.

2. ___3___ I feel relaxed listening to new ideas.

3. ___4___ I am generally overexcited and rattled when others are speaking to me.

4. ___3___ I often feel uncomfortable when listening to others.

5. ___2___ I often have difficulty concentrating on what is being said.

6. ___1___ I seek out the opportunity to listen to new ideas.

7. ___4___ Receiving new information makes me nervous.

8. ___2___ I have no difficulty concentrating on instructions given to me.

9. ___2___ People who attempt to change my mind make me anxious.

10. ___3___ I am generally relaxed when listening to others.

Add up your scores for items 1, 2, 6, 8, and 10 (set #1). Now add up your scores for items 3, 4, 5, 7, and 9 (set #2). Subtract set #2 from set #1 to get a composite score. If this score is positive (between fifteen and twenty), you have a strong tendency toward apprehension across a range of situations. If your score is between five and fifteen, you have an average level of apprehension. If your score is between negative twenty and five, you have a low base level of receiver apprehension.[14]

Understanding your own level of listening apprehension is the first step toward managing anxiety. Obviously, this test was limited in that we did not ask about very many listening situations. Nevertheless, this test should give you a rough estimate of what your general feelings are toward the emotional component in the listening process. It is now up to you to determine those listening situations that may elicit anxiety. Next, prepare for the situation — gather necessary information so that your background knowledge is at the level expected by the source. If you are not able to do this, say so to the source of the message if possible. By controlling anxiety, you are better prepared to move successfully through the subsequent stages of the interactive listening process.

TABLE 4-4
Making the Most of Listening Situations

Area of Improvement	Factors	Technique
Situation control	Setting	Improve seating arrangements. Enhance privacy. Adjust room temperature to comfortable level. Reduce competing messages. Ensure ready access to necessary data.
	Time/timing	Do no overschedule appointments. Ensure enough time to avoid being rushed. Avoid situations that are poorly timed.
Personal control	Emotions	Avoid hasty generalizations. Control emotions by objectifying the situation (this is not about you).
	Patience	Wait until all of the facts are on the table. While you wait to speak, analyze the speaker's points.

Evaluating Your Listening

The final step in this strategic interactive listening process consists of evaluating your success. Although we have placed a detailed evaluation stage at the end of this chapter, you can use these skills to make evaluations at all of the stages of communication. It is important to conduct ongoing evaluations to determine how best to proceed as a listener even as the listening situation evolves. Nevertheless, it is critical that you get into the habit of evaluating listening situations immediately after they occur.

Goal Assessment

The first step in evaluation is to assess whether you were able to achieve the goals you set for yourself. Assessing yourself can be difficult if you do not take an objective approach. Objectivity can be achieved by answering the following questions honestly:

1. To what extent did you fulfill your goal? If you had more than one goal, how many of them did you achieve?

2. Did you adapt your listening behavior during the course of the situation to better achieve your goals?

3. Were the goals that you set for this listening situation realistic?

4. What elements prevented you from achieving part or all of your goals?

5. What can be done in the future to achieve the same goals?

Answering these questions gives you a better picture of how to assess your current listening behavior and how to plan to become an even better listener in the future.

SWOT Analysis

SWOT, a technique for identifying the *s*trengths, *w*eaknesses, *o*pportunities, and *t*hreats of your listening behavior, can be used as a form of listening

---

Interact!

This chapter points out that listening is an active, rather than a passive, skill. To be a good listener, you must concentrate and develop good habits. This exercise challenges your listening skills while demonstrating the organizational consequences of poor listening habits.

Divide the class into groups of at least ten people each, and separate into different parts of the room. Your instructor then hands one member of each group a sheet of paper with a story written on it. The story relates a rumor about an executive in a large company. You and your group members are employees in that company.

The group member who received the story from the instructor reads the story to another person in the group very softly so that no one else can hear it. That person then tells (not reads) the story to the next group member. The story is passed to each group member until everyone has heard it. Only the first group member can read the story; everyone else must pass it along from memory. No notes are allowed, and once a group member begins telling a story, there can be no questions and no interruptions.

The last person in each group to hear the story then leaves the room. One by one, these people come back into the room and tell the class their versions of the story, along with what they think will be the result for the executive and the organization. The instructor will then read the original story and its outcome to the class.

You will probably note substantial differences between the story as it was originally told and the versions given at the end of the exercise. Pay special attention to which details were lost and when.

Consider these questions in a class discussion following the exercise.

1. What accounted for the differences in the story as it was passed from one person to another in each group?

2. Which listening skills or habits seem to be the weakest as demonstrated in this exercise? What can be done to improve these skills and correct these habits?

3. What real-life situations does this exercise remind you of? What are some of the consequences when such a problem occurs in a business or organization?

4. What adjustments do you plan to make as a result of what you learned in this exercise?

You can also try the following variation on this activity:

In each group, have one person make up a story about an event or a person in a fictitious company. The story should be in one of the following categories: good news or praise, bad news or criticism, or a neutral description of a routine event. (Each group should choose a different category.) In each group, rerun the exercise of reading and relating the story among group members, and compare the final version with the original. Compare results among groups to find out if good news, a neutral event, or bad news was reported most accurately. Do your results correspond to experiences you have had in the workplace? What might be some explanations for your results?

evaluation.[15] SWOT is based on your answers to the questions posed in the previous section. *Strengths* are listening behaviors that help to achieve your goals. For example, your answers to the questions may reveal that you have especially strong questioning techniques or that you are quite effective at decoding nonverbal cues.

Every listener has some *weaknesses*. The process of assessing weaknesses can be somewhat depressing if you do not keep it in perspective. Evaluating weaknesses can be productive and profitable if you follow these suggestions: realize that weaknesses are only temporary because you can take action to correct them; understand that weaknesses are actually opportunities to grow and develop your strategic listening skills. Assessing weaknesses may be the most important aspect of the interactive listening process.

Opportunities are additional and unexpected chances for success in the communication process. Opportunities may occur spontaneously as a result of the listening situation. For example, imagine you are in a sales meeting listening to a manager describe a new marketing technique. You are not certain you understand what she is saying. A co-worker raises his hand to ask a question. You can use this opportunity to find out more about the technique *and* about the co-worker who asked the question. You can even get a sense of how the manager feels about unsolicited questions in meetings. Most listening situations present new opportunities; identify and focus on them.

Threats represent dangers and problems to you and your listening ability. Three common threats are yourself, others, and the environment. You may be surprised to think of yourself as a threat, but being uninterested, overemotional, or unprepared for good listening are just a few ways that you can undermine your own ability to listen.

Others can be a threat if they distract your listening concentration, demand too much of your listening ability, or make noise that physically prevents you from listening well. The environment may pose threats, especially noise or inconvenient distance between communicators, that cannot be easily controlled.

You may or may not be able to control threats to effective listening. If you try to control threats without success, you may want to reconsider your original goals and adjust them to the situation.

To carefully conduct a SWOT analysis, use the following guidelines to help you to evaluate listening situations. Use these guidelines as often as possible to get a better feeling for the consequences involved in the listening process.

Strengths: identify those aspects of the listening situation that you knew were strong points in your favor.
Weaknesses: identify those elements of the listening situation in which you recognized a shortcoming in your behavior or skills.
Opportunities: list those chances for success that were identified during or after the listening situation.
Threats: identify those aspects of the listening situation that inhibited, harmed, or threatened your chances for listening success.

Summary

Interactive listening is a complex but invaluable method of communicating with people. As you learned in this chapter, the listening process is a critical aspect of everyday life. Listening is the first communication skill a child learns, and it continues to dominate the other communication processes (talking, reading, writing) in the amount of time spent in each. Although many people take listening for granted, it is a crucial component of personal and professional activity. Much of people's financial compensation on the job is earned by listening, and as a person rises in her or his profession, the percentage of salary earned listening also rises. Skilled listening also avoids such problems for the listener as being perceived by others as less intelligent, costing time and money, and limiting chances for success.

Listening is difficult to conceptualize unless viewed as part of the whole communication picture that includes the elements of perception and capacity to understand others' points of view. The communication process itself is interactive; it depends on at least two people exchanging verbal and nonverbal messages. Successful listening derives from setting appropriate goals for the communication, building motivation, and generating energy to make the most of the encounter. With specific goals as a basis, the masterful listener obtains the necessary situational knowledge, which includes the speaker's communication style, environmental distractions, emotional distractions, and the physical condition of the communicators. Once engaged in the communication, the listener cultivates silence, speaks to ask clarifying questions, and uses nonverbal behavior to communicate empathy and sympathy. But even the most accomplished listener encounters anxiety-producing situations. To deal with these, the listener can use his or her analytic skills to identify and remedy "receiver apprehension" and then follow this up by evaluating what is successful in the communication.

Discussion

1. What is the difference between hearing and listening?
2. What factors influence your listening perception and priorities? What are their implications for organizational communication?
3. How do mental and physical energy levels affect listening ability? What are some techniques for increasing your energy levels?
4. What are some common barriers to listening in an organizational setting?
5. How can questioning techniques and nonverbal feedback improve the interactive listening process for greater productivity?
6. What are some ways to overcome personal barriers to effective listening (the three D's and boredom)?
7. What is receiver apprehension? Why is it a particularly serious problem in business settings?
8. How can a listening evaluation help you to improve your confidence and productivity?

Activities

1. Explain to other members of your discussion group why listening would be important in each of the following business situations:
   a. Conducting an employment interview
   b. Judging an employee's grievance
   c. Deciding whether two employees can trade vacation schedules
   d. Representing your company in a media interview

2. Select three behaviors that you need to concentrate on to improve your own skills in listening. Next to each behavior, devise an action plan you can implement to improve your skills.

3. Make a list of the behaviors you see exhibited by other people when you believe that they are listening to you. Share your list with other class members.

4. This chapter argues that creating or tolerating distractions is detrimental to good listening. Select a recent communication transaction in which you had particular trouble concentrating on listening because of distractions. Ask other members of your discussion group for strategies they might have used in the same situation to be a good listener.

Notes

1. Germaine Knapp in T. Harris, "Listen Carefully," *Nation's Business* 77 (June 1989): 78.
2. M. Buck-Lew, "Making Technology Work for Us," *Boston Globe*, December 4, 1990, p. 48.
3. M. Osborn and S. Osborn, *Public Speaking*, 2nd ed. (Boston: Houghton Mifflin, 1991), p. 57.
4. W. Pauk, *How to Study in College*, 4th ed. (Boston: Houghton Mifflin, 1990), p. 122.
5. V. S. Di Salvo, "A Summary of Current Research Identifying Communication Skills in Various Organizational Contexts," *Communication Education* 29 (1980): 283–290.
6. V. Yates, *Listening and Note-Taking* (New York: McGraw-Hill, 1979).
7. Interview with Captain Robert Dunford, Boston Police Department, December 10, 1990.
8. J. M. Kouzes and B. Z. Posner, *The Leadership Challenge* (San Francisco: Jossey-Bass, 1987), p. 60.
9. B. Goss, *Processing Communication* (Belmont, Calif.: Wadsworth, 1982).
10. B. Goss and D. O'Hair, *Communicating in Interpersonal Relationships* (New York: Macmillan, 1988).
11. Pauk, *How to Study*, p. 127.
12. Harris, "Listen Carefully," p. 78.
13. A. Wolvin and C. Coakley, *Listening* (Dubuque, Iowa: William C. Brown, 1988).
14. This is adapted from L. Wheeless, "An Investigation of Receiver Apprehension," *The Speech Teacher* 24 (1973): 261–263.
15. J. W. Pfeiffer, L. D. Goodstein, and T. M. Nolan, *Understanding Applied Strategic Planning: A Manager's Guide* (San Diego, CA: University Associates, 1985).

Chapter 5

*V*erbal and Nonverbal Skills

OBJECTIVES

After working through this chapter you will be able to:

1. Identify the importance of verbal and nonverbal communication to businesses

2. Understand the relationship among power, status, and nonverbal communication

3. Evaluate the messages sent through clothing choice and be aware of basic guidelines for business attire

4. Improve your use of language

5. Respect gender and cultural differences in communication

6. Employ and interpret nonverbal cues, including paralanguage, facial expressions, and kinesics

7. Manage anxiety in informal communication situations

When you consider how much time a professional spends communicating with others during a normal working day, it is easy to understand the importance of this activity. The ability to send clear and coherent messages to supervisors, co-workers, outside vendors, and even the media and the public is critical to maintaining productivity and a positive image, regardless of the industry. Furthermore, as a person rises in the organization to higher levels of management, the need for communication increases.[1] Strong verbal and nonverbal skills are essential for personal success and the health of the organization.

Verbal communication includes *all* messages composed of words, either spoken or written. In this chapter we focus on the spoken (oral) aspect of verbal communication. Verbal communication is often taken for granted in business organizations because people's lifelong familiarity with words and speaking makes it easy to neglect the importance of planning the oral messages they send to others. As a result, communication failures occur that could have been avoided with some thought and preparation.

Nonverbal communication refers to any message — other than spoken or written words — that conveys meaning, such as how you use your voice, face, and body; how you dress; even how you arrange your office or the seating configuration at a meeting. All these signal meaning to other people.

Whereas verbal communication is, by and large, controllable and intentional, nonverbal behavior is often difficult to manage. Think, for example, of an experience when someone you were talking to did not believe what you were saying. Your words were probably clear and appropriate for the situation ("I'm sorry I was late to class yesterday; I had trouble finding a place to park my car"), yet you may have avoided eye contact; spoken in a soft, hesitant voice; or used facial expressions that contradicted your words.

In this case, you may have suffered only a reprimand from an instructor. In the business world, however, a contradiction in verbal and nonverbal messages can have severe effects: a loss of trust between you and your manager; a failure to close an important deal with a client; a lack of understanding with a co-worker; or even conflict with others who are confused by your communication. Clearly, along with listening skills, verbal and nonverbal skills are the foundation of communication in business.

Successful verbal and nonverbal communication requires careful planning, analysis, execution, delivery, and appraisal. In this chapter we apply the components of strategic communication to the basic process of verbal and nonverbal interaction. Then, we cover verbal and nonverbal strategies you are likely to encounter in business and professional contexts. You will undoubtedly recognize some of these strategies and may already know which you are good at and which you need to work on. We start by discussing goal setting for effective messages.

Goal Setting for Effective Messages

Successful verbal communication depends on identifying the purpose of a message — the idea you are trying to convey and the reaction you are hoping to elicit — and how likely the receiver is to respond accordingly.

When you consider the goal or purpose of a message, you are anticipating the function that you want the receiver to perform in response to the message. Charles Redding has grouped messages according to three purposes or functions: task, maintenance, and human.[2] *Task messages* are those whose intent is to make others accomplish specific goals. Task messages include orders, questions, and even confrontations so long as they promote the primary goals of the organization. Examples of task messages are "Do you have that order ready today?" "When will that shipment of microchips arrive next week?" and "Put those graphs in the report at the end."

Maintenance messages keep the organization in working order so that tasks can be performed. Maintenance messages provide support for people who perform tasks within the organization. For example, statements made about the organization's operations, the role of unions, salary and benefits, and even competitors serve maintenance functions ("Be sure to fill out the departure form in triplicate," or "Jim should contact Janice about the delay").

Human relations messages help employees to fully realize their potential in the organization. Examples include statements such as "Sylvia, I appreciate the way that you always give us more than we ask on special projects; you're a valuable employee," and "I really think you have potential in the area of accounting — why not consider getting a degree?" Human relations messages promote workers' personal development and occur frequently in organizations that emphasize open communication.

When setting goals for oral communication, consider which of the foregoing categories the message fits into. For example, human relations messages generally do not promote extremely specific goals, so do not expect to get a concrete and definite response to such messages. A more appropriate goal for a human relations message might be "I will try to improve the attitude of my work group by making more positive comments." Task messages, however, are used to make direct requests for specific results. When you set goals for task messages, make them definite and concrete, such as "Send three cartons of the new product to Elizabeth Martin in the Ohio office by 10:45 A.M. Wednesday, March 4."

Situational Knowledge: Personal and Environmental Factors

To set effective goals in oral communication, you must consider the person or people who will receive the message as well as the work environment in which the communication takes place. Several characteristics determine how receivers respond to the message, including perceptual differences between you and the receiver and the number of people who will ultimately need to receive the message. If several people need the information that you plan to send, a group presentation may be a more appropriate means of communication. If large numbers of people need to hear your message, you may be most effective if you deliver a public speech. In addition, it is prudent to consider the status of the person receiving the message so you can construct your message appropriately.

Status

Every message carries a great deal of information about how you perceive your relationship with the receiver. Many communication specialists have argued that messages have two parts: a *content element* (what you are trying to communicate) and a *relational element* (how you feel about the person you are communicating with). The relational element of a message can also be considered in terms of its *relational consequences* — that is, how the message will influence your future communication with the receiver.

It is important to anticipate the relational consequences of your message. If you tell a co-worker to "get that report by 5:00 P.M.," you are not only asking for a task to be performed; you are also asserting that you have the power to make such a demand and expect others to acknowledge it. You could have said, "Would it be possible for you to have that report to me by the end of the day?" The relational consequences of such a query would be quite different because you addressed the co-worker as an equal in a cooperative endeavor. (See Chapter 6 for further discussion of work relationships.)

Nonverbal communication can influence perceptions of power and status, or it can be influenced by status and power. Those who have power communicate nonverbally so as to reinforce their relative power position with others. Those who aspire to status and power may try to influence others by using high-status-and-power nonverbal communication. It is therefore important for you to know which nonverbal behaviors are generally associated with status and power so that you can use or respond to these forms of communication in appropriate ways. Table 5-1 summarizes much of the research on nonverbal indicators of status and power.[3]

Table 5-1 can be used as a guide to general nonverbal status and power indicators. You are probably familiar with some of them; others may not correspond to your work or school experiences. Nevertheless, recognizing these behaviors can be a useful starting point for evaluating high- and low-status communicators, provided that you are careful to collect additional cues from the speaker and the communication situation.

TABLE 5-1
Nonverbal Indicators of Power and Status

Powerful and High-Status Indicators	Powerless and Low-Status Indicators
Relaxed posture and body position	Erect and rigid posture and body position
Less attentive to others	More attentive to others
More expansiveness	More restrictiveness
Seated position	Standing position
Dark conservative suit	Light suit or strange clothing
Tall height	Short stature
More access to space	Less access to space
Finger pointing	Receipt of finger pointing
Less direct body orientation	More direct orientation toward superiors
Closed arm position (akimbo)	Open body orientation
Give less/receive more eye gaze	Receive less/give more eye gaze
Sarcastic smiling/laughing	Respectful smiling/laughing
Touch others more/touched less by others	Touch others less/touched more by others
Making others wait for you	Waiting on others (superiors)
Determine meeting time and length	Told of meeting time and length
More flexible time schedule	Rigorous and strict time schedule
Expensive office furniture	Economical office furniture
Larger office in nicest and most private location	Office location dependent on job duties

Perceptions

We discussed the role of perception in listening in Chapter 4. Although perception is most commonly associated with the *receiver* of a message, it influences how messages are sent as well. As you know, perception is the process of creating meaning based on experience. These meanings inform your verbal communication in several ways.[4]

Perception is influenced by your attitude toward the person with whom you are communicating. When you speak to someone you like and respect, your verbal message will probably reflect those positive attitudes — for example (smiling and using a friendly voice), "Jim, could you present a progress report on the XYZ project tomorrow?" If you have negative attitudes about the receiver — that he or she is lazy, untrustworthy, careless — your message will probably reflect that perception — for example (frowning and using a stern voice), "Tom, regardless of your attitude about the XYZ project, I expect you to make a five-minute report on it tomorrow; make sure that you have all the facts straight."

Another factor that influences perception is emotion. When you are highly aroused by emotions such as anger, surprise, joy, or even fear, you are less likely to perceive a situation accurately, and you may confuse others by using excessive or contradictory nonverbal cues. You are influenced by the emotion of the situation itself and by memories of emotions you have experienced before in similar instances. For example, if you experienced an embarrassing lapse of memory in a group presentation, your perceptual attitudes during later presentations are likely to be tainted by that memory.

In all communication situations, especially those that involve strong emotions, attitudes, or the possibility of prejudice, ask yourself if your message is based on accurate and objective perception or if you are letting misperceptions limit your oral communication skills. The following questions will help you to assess your perception:

1. Am I being influenced by my personal attitude toward this person?

2. Are my emotions clouding my objectivity in this situation?

3. Am I making judgments about this situation based on the facts as I know them?

4. Am I ensuring that my biases and personal prejudices are not affecting my verbal communication?

5. Am I being overly optimistic/pessimistic in my verbal communication because of previous experiences in these matters?

Personal Space

The use of space, also known as *proxemics,* plays an important role in communication. Personal space, or the distance between communicators, has two aspects. The first is actual distance, which can be measured in feet and inches, and the second is perceived distance, which can be measured only by how comfortable people feel about the spatial distance between them and their communicating partners. People differ according to their tolerance for personal space. Some prefer very close communicating distances, whereas others require further distances. People from different cultural backgrounds vary a great deal in how they tolerate distance. There are four zones in which communication takes place.[5]

Intimate zone.   The zone where people interact at the closest distances is the intimate zone, which ranges from skin contact to eighteen inches. Business associates very rarely interact at this distance, with the exception of congratulatory hugs, whispering during a presentation, and so on.

Personal zone.   This zone ranges from eighteen inches to four feet and is usually reserved for interactions that are personal or private in nature, although there are a few examples of business interaction. Talking semiprivately, illustrating something to someone on paper, and sharing a handout, chart, or other visual aid in a meeting all occur in the personal zone.

Social zone.   The social zone ranges from four to twelve feet and is used a great deal in business settings. It is a comfortable zone for business interactions given the norms of business and society. Interviews, small meetings, conversations among several people, and chance encounters all usually occur in this zone. At this distance, people communicate in a normal voice, and generally feel comfortable both verbally and nonverbally.

Public zone.   The largest interacting distance space is the public zone, which ranges from twelve feet and beyond. This zone is used for events such as speeches and presentations, large-group meetings, and demonstrations. The public zone reduces the chance for immediate feedback among the participants, and the ability to read facial expression and eye movement is limited. Vocal pitch and volume are usually at high levels, and gesturing may be exaggerated so that everyone within the zone can see.

It is important to recognize the social and cultural norms reflected by these zones. When you violate the rules of personal space as dictated by these zones, you may offend or repulse others. Crowding the intimate zone of a business acquaintance can result in tension or hostility. If, however, you choose to interact at distances that are larger than what the situation calls for, you may be perceived as cold and aloof. In addition, people from differing cultural backgrounds may have different perceptions of these zones. For example, in Eastern Europe and Latin American countries, hugging is an acceptable equivalent to hand-shaking, despite the fact that it occurs in the intimate zone. By gauging the proxemic patterns of people as they interact, you can get a good idea of the norms for each situation that you face.

Territories

Another aspect of personal space is territoriality, or the behaviors or actions associated with the use, maintenance, or defense of physical space as to indicate ownership.[6] Territories are readily recognized in organizational settings, and many people go to great lengths to preserve and protect theirs.

Why is territoriality important to people? Territories provide a space in the business environment that allows people to take comfort and refuge.

Just as you may claim the same seat in this class lecture after lecture, members of organizations look for places that they can call their own. Offices are probably the best examples of territories. Some people strongly identify with their office, cubicle, or desk and may feel personally threatened or violated if others enter without asking or rifle through items on the desk.

Territory can also be a function of habit or routine — for example, a certain table in the cafeteria may be informally reserved by a group of people who sit there day after day and who may become annoyed or angry if another group "takes" the table. Seating positions at a conference room or training center may "belong" to certain people, and violation of their territory may be met with verbal and nonverbal opposition. Parking spaces, chairs, places to stand, and even coffee cups are considered territories. By being observant, you gain information about others' habits, territories, and preferences regarding personal space. You can then demonstrate your competence as a communicator by respecting these preferences.

Cultural background strongly influences perceptions and interpretations of personal space.

Clothing and Dress

Clothing and dress communicate a great deal about the wearer, especially in the workplace. You may have what you refer to as "interview clothes," clothes that you wear only to interviews or formal presentations with possible employers. Special clothes show that you are aware of the importance of an event, whether professional, social, religious, or political.

In business and professional settings, dressing appropriately is critical to success. One reason is that strong impressions of others are formed in the opening moments of communication. According to Leonard and Natalie Zunin, human relationships are established, reconfirmed, or denied within the first four minutes of contact.[7] The most important cues that can be picked up in that time are your appearance and manner.

A number of best-selling books have been published instructing employees in the art of proper attire at work.[8] One of your authors once overheard a superior remarking to a subordinate, "If you want to fit in around here, you need to buy a 'dress for success' book and live by it!"

Most business dress etiquette books convey the same basic message: understated, conservative dress is the most accepted and safest course of action. For men, this means a dark suit, light shirt, and conservative tie; for women, it suggests a skirted suit or jacket-and-skirt combination with a light blouse. The standards for women's professional attire have been modified noticeably during the past two decades, with women often wearing clothes that do not necessarily imitate men's styles. Men's styles have also become slightly more open to interpretation, although the benchmark remains the conservative gray suit. As a way of summarizing the numerous "authorities" on professional dress, we present Table 5-2 to depict what is considered acceptable attire for the office.[9]

The guidelines in this table are quite conservative and may not hold for all occupational and professional settings. We suggest that you observe what others are wearing and consider the climate of organization (formal? friendly? traditional? trendy?) when choosing what to wear to work.

The organizational context may suggest that variations can be made in standard dress. For example, many companies expect their employees to wear suits to work, yet as soon as they arrive at work, people hang their coats on their doors and do not don them again until they leave the office. Because everyone does it, the context has allowed a modification in the dress code. Some occupations do not have any set standards for dress and simply rely on the context to determine appropriate clothing. For example, some of your professors probably dress more formally on the days they teach than on the days they work in the office or library. On the other hand, an organization may go to court to uphold its right to enforce a dress code.[10] The following are just a few examples of dress code regulations that have been upheld in court.

TABLE 5-2
Acceptable Office Attire

Clothing Article	Females	Males
Suits	Conservatively cut suits, with just-below-the-knee skirt length. Patterns — solids, tweeds, plaids. Fabrics — wool, linen. Colors — gray, navy, medium blue, beige, camel, dark brown.	Conservative, American-cut suits. Fabrics — wool or wool blend. Design — two-button, single vent. Colors — navy, gray.
Shirts	Solid color, cotton or silk blouse. Simple cut with no frills or lace.	Long-sleeved, cotton or cotton blend shirt. Colors — white, light blue, pinstripe.
Ties	Bow ties and ribbon ties.	Maroon, light gray, blue, navy. Choose ties with a simple pattern (avoid solid-color ties).
Shoes	Black, navy blue, or burgundy medium-heel pumps.	Black laced shoes.
Socks/hose	Neutral-colored or skin-tone hose. No patterns.	Black or dark gray socks.
Accessories	Simple and functional jewelry. Finger jewelry only on the ring finger. The less jewelry, the better.	Same as females.
Make-up	Use as little make-up as possible.	Avoid make-up.
Hair	Medium to short cuts. Avoid excessive curls.	Short, well-groomed cuts.

No tight-fitting clothes

No excessive make-up

No long hair (men and women)

No facial hair (mustaches, beards)

Jackets to be worn during meetings

No braided hair

Suits only

Required neckties

No earrings for men

No long sideburns

Clean-shaven faces

Generally conservative dress

Approriate dress depends in large part on the job and the organization. In this photo, the owner of a contracting business and the surveyor wear standard attire. Although each person is dressed appropriately, their styles are very different.

Dress codes and the supportive court rulings regulating appearance and attire may seem harsh to those of you who feel strongly about individuals' rights. If you know that you will have difficulty with certain types of dress codes, you would be wise to check into a prospective company's policy on dress before accepting a position. It is better to pass up a job that is not suited to you than to take a position that will make you unhappy and cause you to search for other employment in a short time.

Environmental Factors

Knowledge of individual receivers is necessary for you to set goals but does not provide enough information to design an effective message strategy. You must also take into account the influence of organizational culture and setting.

Environmental space refers to how people perceive, construct, and manipulate physical space in business and professional settings. Office ar-

A person's office conveys many messages about work style, responsibilities, habits, personality, and organizational culture. The stock broker shown here has easy access to the tools of the trade—quotetron, telephone, and lots of paperwork.

rangements, reception areas, and even furniture, lighting, fixtures, colors, floor coverings, music, and live plants are carefully placed in a professional setting.

When visitors approach a building or office setting, they cannot help but form impressions of the organization based on how the building or office looks. Think of any experiences you have had in visiting a building or office for an interview, a tour, or a meeting with a friend. What sorts of impressions did you have of the company before you even entered the front door? There are several criteria that you may use to measure the location and building: Is the organization located downtown in the epicenter of business and financial affairs? Is the building's architecture traditional or contemporary? Is it old or new? Is it cold and foreboding or warm and inviting?

Estimates suggest that about $70 billion was spent in 1988 to design and equip offices and that this amount will grow each year.[11] The distribution of spending on offices and their furnishings signals important information about the status of the office occupants.

Larger, prestigiously decorated and furnished offices are usually reserved for those in the upper rungs of the organization. Those at the bottom of the pecking order are usually provided work stations that are very visible and accessible to large numbers of people, small areas that are more functional than aesthetic, and offices that usually are noisier and less private than the offices of superiors. Again, office design must be functional, but at the same time it must contribute positively to the impressions formed by occupants of and visitors to the office settings.

In an era of declining office size resulting from the rising costs of office space, design is one area that can increase efficiency by creating the proper atmosphere for those who work and visit there. It is expected by industry experts that flexibility will be the key word in the office design of the future, with modular designs becoming more and more commonplace.[12]

Probably the most important factor is whether you and your environment fit together smoothly and project a capable and businesslike image. When you enter an office, ask yourself the following questions: Does the place communicate pleasant feelings? Is the design highly functional? Do employees appear to enjoy privacy? Do they feel comfortable talking to you about their organization? Does the company seem to have the technology and equipment necessary to do an effective job? Does your personality seem to fit the office and building?

Communication Competence: Verbal and Nonverbal Skills

To develop the skills at work in verbal and nonverbal communication, you must first make decisions regarding the physical dimensions of your message — where, when, and how long it will be. Then, choose appropriate words and nonverbal gestures and avoid such bad-language habits as overuse of jargon, euphemisms, and racist or sexist language.

Choose the Setting for Communication

Consider the following communication situation.

> Sam was anxious because his boss, Sandy, had not informed him of his raise for next year. He had spent a lot of time thinking about how much he needed and deserved a raise and how to phrase his request to Sandy. The issue was so important to him that when he saw Sandy talking to some employees in the hallway, he immediately approached her and asked if she had made a decision about his raise. He did not pause to think about the appropriate setting for the request. Sandy wheeled around and in a hostile tone said, "I can't talk about that right now!"

It is important to plan the setting in which a message will be sent and received. A message that is received in the privacy of an office is likely to elicit a different reaction from that received in the company cafeteria or in the presence of casual bystanders. Messages sent and received in formal settings such as a class or a meeting sound different from messages communicated in informal settings, such as hallways. Three different variables are worthy of consideration when you are choosing the setting: the potential for bystanders to receive the message unintentionally; the physical characteristics of the setting — high echoing ceilings, possible sources of noise, and so on; and the formality of the situation as dictated by social or company norms.

You will be able to increase the effectiveness of your spoken communication by thinking about these variables beforehand. If Sam had done so, he would have realized that the hallway was an inappropriate setting for a discussion of his raise, for several reasons. First, money and salary issues are generally sensitive and private and should not be discussed in front of others unless the organizational culture promotes such discussions. Second, the hallway is generally not an appropriate setting for lengthy discussions because such talk can distract others or interfere with their work. Third, most companies have specific procedures for giving raises. Sam should have familiarized himself with his company's formal procedures before confronting Sandy.

Time the Message Carefully

Most people do not consider how long a message actually needs to be in a particular circumstance. You have undoubtedly suffered through excessively long and wordy messages that could have been condensed without losing meaning. There are several good ways to practice concise communication. For example, you can write out your message on a piece of paper. Then go through and circle the key words, crossing out all unnecessary words. You will be surprised by how much shorter the message can be. Communicators in professional settings often provide extra details and elaboration to impress the receiver, when in fact most receivers are busy and want the most efficient exchange possible.

Another way to check your message length is to see if the message can be broken into two or more separate messages. Frequently, people try to communicate too many ideas at once. Your communication will be much more successful if you send several short, self-contained messages instead of one long message that wanders from point to point. Nevertheless, your message must be long enough to contain the necessary information.

We mentioned in Chapter 2 the importance of messages arriving at their destination at the appropriate time. The timing of messages is something of an art in that it is difficult to gauge when receivers can best handle the message you wish to send. In deciding when to send your messages, you are wise to consider three elements of timing: when messages may pile up, what the receiver's schedule is, and whether all aspects of your message are in sync.

Know the organization well enough to understand when messages are likely to pile up all at once. In the university setting, messages are more frequent at the beginning and end of the semester. Likewise, telephone or personal calls are likely to be more congested during midmorning and midafternoon.

Know the schedule of the receiver in question. Find out if her or his duties and responsibilities are seasonal or cyclical. You can determine some of this information from the receiver or her or his assistant.

Think of yourself, the receiver, and your message as a package or a team; all three must be sync before you send the message. Receivers are always curious about your motive for sending messages, and the more they agree with the timing of the message, the more likely you are to get an appropriate response. In other words, receivers need to believe that now is the best time to receive your message.

Use Language Effectively

Language is created by assigning symbols or words to people, places, or things. It is not always easy to use language effectively, particularly in business and professional communication settings. Problems with language stem from its arbitrariness — words stand for ideas and objects but have no real physical or logical connection to those things. The relationship between a word and what it represents is not based on real or concrete shared characteristics that can be analyzed or predicted. Essentially, the learning of language is a word association and memorization process. You can increase your skill in using language by continually learning new ways to say what you mean.

One way to familiarize yourself with appropriate language is through reading trade journals in the field you plan to enter. Another technique is to write down new words and their definitions when you come across them. The act of writing helps you to remember the word and how it was used. It is in your best interest to be familiar with as many different word choices as you can.

Language varies in its preciseness. Some forms of language, such as legal, medical, or technical language, are very specific and not open to a wide range of interpretations. Other forms can be vague or abstract or given to multiple meanings. Both extremes are likely to cause receivers trouble. When you formulate a spoken message, choose words that are neither too specialized nor too general. Be accessible without being ambiguous, and pay attention to the difficulties that you are likely to encounter if you use jargon, euphemisms, tag questions, or sexist or racist language in your message.

Jargon.   Jargon is the specialized language used by professionals to communicate more efficiently among themselves. Jargon is also "nonsensical, incoherent, or meaningless talk."[13] The contrast between these two meanings shows the potential and the limits of jargon quite vividly. At its best, jargon makes communication among members of a group more efficient and precise and has definite advantages for shared meaning in such a context. For instance, medical care personnel cannot live without specialized vocabulary ("Myocardial infarction in the later stages of pulmonary edema suggests a code four procedure"). The use of jargon in inappropriate situations, such as around people who are unfamiliar with it, however, tends to result in an undesirable image — silly, inconsiderate, out of touch — for the communicator and more importantly, in failure to achieve shared meaning.

Euphemisms.   Euphemisms attempt to use agreeable, neutral, or acceptable phrases to describe unpleasant events. For example, when a vice-president says, "Because of declining sales, we will have to implement a retrenchment program that might temporarily displace some people," she or he is really saying, "A drop in sales means we will have to cut costs and fire people." Some euphemisms have become mainstream terminology and therefore require euphemisms of their own. An example of this is the succession of terms for the act of firing. In the 1970s people were no longer fired but "laid off"; the term was so widely adopted that it was no longer effective as a euphemism. New euphemisms were invented to replace "layoff"; these included "temporary displacement," "voluntary retirement," and "downsizing."

Although euphemisms are often used to soften the blow of communicating bad news to others, they can also be used in less altruistic ways. Some speakers use euphemisms to create ambiguity or vagueness in their messages. Stressful or difficult circumstances promote white-washing or distorting explanations so as to avoid confrontations or criticism. These motives result in loss of the communicator's integrity. Use euphemisms with care, and employ them only in those circumstances in which you are making an honest effort to help others.

Tag questions.   When you consistently tack qualifying questions onto the end of your statements, you undercut the effectiveness of your message. Such examples as "These cost overruns are killing us, don't you think?" "I am really feeling the heat from the accounting department, know what I mean?" and "It is disgraceful that we have to attend this meeting, isn't it?" demonstrate that tag questions soften the original statement to the point of feebleness. Such weak language use does not create respect for you as a communicator or advance important points. It makes you look overly dependent on the opinions of the receivers.

Avoid Racist and Sexist Language

With time, certain words or phrases take on new and controversial meanings. Referring to a female employee as a "girl" or a male African-American employee as a "boy" may have been common earlier in this century, but the usages are unacceptable now. Many other words or phrases are equally inflammatory. For example, the term *secretary* is being replaced with "assistant," "associate," or even "project manager."

Regardless of your position, you are smart to cultivate mutual respect for those you work and communicate with. The guidelines for nondiscriminatory communication are easy to understand and remember: respect and be considerate of others and commit yourself to thoughtful language choice. This means that you do not immediately say the first words that come to mind; rather, you consider the values and assumptions the words imply. A quick check before speaking will prevent you from promoting stereotypes and making damaging generalizations. If your language does not stand up to personal scrutiny, it is probably not the most effective way to express your message.

These basic values are critical to successful communication. Even if you are convinced that the people you are speaking with "don't care" about such issues, you are limiting your communication ability by making that assumption, particularly because you will not be prepared to communicate effectively with those who do care and care very strongly. Racist or sexist language is likely to cause many receivers to refuse your message and can easily cause others to perceive you as incompetent or insensitive. The following is a list of commonly used racist and sexist terms, with suggestions for neutral alternatives:[14]

Adman	ad agent or ad writer
Airman	flier or pilot
Anchorman	anchor
Black man/woman or black	African-American
Businessman	executive
Chairman	chair
Chinaman or Oriental	Asian or Asian-American
Cleaning girl	cleaner or maintenance worker
Congressman	representative
Fireman	firefighter
Foreman	supervisor
Gentleman's agreement	honorable agreement
Headmaster/headmistress	principal
Maiden voyage	first voyage or premier voyage
Mailman	letter carrier or postal worker
Manhandle	subdue
Manpower	staff, labor, personnel
Salesman	salesperson

Interpret Nonverbal Cues Accurately

Nonverbal communication accompanies verbal communication. Nonverbal behavior can repeat what is said verbally (smiling while saying that you are satisfied with a business report), it can help to regulate verbal behavior (breaking eye contact to signal that a conversation is about over), it can complement oral communication (talking very slowly and deliberately to make an important point), it can substitute for verbal behavior (nodding, winking, or gesturing your approval), and it can even contradict what you say verbally (saying you are really glad to meet someone without establishing any eye contact with that person). There are three areas of nonverbal expression that require accurate interpretation: paralanguage, facial and eye expressions, and gestures and body movement.

Paralanguage.   Paralanguage refers to how you use your voice. You are probably familiar with the following *voice qualities,*[15] or characteristics of speech such as pitch (how high or low the voice is), tempo (rate of speaking), volume (loudness of voice), rhythm (timing and emphasis on words), and articulation (how clearly words are pronounced). You can get a good idea of the personality and mood of a speaker by paying attention to his or her voice qualities. Rapid, high-pitched speech often signals that the speaker is excited or distressed. Poor articulation may suggest fatigue, lack of interest in the topic, physical handicaps, or other problems.

Paralanguage has significant effects on communication. You often inadvertently communicate certain ideas to others through the sound of your voice rather than the words you use. It is important to monitor how your vocal cues are signaling what you think and feel to other people.

For example, changes in vocal tone and rate can help to manage conversation. When you want to signal to others that you are ready to give up the floor of conversation, you can use a rising vocal inflection to indicate a question or a falling inflection to show the end of your message.

You can also use paralanguage to communicate your feelings toward others. When you greet someone with an appealing tone of voice, you reinforce that you are glad to see that person. An expressionless greeting gives a person the impression that she or he is unwanted. Either way, paralanguage gives people an idea about your feelings toward them.

Facial and eye expressions.   The face is the most expressive outlet for nonverbal communication; it can display more than one thousand different expressions.[16] That the face serves as a conspicuous mode of communicative expression is both advantageous and problematic. It is good that you have the ability to express how you feel through your face, yet it is challenging to interpret others' facial expressions.

Understanding the facial expressions of co-workers can give you an opportunity to determine the real motivations and intentions behind their actions. But simply observing another person's face for emotional cues is probably not enough to establish a high degree of accuracy; rather, you must act like a detective by putting together a number of cues that help to paint a complete picture of the person's emotional state.

Eyes are another important source of information. Because humans are so visually oriented, the movement of the eyes and how they are focused on other people and objects reveal a great deal of information. It is only natural to search the eyes of other people in an effort to understand their feelings, intentions, and motives.

The eyes are also an important tool for regulating the flow of communication among people. For example, you can use a direct look to notify someone else that you are ready to communicate. Eye contact is also useful when you wish to influence others. When a salesperson is trying to convince a buyer to make a purchase, he or she seldom resorts to letters or telephones. This is particularly true when closing a sale, because the salesperson needs to read the buyer for signs of support, anxiety, or hesitancy. Lack of direct eye contact, a shifting gaze, or a fixed stare can signal that the buyer has doubts about you, the product you are selling, or simply is no longer interested in the sale. In any instance where you are trying to influence another person, it is worth your while to communicate in person so that you can use the other's eye behavior as a source of information to help your case.

The following factors also relate to eye behavior and the regulation of communication:[17]

◆ People have a tendency to "match" the gaze duration of their conversational partners.

◆ Speech rate is higher when the speaker looks at the listener.

◆ Eye gaze increases when the information being communicated is positive and decreases when it is negative.

◆ Smiling causes a decrease in eye gaze.

◆ People in groups tend to look more while speaking and less while listening (the opposite effect occurs when only two people are talking).

◆ People who gaze longer are better liked.

◆ Increased gazing causes favorable impressions when positive information is communicated and unfavorable impressions when negative information is revealed.

◆ People with lower status (power) look more when listening than when speaking compared to high-status people.

◆ Females gaze more than males.

◆ Females are looked at more than males.

◆ Females are more uncomfortable when they are unable to see their conversational partner.

Gestures and body movement.   Often referred to as *kinesics,* gestures and body movement can be intentional or unintentional. Although it is difficult to monitor what you are doing with your hands and body at all times, familiarizing yourself with the following types of nonverbal cues can enable you to be more aware of the messages you are sending to others.[18] These behaviors represent only a partial sampling of the extensive research that has been done in kinesics.

Emblems are movements that substitute for words, such as a thumbs up signal indicating "Go ahead," "Good job," or "Keep up the good work"; a thumbs down signal indicating disapproval or disagreement; a circle with the thumb and index finger signaling, "O-kay," or "I understand." Emblems are intentional nonverbal acts and are usually reserved for people who know their meaning. If you try to use emblems with people who are unaware of their meanings, you risk miscommunicating or even insulting them.

Illustrators are body movements that amplify, accent, or supplement what is being said orally. Illustrators generally are less intentional than emblems and are often used without conscious thought. A friend of ours has a habit of waving his arms wildly when he is trying to make a point and has no idea how flamboyant he appears to others.

In business and professional settings, illustrators function as a double-edged sword. Illustrators can be helpful in making verbal communication more meaningful as long as they clearly *correspond* to the message. But some illustrators may actually *contradict* the verbal message. Consider the following situation.

> Karla had a habit of smiling when she presented material to a group of co-workers. She learned to smile while speaking publicly at a company seminar several years previously. On one occasion, she was asked to provide her workers with news of an impending plant closing. As she spoke about the closing, her co-workers looked at each other wondering what was so pleasant about the news she was relaying because Karla was smiling the entire time.

Consider your own use of illustrators. How often do you illustrate with your hands, arms, and body without really thinking about it? Do people readily recognize and understand your illustrations? You can improve your illustrating behavior by observing others who are good at illustrating and modeling what they do. For example, some people use their fingers in a very detailed manner; others use their hands and arms to depict a thought they have. By copying the effective illustrators you observe, you will be in a position to enhance your overall communication ability.

Regulators are nonverbal, usually automatic acts that help to maintain

"Say what's on your mind, Harris—the language of dance has always eluded me."

Drawing by Mankoff; © 1991 The New Yorker Magazine, Inc.

the flow of a conversation. Communicators are often unaware of how these nonverbal behaviors control conversation. Regulators function in a number of ways. You can signal to others that you are ready to give up the floor of conversation, for example, by opening your palms, reducing your gestures, or even motioning toward another person to encourage him or her to take a turn. You can signal to others that you would like to keep talking by increasing your gesturing, holding up your hands, or leaning toward your conversational partner. You can request a turn by raising your index finger or hand or rapidly nodding your head. You can even deny someone else the chance to speak by holding up your hand or shifting your posture away from that person.[19]

Monitoring nonverbal cues will help you to respond appropriately to the needs of friends and co-workers. If you work to become aware of the variety of nonverbal cues that people communicate with, you will be developing skills that will improve your strategic communication.

Anxiety Management

If you associate anxiety with formal speaking presentations and large groups of people, you will be surprised to learn how many speech problems caused by nervousness occur in your everyday speech. For example, if you are speaking to a person of higher authority, or discussing an important subject or a topic that you are uncomfortable with, your voice may climb to a higher pitch, you may stammer, or you may speak more softly. There are several skills that can help you to manage these symptoms of nervousness.

One tactic is to identify particular weaknesses in your spoken communication. The best way to do this is to tape-record yourself. Choose a topic that is important to you, such as asking for a raise. Record your reasons for requesting the raise; then play back the tape. Did your voice sound convincing? Even if your reasons are valid, you can undermine their effectiveness by speaking softly, stammering, or choosing inappropriate language (such as adding tag questions to your statements). Although it may be painful to listen to yourself, it is the only way to recognize the impact of anxiety on your speech.

One of the most effective ways to control anxiety is to breathe deeply and regularly. Indeed, if you breathe shallowly, the build-up of carbon monoxide in your bloodstream may cause you to feel dizzy and disoriented in addition to being nervous.

Another tactic is to slow down your communication and consciously focus on one idea at a time. As you well know from your school experience, a workload can sometimes seem so overwhelming that you do not want to begin tackling it. The same can be true in communicating — you have much to say but do not know where to begin. If you say nothing, your anxiety will only increase. Just as you prioritize your schoolwork and tackle one project at a time, you can sort out which ideas are most important and concentrate on communicating them first.

Finally, do not be too hard on yourself in communication. If you create unrealistic scenarios ("I'll instantly win my co-workers' respect by telling them about my dedication to the organization") rather than appropriate goals ("I'll speak to others with respect and plan my messages so that they are clear and effective"), you are more likely to be anxious when you communicate. Realize that although all communication skills can be improved, you will always be stronger in some than in others, and accept the way you are.

Message Strategies

Message strategies are combinations of skills designed to communicate specific ideas to achieve a goal. A vast array of message strategies are used in business and professional settings. Although we do not have the space to discuss all the possible variations, we have analyzed several basic strategies. As you read about these strategies, reflect on how they incorporate the skills you learned in the first half of the chapter.

Conversation

Many people feel that they are good conversationalists, with the ability to talk about a wide range of topics with ease. Nevertheless, in professional settings, conversation must be handled carefully. Conversation is an important message strategy system because the business and professional environment provides so many opportunities for it to occur.

Conversational turns.   Turn taking is one of the most important elements of conversation. Turns may vary in length and intensity but are necessary to maintain a conversation. You come to understand the "rules" associated with conversational turn taking by watching others engaged in conversation. An *interruption* occurs when the challenging speaker is successful in taking an unsolicited turn in the conversation. Interruptions are useful for correcting inaccurate information or verifying what someone has said. Other reasons for interruptions include disagreement ("Wait a minute, I think that there are four, not three, departure points for that supply order"), agreement ("Yes, you're absolutely right in hiring her!"), and changing the subject ("Excuse me, but aren't we late for that meeting with Scott?").[20]

It is important to realize that although interruptions can serve important functions, as we have just described, most people do not appreciate being interrupted when they are talking. If you have a tendency to interrupt without thinking, consider if the interruption is worth the risk it entails before you jump into the conversation. Many times you will realize that it is better simply to wait for your turn in the conversation to get your point across. If you find yourself being interrupted, you can try to prevent it by using stronger and more active language. You can also assert yourself in conversations simply by speaking up more often.

Conversations between women and men.   Researchers have observed several differences in the way women and men participate in conversation. Men interrupt more often than women do; thus men control conversations more often than women do. Men also talk more than women do, both by taking more conversational turns and by taking longer turns. Women are generally more informative, more receptive to ideas, and more concerned about others in their conversations than men are. What does this mean for communication between co-workers?

Another difference in men's and women's conversational patterns is in giving orders. According to Deborah Tannen, women are less comfortable with hierarchy than men are and generally prefer to achieve goals through consensus. Men are more likely to give orders without options. This difference causes confusion. Men may feel confused or manipulated if a woman does not give a direct order but still expects results. Women may be put off by a man's use of rank, authority, or power in giving orders.[21]

FOCUS on Corporate Communication

WARNER-LAMBERT CO.

You will probably recognize many of Warner-Lambert (W-L) Company's brand names: Parke-Davis pharmaceuticals, Halls cough tablets, Schick shaving products, Listerine mouthwash, Trident chewing gums, even Tetra aquarium products. The organization is dedicated to developing, manufacturing, and marketing quality health care and consumer products, but its commitment to "good health" extends beyond its product lines. A healthy communication environment and a strong interest in employee health and growth form the basis of corporate culture at Warner-Lambert.

The organization has a global operation, with 34,000 employees in approximately 130 countries. You may wonder how a large and diversified corporation handles communication so that information is consistently accessible to people everywhere in the organization. At W-L, the Warner-Lambert Creed provides the foundation for both the corporate culture and the processes through which communication takes place. The creed is vital to W-L's identity: printed in the languages of all employees' countries, in all external and most internal publications, it is frequently cited as the source of growth and career development for individual employees.

The creed begins with a mission statement: "To achieve leadership in advancing the health and well-being of people throughout the world." This statement is followed by five commitments — to customers, employees, shareholders, suppliers, and society — that outline how to work toward the mission goal. In particular, the commitments to employees and to society provide challenges and opportunities for communication.

To meet these challenges and to take advantage of opportunities, W-L maintains a communications network of seventy employees from company locations worldwide whose job it is to transmit information, news, and concerns from their home sites to the corporate headquarters in Morris Plains, New Jersey. In addition, the employee communications department in Morris Plains coordinates a variety of communications programs for employees and provides marketing and public relations support on key issues. Each semester, the department hires a college intern to assist in the production of newsletters, bulletins, and magazines and in the fulfillment of other communication functions.

In addition to printed communications,

Intercultural conversations. In their study of communication between African-Americans and whites, Michael Hecht and his colleagues noted that culture influences communication and can therefore lead to communication differences. They identified the following strategies for improving interracial conversations: openmindedness — considering others' ideas rather than dismissing them too quickly; treatment as an equal — not taking a superior or self-righteous attitude toward the conversation; avoidance — acknowledging that certain conversations should not take place; interaction management — regulating the amount of talk and the rate so that both partners

bulletin boards, and electronic mail, employees can view quarterly video releases. Each video covers two or three subjects, such as research in progress, benefits programs, and corporate donations. The video topics are selected with help from employees' suggestions. Videos are moving toward in-house production, and they are copied and sent to every company site. Site managers can decide for themselves the most appropriate time and setting for showing the video to their employees.

The employee communications department sponsors special events as well. These events tie in to W-L's commitment to an open and participatory environment. For example, the theme of a recent employee photo contest, which resulted in eleven hundred submissions, was "the world around us." Employees were encouraged to send in photos illustrating work in their particular areas of W-L and the world. The collage of images showed the great variety of work experiences and perspectives. To share these perspectives and photos, the top photos were used in a calendar, with month names printed in different languages. Each employee received a copy of the calendar along with a letter from the chief executive officer.

Warner-Lambert's Creed also provides the basis for commitment to employee development and growth inside and outside the organization. In the area of communication, this commitment is expressed through an impressive training program that offers in-house courses on language skills, presentation skills, improvement of work relationships, and participation in a diverse work force. Employees are encouraged to take elective courses to improve their communication skills. As one employee wrote, "Quality improvements . . . can't be purchased like capital equipment, bargained for like benefits or mandated by executive edict. They can only be given to ourselves by ourselves as we work to improve our daily interpersonal skills" (Dan Morris, Packaging Supervisor, "The True Quality of Work Life," *World* [Winter 1991]).

Further highlighting the importance of communication in leadership are courses such as Performance Management Skills, which covers the fundamentals of performance evaluation interviews, and Managing at Warner-Lambert, a required course for managers. Employees are given many opportunities to build on basic skills and are rewarded for commitment to positive and effective communication.

are comfortable with the communication; and other orientation — attempting to involve the other person, find common ground, and create identification.[22]

Successful intercultural conversations show concern for others as individuals and do not expect them to speak for an entire group. Treating others with respect and acknowledging their professional status can also help to bring about mutual shared meaning. Most importantly, always avoid lazy and thoughtless communication based on broad stereotypes instead of active consideration of the person (e.g., not all British citizens are stuffy, not all Hispanics enjoy Mexican cuisine, there are many Italians who are not touch sensitive).[23]

Conversational ethics.   Conversational turns should contain enough background information so that listeners have a frame of reference for what you are talking about.[24] As you recall from our earlier reviews of general ethical guidelines, it is unacceptable in most organizations to manipulate listeners by giving them only partial information. It is generally unproductive as well because receivers who discover that they were treated unethically in conversation may refuse to work with you or may tell co-workers that you cannot be fully trusted.

Conversational messages should also be truthful. Speakers can sometimes get into a trap of providing false information to accomplish some goal or make claims for which they lack evidence. In both instances, the conversationalist is violating the principle of truth. Deceiving or lying to others is unfortunately a common practice in professional settings, yet rarely does it produce the desired results over the long term. Invariably, lies are found out and do more harm than the truth.

The final rule of conversation is clarity. When you converse with others, articulate your thoughts and ideas in ways that reduce the uncertainty others may have about you and your messages. You can accomplish this goal by avoiding obscure language, making points logically, and eliminating extraneous information that may distract receivers from your primary message.

Understanding and agreement.   Conversationalists do not always understand or agree with one another as they interact. Everett Rogers and Lawrence Kincaid proposed that four combinations of understanding and agreement can occur.[25]

Mutual understanding with agreement: with this combination, communicators understand each other's point of view and agree with it. This is a very common type of casual, social, and nonconfrontational conversation.

Jose: Why don't you send me your notes on the Atwater project?
Menachem: You mean you think it is a viable alternative to our problem?
Jose: Of course. I know that your department undertook all the necessary steps to deliver the report.
Menachem: Thanks. I appreciate your vote of confidence.
Jose: Sure.

Mutual understanding with disagreement: this combination suggests that conversationalists understand each other's viewpoint but disagree with it. This is a case of honest disagreement between parties.

Rob: Maria, don't you think the copy machine needs to be replaced?

Maria: No. Obviously it doesn't make great copies, but an adjustment would fix the problems.

Rob: Well, this has been happening for some time; besides, it's an old machine.

Maria: It may be old, but the problem is in the feeder, which has needed adjusting for some time.

Rob: I wish something could be done.

Mutual misunderstanding with agreement: as a polite way of carrying on conversation, participants may act as if they understand each other's viewpoint (agreement) but actually do not. Or conversationalists may agree with what each is saying but do not understand the purpose or deeper meaning of the topic.

Don: I will be glad when we are able to hire additional personnel (thinking: to keep pace with our orders).

Leon: Yes, we have been needing more people for more than nine months (thinking: to bring younger, more energetic people on staff).

Don: More people will improve our ability to achieve the goals we set in January (thinking: greater production rates).

Leon: Exactly. That is something that the home office will be excited to hear about (thinking: better morale and energy among workers).

Mutual misunderstanding with disagreement: this is the classic case of confrontation in which participants in a conversation have no understanding of each other's viewpoints and demonstrate no agreement with the issues. This is a stalemate situation until both parties agree to respect and sympathize with the other's position.

LaVerne: All I know is that we are behind schedule because your people take too many breaks.

Kelly: Hogwash! We're not any more behind than the other departments; besides, if there has been a delay, it's because your people have been tardy in getting materials to us. What's the holdup?

LaVerne: Who are you kidding? We are always on time in delivering materials, and if you guys don't get on the stick, all of us will suffer.

Kelly: The only suffering you guys do is having to look at each other's faces each day.

Keep these four possible outcomes in mind when you are speaking to others. Do not assume that a person who agrees with you necessarily understands what you have said. Do not jump to the conclusion that people who disagree with you should be dismissed as irrelevant. The best way to achieve mutual shared meaning is to make sure you have answered the basic questions (those relating the "what," "where," "who," "when," "why," and "how" of the subject) in the conversation and that you and the receiver agree on the answers to those questions.

Making Requests and Giving Directives

Making requests is a crucial activity on the job, particularly when you are a new employee. Consider your past working experiences — the first few weeks at a job were undoubtedly characterized by the large number of questions you needed to ask just to do the basic requirements of your position. Many people are reluctant to request information or help for fear of appearing unintelligent or helpless. But you can phrase requests so that they benefit you by giving you necessary information and resources and by giving you a positive image that shows curiosity and enthusiasm for your job.

Several skills are involved in effective requests. First, be specific. Second, be sure you are asking the right person for the information. If you're not sure, ask an exploratory question first, such as "Are you in charge of accounts?" If the answer is affirmative, make your request — for example, "How do I allocate the money for next month's regional meeting?" Third, be confident in your requests — if you have tried to find the information or complete the job yourself without success, you are justified in asking for help. Others are usually more than willing to cooperate, particularly if you know exactly what you are asking for and phrase your request in clear and friendly language.

Giving directives is another important verbal strategy, particularly when it complements a positive style of making requests. Regardless of your position in the organization, you are likely to need both of these strategies to achieve your goals. The following list shows the difference between requests and directives:

Requests	Directives
"Can you help me solve this problem?"	"Be sure you finish this project today."
"Can we meet sometime today?"	"See me at 10:30."
"Which file should this go in?"	"File this."
"Is there any way we can finish this project today?"	"I am expecting the report today."
"Can you help me find the XYZ file?"	"Find the XYZ file now."

Making requests creates a supportive climate and gives the impression that people have a choice in carrying out their responsibilities. Those who are carrying out the requests will probably have a better attitude and are likely to perform their duties in a more effective manner.

Nevertheless, in situations that call for specific action, directives may be more appropriate. It is possible to give directives in a positive way that does not assume a power imbalance. You can do this by giving the reason for the directive. Do not simply make a demand without telling co-workers why it is important that they do what you say. Indeed, if you give a directive, you should have an important reason for doing so and be willing to explain it to others. They are much more likely to cooperate when they see the need for such action. The directives in the preceding list can be rephrased as:

"Be sure you finish this project today."	"Be sure you finish this project today. Lisa needs the results tomorrow morning."
"See me at 10:30."	"See me at 10:30. We need to discuss the plans for the sales meeting."
"File this."	"File this. I am expecting an important call."
"I am expecting the report today."	"I need the report today because it is important that we stay on schedule."
"Find the XYZ file now."	"Please find the XYZ file. I have my hands full looking for the Logan file."

Summary

This chapter exposed you to a number of skills and methods of verbal and nonverbal communication. As you learned from our discussion, a great deal of care must be taken when anticipating, preparing for, delivering, and evaluating verbal messages. Problems with communication can usually be traced back to people who take this important process for granted.

The oral communication skills you can develop to avoid these problems can be categorized by their relation to the model of strategic communication. Skills related to goal setting include identifying your purpose, analyzing your target, and understanding the influence of perception. Situational knowledge skills relate your communication to the organizational culture as a whole. Communication competence includes choosing the appropriate setting, deciding on the length and timing of the message, using language effectively, and avoiding racist or sexist language. Anxiety management can, and should, be accomplished in your daily communication with others.

As you consider your chosen career, your attention is likely to center on the specific talents and expertise that are necessary for being successful in that field. We cannot stress enough the importance of good communication skills for any professional position. Surveys indicate that specific occupational skills and talent are necessary but not sufficient for success. You must be able to communicate effectively and appropriately so that the knowledge you are acquiring in college and elsewhere is apparent to others. We encourage you to practice the skills discussed in this chapter to enhance your career even before it begins.

Discussion

1. In your experience, which of the nonverbal status indicators in Table 5-1 are most prevalent in business communication? How might cultural differences result in misinterpretation of these behaviors?

2. How do office design and arrangement affect communication and perceptions of status? In your experience, is office design an accurate predictor of an organization's communication climate?

3. Have you worked in an environment where a dress code was enforced? Did the dress code have an effect (either positive or negative) on morale, communication patterns, and organizational climate?

4. What specialized jargon do you use on the job or as a student? How might it cause problems for others who are not familiar with its meaning?

5. Can you think of a situation in which a co-worker's nonverbal communication contradicted his or her words? Which message was stronger to you? How did the contradiction affect your trust in the other person?

6. Discuss the effect of gender and cultural differences on communication. How have you handled such differences (successfully or unsuccessfully) in your work experience?

7. Explain the complementary nature of requests and directives. When should each be used?

Activities

1. Write an essay in which you react to the statement "One cannot *not* communicate."

2. Describe some typical settings in a business or organization in which the following space zones would be appropriate:
   a. Intimate   c. Social
   b. Personal   d. Public

3. In a small-group discussion, explain to your classmates how important you believe "correct" business dress is to a person and to an organization.

4. Think of some of the consequences to an employee who violates standards of nonracist and nonsexist language in an organization.

5. List at least five circumstances in which a manager is wise to use a request, rather than a directive, in organizing and planning employees' work.

Notes

1. J. C. Bennett and R. J. Olney, "Executive Priorities for Effective Communication in an Information Age," *Journal of Business Communication* 23 (1986): 13–22; V. S. Di Salvo and J. K. Larsen, "A Contingency Approach to Communication Skill Importance: The Impact of Occupation, Direction, and Position," *Journal of Business Communication* 24 (1987): 3–22; S. Tegmeyer, "Survey of College-Educated Managers in the Southwest" (Las Cruces, N.M.: 1989, unpublished study).

2. W. C. Redding, "The Organizational Communicator," in W. C. Redding and G. A. Sanborn (eds.), *Business and Industrial Communication* (New York: Harper & Row, 1964), pp. 29–58.

3. For further reading on this subject, see P. Anderson and L. Bowman, "Positions of Power: Nonverbal Influence in Organizational Communication," in J. De Vito and M. Hecht (eds.), *The Nonverbal Communication Reader* (Prospect Heights, Ill.: Waveland Press, 1990), pp. 391–411; A. King, *Power and Communication* (Prospect Heights, Ill.: Waveland Press, 1987); J. T. Molloy, *Dress for Success* (New York: Warner Books, 1975); B. Linkemer, *Polishing Your Professional Image* (New York: American Management Association, 1987).

4. O. Hargie and P. Marshall, "Interpersonal Communication: A Theoretical Framework," in O. Hargie (ed.), *A Handbook of Communication Skills* (New York: New York University Press, 1986).

5. E. T. Hall, *The Hidden Dimension* (Garden City, N.Y: Doubleday, 1966).

6. M. Knapp, *Nonverbal Communication in Human Interaction* (New York: Holt, Rinehart & Winston, 1972).

7. L. Zunin and N. Zunin, *Contact — The First Four Minutes* (New York: Ballantine Books, 1972).

8. J. T. Molloy, *Dress for Success*; J. T. Molloy, *The Women's Dress for Success Book* (New York: Warner Books, 1977).

9. Ibid.; Linkemer, *Polishing Your Professional Image.*

10. E. Matusewitch, "Tailor Your Dress Codes," *Personnel Journal* (February 1989): 86.

11. K. Evans-Correira, "Getting the Right Office Fit," *Purchasing,* April 28, 1988, p. 92.

12. Ibid.; W. Taubert, "Open and Closed Offices: Designing for Productivity," *The Office* (October 1989): 81; G. Mong, "Work Stations: Building Blocks in Office Design," *The Office* (December 1989): 14; P. Fernberg, "Modular Systems: Divide and Conquer Space," *Modern Office Technology* (September 1989): 84.

13. *American Heritage Dictionary,* 2nd college ed. (Boston: Houghton Mifflin, 1985), p. 686.
14. Bobbye D. Sorrels, *The Nonsexist Communicator* (Englewood Cliffs, N.J.: Prentice-Hall, 1983), pp. 124–142.
15. G. Trager, "Paralanguage: A First Approximation," *Studies in Linguistics* 13 (1958): 1–12.
16. P. Ekman, W. Freisen, and P. Ellsworth, *Emotion in the Human Face: Guidelines for Research and an Integration of the Findings* (New York: Pergamon Press, 1972).
17. R. Harper, A. Wiens, and J. Matazzaro, *Nonverbal Communication: The State of the Art* (New York: John Wiley & Sons, 1978), p. 173.
18. P. Ekman and W. Friesen, "The Repertoire of Nonverbal Behavior: Categories, Origins, Usage, and Coding," *Semiotica* 1 (1969): 49–98.
19. Knapp, *Nonverbal Communication.*
20. C. Kennedy and C. Camden, "A New Look at Interruptions," *Western Journal of Speech Communication* 47 (1982): 45–58.
21. "Power Talk," interview with Deborah Tannen by Lee Lusardi, *Working Woman* (July 1990): 92–94.
22. M. L. Hecht, S. Ribeau, and J. K. Alberts, "An Afro-American Perspective on Interethnic Communication," *Communication Monographs* 56 (December 1989): 386–399.
23. M. J. Collier, "A Comparison of Conversations Among and Between Domestic Culture Groups," *Communications Quarterly* 36 (Spring 1988): 130–148.
24. H. P. Grice, "Logic and Conversation," in D. Davidson and G. Harmon (eds.), *The Logic of Grammar* (Encino, Calif.: Dickenson Publishing, 1975).
25. E. M. Rogers and D. L. Kincaid, *Communication Networks: Toward a New Paradigm for Research* (New York: Free Press, 1981).

*I*nterpersonal Communication Strategies

Part 3 applies the theory and skills developed in Parts 1 and 2 to one-to-one communication in a variety of settings. Although often taken for granted, it can be one of the more difficult aspects of communication both for employees and for those who strive to join the organization through selection interviews.

❑ Chapter 6 explains the skills needed to maintain constructive relationships with superiors, co-workers, customers, and others.

❑ Chapter 7 focuses on basic principles of interviewing, including types and sequencing of questions and responses.

❑ Chapter 8 covers key interviews common in a business environment, giving special attention to the roles and regulations of employment interviews.

*W*ork
Relationships

OBJECTIVES

After working through this chapter, you will be able to:

1. Understand the importance of work relationships

2. Describe the characteristics of strong manager-employee relationships

3. Resolve relational difficulties with co-workers

4. Develop productive relationships with customers

5. Initiate a mentoring relationship with an experienced employee

6. Understand the positive and negative aspects of romantic relationships at work

Interpersonal relationships are critical to achieving organizational goals. In your work experience you have probably encountered many of the relationships we discuss in this chapter but may have been unaware of their importance to you and the organization itself. The following are just two examples of how relationships can promote organizational goals and values.

Paul, an employee at Delen Corp., was strongly committed to Delen's mission statement, which emphasized providing service to customers and promoting good relations with the local community. He frequently thought about how business practices and community relationships might be improved. Nevertheless, he usually felt a little nervous about suggesting changes. Paul's supervisor, Angela, was an experienced employee who knew the organization well. Her opinions and decisions were generally well respected, and she had achieved a reputation for supportiveness and honesty. Paul approached her with some ideas, and the two of them worked out a plan for starting an educational partnership with the local high school and providing internships for college students. In doing so, they increased Delen's visibility in the community and ensured that young, well-educated people would be attracted to working for the organization.

Amy, a sales manager in a large department store, noticed that customers frequently became annoyed when approached by clerks. She knew the clerks were trying to provide prompt and courteous service yet she also understood the customers' desire to be undisturbed. She resolved the situation by suggesting that the clerks remain alert, attentive, and visible to customers but refrain from approaching unless invited by a customer. She emphasized that when clerks did interact with customers, they should strive to be friendly and responsive at all times. In the weeks after her suggestions were implemented, several customers commented to Amy on the wonderful service in her department. Amy had succeeded in identifying and providing the level of service customers wanted and needed.

Despite their importance, building strong positive relationships can be difficult and it is an area frequently neglected in the quest for greater productivity. Increasing dependence on technology-mediated communication creates a less personal environment that may discourage relational growth. "Office politics" or striving to get ahead may create friction between co-workers. The organizational culture may discourage dynamic relationships, or it simply may not correspond to individuals' communication styles. Strong interpersonal skills can help you to overcome these difficulties and develop relationships that benefit you and the organization in which you work.

Most work relationships, such as the relationship between a salesperson and a customer, must follow norms, standards, and rules. In a larger sense, though, all work relationships rely on ethical communication. Commitment

Strong work relationships complement technical skills and expertise. Here, layout editors work on the next edition of USA Today.

to communication ethics in relationships includes refraining from "killer comments," gossip, or careless communication that reveals sensitive work information. It means being straightforward and honest with co-workers, customers, and supervisors at all times. It means avoiding delays, distortions, hiding information, or manipulating a relationship for personal gain. Finally, it means recognizing that work relationships exist for the primary purpose of achieving organizational goals, and acting on this principle when and if a conflict of interests arises. These guidelines apply regardless of the type of relationship in which you are involved.

In the following sections, we cover the basic elements of several types of relationships common in business and the professions. These include relationships between managers and employees (also known as superior-subordinate relationships), relationships between co-workers (cooperative and uncooperative), employee-customer relationships, mentoring relationships, and romantic relationships. We begin with the most prevalent of all work relationships, the manager-employee relationship.

Manager-Employee Relationships

Relationships between managers and employees are vitally important in the workplace, for the simple reason that everyone (except perhaps the chief executive officer!) has a boss. Considerable study of this special type of relationship in recent years has revealed a number of issues that deserve attention.

Figure 6-1 shows that the manager-employee relationship takes place within the communication *climate* produced by the behaviors and attitudes of each person. Important factors in creating the climate are the communication patterns (upward and downward) and personal characteristics of the manager and employee. The center of the figure shows outcomes of the relationship: *mutual influence* and *power sharing*.[1] These basic components are common to most strong manager-employee relationships.

Climate

As we discussed in Chapter 2, *climate is affected by manager-employee relationships,* especially by how decision-making power is shared and how supportive supervisors and workers are toward each other. Climate is changeable because organizational members' behaviors and their attitudes toward the organization change.

Climate affects manager-employee relationships as well. It either encourages or discourages employees' communicating in the organization, exerting control over matters that affect them, and obtaining satisfaction from the responsibilities they carry out.[2] A healthy climate is one in which managers and employees communicate effectively with each other and support each other.

Effective managers possess a number of characteristics that make their communication successful. Managers who experience healthy relationships with their employees are approachable, sensitive, credible, supportive, confident, and honest. Their communication (the downward communication in the organization) demonstrates frankness, respect, empathy, and calmness. Effective managers are quick to explain decisions, are articulate and clear in their messages, and encourage information and input from employees.

Managers are most pleased with employees who display the following characteristics: good job performance, ability to handle pressure, help in promoting the boss's success, cooperativeness, honesty, and supportiveness. Subordinates who enjoy good relationships with their bosses provide feedback about how superiors perform their jobs (upward communication), demonstrate appropriate forms of persuasion, disagree in a constructive manner, and confirm the messages that are sent downward.

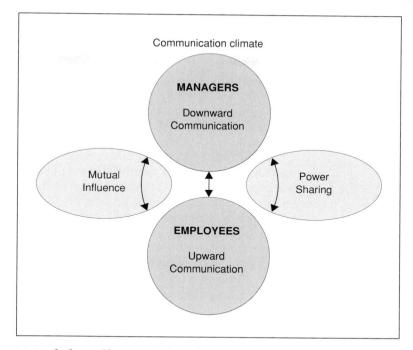

FIGURE 6-1   Characteristics of strong manager-employee relationships include communication, mutual influence, and power sharing.

Mutual Influence

Managers and employees rely on each other to get their jobs done. When they possess the foregoing characteristics and display open and appropriate communication styles, they do more than simply work together; frequently they positively influence one another.[3] It is not enough to consider the relationship only from the manager's point of view; the more we know about organizational communication, the more certain we are that employees have a significant effect on their bosses. Employees' actions, attitudes, performance, and communication style play a very large role in how managers conduct their own business. Managers cannot do the job of their unit or department without the cooperation of employees and therefore must rely on this important relationship to accomplish goals.

Mutual influence is an informal negotiation process between managers and employees. Managers provide approachability, sensitivity to employees' needs, and supportiveness; and employees respond with feedback about their concerns, improved work performance, and an honest effort to cooperate with the boss. The two parties can recognize and understand each other's needs and work toward these mutual goals at the same time.

Power Sharing

A casual glance at an organizational chart may appear to show that people in management hold all the power and that those they manage possess none. Actually power holding can be distributed in four ways: managers hold all the power and workers hold none, neither supervisors nor workers have much power, workers hold most of the power with supervisors holding little, and managers and workers share power.[4] Let us briefly consider each of these.

Organizations in which management holds all the power are rare now, but they were common in the early part of the twentieth century and were described by Frederick Taylor, Max Weber, and Henri Fayol (see Chapter 2 for a review of classical organizational theory), among others. These organizations are characterized by rigidity, strict adherence to process, and downward communication.

Organizations in which neither managers nor employees have much power suffer numerous problems. According to James Kouzes and Barry Posner, "People who feel powerless, be they managers or subordinates, tend to hoard whatever shreds of power they have. Powerless managers also tend to adopt petty dictatorial management styles. Powerlessness creates organizational systems where political skills become essential and 'covering' yourself and 'passing the buck' become the preferred style for handling interdepartmental differences."[5]

Organizations in which subordinates hold most of the power are also rare, but they are becoming somewhat more common as the demands on business for innovation and competitiveness increase. For example, companies such as Ben & Jerry's, Next, and Honda put most of the power in the hands of the employees. These companies deemphasize differences in status between managers and employees and encourage employee input through lateral communication. Such a structure may be too loose or decentralized for some companies.

Organizations in which managers and subordinates share power enjoy workers' satisfaction and commitment without losing direction. When people feel they have some control and influence over the ways decisions are made and actions are carried out, they are more energetic in accomplishing the goals of the unit and the organization. Managers, in turn, have enough power to effectively manage the unit.

As with mutual influence, power sharing between supervisor and worker has to be negotiated. Management expert Rosabeth Kanter identified four methods for sharing power:[6]

1. Give people important work to do on critical issues.

2. Give people discretion and autonomy over their tasks and resources.

3. Give visibility to others and provide recognition for their efforts.

4. Build relationships for others, connecting them with powerful people and finding the sponsors and mentors.

In return, employees actually increase their productivity and strengthen their relationships with managers.

Remember that power and power sharing occur on a unit or department level as well. Power that is earned or bestowed on any member of a unit, whether manager or subordinate, is essentially the unit's power. Conversely, when a worker is denied power, the entire unit suffers.

"Managing Diversity"

Manager-employee relationships are also affected by issues of gender and ethnicity. Since 1972, the number of female managers in the United States has nearly doubled.[7] Women and members of minority groups are expected to make up 85 percent of the net increase in the size of the U.S. work force by the year 2000. With a greater influx of managers and workers from a wide variety of backgrounds, special attention has focused on the relationships between male and female managers and male and female subordinates and on how people of different cultural backgrounds can make the most of their work relationships, a concept known as *managing diversity* or *valuing diversity.*

The question of gender, culture, and managerial preference really focuses on two issues: stereotypes and competence. Different experiences, opportunities, and educational preparation may account for varying levels of managerial skills in people, but these differences are not specific to either gender or culture.

What are specific to groups are the stereotypes associated with them. Stereotypes associated with male and female managers are fueled by societal stereotypes about males and females in general, which may exist because of misunderstanding or failure to consciously question their validity.[8] Men have been stereotyped as competitive, ambitious, assertive, risk taking, and power seeking. Women have traditionally been stereotyped as soft-spoken, passive, emotional, understanding, and sensitive. Problems can arise when women and men do not behave as these stereotypes suggest they will. Consider the following example.

> Amber and Kelly were recently hired as manager trainees for a fast-food company. Most of the employees they supervise have never had a female manager before. Amber decided the best way to advance in the company would be to emulate the management style of her two bosses, Fred and Juan. Fred and Juan are very task oriented; they rarely socialize or even show their emotions when on the job.

Modeling these men, Amber maintained her distance from her line employees; she answered questions but never volunteered additional information, and she tried not to get involved in her workers' personal problems. She figured that her efficient demeanor would ensure that her shift performed professionally.

Kelly, however, treated her line workers in a warm and informal manner. She asked about their personal lives and attempted to establish close relations. She figured that her obvious care for her workers would ensure their doing a good job for her.

At their semiannual evaluations, both Amber and Kelly were informed by upper management that their relationships with employees needed improvement. Line workers had complained about how they were treated. Amber and Kelly were stunned by these comments. What were the causes of the line workers' complaints?

Although feminine stereotypes are not necessarily inherently negative, they can cause problems for women in management, especially if the organization has only recently moved women to management positions. If a female manager possesses stereotypic traits, some may assume that she is too "feminine" to be effective. If she does not conform to stereotype and possesses more "masculine" traits, some may be suspicious because she does not appear to "act like a woman." This phenomenon is termed *gender role congruency.*[9] Behavior that deviates from others' expectations for a particular gender can arouse mistrust, or even hostility, if neither person attempts to view the other as an individual.

In the same sense, members of ethnic or cultural groups are also frequently stereotyped. For example, African-Americans who assert their beliefs may be labeled "aggressive," Asian-Americans may be considered too "polite" or "passive," and Hispanic-Americans may be thought "slow." It is difficult for members of the majority to recognize subconscious stereotyping, yet it is nearly always present. The most destructive approach to managing diversity is to claim lack of prejudice because the claim usually masks a failure to acknowledge biases that are apparent to others or a dismissal of others' perception of bias as misguided. Each person, regardless of gender or cultural status, is far more complex than any stereotype begins to describe.

The double bind that minority and female managers experience can be minimized and is already changing. As more minorities and women enter the work force and become managers, the behaviors associated with those stereotypes will become more common and are likely to be perceived as positive. As you recall from Chapter 3, the most effective managers and leaders are sensitive to employees' needs, take a personal interest in their subordinates and nurture them, and are passionate about the goals and values of the organization. Such positive traits are appreciated by most subordinates.

Research has also revealed that women increasingly prefer female managers.[10] As women make up a larger percentage of the work force, this subordinate support will make a big difference in the success of female managers overall.

The best approach to managing people effectively seeks to get the most from all employees based on their individual strengths. Most managerial jobs require a certain level of competitiveness, risk taking, and power seeking as well as sensitivity, empathy, and emotional involvement. Good managers have always recognized this fact. Women and men who follow the leadership principles outlined in Chapter 3 are a step ahead of their managerial cohorts. An approach that stresses goals, situational knowledge, communication competence, and anxiety management yields a higher level of excellence for any manager.

Co-worker Relationships

Co-worker relationships are truly the glue that holds an organization together. Positive and constructive co-worker relationships enhance productivity, creativity, and teamwork as well as make work an agreeable place to be! Of course, co-worker relationships can be voluntary or involuntary. In the latter case, you do yourself a considerable service if you understand how co-worker relationships develop so that you can work out a method for dealing with involuntary relationships that could undermine your productivity. There are many bases for co-worker relationships, including proximity, shared interests, shared tasks, and satisfaction of needs. Figure 6-2 conceptualizes these basic components.

Proximity

One of the fundamentals of relational development is that the closer physically you are to people, the more likely it is that you will develop relationships with them. Officemates form friendships and alliances simply because of their *proximity,* or closeness, to one another. (Of course, common lounges, meeting areas, restrooms, and hallways are places you can meet people who do not work in your area.) Think about the classes you are taking. You have probably become friends with the people who usually sit near you in the classroom.

Shared Interests

It is not difficult to see that people like to be with others who share the same interests. Working in the same organization automatically provides a number of common interests on which to build work relationships. Co-

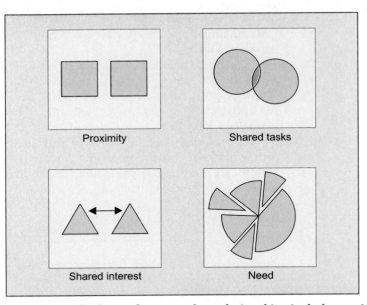

FIGURE 6-2   The bases for co-worker relationships include proximity, shared tasks, shared interest, and need.

workers share a corporate identity, work location, possibly even the same bosses at times. Relationships often develop naturally around these common interests. The grapevine is one expression of shared interest relationships among co-workers.

Shared Tasks

More and more jobs require the joint effort of two or more people. Work groups, task forces, and team projects show that cooperation is an increasingly popular way to solve problems and address complex issues. People are usually assigned to particular work groups because of their talents and expertise and regardless of whether they like the other group members.

Working with people on common tasks can provide a great deal of relational satisfaction, along with professional enrichment. The more often you communicate with co-workers, the more likely you are to understand them on a personal level and form friendships with them. Unfortunately, the opposite is also sometimes true — the more you work with someone, the more you may dislike her or his personal qualities.

Regardless of your personal feelings about your co-workers, several guidelines can help you to form positive shared-task relationships:

◆ ignore personal idiosyncrasies as much as possible;

◆ stay focused on mutual goals — the organization's success depends on employees working well together;

◆ know your responsibilities, and be accountable for your performance; and

◆ share credit for success with co-workers and take your share of the blame for failure.

These guidelines will help you to establish strong organizational relationships and overcome even difficult or uncooperative co-workers. You may just discover that someone you initially disliked for personality reasons is actually very good to work with.

Satisfaction of Needs

One of the more common reasons that relationships develop at work is to satisfy basic needs. In addition to basic subsistence needs such as food, clothing, and shelter, you have emotional and intellectual needs at every point in your life; for example, as a student you are fulfilling your need for knowledge and skills.

Needs do not go away when you join an organization. Your needs for affiliation, social exchange, and sharing of ideas with others are just as prevalent at work as they are in your personal life. Many people spend half or more of their waking hours at work, so it is only natural to satisfy these needs through their jobs. Most of the needs that can be fulfilled at work can be grouped into four areas: support, power, expertise, and social exchange.

Support.   The need for support can take various forms. People need professional support to ensure they are performing correctly at work. They need friends at work who can provide professional support by serving as a sounding board for new ideas, giving suggestions, and acting as cheerleaders. On-the-job friends can also provide personal support. A friend can give you a lift after you have had a disagreement with your boss or have found out that you did not get the promotion or raise you were counting on.

Power.   People often leave their jobs because they feel powerless. To accomplish professional goals, workers need power, and sometimes relationships are the best source of acquiring power and control. Although power relationships can be abused, there is nothing inherently wrong in forming them.

Co-workers who have attained a certain level of power can serve as resources for learning how the organization's power structure operates. You can learn from those who have power by observing their actions and deciding if their methods are acceptable to you. Some powerful people may use unethical means, and we encourage you to avoid mirroring them. Nevertheless, you may want to observe unethical behavior to protect yourself from it.

Expertise.   You have probably found that you sometimes need the expertise of others to achieve a goal. It is worthwhile to keep track of your co-workers' areas of expertise so that you know whom to call when you need help. For example, some people may be mathematical or statistical whizzes who can help interpret quantitative trends, others may be experts in budgeting matters, and still others may possess computer skills.

Remember that asking for expert advice is a reciprocal process, a two-way street. Some people are eager to share their expertise without any strings attached. Others may agree to help but are interested in getting something tangible in return. When asking someone for expert advice, think of some way you can offer some specialized help in return. A commitment to helping others increases your chances of receiving their expertise when you need it.

Social exchange.   Humans have a basic need for social interaction with others; the need does not go away when they enter the work environment. Some socializing occurs at coffee breaks, at lunch, or in the lounges of the organization. Socializing also occurs during work, often to the chagrin of corporate leaders.

Socializing reflects the desire for self-expression and for knowledge of co-workers. Many people feel comfortable telling co-workers their thoughts, feelings, and opinions on any number of topics — politics, company policies, marriage, children, economics, finances, and even religion. Socializing helps people to handle the stress of a hectic, fast-paced work environment.

Relationships with Difficult Co-workers

Just about every organization is going to have employees who are difficult to deal with. Some people cannot get along with anyone, others get along only with a few people, and still others have good relations with everyone but you. The chances are very good that you will have to work and associate with someone you consider difficult.

The maintenance of appropriate work relationships with difficult people can be accomplished in several ways if at least one of the parties is willing to work out the problems. The following outline summarizes the steps to take when you deal with difficult people.[11]

Steps for Improving Relationships with Others

A. Make sure you are not the difficult person.
B. Ensure that you are doing your job.
C. Ascertain the goals of the "difficult" person.
D. Assess perception levels.
E. Accept the difficult person for what he or she is, not for what you want that person to be.
   1. Forget the past, and focus on the future.
   2. Do not sweat the little things.

F. Confront the person.
   1. Take the initiative toward good relations.
   2. Ask questions.
   3. Ask for input/suggestions.
   4. Listen carefully.
   5. Focus on job-related issues as much as possible.

G. State how you feel.
   1. Express your goals.
   2. Do not apologize if you are certain you are right.
   3. Demonstrate political sensitivity.

H. Give recognition when the other person deserves it.
I. Maintain a professional demeanor during interactions.
J. Seek mediation if all else fails.

You may find yourself in situations that require all of the preceding steps; less complicated situations may require only two or three steps for resolution. The following scenario shows how Della is able to use steps one through eight to resolve a conflict with Victor.

Della and Victor are co-workers who share a large office suite with four other employees. Although they usually work on different projects, their work often overlaps, and they depend on each other's commitment to doing a good job. Lately, Della has perceived Victor's behavior to be increasingly unfriendly and aloof. Della has also heard rumors (apparently spread by Victor) that Della was not doing her share of the work on their joint projects. Even Della's boss remarked that Della and Victor should work things out.

   Della did not see that she had done anything to upset Victor, and after evaluating her performance on their joint projects, she decided she was certainly pulling her weight. She thought about her goals and wondered if the two of them were striving for different results. She also suspected that they did not perceive the value of these projects in the same way. Although Della had other independent projects that concerned her, she knew that Victor placed the highest priority on their joint projects.

Della decided to approach Victor with an open mind and to listen sincerely to his complaints. At first Victor refused even to talk about the matter, but after a while he told Della that he was upset because Della appeared to give their projects low priority and sometimes was not available when Victor wanted to work together on them. Della acknowledged Victor's complaints. Although Della did not feel that an apology was required, she did agree to be more cooperative with Victor.

Later, when one of their joint projects enjoyed great success, Della openly and generously credited Victor for his role in the achievement. Although Victor and Della never became personal friends, their professional relationship grew stronger as they understood each another better.

Of course, not all difficult relationships can be untangled in the same productive manner as Victor and Della's. When you are dealing with people who are simply impossible and who refuse to work at resolving the difficulties, maintain a professional demeanor — be patient and do not lose your temper; remain task oriented — focus on the goals you are trying to achieve; and seek third-party mediation from a boss, co-worker, or counselor. There is no reason to allow others to affect your performance when they are unwilling to reason things out. You have a right to be productive without the distraction of a hateful co-worker.

Customer Relationships

"Stay close to the customer" was one of the tenets of *In Search of Excellence,* the best-selling book describing the pathways to business success.[12] Knowing who the customers are, what they want, and how they will react to products or services is one of the most basic goals of businesses. This is especially true when you consider that the economy has shifted from a manufacturing to a service orientation. With more than three-quarters of all jobs created in the United States in the last ten years devoted to service industries, customer relations are a high priority for organizations and are likely to be part of your work experience as well.[13]

Interpersonal communication is at the heart of customer relations. Customers must feel that the people they give their business to can listen carefully to and understand their needs. There are five basic rules of conduct that can ensure successful customer relationships: know the customer, take responsibility for customer satisfaction, avoid unresponsive behavior, employ effective communication skills, and treat difficult customers with respect.

"Really, I promise you that I'll always be your very own personal banker, but please try to understand that I must be that to others, too."

Drawing by D. Reilly; © 1990 The New Yorker Magazine, Inc.

Know the Customer

It is difficult to please customers if you are ignorant of their needs. All too often excellent products, produced with hard work, fail because customers are not convinced that they need such products. Successful organizations work to find out what customers want and to provide it.[14]

You can work toward the same goal in your relationships with customers. Knowing the customer in an organizational sense depends to a great extent on the openness and honesty of the relationships between people. Successful relationships help you to discover the customer's characteristics and idiosyncrasies so that you can respond to specific customer desires.

Customer relationships can entail problem solving to help customers obtain goods and services that are right for them. You become their partner in solving their problems. Often, this problem-solving process means planning for the customer's future needs and desires; changes in tastes, technologies, and economic outlooks are constants in the business environment.

Customer relations also include mutual goal setting by employees and clients. By understanding customers' present and future needs, you have a better opportunity to plan for the services you will have to deliver. Knowing the customer well enough to set effective goals requires establishing a relationship that is focused on understanding and cooperation.

Take Responsibility for Customer Satisfaction

Customers enjoy doing business with organizations that personalize their service. Personalized service at its best means ongoing attention from a specific person. When customers call to place an order, make a complaint, specify a correction, or even give a compliment, they want to deal with someone they know who takes a personal interest in them.

Customer satisfaction can be monitored in a variety of ways. Many organizations provide comment cards as a means of gauging customer satisfaction. Surveys, studies by market research firms, and analysis of sales data can also give clues about customers' level of satisfaction.

The most effective means is actually calling or meeting with clients to determine the exact nature of their satisfaction. Questions such as "How do you like our new product line compared to the last?" "What would work better for you?" and "What are your most important concerns about the services that you use?" show the customer that you care about his or her satisfaction.

Taking responsibility for customer satisfaction also involves follow-up actions. Attention to details, such as keeping customers notified about work in progress (even misplaced orders or other setbacks), sending holiday greetings, giving advance notice of specials, and taking interest in their personal lives, gives customers a feeling that someone is looking out for them. Loyal customers are usually the result.

Avoid Unresponsive Behavior

Customer relations can be enhanced significantly if you make the effort to avoid unresponsive behavior.[15] You may have seen problems caused by unresponsiveness in the organizations that you do business with.

Apathy, or lack of emotional involvement in the job, usually results in employees failing to treat customers with care and concern. The best way to avoid apathy is to learn about each customer. Remembering a frequent customer's name and expressing interest in his or her job or family can show customers that you see them as more than simply a source of income for the organization.

Coldness also damages customer relations. Coldness can be displayed in several ways. Condescending answers to legitimate questions or concerns, negative facial expressions, or demeaning comments indicate to customers that they are not your highest concern. Sometimes you may give an impression of coldness unintentionally, especially if you are tired, under stress, or nervous about the customer relationship. Although it is difficult to keep personal frustrations and concerns hidden, revealing them to customers usually hurts relations with them.

Robotism, or rigid and inflexible behavior toward customers, is another form of unresponsive behavior. Rules and procedures may encourage robotism, but customers will usually attribute rigidity to you personally. Some examples of robotism include being systematically put on hold or transferred from department to department when you are calling with a question or continuing to receive "junk" mail or solicitations long after you have called to cancel a subscription to a publication.

Avoiding robotism means keeping an open mind about how customer desires can be handled within the context of current policies and regulations. There is nearly always some flexibility available in even the strictest standards, and recognizing occasions when customers deserve special consideration will keep them better satisfied.

Employ Effective Communication Skills

Customers prefer to establish relations with company representatives who display effective communication skills. Successful customer relationships are based on assertive, open, and friendly communication. Such communication is effective because customers expect to be well treated by someone who clearly knows what she or he is talking about, can explain problems, and does not make the customer feel ignorant or pushy for asking questions. You can convey a successful communication style by smiling, making eye contact, asking pertinent questions, answering questions promptly and accurately, and using encouraging nonverbal communication.

Treat Difficult Customers with Respect

Handling difficult or hostile customers is a thankless job. Nevertheless, there are few job duties more satisfying than turning an angry customer into a happy one. Your ability to handle difficult customers is vital to maintaining successful customer relationships in general because even the best customer relationships sometimes hit snags, and you are wise to be prepared for them.

You may think it is not worth your time and energy to appease difficult customers. Statistics show, however, that hostile customers, through word of mouth, can reduce a company's business by 2 percent — certainly an

FOCUS on *Corporate Communication*

HEWLETT-PACKARD CO.

*I*t may seem contradictory that a company as committed to high technology as Hewlett-Packard (HP) would consider face-to-face communication one of the most significant characteristics of its corporate culture. At HP, the personalized relationships between management and employees have two strong underpinnings: the tradition of openness established by the company's founders and the strong belief that open communication leads to greater productivity and job satisfaction.

Both communication and work at HP, a manufacturer of measurement and computation products and systems that employs 91,000 people worldwide, are based on the central value of empowerment. HP's founders believed that people want to do a good job, and given the right tools and support, they will do so. In terms of communication, that support usually takes the form of one-to-one interaction between employees and managers.

The pattern of growth at Hewlett-Packard has done a lot to encourage strong interpersonal communication. Originally, divisions were responsible for individual products, and each division manager was equivalent to the chief executive officer of a small indepen-dent company. In the past fifteen years, HP's move into systems has changed that structure. Increasingly, divisions work together, each producing one component of a system. As a result, managers work with multiple work teams, and work teams share multiple tasks. A lot more communication is necessary to prevent confusion over responsibilities, coordinate schedules, take advantage of ideas, and keep up productivity.

At HP, managers walk around and talk to employees regularly, encouraging people to voice ideas that they may not have felt comfortable bringing to management themselves. This interaction, an example of "management by wandering around," helps managers collect the information they need to do their jobs well and provides workers with individual support.

Communication takes other forms as well. One of the most widely used is the "coffee talk." Coffee talks are informal presentations by managers to their people about job concerns, the financial state of the company, product development, and new responsibilities. Most important, they are an opportunity to solicit questions or suggestions from employees. Coffee talks vary in frequency from as often as once a week to once a month, depending on the amount of information managers have to discuss and the level of employee demand for it. The coffee talks

amount worth considering.[16] The key to improving your relationship with a troublesome customer is a conscientious communication style. The following guidelines can help you work through difficult situations with customers:[17]

1. Let customers talk. Listen carefully and with an open mind to their complaints, making note of instances in which your company may be at fault.

function as ongoing forums to discuss issues and exchange questions and answers.

One of the most important functions of the coffee talk occurs when HP makes an earnings announcement. Along with a standard press release, managers receive packages of support materials — slides or other visual aids and "talking points" — for presentation to their people. The manager's presentation includes an organizational overview and a discussion of how the local unit contributed to the company's performance, what the company's performance means for the unit, and what the results will mean for employees as individuals. Managers try to schedule coffee talks as soon after the earnings announcement as possible, often on the same day.

Managers are increasingly using voice mail (sophisticated answering-machine technology) as a supplementary form of coffee talk. Employees can choose to access a voice mail program that plays a three-to-five-minute message related to a current issue, then gives a number to call to record a response. The manager can sign onto the voice mail program, collect the employees' input, and issue a response or make a note of topics for future coffee talks.

Some concern exists that voice mail may eventually replace, rather than enhance, coffee talks. As with any new technology, voice mail's functions are being adapted to fit people's needs, and it is a challenge to continually improve communication technology and simultaneously support and maintain the open, people-oriented culture at HP.

The key is to use multiple media that support, not undermine, each other's functions. For example, voice mail can be more useful than face-to-face communication in some circumstances. Through call-in message pickup, voice mail can help to maintain some manager-employee contact even when a manager is out of the office. Voice mail also allows routine concerns and uncomplicated questions to be handled more quickly and easily, and information can be made available constantly because the recorded message can be monitored and updated by the manager from anywhere in the world.

One of the most important uses of multiple media is to reach the broadest range of employees possible to allow them to work well together. In addition to traditional media, HP uses worldwide electronic mail, an electronic newsletter, a fifteen-minute bimonthly video magazine, and an occasional tele-conference for major events. People choose the media that work best for them. Ultimately, multiple media give people the information they need to interact on a face-to-face basis.

2. Reassure customers that their concerns will be heard and addressed.

3. Do not personalize the issue. Recognize that customer anger is not directed personally at you. People who go to the trouble of making a complaint are usually concerned with getting satisfaction rather than with making employees feel bad.

4. Acknowledge instances in which the customer is correct. Customers like to be told that they are right when they are.

5. Apologize and provide immediate satisfaction if you determine that the company was wrong. If blame cannot be determined immediately, promise the customer you will respond at a specific time, and be sure you follow up.

6. Ask the customer to suggest how problems could be avoided in the future.

By giving the unhappy customer the attention he or she is seeking, you may be able to turn an enemy into a friend. In the following situation, the clerk successfully resolves a customer's anger about a damaged product.

Clerk: Can I help you?

Customer: I want a refund. The radio I bought here is defective.

Clerk: I'm sorry you're not happy. What exactly is the problem?

Customer: Quite a few things. The left speaker is giving off a lot of static, and I can't get my favorite station clearly enough. I want my money back!

Clerk: Sometimes static can be easily eliminated by tightening the wires inside the speaker, but just in case it's a more serious problem, I'll be happy to get you a new radio and send this one back to the manufacturer to be checked out.

Customer: Well, okay. Thanks. I need a few other items while I'm here, too.

Clerk: I'm sorry about this inconvenience. Always let us know when you're not completely satisfied.

Customer: Yes, I will.

Mentoring Relationships

One of the most valuable relationships you can establish early in your career is with a mentor. Mentors are experienced, mature, and successful employees who give help and guidance to newer employees (protégés) in many areas, including knowledge, skills, and appropriate attitudes and behavior.[18] The mentor acts as a role model who demonstrates how the new employee can develop and become successful.

You may have already experienced the benefits of a mentor in the places you have worked. If so, you can compare this information to your experience and learn more about the workings of mentor relationships. For those of you who have not enjoyed a mentoring relationship, the following provides a number of key suggestions for becoming involved with a mentor when you take a job after graduation.

Importance of Mentoring Relationships

Successful mentoring relationships usually benefit everyone involved — the protégé, the mentor, and the organization. According to Rosabeth Kanter, if an organization wants to be more successful, it should encourage mentor-protégé relationships.[19] Young employees can develop faster when they have the help of a mentor. John Kotter championed the cause for these relationships when he stated, "Virtually all of the successful and effective executives I have known have had two or more of these kinds of relationships early in their careers. Some have had upwards of a dozen people they were able to rely on for different needs — some provided important contacts, others gave key information in specific areas, and still others taught them certain valued skills."[20]

Benefits to the protégé.   Once a mentoring relationship has been established, the protégé has access to opportunities that may otherwise be unavailable. Benefits from mentoring relationships include receiving support from the mentor, having the mentor influence others on behalf of the protégé, getting public recognition from the mentor, having the mentor as a friend and role model, obtaining greater knowledge of the politics of the organization, and being promoted by the mentor.[21] The results of these benefits include more rapid promotions, higher salaries, more challenging work assignments, more career mobility, and more work satisfaction. Although mentoring relationships usually require more dedication to a job and possibly longer work hours, if you are serious about the "fast track," they can be extremely valuable.

Benefits to the mentor and organization.   Mentors can obtain a great deal of satisfaction from helping a younger employee. They may learn from the protégé. They may also increase their own value to the organization by demonstrating an ability to help new employees to develop.

The organization benefits from mentoring because protégés tend to develop faster, have stronger leadership skills, demonstrate teamwork and shared values, and are less likely to leave the organization for other opportunities.[22] The following example shows how mentoring can benefit everyone involved.

> Connie worked part-time as an inventory clerk at Brooks, Inc. while attending City College. Brooks had a good reputation, and Connie hoped that if she proved herself as a part-time employee, she might land a job with the company after graduation.
>
> She noticed that Roger, an inventory manager, was competent, well liked by others, and friendly. Connie took on some paid overtime tasks in inventory control (a new area for her) and asked Roger for some advice on how best to do the work. Roger really appreciated having help from an

enthusiastic worker and took time to teach Connie what she needed to know to handle inventory control. Soon, they were taking their breaks together to discuss various company and professional issues.

Connie learned a lot about Brooks from Roger, and after her graduation she started work full time — bringing to the job experience, knowledge, and contacts that made her a valuable employee from the start.

Characteristics of the Mentor and Protégé Roles

The mentor is usually older (eight to fifteen years) than the protégé and enjoys a secure, often prestigious position with the organization. The protégé is usually new to the organization or unit and is interested in career advancement.[23] Although assigned mentoring relationships exist in some organizations, prevailing opinion suggests that voluntary relationships are best, as required relationships may be viewed as a burden by one person or the other.[24]

Mentoring relationships require both partners to agree on their relative roles and understand each other well. Mentors must possess the knowledge and skills necessary to benefit protégés, and protégés must be willing and skillful learners. For a successful and productive relationship, mentors must also be confident, approachable, successful, skillful in communication, able to make decisions, secure, and possessed of strong interpersonal skills; protégés must be ambitious, eager to learn, openminded, loyal, talented, energetic, and communicative.[25]

Mentoring Phases

Mentoring relationships go through phases. Like all relationships, changes in a person's knowledge, status, abilities, or work experiences can alter the nature of a mentoring relationship. Most mentoring relationships include the following four phases, although the amount of time spent in each stage may vary quite a bit.[26]

Initiation. The protégé learns to appreciate the talents and expertise of the mentor. The mentor demonstrates support and interest by coaching, teaching, and listening to the protégé. The protégé exhibits loyalty, intelligence, and energy as she or he responds to the direction and advice of the mentor.

Cultivation. Interpersonal bonding occurs between mentor and protégé. As the mentor coaches, protects, and promotes the protégé, their mutual admiration increases.

Mentoring relationships often benefit the employee and the organization by promoting greater job satisfaction and productivity. Mentors are usually in positions of authority, such as this franchise owner, and can offer support and knowledge to protégés.

Separation. The mentor and protégé drift apart because of physical separation (for example, one may travel more than the other), promotions, or greater independence on the part of the protégé.

Redefinition. The (former) mentor and protégé reestablish a relationship based on different criteria. The mentor may still fulfill some of the old responsibilities, such as providing advice and expertise, but more likely the two see each other as peers. By this time they may hold similar positions in the organization. Not all mentoring relationships experience the last phase because protégés may be reassigned through promotion or leave the organization for a different job.

Gender and Cultural Issues

Minorities and women can particularly benefit from mentoring relationships. Even if an organization's corporate culture is geared toward white male norms and attitudes, a personal relationship with a successful person of the same gender or ethnic group can help you to adapt much more successfully.

Unfortunately, it may be more difficult for women and minorities to find such mentors because of their relatively low representation in management. Currently, there are not enough women and minorities in upper and middle management positions to act as mentors.

Although there is nothing inherently problematic with male-female or cross-cultural mentoring relationships, the potential for controversy can restrict opportunities for the protégé. Suggestions of romantic involvement, fraternization, and sexual intimacy may scare off male mentors. In mentoring relationships between white mentors and black protégés, whites are sometimes afraid to correct their protégés out of a fear of appearing racist. Members of minority groups may also resent special attention if it appears to be presented as remedial help.[27]

The lack of mentors for female and minority employees is especially unfortunate because the absence of such relationships may significantly reduce job effectiveness.[28] The research that does exist on cross-gender mentoring relationships suggests that a large share of successful female executives benefited from mentoring by male role models.[29] In addition, many professional organizations such as the National Consortium for Black Professional Development, the American Society of Professional and Executive Women, the Hispanic Organization of Professionals and Executives, and the National Association of Asian-American Professionals can provide mentor-like support and networking opportunities for women and members of minority groups.

Finding a Mentor

If you are new to an organization and want to benefit from a mentor, what do you do? The following steps may be useful in securing an appropriate mentor in your first job.[30]

1. Ask the personnel or human resources department about formal mentoring programs in the organization.

2. Identify people who have the same specialization and interests you do. Try to determine if they possess the "mentor characteristics" listed here.

3. Approach some of those people whom you have identified and act

interested in what they do. Ask questions that reveal your enthusiasm for their jobs. If appropriate, volunteer for tasks that would facilitate their jobs and careers.

4. Disclose information about yourself that gives them an impression that you are upwardly mobile and interested in learning as much as you can about the profession and the organization.

5. Ask for advice on matters where their expertise would improve your productivity.

6. Ask them if they would be interested in sponsoring you. Explain why you might be a good choice. Indicate your confidence and admiration and the appeal their career track has for you.

Romantic Relationships in the Workplace

Have you ever been romantically attracted to someone you worked with? Have you ever dated someone from work? If you answered yes to these questions, you are not alone. The number of romantic relationships in the workplace is increasing each year as more women enter a once predominantly male work force.[31] Although only limited study has been made in this area, it is clear that romantic relationships in the workplace have the potential for creating widespread controversy if handled in inappropriate ways. It is therefore important for you to be aware of the issues involved in organizational romance — whether you are a participant or an observer.

Pervasiveness of Organizational Romance

You may be wondering whether organizational romances are really all that prevalent. James Dillard and Katherine Miller defined organizational romance as an intimate interpersonal relationship between employees of the same organization that can be characterized by a substantial degree of mutual sexual attraction.[32] According to research conducted in the last several years, two-thirds of workers surveyed observed romantic relationships where they worked, and one-third of those surveyed claimed to have been involved in such a relationship.[33]

If you think about the workplace as a dynamic environment where people are interacting with one another for extended amounts of time, it is little wonder that close personal relationships form. As we mentioned earlier, work may be the best available opportunity for meeting and socializing with people. Romance can often spring from close interaction.

Consequences of Organizational Romance

Negative and positive consequences can result from romantic work relationships.[34] Problems resulting from organizational romance can appear in task and relational areas and can include tardiness, absenteeism, poor work quality, and absent-mindedness. In addition, when people become involved in romance, their goals and emphasis in the workplace may become personal where they were once organizational.

Relational problems may also emerge. If the romance hits a snag, relational partners may become distracted by their personal problems and neglect their other responsibilities. If the relationship is severed, the former romantic partners may be reluctant to work together.

Co-workers may also have problems with the romantically involved couple. Co-workers may feel envy, jealousy, or even disgust toward the romance. In extreme cases, disapproving co-workers may shun or ignore the couple.

Nevertheless, there are several positive consequences associated with organizational romance. In a number of studies, organizational romance either did not affect the work performance or attitudes of participants or actually improved their behavior at work.[35] Participants in these relationships were easier to get along with, worked better in teams, improved their work flow, and were generally more productive. From the best available evidence, it appears that the nature of the consequences stemming from romantic relationships depends on the particular couple.

Summary

Developing and maintaining relationships in the workplace are not simple tasks. Relationships require a certain amount of planning and effort to be desirable and productive. Ethical communication is vital to all forms of work relationships.

The workplace promotes a variety of relationships, including those between managers and employees, co-workers, employees and customers, mentors and protégés, and lovers. Manager-employee relationships are affected by the communication climate of the organization, the communication patterns and personal characteristics of the two parties involved, and the degree of mutual influence and power sharing in the relationship.

Co-worker relationships develop through proximity, shared tasks, shared interests, and satisfaction of needs. Some co-worker relationships are involuntary and may involve working with difficult people. Getting along with these people requires that you keep focused on the job at hand and maintain a professional demeanor.

Employee-customer relationships benefit from knowing the customer as well as possible, taking responsibility for customer satisfaction, avoiding common pitfalls, employing effective communication skills, and treating difficult customers with respect.

Mentoring relationships provide valuable benefits for new employees, such as support, influence, recognition, friendship, role models, organizational knowledge, and even promotions. The drawback to mentoring relationships is the difficulty of finding a willing mentor, especially in organizations that do not have structured mentoring programs in place.

Romantic relationships are a potential source of controversy in the workplace; occurrences of romantic relationships between employees are reported to be increasing. Positive and negative consequences of romantic relationships in the workplace have been reported.

Discussion

1. Why are strong interpersonal relationships important to businesses? What are some obstacles to such relationships? Discuss these questions in relation to each type of relationship covered in the chapter.

2. What are the implications of power sharing for manager-employee relationships?

3. What is meant by the concept "managing diversity"? In your experience, in what ways has the concept translated into practice?

4. Discuss the process of improving relations with difficult co-workers. What factors (personal or organizational) may make the process a challenge?

5. What are some of the problems caused by employee unresponsiveness toward customers? Have you experienced any of these or others? How did they affect your opinion of the organization?

6. Who benefits from a mentoring relationship? How do the work and communication styles of managers and trainees affect the development of mentoring relationships?

7. What are some of the potentially positive and negative consequences of romantic relationships in the workplace?

Activities

1. Pretend for a moment that you supervise five employees who range from five years younger to seven years older than you. What kinds of personal/work relationships do you believe you would develop with this group?

2. What do you usually do when you encounter a difficult person? Would you react any differently in a work setting?

3. What challenges does each of the following classes of diversity present to workers in modern organizations? Share your opinions with your classmates in a small discussion group.
   a. Older citizens as co-workers
   b. Women as managers
   c. Japanese philosophies stemming from foreign ownership
   d. Mixed-ethnic work teams

4. Many co-workers become frustrated with one another in nonwork settings because of their tendency to "talk shop," or primarily discuss work issues. Spouses and guests are often alienated as well. Can you think of any other negative consequences?

Notes

1. For further reference, see F. M. Jablin, "Superior-Subordinate Communication: The State of the Art," *Psychological Bulletin* 86 (1979): 1201–1222; G. Goldhaber, *Organizational Communication* (Dubuque, Iowa: William C. Brown, 1990); F. Dansereau and S. E. Markham, "Superior-Subordinate Communication: Multiple Levels of Analysis," in F. Jablin et al. (eds.), *Handbook of Communication Science* (Beverly Hills, Calif.: Sage, 1987), pp. 343–388; R. Klauss and R. Bass, *Interpersonal Communication in Organizations* (New York: Academic Press, 1982).

2. W. C. Redding, *Communicating Within the Organization: An Interpretive Review of Theory and Research* (New York: Industrial Communication Council, 1972); T. L. Albrecht, "The Role of Communication in Perceptions of Organizational Climate," in D. Nimmo (ed.), *Communication Yearbook 3* (New Brunswick, N.J.: Transaction Books, 1979), pp. 343–357; Jablin, "Superior-Subordinate Communication."

3. H. P. Sims and C. C. Manz, "Observing Leader Verbal Behavior: Toward Reciprocal Determinism in Leadership Theory," *Journal of Applied Psychology* 69 (1984): 222–232.

4. J. Kouzes and B. Z. Posner, *The Leadership Challenge* (San Francisco: Jossey-Bass, 1987).

5. Ibid., p. 162.

6. Ibid., p. 175.

7. O. C. Brenner, J. Tomkiewicz, and V. E. Schein, "The Relationship Between Sex Role Stereotypes and Requisite Management Characteristics Revisited," *Academy of Management Journal* 32 (1989): 662–669.

8. V. Wheeless and C. Berryman-Fink, "Perception of Women Managers and Their Communicator Competencies," *Communication Quarterly* 33 (1985): 137–147.

9. P. Johnson, "Women and Power: Toward a Theory of Effectiveness," *Journal of Social Issues* 32 (1976): 99–110; B. Ragins, "Power and Gender Congruency Effects in Evaluations of Male and Female Managers," *Journal of Management* 15 (1989): 65–76.

10. Wheeless and Berryman-Fink, "Perception of Women Managers."

11. This outline was partially developed from material in A. J. Di Brin, *Effective*

Business Psychology, 2nd ed. (Reston, Va.: Reston Publishing, 1985); Kouzes and Posner, *The Leadership Challenge.*

12. T. J. Peters and R. H. Waterman, *In Search of Excellence: Lessons from America's Best-Run Companies* (New York: Warner Books, 1982).

13. K. Albrecht, *At America's Service: How Corporations Can Revolutionize the Way They Treat Their Customers* (Homewood, Ill.: Dow Jones–Irwin, 1988).

14. Peters and Waterman, *In Search of Excellence.*

15. Albrecht, *At America's Service.*

16. Dan Finkelman and Tony Goland, "The Case of the Complaining Customer," *Harvard Business Review* May/June 1990: 9–21.

17. This list is adapted from ibid.

18. R. A. Noe, "Women and Mentoring: A Review and Research Agenda," *Academy of Management Review* 13 (1988): 65–78; K. E. Kram, *Mentoring at Work: Development Relationships in Organizational Life* (Glenview, Ill.: Scott, Foresman, 1985); R. J. Burke and C. A. McKeen, "Developing Formal Mentoring Programs in Organizations," *Business Quarterly* 53 (1989): 76–79.

19. R. Kanter, *The Change Masters* (New York: Simon & Schuster, 1984).

20. J. Kotter, *Power and Influence* (New York: Free Press, 1985).

21. Noe, "Women and Mentoring"; T. Daniels and B. Spiker, *Perspectives on Organizational Communication* (Dubuque, Iowa: William C. Brown, 1987); E. A. Fagenson, "The Mentor Advantage Perceived Career/Job Experiences of Protégés vs. Nonprotégés," *Journal of Organizational Behavior* 10 (1989): 309–320.

22. J. Lawrie, "How to Establish a Mentoring Program," *Training and Development Journal* 41 (1987): 25–27.

23. Noe, "Women and Mentoring."

24. Ibid.; Burke and McKeen, "Developing Formal Mentoring Programs."

25. Some of these characteristics come from N. Colwill and M. Pollock, "The Mentor Connection Update," *Business Quarterly* 52 (1987): 16–20.

26. K. E. Kram, "Phases of the Mentor Relationship," *Academy of Management Journal* 12 (1983): 608–625.

27. G. Haight, "Managing Diversity," *Across the Board* (March 1990): 22–29.

28. Noe, "Women and Mentoring."

29. Burke and McKeen, "Developing Formal Mentoring Programs."

30. Noe, "Women and Mentoring."

31. H. Wittemann, "Organizational Romance: Whose Problem Is It?" (Paper presented at the annual meeting of the Western States Communication Association, Salt Lake City, Utah, February 1987).

32. J. P. Dillard and K. I. Miller, "Intimate Relationships in Task Environments," in S. Duck (ed.), *Handbook of Personal Relationships* (Sussex, England: John Wiley, 1988), pp. 449–465.

33. Ibid.

34. J. Dillard and K. Miller, "Intimate Relationships"; R. E. Quinn, "Coping with Cupid: The Formation, Impact, and Management of Romantic Relationships in Organizations," *Administration Science Quarterly* 22 (1977): 30–45; Witteman, "Organizational Romance."

35. Quinn, "Coping with Cupid"; C. Anderson and P. Hunsaker, "Why There's Romance in the Office and Why It's Everyone's Problem," *Personnel* 62 (1985):

57–63; J. P. Dillard and S. M. Broetzman, "Romantic Relationships at Work: Perceived Changes in Job-Related Behaviors as a Function of Participant's Motive, Partner's Motive, and Gender" (Paper presented at the annual meeting of the Western Speech Communication Association, San Diego, California, February 1988).

Chapter 7

*P*rinciples of Interviewing

OBJECTIVES

After working through this chapter, you will be able to:

1. Describe the nature and importance of the interview in business and the professions

2. Identify appropriate goals for the interviewing process

3. Specify effective strategies for preparing for an interview

4. Structure the opening, body, and close of an interview to enhance the achievement of your goals

5. Develop appropriate questions for an interview in terms of meaning, form, and sequence

6. Select effective ways of reacting to the responses of the other party in the interview

7. Manage communication apprehension in a dyadic setting

In the world of business, "as soon as you move one step up from the bottom, your effectiveness depends on your ability to reach others through the spoken word."[1] So said Peter F. Drucker, a management consultant. Although Drucker was not talking specifically about the communication skills involved in interviewing, he might well have been. Indeed, John and Merna Galassi, summarizing sixty years of research on the most important factors in employment interviews, concluded, "Researchers consider communication and interpersonal skills as the single most important set of factors in the interview."[2] Not only are interviewing skills crucial for obtaining jobs; they are equally important for success and promotion once a position has been secured. In a recent research report, Dan Curtis, Jerry Winsor, and Ronald Stephens identified more than thirty studies of employers' needs conducted between 1972 and 1990 that agreed that the skills most valued in the contemporary job market are the ability to communicate and work effectively with other people.[3] Not only do leaders in business and industry articulate this view; they support their beliefs financially. Anthony Carnevale, Leila Gainer, and Janice Villet reported that "employers spend $30 billion on formal training and approximately $180 billion on informal on-the-job training each year" — about the same amount spent for education at the primary, secondary, and college levels.[4] By far the most common type of training is that focused on interpersonal communication skills — more than 90 percent of business organizations provide communication training for their employees.[5]

The Interview

A major target of these significant efforts and expenditures by business and industry is the improvement of interviewing skills. To get a feel for what makes up interviewing skills, let us look at a random sampling of definitions:

◆ "The interview is a form of oral communication involving two parties, at least one of whom has a preconceived and serious purpose, and both of whom speak and listen from time to time."[6]

◆ "We define interviewing as a process of dyadic, relational communication, with a predetermined and serious purpose designed to interchange behavior and involving the asking and answering of questions."[7]

◆ "An interview occurs when there is planned conversation (give-and-take) between two (and, at times, more) people."[8]

◆ "We define an interview as a specialized form of oral, face-to-face communication between people in an interpersonal relationship that is entered into for a specific task related purpose associated with a particular subject matter."[9]

◆ "Here are ten general characteristics of interviews: (1) a serious purpose, (2) planned interaction, (3) oral interaction, (4) face-to-face interaction, (5) dyadic interaction, (6) inquiry and response, (7) objective and subjective information, (8) role differentiation, (9) alternating roles, and (10) multiple measures of success."[10]

◆ "Interview: a form of goal-oriented, dyadic human interaction involving primarily oral/aural communicative behavior."[11]

While emphasizing different features, these definitions share a common emphasis on three defining characteristics of the interview. The interview is a process of planned, dyadic, interactive discourse. Let us explore each of these features briefly.

Planned Discourse

The interview has a purpose beyond the initiation and development of a relationship between the two parties involved in the interview. Even though the interpersonal relationship is important to the interview, at least one of the two parties (sometimes both) has a predetermined goal (e.g., to share information, persuade, solve problems). That goal existed before the start of the interview, thereby allowing for advance planning concerning how best to initiate and conduct the interview.

Dyadic Discourse

In the interview there are *two parties;* there is no third party to act as a mediator or arbiter should the two parties not agree. Although each "party" is typically a single person, there can be more than one person in each party. Thus, for example, in the employment interview, multiple representatives of a firm may interview a job applicant in a "group interview" (or, less commonly, a representative or representatives of a firm may interview multiple applicants simultaneously).

Interactive Discourse

An interview is a dialogue rather than a monologue. It involves the two-way interaction of two parties in which both speak and listen. As a result, the interview requires adaptation by both parties to the verbal and nonverbal messages being exchanged. Although the interview normally occurs face to face, it also can and does take place over the phone or via computer.

Given a basic understanding of the interview as a process of planned, dyadic, interactive discourse, it should be easy to see that a strategic approach to communication can apply very well to interviewing. To illustrate this fact, let us look in on Communication Design, a small advertising studio with multiple clients, and identify a small number of interview possibilities. As we look around the office, we see:

> Young Kim, a recent college graduate, participating in a job interview with the owner, Rena Rae (employment interview)
>
> Andy Garber, the personnel manager, explaining insurance benefits to new employee Sally Jackson (orientation interview)
>
> Account executive Jeanne Kovac gathering information from potential client Larry Wieder, the chief executive officer of Emerald Film (research interview)
>
> Lynda Morris, office manager, conducting an evaluation interview with graphic artist Robert Norton (appraisal interview)
>
> Art director Joe Walther talking with client Serena Tonelli, who is very unhappy with the design of a brochure for the State Arts Council (grievance interview)
>
> Two copywriters, J. D. Wilson and Barbara Epstein, meeting to discuss potential copy for a new advertisement for the international journal *Calligraphy Review* (problem-solving interview)
>
> Alysha Jamal, account executive, attempting to convince Ed Nuttal of Star Manufacturing that it is time to redo the company's full-page advertisement for *Picture Framing Magazine* (persuasive interview)

In each of these examples, the two parties in the interview are striving to achieve goals. They bring information to the interview and increase their knowledge as the interview progresses. They must employ appropriate questioning, responding, and listening skills, and regulate their levels of apprehension. These are general principles that are applicable across all types of interviews, as we illustrate in the next chapter. We begin our discussion of these basic principles with the first component of the model: setting goals.

Goal Setting: Dyadic Communication

Given the wide variety of interviews, there are no universally recognized labels to identify the two parties involved. The most common or general designators are interviewer and interviewee, but in certain situations the parties are more accurately and specifically described as persuader/persuadee, counselor/client, or employer/applicant. In some interviews it is possible to designate one party as carrying the major responsibility (the therapist in a counseling interview, the pollster in a public opinion survey, the persuader in a sales pitch); in a small number of situations these labels become problematic. To illustrate, in a problem-solving interview (e.g.,

Tell me what you really think . . . Market researchers interview customers to gather information about their needs and their reactions to products. Here, a customer responds to questions during a televisied interview.

Communication Design's J. D. Wilson and Barbara Epstein discussing potential copy for an ad), the responsibilities for the interview may be equally shared. Even in the employment interview, it may not always be clear who should have the major responsibility: The employer? The employee? Or either one, depending on the tightness of the job market?

Even where the interviewer and interviewee can be clearly specified, their relationship may not be quite so easy to determine. In fact, the initiation and development of the relationship between the interviewer and interviewee are not the key features of the interview. The interview usually has another, more specific purpose, and goal setting brings this purpose into focus: is the goal of the interview, for example, to gather information, give information, counsel, or persuade? The nature of the purpose then shapes the relationship between the interviewer and interviewee. For example, if you decide that the goal of a particular interview is to gather information, you must then consider what type of relationship between the interviewer and interviewee will facilitate that goal. Without goal setting, you are likely to focus too much attention on interpersonal concerns (e.g., because you want to be friends with the other person, you hesitate to ask provocative but necessary questions) or too little attention (e.g., you ignore nonverbal feedback that the other person does not understand your questions). In either case, your decision to emphasize or deemphasize the interpersonal relationship interferes with the achievement of your goal — gathering information.

With the reasons for engaging in an interview in the foreground, you can move onto the next task: identifying potential barriers to the achievement of the goals of the interview. Such obstacles can include insufficient preparation on the interviewer's part or biases, misperceptions, or preconceived notions about the interviewee that can interfere with the interview. On the interviewee's side, obstacles can take the form of an inability or unwillingness to contribute to the achievement of the interviewer's goals; demographic, social, or psychological factors that detract from the interview; or a negative response to the interviewer.

The setting can also prove to be a hindrance. The time of day or week, location of the interview, and/or seating pattern can diminish the effectiveness of the interview. Of course, careful preparation by the interviewer (and often by the interviewee as well) usually pinpoints these potential hindrances and remedies them. The following list shows possible barriers to effective communication in interviews. One goal common to both the interviewer and the interviewee is to anticipate and minimize these obstacles as much as possible.

- ◆ Competing demands
- ◆ Ego threats
- ◆ Lack of courtesy
- ◆ Trauma

- ◆ Forgetfulness
- ◆ Confusion
- ◆ Jumping to conclusions
- ◆ Distracting subconscious behaviors

Situational Knowledge: Structuring the Interview

Because an interview is produced by the interaction of two parties, its structure is not easily specified in advance. Although each party may prepare in advance, each must be ready to employ the second component of strategic communication — gathering situational knowledge — to maximize the smooth exchange of valuable information during the interview. It is useful to think of an interview in terms of three identifiable parts: the opening moments, the body of the interview, and the closing moments. Each part provides an opportunity for the interviewer and the interviewee to increase their knowledge of each other, the purpose of the interview, and the direction it takes. Although there are no hard-and-fast rules — or time limits — for any of these components, consider the functions they potentially serve.

The Opening

The opening moments of an interview are useful for addressing three issues that may concern the interviewee: credibility (Will I like and can I trust this person?), orientation (What will this interview be about?), and motivation (What will I gain from participating in this interview?). Answers to these questions may be provided by the context of the interview, but that is not always the case. Thus, the interviewer can use these three questions to determine whether it is necessary to address one or more of the issues specifically.

If, for example, the interviewer and interviewee are getting together for the first time, issues of credibility will be important. When this is the case, the interviewer and interviewee are wise to consider and adapt to what Judee Burgoon and her colleagues described as the key principles of impression formation:[12]

1. People develop evaluations of one another from limited external information.

2. First impressions are partly based on the stereotypes held by the perceiver.

3. First impressions are often initially based on outward appearance cues.

4. Initial impressions form a baseline of comparison for subsequent impressions and judgments.

5. Impressions consist of judgments on at least three different levels: physical (e.g., age, gender, race), sociocultural (e.g., socioeconomic status, education level, occupation), and psychological (psychological make-up, temperament, moods).

Given these principles and considering the importance of situational knowledge, when an interviewer meets an interviewee for the first time, both must be sensitive to knowledge exchange based on nonverbal assets and liabilities. The astute interviewee asks herself or himself such questions as: What is an interviewer likely to conclude as a result of my physical appearance, body motion, vocal cues, use of space, and so on? Are there any of these characteristics that I can modify? Do I want to do so? For those elements that cannot be changed, is there anything I can do to moderate their effect?

An interviewer is smart to ask herself or himself similar questions concerning orientation and motivation. Will the interviewee know what the interview is about? If not, how can I provide orientation to the interview? Will the interviewee want to participate in the interview? If the desire to participate is weak, what sources of motivation (e.g., humanitarian appeals,

Employment interviewing can be highly stressful, but the interviewer and interviewee can use a variety of methods to defuse tension. This candidate for a community service job receives information about the position during the orientation segment of the interview.

promises of rewards, fulfillment of expectations, recognition, sympathy, and understanding) can I use to strengthen the interviewee's involvement?

Credibility, orientation, and motivation are, of course, not independent; techniques for achieving one may serve the others as well. As you consider the unique requirements of your situation, you may find one or more of the following common opening techniques applicable:

1. Make a brief statement or rapid summary of the problem, issue, or need. (This is appropriate when the interviewee is vaguely aware of a problem but not well informed on details.)

2. Briefly explain how you happened to learn about the problem, and suggest that the interviewee will want to discuss it. (This avoids the appearance of lecturing or talking down to the interviewee and encourages a spirit of cooperative, objective discussion of a mutual problem.)

3. State an incentive (goal or outcome) desired by the interviewee that may reasonably be expected if the proposal is accepted. (This is potentially the most powerful opening of all but is easily abused — it is frequently too obvious or exaggerated. Avoid sounding like someone

giving a high-pressure "sales pitch," and emphasize honesty and sincerity!)

4. Request the interviewee's advice or assistance on a problem. (This is good when it is sincere. Do not use this technique as a slick gimmick.)

5. State a striking, dramatic fact. (Again, this is a potentially powerful opening, but it can be "corny." This opening must be sincere, logically justified, and related to the interviewee's motivations; it can easily be tied in with incentives. This technique is particularly appropriate when a real emergency exists and when the interviewee is apathetic and must be aroused.)

6. Refer to the interviewee's known position on a given problem situation. (This is the common-ground approach. It is excellent to use when the interviewee has taken a public position or has already asked you to bring in proposals, etc.)

7. Refer to the background (causes, origin, etc.) leading up to the problem (but do not state the problem itself) when the interviewee is fairly familiar with this background. (This is another application of common ground that may be useful when you expect the interviewee to react in a hostile manner when you reveal the purpose of your proposal.)

8. Identify the person who sent you to see the interviewee. (This is appropriate when the interviewee is a stranger and an "entrée" is necessary; it can be used, of course, only when you are a stranger and when the third party is respected by the interviewee.)

9. State the company, organization, or group you represent. (This is appropriate when added prestige is needed or when you have to explain why you are there.)

10. Request a specified, brief period of time (e.g., "ten minutes of your time"). (Note, however, that this opening can be too apologetic. Use it only when necessary; for example, when dealing with an impatient, irritable, or very busy interviewee.)[13]

The Body

Whereas the opening sets the stage for the interview by establishing credibility, orientation, and motivation, it is in the body of the interview that the participants' goals are (or are not) achieved. In developing the body of an interview, the interviewer can choose from a spectrum between two contrasting approaches: directive and nondirective.

With a directive interview, the interviewer controls the purpose, structure, and pacing of the interview. Interviews that lend themselves to a directive approach include public opinion polls, employment interviews, and sales interviews. As an interviewer plans for a directive interview, the choices range from "nonscheduled" to "highly scheduled, standardized."

In a *nonscheduled* interview, the interviewer prepares an interview guide that lists potential topics and subtopics. These topics may or may not

Interact!

This chapter argues that interviewing situations require strong listening skills. Good listening habits help the interviewer to properly evaluate and assess information and to enable her or him to ask proper follow-up or probing questions.

One skill distinguishing effective from ineffective interviewers is the use of probing questions. Probes are used to clarify information in an interviewee's answer ("You mentioned running out of time on the project. Did you mean you need increased support?"), to obtain more information from an incomplete answer ("Were any other factors involved? Can you tell me more about the problem?"), or to assess the interviewee's opinions and attitudes about the factual information presented in a response ("I see we are running a deficit; how do you think it will affect our operations?")

Effective probing questions do not occur automatically. When formulating probes, the interviewer must concentrate on the interviewee's answer to a question and *decide what he or she wants to know next*. In this exercise, you practice probing questions that can improve your success as an interviewer, as well as show you the type of questions you can expect as an interviewee.

Imagine that you are the CEO of a small retail business. You have sent one of your managers to a two-day seminar on improving work relationships, and he or she has just returned. You are interviewing the manager to find out how the class went, what was learned, whether you should send others who work for you to the same class, and so forth. Your goal is to find out as much as possible (in detail) about the seminar.

The class should divide into groups of three for the exercise. One person will be the interviewer, another the interviewee, and the third person an observer. You can repeat the exercise, switching roles so that everyone in the group has a chance to play all of them.

Choose five of the following questions to create an interview schedule.

1. Who attended the seminar?
2. What topics were covered?
3. What presentations were made?
4. How was each day organized?
5. What did you do first?
6. Should any of our other employees attend in the future?
7. Was the seminar well planned?

8. What did you learn that can help our organization?

9. How does our way of doing things compare with others'?

10. What were the general attitudes of the leaders and participants?

11. What did you learn about a) manager-employee relations, b) co-worker relations, c) customer relations, d) mentoring, e) romantic relations in the workplace?

12. What were some new insights you received?

13. What do you think we should do differently with regard to work relationships?

14. How would you compare the seminar to others you have attended?

15. What would you have changed about the seminar?

Take a few minutes to think about your schedule before beginning the interview. The interviewee responds to each question realistically; i.e., giving only information that is asked for. It is the interviewer's responsibility to follow up with probes in order to gather more information.

Based on the interviewee's response to each question, the interviewer can use probing questions to clarify, seek more information, or discern opinions and attitudes. Specific probing questions cannot be framed in advance because they depend completely on what response you get to the general question.

The observer listens to the questions and answers and evaluates the appropriateness and effectiveness of each probing question that is asked. The evaluation can be based on the quantity and quality of information gathered by the interviewer and noted by the observer. The observer should give feedback (such as any unanswered questions, which probes seemed particularly effective in leading into new topics or completing a thought, probes that were not effective for some reason) to both parties at the end of the exercise.

After everyone has had a chance to work through the exercise, consider the following questions:

1. Do you believe asking probing questions in an interview is difficult? Why or why not?

2. What communication skills are necessary for good probing questions?

3. Based on the probing questions you heard in the exercise, what were some characteristics of effective versus ineffective ones?

4. What factors made some probing questions more effective than others in this exercise? What do you need to concentrate on to be more effective in probing?

be covered in the actual interview and may or may not be covered in the listed order. What actually happens in the interview depends more on the interviewee's responses than on the interviewer's interview guide.

In a *moderately scheduled* interview, the interviewer prepares an interview guide that includes all major questions, with possible probe questions under each major question. The questions are asked in the order they are listed, but the probes may or may not be used.

In a *highly scheduled* interview, the interviewer prepares an interview schedule that contains all the questions that will be asked (including all probe questions) and the exact wording that will be used with each interviewee. Every interviewee receives exactly the same questions in exactly the same order.

In a *highly scheduled, standardized* interview, the interviewer prepares an interview schedule that includes not only all questions but also all answer options. The answer options normally ask the interviewee to select one of a number of alternatives (e.g., "Do you intend to vote in the school board election?" "Yes," "no," "undecided").

In contrast to a directive interview, in a nondirective interview the interviewer chooses to cede control of the purpose, structure, and pacing of the interview to the interviewee. This is the option typically chosen for such interviews as problem solving and counseling. In such situations, the interviewer either does not have enough knowledge to structure the interview or feels that more reliable and valid responses will be gained by allowing the interviewee greater latitude to participate in structuring the interview. In a counseling interview, for example, the interviewee may be asked to describe the nature of the problem to be confronted and possible solutions to be considered. The interviewer, instead of executing a structure planned in advance of the interview, may react to the needs and thoughts developed by the interviewee during the interview, incorporating situational knowledge as revealed by the interviewee.

The choice of a directive or nondirective approach depends in large part on the interviewer's situational knowledge (which has increased during the opening of the interview). Once the decision has been made, it affects greatly the amount and kind of situational knowledge that may be discovered and employed in the remainder of the interview.

The Closing

Effectively closing an interview requires as much careful thought as does opening an interview. Even though it may be tempting to quickly move the process to a close once the purpose of the interview has been achieved, an abrupt ending can do long-term damage to the relationship between the two parties. Thus, it is important to think through the functions of a closing and the nonverbal and verbal strategies that can fulfill these functions.

Mark Knapp, Rod Hart, Gus Friedrich, and Gary Shulman studied the functions and norms involved when people take leave of each other.[14] Within the interviewing context, these functions can be described as concluding (signaling the end of the interview), summarizing (recapitulating the substantive portion of the interaction), and supporting (expressing pleasure with the interaction and projecting what will happen next). These functions can be accomplished verbally as well as nonverbally (e.g., breaking eye contact, straightening up in your seat, leaning toward the exit, smiling, rapid nodding, looking at the clock). The following closing techniques capitalize on both verbal and nonverbal strategies:

1. Offer to answer questions. Be sincere in the desire to answer questions, and give the interviewee adequate time to ask. Do not give a quick answer to one question and then end the interview.

2. Use clearinghouse questions, such as "Does that cover everything?" The clearinghouse question allows you to determine if you have covered all topics or answered all the interviewee's questions. It can be an effective closing if your request is perceived not as a formality or an attempt to be sociable but as an honest effort to ferret out questions, information, or areas of concern not discussed adequately.

3. Declare the completion of the purpose or task. The four-letter word *well* probably brings more interviews to a close than any other phrase. When people hear it, they automatically assume the end is near and prepare for leave taking.

4. Make personal inquiries. Personal inquiries are pleasant ways to end interviews, but they must be sincere and show genuine interest in the interviewee. Interviewees judge sincerity by the way interviewers listen and react verbally and nonverbally.

5. Signal that time is up. This closing is most effective when a time limit has been announced or agreed on in the opening. Be tactful in calling time, and try not to give the impression that you are moving the interviewee along an assembly line.

6. Explain the reason for the close. Tell why you must close the interview, and be sure the justifications are real. If an interviewee thinks you are giving phony excuses, any future interactions will be strained.

7. Express appreciation or satisfaction. A note of appreciation or satisfaction is a common closing because interviewers usually have received something — information, help, a sale, a story, and so on.

8. Exhibit concern. Expressions of concern for the interviewee's health, welfare, or future are effective if they are sincere, not merely habitual.

9. Plan for the next meeting. It is often appropriate to arrange the next interview or reveal what will happen next, including date, time, place, topic, content, and purpose.

10. Summarize the interview. A summary is a common closing for informational, appraisal, counseling, and sales interviews. Summaries may

repeat important information, stages, and agreements or verify accuracy or agreement.[15]

Communication Competence: Asking Effective Questions

In addition to setting interview goals and gathering situational knowledge before and during the interview, both the interviewer and interviewee need to be able to formulate effective and appropriate questions and responses. The ability to do so — and to employ verbal, nonverbal, and listening skills to maximize the flow of information — comprises the third component of the model of strategic communication.

In *The Art of Asking Questions,* Stanley Payne made the important point that asking the right question in the right way is central to the success of the interview process.[16] Doing so requires that all participants in the interview master three important characteristics of questioning: the question's meaning, form, and sequence.

Question Meaning

A favorite saying of computer junkies is "garbage in, garbage out" — that is, what you get out of the computer can be no better than what you put in. Because this principle applies just as strongly to questions and answers in the interview, consider the wording of each question to be asked in terms of clarity, relevance, and bias for the person expected to answer it.

Clarity.   The first concern of the questioner should be whether the respondent will understand the words used in the question. To maximize the possibility of a positive response to the question, Payne suggested a number of strategies:[17]

1.   Start by making sure you have a clear understanding of the issue yourself. This means defining the issue precisely regardless of the general understandability of the words. To achieve this, ask yourself the stock journalistic questions: who, what, when, where, and how?

2.   Once you have stated the issue precisely, turn to the dictionary to determine whether the question can be restated more directly or more simply. Look up each word, asking four questions about it: Does it mean what you intend? Does it have other meanings? If so, does the context make the intended meaning clear? Is a simpler word or phrase suggested (either in the dictionary or in a thesaurus)?

3.   Try to keep questions somewhere in the neighborhood of twenty words or less. A study that compared "tight" questions with "loose"

questions found that, on average, loose questions were one and one-half times as long as tight ones — thirty-one words to twenty-two words.[18]

4. Phrase questions positively. Research indicates that questions that are understood when stated in a clear, positive manner are highly confusing when stated negatively.

Relevance.   Writing in *Tide* magazine, March 14, 1947, Sam Gill reported the results of a public opinion poll in which he asked respondents "Which of the following statements most closely coincides with your opinion of the Metallic Metals Act? (a) It would be a good move on the part of the United States. (b) It would be a good thing but should be left to individual states. (c) It is all right for foreign countries but should not be required here. (d) It is of no value at all." Seventy percent of the respondents chose one of the alternatives; 30 percent said they had no opinion.[19] The surprising feature of this poll was that the Metallic Metals Act was a fictitious issue — a creation of Sam Gill's imagination.

The penchant of many respondents to answer questions that have no meaning for them has been demonstrated many times since 1947. George F. Bishop and three colleagues asked 467 people eighteen and older in Hamilton County, which includes Cincinnati, Ohio, the following question: "Some people say that the Public Affairs Act should be repealed. Do you agree or disagree with this idea?" Even though the Public Affairs Act was fictitious, a full one-third of the group firmly gave an opinion. The people who were more likely to volunteer opinions were those with the least education.[20]

Given this propensity of respondents to answer meaningless questions, then, it is not enough to develop questions that are clear and understandable for the respondents; it is equally necessary to ensure the relevance of questions for these respondents. Two strategies for accomplishing this are the use of pretests and filter questions. In pretesting, a small number of people who are representative of the eventual respondents are asked the target questions that will be included in the interview and asked what they think the questions mean. Proper pretesting is an excellent way of exposing meaningless questions in advance of the interview. The second strategy, filter questioning, recommended by George Gallup in his "quintamensional" plan (which we discuss shortly), asks respondents to define terms or give examples before answering the question as a means of sorting out people for whom the target question would be meaningless.

Bias.   Once you have phrased a clear and relevant question, the last task is to locate unintended potential bias. The issue here concerns whether the wording of the question will lead some respondents to give different answers than they would give to a different wording of what was intended to be the same question. When a question provides no hint to the respondent concerning the expected response, it is labeled *neutral;* when it either subtly or blatantly clues the respondent concerning the expected response, it is labeled *directed.* Directed questions can be either leading or loaded. When the cue is subtle (e.g., "You like ice cream, don't you?"), the question is labeled *leading;* when the cue is blatant (e.g., "Are you a women's libber?" or "When was the last time you got drunk?"), the question is called *loaded.* Loaded questions usually involve the use of emotionally charged words or name calling ("women's libber") or the asking of one question that is really two questions ("Have you ever been drunk?" "When was the last time you were drunk?").

There are many ways in which questions can produce unintended bias. One of the most commonly recognized forms of bias is that which appeals to the very human desire for prestige. Probably the strongest and most common prestige influence in interviews is something we have already discussed — the feeling of respondents that they should have an opinion. The prestige influence often operates in a very subtle fashion, and its effects are sometimes unexpected. A most straightforward question such as "Do you own a computer?" can, for example, be loaded with prestige.

The words used to state alternatives have an effect on the proportion of middle-ground and undecided replies. The less extreme the choices are, the more willing people are to report a commitment. For example, people who are asked if they prefer/do not prefer an idea are more likely to express a commitment than are people asked whether they would vote for or vote against the same idea.

Given a list of numbers, respondents are prone to choose those near the middle of the list. Therefore, when you use a list of numbers as a test of knowledge, it may be a wise precaution to put the correct figure first or last.

Given a list of ideas or statements, respondents tend to select the statements at the extreme position rather than those near the middle, and they favor the top of the list more than the bottom. When you ask respondents to select from a list of ideas, therefore, rotate the order of the ideas for different respondents.

Questions that emphasize the existing situation take advantage of a strong disposition to accept things as they are. Thus, such phrases as "as it is now," "or should it be changed," or "as you know" are likely to lead to higher approval than the idea would receive without this advantage.

When there are two alternatives, it is safer to state both choices rather than one. For example, the following versions of the "same" question are likely to produce different results: Do you think the United States should allow instant press coverage of wars? Do you think the United States should forbid instant press coverage of wars? Do you think the United States should allow or forbid instant press coverage of wars? Additionally, the list of alternatives should be exhaustive if it intends to cover the range of possibilities. Otherwise, an idea may be underplayed not because it ranks low in the respondent's thinking but because the questioner either overlooked it or happened to consider it insignificant.

It is normally best to avoid all-inclusive or all-exhaustive words such as "all," "always," "never," and "none" because such words usually produce an overstatement. Many people will go along with the idea, accepting it as a form of literary license, but purists may either refuse to give an opinion or choose the other side in protest.

The questioner must realize that the very act of bringing up some questions is a form of bias. In addition, a response to a question does not necessarily report what the respondent is thinking; more often, it captures what the respondent would think if asked the question.

Our discussion of bias in question wording to this point could easily be taken as a blanket prohibition against directed questions (either leading or loaded). Such is not the case. Although they should never be used unintentionally, there are circumstances in which these questions can be put to good use. The interviewer may, for example, be dealing with an ego-threatening topic and may wish to convey to the respondent that the response will not shock the interviewer. Thus, a question such as "When was the last time you cheated on a test?" may under certain circumstances produce a more truthful answer than a neutral strategy for asking the same question. There are also circumstances in which the interviewer may wish to use directed questions to explore how the respondent reacts to stress. The key point, then, is to recognize the difference between neutral and directed questions and to use directed questions only when they facilitate an unbiased response from the respondent.

Question Form

In addition to considering the meaning of a question, the questioner must also consider the form. It is possible to identify numerous characteristics of questions, but here we restrict our treatment to two dimensions: open/closed and primary/secondary.[21] Each and every question in an interview can be characterized in terms of both dimensions.

Open/closed. The distinction between open and closed questions can be drawn in at least two ways: form of response and latitude of response. For form of response, open questions ask respondents to answer in their own words from alternatives they construct (e.g., "If you could create your ideal job, what would it be?"). Closed questions ask respondents to select from a list of offered alternatives (e.g., Answer "yes," "no," or "no opinion" to the following question: "Do you believe that women should be allowed to be in combat roles in the military?").

Distinguishing open and closed questions on the basis of latitude of response requires more judgment on the part of the person making the discriminations. In this view, the most closed question is a question that typically asks respondents for a "yes" or "no" answer (e.g., "Did you vote in the last election?"). At the other end of the spectrum are questions that allow respondents almost unlimited freedom in terms of the amount and kind of response (e.g., "What do you believe are the most important problems facing the United States today?").

In terms of open versus closed questions, there are advantages and disadvantages to questions that fall at either end of the continuum. Open questions allow respondents the greatest amount of freedom and are thus useful when the questioner is initiating a topic, knows less about the topic than the respondents, or wants to get an uninfluenced view of respondent thinking. Because there are normally no incorrect responses to an open question, respondents are also less likely to be threatened by it. Such advantages are, of course, purchased at the cost of increased time per interview and answers that are difficult to summarize and compare. Thus, when the situation requires greater control by the questioner or when the questioner plans to compare the responses of numerous respondents, questions of a closed nature are normally the better choice.

Primary/secondary.   Primary questions introduce new topics or areas of questioning; secondary questions develop topics or areas introduced by primary questions. You can start an area of questioning by asking, for example, "If you could create the ideal job for yourself, what would it be?" and then follow up or probe with a number of secondary questions (e.g., "Where would the job be located?" "Do you think, then, that it is important to work with like-minded individuals?" "Can you tell me more?").

Although a secondary question can assume many forms, among the more useful are:

1.   Clarification: directly requesting more information about a response (e.g., "Could you tell me a little more about the kind of person you would like to work for?")

2.   Elaboration: directly requesting an extension of a response (e.g., "Are there any other features of location that you would consider important?")

3.   Paraphrase: putting the response in the questioner's language in an attempt to establish understanding (e.g., "Let's see if I've understood what you're saying — do you consider the type of people you work with more important than salary and benefits?")

4.   Silence: waiting without speaking for the respondent to begin or resume speaking

5. Encouragement: using brief sounds and phrases that indicate attentiveness to, and interest in, what the respondent is saying (e.g., "Uh
   huh," "I see," "That's interesting," "Good," and "Yes, I understand")

6. Mirror: repeating the response using the respondent's language (e.g.,
   "You say, then, that it is important to you to be located near a
   university")

7. Summary: summarizing several previous responses and seeking con-
   firmation of the correctness of the summary (e.g., "Let's see if I've
   got it: your ideal job involves an appreciative boss, supportive colleagues, interesting work, and living in a large metropolitan area")

8. Clearinghouse: asking if you have elicited all the important or available information (e.g., "Have I asked everything that I should have
   asked?")

Question Sequence

Once the interviewer is sure that questions are clear, relevant, and unbiased
for the respondent (meaning) and that issues related to choices between
open/closed and primary/secondary questions (form) have been resolved,
he or she then considers the manner in which questions can be best sequenced to develop the topics of an interview. A common way of thinking
about the sequencing of questions looks at three organizational patterns:
funnel, inverted funnel, and tunnel.

Funnel. With a funnel sequence, the questioner starts with broad, open
questions and moves toward narrower, closed questions — hence the label
funnel (an object that is broad at the top and narrow at the bottom). An
interviewer interested in exploring a personnel manager's view of how best
to conduct a job interview, for example, can use a funnel sequence such as
the following:

1. Can you tell me about the experiences you've had conducting job
   interviews?

2. How do you prepare for a job interview?

3. What are some of the strategies that work for you during the actual
   interview?

4. What kinds of questions do you ask the applicant? Is there any special sequence to these questions?

5. How much of the talking do you do in an employment interview?

6. Do you ask applicants how they developed an interest in the job?

7. Do you ever worry about asking applicants an illegal question?

As this example illustrates, the funnel sequence is an excellent choice for situations in which the interviewee has more knowledge on a topic than the interviewer does. In such situations, a funnel sequence allows the interviewee to begin talking about an area in an unbiased, nonthreatening way — thus opening up avenues that the interviewer can then explore with narrower secondary questions that probe for clarification and elaboration.

Inverted funnel.   The inverted funnel sequence turns the funnel sequence upside down. That is, it begins the questioning process with a closed, perhaps bipolar, question and gradually moves toward broad, open questions. For example, assume you are exploring the use of computers in a small business organization. You can, for example, ask the owner a sequence of questions such as:

1. Do you use a computer in your business?
2. What is the brand of your computer?
3. What kinds of software do you use?
4. What are the major functions that you use a computer to perform?
5. What kind of training have you and others in your organization received on computer use?
6. How central is the use of computers to the success of your business?
7. Is there anything else you can tell me about the use of computers in your organization?

The inverted funnel sequence assumes that the interviewer has enough information about the topic and the interviewee to frame specific, narrow questions. It is a useful sequence when the interviewee's memory requires focusing — a series of closed questions can jog the interviewee's memory on the topic and provide the motivation to respond to more open questions. This can be especially true when the topic involves an unpleasant event or when the interviewee may feel otherwise threatened or inadequate to comment on the topic.

Tunnel.   The tunnel sequence continues the visual metaphor — that is, it involves a series of questions at a similar level of openness or closedness. Most frequently, the response level is at the closed end of the continuum, and the interviewer asks of a number of people a series of yes-no and multiple-choice questions. Because responses to open questions are difficult to replicate, code, tabulate, and analyze, interviewers who ask questions of more than one person and then summarize the results typically ask closed, rather than open, questions. An example follows.

Use the following scale (VF = very frequently, F = frequently, O = occasionally, R = rarely, and N = never) to indicate how often you have participated in the following types of interviews:

Employment	VF	F	O	R	N
Information giving	VF	F	O	R	N
Information gathering	VF	F	O	R	N
Disciplinary	VF	F	O	R	N
Appraisal	VF	F	O	R	N
Problem solving	VF	F	O	R	N
Persuasive	VF	F	O	R	N

Special purpose. The three sequences (funnel, inverted funnel, and tunnel) can be put together in various combinations within an interview. Thus, an interviewer may start with a funnel sequence, develop the next two topics with a tunnel, and conclude with an inverted funnel.

There are also sequences that cannot be described by any of the three labels. Perhaps the best known of these is one developed by George Gallup for use when conducting public opinion polls aimed at determining intensity of opinions and attitudes. Labeled the *quintamensional plan,* it comprises a five-step process:[22]

1. Awareness of the topic is first ascertained by a free-answer, knowledge question (sometimes labeled a filter question): "What, if anything, do you know about the use of computer conferences for problem solving in business?"

2. Uninfluenced attitudes on the subject are next developed in a free-answer question: "What do you perceive to be the advantages and disadvantages of using computer conferences for business problem solving?"

3. Specific attitudes are then elicited through a two-way or a multiple-choice question: "Do you approve or disapprove of the use of computer conferences for problem solving in business?"

4. Reasoning behind the attitudes follows in a free-answer, reason question: "Why do you feel this way?"

5. Intensity of feeling comes last in the form of an intensity question: "How strongly do you feel about this: strongly, very strongly, or 100 percent committed?"

Responding and Providing Feedback

When it comes to the reaction phases of the interview, the interviewer can benefit from the information gleaned by Carl Rogers in a series of research studies concerning how people communicate with each other in face-to-face situations.[23] He found that when one person reacts to what another has said, 80 percent of all responses can be classified into five categories. The first category, *evaluative,* is made up of responses that indicate that the interviewer has judged the relative goodness, appropriateness, effectiveness, or rightness of the interviewee's response; the interviewer in some way implies what the interviewee might or ought to do. In the *interpretative,* or second category, responses indicate that the interviewer's intent is to teach or tell the interviewee what the response means, how the interviewee really feels; the interviewer either obviously or subtly implies what the interviewee might or ought to think. In the third, *supportive* category, responses indicate that the interviewer's intent is to reassure, pacify, or reduce the interviewee's intensity of feeling; the interviewer implies that it is either appropriate or not necessary for the interviewee to feel as she or he does. The fourth category, *probing,* includes responses that indicate that the interviewer's intent is to seek further information or provoke further discussion. In the *understanding,* or fifth, category, responses indicate that the interviewer's intent is only to find out whether he or she correctly understands what the interviewee is saying.[24]

To illustrate Rogers's categories, consider the following situation:

Interviewer: "How do you go about motivating employees?"

Interviewee: "Well, that varies with the employee. For some, rewards are intrinsic to the job itself — things like the satisfaction of knowing they are doing a good job. For others, motivators are more extrinsic — things like pay, benefits, vacation. . . ."

Evaluative response: "That doesn't seem like a very practical way of thinking to me. How can you get any work out of employees if you spoil them?"

Interpretative response: "I guess that means that you think you need to be fair but firm with your employees. You find out what motivates them but make sure they understand your expectations for job performance."

Supportive response: "I've noticed the same things where I work. Some people are intrinsically motivated; others, extrinsically."

Probing response: "What are some of the best ways to motivate employees who are motivated extrinsically?"

Understanding response: "So the first step is to find out if the employee is intrinsically or extrinsically motivated."

Carl Rogers discovered that people in a wide variety of settings use the five alternatives in the following order of frequency (from most to least): evaluative, interpretative, supportive, probing, and understanding. He also discovered that if a person uses one category of response as much as 40 percent of the time, others will see that person as always responding that way.

The message of Rogers's research is not that a person should prefer (or avoid) one type of response in preference to another. All five types of response are useful to an interviewer. Overuse and/or underuse of a category, however, or a failure to think through the relevance of a category for a specific situation may well be dysfunctional. Thus, an interviewer should know how to produce all five types of responses and when they are appropriate. In many situations it may be best to start with probing and understanding responses before moving to evaluative and interpretative ones.

Anxiety Management: Interviewer and Interviewee

Interviewing is a source of communication anxiety for many reasons. As you recall from Chapter 2, anxiety is "situational" for many people. In other words, some people may be more anxious in specific settings than others or may find that their normal levels of communication apprehension are heightened by such factors as being in a new setting, speaking to an unfamiliar person, being the focus of attention, or having important decisions or outcomes rest on the success of their communication. Interviewing can be a source of many of these anxieties, both for the interviewer and the interviewee.

A competent interviewer can take steps to ensure that neither party's apprehension undermines the goals of the interview or damages the interaction between interviewer and interviewee. The following guidelines for interviewers can help defuse tension inherent in interview situations and put the interviewee at ease.

1. *Be prepared.* Know the specific purpose and goal of the interview, and review it for the interviewee at the very beginning of the time period. Plan questions in advance, and ensure that the interview is long enough to accommodate all of them without rushing the interviewee.

2. *Listen well.* Give appropriate and direct responses and use question forms and sequences discussed earlier in the chapter to gather additional information. Show sincere attention by nodding or leaning forward. Suppress distracting gestures such as tapping, crossing or uncrossing legs, or shifting in the chair, which may unsettle the interviewee.

3. *Treat the interviewee as an equal.* Set up the interview so that both parties have equal access to each other. Do not slouch behind an imposing desk or have the interviewee stand while you remain seated.

4. *Be personable, not personal.* Maintain a friendly demeanor, but do not become distracted by or comment on the interviewee's appearance, speech patterns, or gestures, which may cause extreme self-

consciousness for the interviewee. Apart from warm-up small talk, keep all questions and responses targeted to the interview goal.

5. *Respond to nonverbal as well as verbal cues.* Offer clarification if the interviewee appears worried or confused. Employ supportive questions to offset the interviewee's anxiety. Seek further clarification if nonverbal gestures such as a furrowed brow or a shrug indicate the interviewee has more to say but is too nervous or unsure to do so.

6. *Show respect for the interviewee.* Do not ask demeaning or belittling questions, lose your temper, use threatening or offensive language, listen halfheartedly, or attempt to intimidate the interviewee.

Nervousness is natural and often productive: the tension of an interview can charge a performance and make the experience more dynamic. Nevertheless, uncontrolled apprehension in an interviewee can make the interviewer's job more difficult and negatively influence the interviewer's responses. If you are the interviewee, attention to the following points can aid you in adjusting your level of apprehension so that it improves, rather than undermines, your performance.

1. *Practice possible responses before the interview.* If you know what the interviewer is likely to ask, work in advance on giving competent responses to those questions. For example, if you are preparing for an orientation interview, make a list of the major points you would like to know about the organization. If you are participating in a research interview, be sure that you have gathered and reviewed the appropriate data. These are just two examples; in the next chapter, we discuss specific questions to expect in employment, appraisal, disciplinary, and media interviews.

2. *Concentrate on what you have to say.* Focus on both the question at hand and the "big picture" — that is, how the interview furthers organizational goals. Keep the interview in perspective — it is unlikely to make or break your career.

3. *Listen carefully to questions.* Do not respond until you have heard the complete question and thought about it carefully. Is it a funneled question, narrowing in on a particular area? Is it closed or open? Primary or secondary? The questions themselves can reveal much about the interviewer's goals and the direction the interview is taking. This knowledge can help to put you at ease.

4. *Mentally review and summarize your responses* before beginning to speak. Do not blurt out the first thing that comes to mind. Take time to pause, collect your thoughts, and then reply.

Remember, the interviewer requested a meeting with you because she or he believed you were worthy of her or his time — and you are! Anxiety is not a devastating problem; it is just one more factor that can be anticipated and prepared for to ensure that the interview is successful. Both interviewers and interviewees can benefit from taking steps to defuse the apprehension of an interview.

Summary

This chapter covered basic principles of interviewing that apply generally to all dyadic communication. The interview is a process of planned, dyadic, interactive discourse. Goals for interviewers may include gathering information, solving problems, persuading, counseling, or giving information. Preparation and cooperation by the interviewer and interviewee are essential to the achievement of any of these goals.

Most interviews follow a basic three-part structure that is made up of the opening, the body, and the closing. In each of these parts, the interviewer and the interviewee use verbal cues and nonverbal impressions to increase their knowledge of the situation and respond more accurately to each other.

Communication competence in interviews comprises the ability to ask meaningful questions, phrased appropriately, in an effective sequence. Questions should be clear, relevant, and unbiased. They may take either an open form (respondents answer in their own words) or a closed form (respondents choose from a set of offered alternatives), and they may be classified as primary or secondary. Primary questions introduce new topics; secondary questions develop topics introduced by primary questions.

Questions can be sequenced in funnel, inverted funnel, or tunnel patterns. A funnel sequence moves from broad questions to specific, closed questions. An inverted funnel sequence begins with a closed question and moves toward open questions. The tunnel sequence includes a set of questions at the same level of openness or closedness.

The interviewer's responses can indicate a range of intentions and implications. People tend to use evaluative and interpretive responses most frequently. Overuse or underuse of one type of response can skew the interviewee's perception of the interviewer in a negative direction.

Anxiety is a common element in interview situations. It can affect the interviewer, the interviewee, and the success of the interaction. Anxiety can be controlled through conscious effort on the part of both the interviewer and the interviewee to be prepared, listen well, and communicate clearly and considerately. In the next chapter, we apply these basic principles to a variety of interviews that occur frequently in business and professional settings.

Discussion

1. What are the three distinguishing features of an interview? How does each affect the nature of communication during an interview?

2. What are some considerations for the interviewer in setting goals for an interview? How might the time and setting affect the outcome of the interview?

3. How is the situational knowledge element of an interview (including credibility of the interviewer, first impressions of both interviewer and interviewee, knowledge level of the interviewee, sources of motivation for the interviewee) developed during the opening section of the interview?

4. Describe the differences among nonscheduled, moderately scheduled, highly scheduled, and highly scheduled, standardized interviews. In which situations would an interviewer most likely use a directive interview? A nondirective interview?

5. What makes an effective question? Be sure to discuss the importance of relevance, clarity, and avoidance of potential bias in the formulation of meaningful questions.

6. What are some ways that bias can unintentionally be introduced in a question? How can they be avoided? When is it acceptable to use a biased question?

7. What are the differences between open and closed, and primary and secondary, questions?

8. Discuss the funnel, inverted funnel, and tunnel sequences for questioning. Which sequence would be most appropriate in the following situations: an interviewer interested in finding out the daily routine of a communications manager; a market researcher exploring many customers' reactions to a new product; a supervisor interviewing an employee to determine the success of a computer-training seminar?

9. Discuss the five categories of response described in the chapter. Why is it important to be able to employ all five types of responses?

Activities

1. Construct a series of questions you would ask in the *opening* portion of the following types of interviews:
   a. To obtain information from a county official about building permits for a report you have been assigned to deliver to senior management
   b. To write a biography of a longtime employee for a special presentation at her retirement party

    c. To counsel a subordinate about a problem he or she is having keeping his or her business expenses within budget guidelines

2. How does the nature of directive versus nondirective interviewing seem to match your own communication tendencies? Share your answer with your classmates.

3. With a partner, attempt to conduct an interview using *only* open or closed questions. How successful were you in gathering appropriate, useful, and detailed information? Was the experience frustrating? Why?

4. Select an important social topic that is worthy of a public opinion poll. Use the quintamensional plan discussed in this chapter, and devise appropriate interview questions for the poll.

Notes

1. Peter F. Drucker, "How to be an Employee," *Fortune* (May 1952). Reprinted in N. B. Sighand and D. N. Bateman, *Communicating in Business* (Glenview, Ill.: Scott, Foresman, 1981), p. 454.

2. J. P. Galassi and M. Galassi, "Preparing Individuals for Job Interviews: Suggestions from more than 60 Years of Research," *Personnel and Guidance Journal* 57 (1978): 188–192.

3. D. B. Curtis, J. L. Winsor, and R. D. Stephens, "National Preferences in Business and Communication Education," *Communication Education* 38 (1989): 6–14.

4. A. P. Carnevale, L. J. Gainer, and J. Villet, *Training in America: The Organization and Strategic Role of Training* (San Francisco: Jossey-Bass, 1990).

5. P. Page and S. Perelman, *Basic Skills and Employment: An Employer Survey* (University of Wisconsin System, Madison, Wis. Interagency Basic Skills Project, 1980).

6. R. S. Goyer, W. C. Redding, and J. T. Rickey, *Interviewing Principles and Techniques: A Project Text,* rev. ed. (Dubuque, Iowa: William C. Brown, 1968), p. 6.

7. C. J. Stewart and W. B. Cash, Jr., *Interviewing: Principles and Practices,* 6th ed. (Dubuque, Iowa: William C. Brown, 1991), p. 3.

8. G. T. Hunt and W. F. Eadie, *Interviewing: A Communication Approach* (New York: Holt, Rinehart & Winston, 1987), p. 4.

9. C. W. Downs, G. P. Smeyak, and E. Martin, *Professional Interviewing* (New York: Harper & Row, 1980), p. 5.

10. W. C. Donaghy, *The Interview: Skills and Applications* (Glenville, Ill.: Scott, Foresman, 1984), p. 2.

11. R. S. Goyer and M. Z. Sincoff, *Interviewing Methods* (Dubuque, Iowa: Kendall/ Hunt Publishing, 1977), p. 2.

12. Adapted from J. K. Burgoon, D. B. Buller, and W. G. Woodall, *Nonverbal Communication: The Unspoken Dialogue* (New York: Harper & Row, 1989), pp. 221–224.

13. This is a slightly modified version of Goyer, Redding, and Rickey, *Interviewing Principles,* p. 10.

14. M. L. Knapp, R. P. Hart, G. W. Friedrich, and G. M. Shulman, "The Rhetoric of Goodbye: Verbal and Nonverbal Correlates of Human Leave-Taking," *Communication Monographs* 40 (1973): 182–198.

15. Stewart and Cash, *Interviewing,* pp. 48–49.

16. S. L. Payne, *The Art of Asking Questions* (Princeton, N.J.: Princeton University Press, 1951).

17. S. L. Payne, "Thoughts About Meaningless Questions," *Public Opinion Quarterly* 14 (1950): 687.

18. S. L. Payne, "Case Study in Question Complexity," *Public Opinion Quarterly* (Winter 1949–1950): 653.

19. S. L. Payne, *The Art of Asking Questions,* pp. 17–18.

20. George F. Bishop in C. T. Cory, "Newsline," *Psychology Today* (November 1979): 21.

21. Stewart and Cash, *Interviewing.*

22. G. Gallup, "The Quintamensional Plan of Question Design," *Public Opinion Quarterly* 11 (1947): 385.

23. Rogers's research is discussed in D. W. Johnson, *Reaching Out: Interpersonal Effectiveness and Self-Actualization* (Englewood Cliffs, N.J.: Prentice-Hall, 1972), pp. 117–140.

24. This is paraphrased from ibid., p. 125.

Chapter 8

*I*nterviews in Business Settings

OBJECTIVES

After working through this chapter, you will be able to:

1. Understand the roles and responsibilities of an employment interviewer and interviewee

2. Prepare for and participate in an employment interview

3. Understand the importance of appraisal interviews

4. Conduct an effective appraisal interview

5. Explain the concept of progressive discipline and elements of a disciplinary interview

6. Describe the purposes and types of media interviews

The last chapter introduced you to the principles and procedures that constitute the interviewing process, including the importance of goals and situational knowledge for structuring the interview, the use of questioning techniques, appropriate reactions, and responses, and the handling of communication anxiety in a dyadic setting. In this chapter we apply these basic skills to a variety of business and professional interviewing situations.

Our first focus is on selection or employment interviews, which are likely to be of immediate importance to you, whether you are actively job hunting, considering the possibilities for summer or part-time employment, or anticipating your next move after graduation. Once you are established in your career, you will probably take part in selection interviews for hiring employees for your organization. Next, we cover appraisal interviews, which are vital to maintaining strong and positive manager-employee relations, and disciplinary interviews, which serve to "troubleshoot" the organization and prevent work problems from getting out of hand. Last, we discuss an increasingly important and frequent setting, the media interview. As you will observe, the skills and techniques you learned in the last chapter are applicable to each of these interviewing contexts. The focus in this chapter is on using those skills to achieve the goals specific to each of these settings.

Employment Interviews

There is an old saying that "your education, experience, and preparation will get you the interview, but it is your performance in the interview that will get you the job." In other words, there are dozens of other candidates with similar experience and education who will also get a chance to interview with the companies in which you are interested. It is the interview itself that will separate you from the pack.

Employment interviewing is probably the one work experience that everyone in the work force has in common. If you have gone through a job interview and have felt it was the most stressful event of your life, you are not alone. Most people are particularly anxious in this communication setting simply because the stakes are high. Your future and career may appear to depend in part on a successful job interview. Even interviewers are likely to be nervous — the success of their organization or department depends on their choosing correctly among a number of candidates, many of whom appear to be equally qualified — a difficult decision.

Although selection interviews vary in their sophistication, comprehensiveness, and formality, interviewers all have at least one goal in common: to select the best possible person from the available pool of applicants. Of equal importance in the interview is the interviewee's ability to sell the interviewer on his or her value to the organization and ensure that the job is one the interviewee is qualified to handle and will satisfy him or her.

Both the interviewer and the interviewee have responsibilities in the employment interview. As an interviewee, you will need a thorough knowledge of interviewing to successfully land a job. By understanding the responsibilities of job interviewers, you gain situational knowledge that can improve your performance as an interviewee. You will have a much better idea of what to anticipate during selection interviews. And as you move up in the organization you will find yourself interviewing more and more people: interviewing skills will come in handy for a long time.

Interviewer's Responsibilities

In the next few years, organizations, recruiters or "headhunters," and personnel departments will be facing a shrinking labor market that will be more diverse and will contain fewer people with highly developed job skills than ever before.[1] This is not to say that there will be a shortage of job applicants, just that it will be more difficult to find and win those who have top qualifications. In trying to attract, recruit, and hire the best available people, businesses will be facing quite a challenge. This challenge can be made much easier through effective preparation and interviewing techniques.

Developing Job Specifications

When a position is to be filled, the person responsible for doing so must first develop job specifications, which are commonly referred to as *bona fide occupational qualifications,* or BFOQs. These include the necessary experience, educational background, and skills — the concrete requirements — for performing the job. Some BFOQs are highly specific because of the technical nature of the position: for example, an auditing accountant position that requires applicants to be certified, with three to five years of experience in tax law in the state of Illinois; or a quantitative marketing position that requires applicants to possess strong communication skills, two years of experience in computer systems sales, a degree in applied mathematics, and superior analytic ability.

It is helpful for the interviewer to define the minimum qualifications necessary for the job as well; for example, a sales representative position that requires a B.A. degree in business or communication and one year of sales experience in any industry. Candidates with additional experience and demonstrated management ability might also be welcome to apply, but it is important that the hiree be able to grow in the job. Interviewers who select overqualified candidates are likely to end up with bored and frustrated employees. When describing a position for a specialized area, the interviewer is wise to review past and current job descriptions similar to the one in question. Such a review is also an opportunity to redefine positions that have become outdated.

Regardless of the industry, organizations want to hire people who are honest, self-motivated, conscientious, and intelligent — characteristics important for any job. In a recent survey, respondents reported that the personal characteristics most important for supervisory positions are general competence, leadership abilities, oral communication skills, and human relations skills.[2] It is important to translate the job qualifications in terms of these less tangible personal qualities that will make the difference between a successful employee and another turnover statistic. For example, if one duty is "to review sales reports and make regular presentations to management on profits and losses," the best candidates will have strong analytic and oral presentation skills.

Advertising the Position

Most midsize to large organizations have full-time personnel departments whose main concern is to advertise job openings, hold recruitment sessions on college campuses, screen and interview applicants, and make formal offers of employment. For countless other businesses, especially small organizations or highly specialized firms, recruiting and hiring employees are more problematic. Interviewers may not be well trained in selection interviewing techniques, or they may be distracted by numerous other responsibilities in addition to interviewing. They may rely on standard newspaper advertisements, which result in enormous numbers of responses that have to be sifted through. Although advertising in newspapers, magazines, and professional journals can be an acceptable approach to finding employees, recruiters generally agree that it is not the best way. How can organizations avoid the expense and hassle of overresponse while still reaching a good number of qualified people? Several popular methods include networking, providing internships, and using employee referrals.

Networking, or finding a job through personal contacts at other organizations, highlights the fact that many, possibly most, people get their jobs because they "know someone." It is estimated that blue-collar workers find out about jobs through friends, family, and co-workers about 80 percent of the time; about 60 percent of white-collar workers initially use networks for job finding, and the number increases as they advance in their careers.[3] Employers can build their own networks through cooperation with college career centers, attendance at job fairs or community career days, or work with government employment agencies.

Internships are an important resource for organizations and job seekers alike. Internships provide organizations with an opportunity to see how potential employees will behave on the job and adapt to the corporate culture; as an extra benefit to the company interns usually work for significantly smaller salaries than permanent employees. Internships are especially useful in attracting and providing experience to women and members of minority groups who may be less connected to "networks" while at the same time providing these candidates with contacts for building a strong network.

Employee referrals are generally a source of good candidates simply because an employee who recommends the organization is likely to believe in its values, support its goals, and be acquainted with others who will feel the same way. Companies frequently encourage employee referrals by giving cash bonuses to people who bring in successful candidates.

Reviewing Résumés

Once applicants have responded to the job opening, you as the interviewer must review the materials provided by these applicants. Your primary goal is to reduce the applicant pool to a manageable size so as to bring only top candidates in for interviews. Many companies may interview eight to ten candidates from a pool of two hundred, and of those perhaps three to five may be offered the "callback" interview on which the selection will be based. In fact, résumés actually screen out 90 percent of all job candidates.[4]

What should a well-prepared interviewer look for on an applicant's résumé? Several areas can reveal whether a candidate is appropriate for the job. First, consider the applicant's *work experience*. Does the progression of positions show increasing levels of skill and responsibility? If not, what might be the reason? Are there any periods in which the applicant did not work? What were the reasons? Has the applicant switched careers? Why?

Next, look at *educational background*. Is the level of education adequate (i.e., possesses a B.A. or B.S. degree if required; is certified to practice in a particular field if required)? Does the candidate's background correspond to the knowledge and skills required for the job?

Then, look for demonstrated basic skills in addition to standard labels and titles. For example, for an entry-level marketing position, it is wise to look beyond the candidate's college major and consider the basic skills that make up such a field of study. A major in English literature could signal that the applicant possesses skills in analysis, writing, and organization. Considering only applicants who possess marketing majors could seriously limit the possibilities for new insight and growth in the position. The best way to assess educational background is in light of the demonstrated skills and abilities that are shown by the applicant's work experience.

References provide a "second opinion" for the interviewer. Are any of the names familiar to you? What professional backgrounds do the reference people possess? What was the reference person's relationship to the applicant? If you are seriously considering a candidate, it is a good idea to contact several of the names given as references to get additional information on his or her skills, experience, and career goals.

If applicants are required to complete a standard application form provided by the company, information from this form (which will most likely conform to the content of the résumé) can also be used to identify the most qualified candidates and to eliminate those who do not meet the minimum requirements. Once a manageable list of candidates is compiled, it is time to invite them in for interviews.

Communicating with Interviewees

Contact the interviewees in writing, and follow up with a phone call. Be sure the candidates know the exact location of your office and the times of their interviews. When scheduling interviews, you might keep in mind the nature of the position. For example, if the job is one that requires alertness early in the morning, try to schedule the interviews so that you can assess the candidates' energy levels at that time of the day.

Preparing an Interview Schedule

Before the candidates arrive for their interviews, prepare a schedule or list of questions to guide and organize the interview. Several benefits of doing so include maintaining control of the interview, ensuring that you question candidates consistently, and focusing the interview on the areas that you have identified as important to the job.

The first step is developing prcliminary questions that elicit information about job qualifications, interest in the company, and personal characteristics. Keep in mind that you want to pose questions that obtain information that was not available on the application form, cover letter, and résumé. Otherwise, you will merely collect duplicative information and will learn little that is new about the applicant. The interview is the opportunity to round out the knowledge you have gained from the résumé, cover letter, and any phone contacts with the candidate.

The second step in preparing the schedule is to compose specific questions that are direct, yet conversational, and that conform to all legal requirements. Avoid questions that can be answered simply "yes" or "no"; also stay away from leading questions. For example, the question "Do you think you'd like to work for our organization?" is ineffective — 99 percent of applicants will simply say, "Yes!"

In a selection interview, avoid skewing a candidate's answer or carelessly soliciting deceptive responses by hinting at the "correct" reply, which the interviewee may then be very tempted to give. Leading questions such as "We certainly encourage good relations between managers and employees — would you be likely to criticize your supervisor or co-workers?" may make the candidate hesitate to answer affirmatively even if he or she feels that constructive criticism and the expression of opinions are valuable on the job.

It is generally best to begin with openended questions to warm up the interviewee and then move to more complicated questions that require thought and analysis. The interview is your chance to assess the candidate's ability to think on his or her feet.

Legal issues.   The process of obtaining information from job candidates is regulated by laws, and it is critical that these regulations be followed in both letter and spirit. The responsibility for conducting an interview legally rightly rests with the employer, not the interviewee.

Title VII of the 1964 Civil Rights Act prohibits discrimination in employment on the basis of color, race, religion, sex, or national origin. This law has recently been supplemented by the Americans with Disabilities Act, which bans discrimination against the nation's disabled citizens.[5] Interviewers have to be particularly careful when asking questions of a candidate to maintain a legal profile conforming to the spirit of the law.

The official source for legal guidance in hiring is the Equal Employment Opportunities Commission's *Uniform Guidelines on Employee Selection Procedures*.[6] This guide provides prescriptive advice for avoiding potentially discriminatory practices during the interview process. It is a good idea to become familiar with its guidelines and be aware of changes because they occur quite frequently.

As an interviewer, you must adhere to two general legal requirements: the same basic questions must be posed to all candidates, and all questions (even those touching on personal qualities, goals, hobbies, affiliations) *must* be job related. Technically, questions that touch on personal or non-work related issues are not illegal in themselves; it is the interviewer's action on the information that constitutes discriminatory hiring practice. The following list gives examples of legal and discriminatory questions.

Legal Questions	Discriminatory Questions
Have you been convicted of a felony?	Have you ever been arrested?
Would you mind working overtime?	Would your husband mind if you worked late?
What three adjectives best describe you?	Would you consider yourself to be happily married?
Where do you see yourself in five years?	Will you need to arrange child care?
	Where were you born?

Are you a U.S. citizen?

Do you speak any languages fluently?

Would you be willing to relocate?

Why do you feel qualified for this position?

What do you like and dislike about your current (or previous) job?

Why should we hire you?

Can you give me some indication of your communication skills?

Where did you learn to speak Spanish?

Could your family relocate with you?

How old are you?

Do you get along well with members of the opposite sex?

Do you qualify for minority status?

Would you continue to dress like that once you are hired?

There is an additional aspect to selection interviewing and the law that has significant implications for anyone responsible for conducting employment interviews. A flurry of lawsuits by customers, clients, or co-workers accusing companies of negligent hiring practices has recently been introduced in court. For example, a plaintiff in Texas won a $4.5 million suit against a taxi company when she was abducted and raped by one of the company's drivers.[7] The court found that the company was negligent in hiring this driver because he had had a criminal record prior to his employment with the company. In other words, the company should have known about his past and not hired him in the first place.

This situation is difficult for employers, especially if they are committed to protecting the rights of interviewees. But if they hire someone based on incomplete information or knowledge, they are leaving themselves open to litigation. Again, the most reasonable solution to this paradox is to be an effective interviewer: ask legal questions that elicit valuable information from a job candidate, and check references.

Creating a Comfortable Atmosphere

Nervous candidates are less likely to open up and fully disclose the information you need to accurately assess them for a job. An atmosphere in which candidates can feel comfortable talking about themselves and their career goals is therefore essential. How do you accomplish this?

Begin by looking at the setting in which the interview will take place. Is the office drab, sterile, or uninviting? If so, you may get responses to match. One interviewer we know has a very small, poorly lit, and crowded office, so when he interviews someone for a job, he reserves a conference room that is wood paneled, well lit, and comfortable. Of course, interviewers should avoid misleading candidates about the physical environment of the organization during the interview. If the candidate will be expected to work in a small, cramped office, he or she should be told of that condition regardless of where the interview takes place. The interview area should be neat, free of distractions, private, and arranged so that the interviewer and interviewee feel equal.

Positive communication can also decrease a candidate's nervousness and put her or him at ease. When a candidate first comes in, smile, introduce yourself by name and title, engage in direct eye contact, shake hands, and express sincere interest and attention.

Once seated, provide a succinct orientation to the interview, including a brief recap of the job description, expected responsibilities, an overview of the interview schedule, and approximately how long the interview will last. This information puts candidates more at ease by showing what is ahead.

Sequencing Questions

Within the general boundaries of the interview schedule, plan questions in a sequence that accomplishes a specific goal. For example, asking opening questions about topics that seem particularly outstanding on a candidate's résumé is effective in helping him or her to get over any anxiety and focus on relevant matters. Difficult and thought-provoking questions are usually best posed after a candidate has warmed up. Table 8-1 compares a variety of questions that might be used during the course of an employment interview.

Select an interview style that is best for the situation. A nondirective style allows a great deal of flexibility in the choice and order of questions; as a result, you may not ask all questions of all interviewees. A nondirective approach can decrease an interviewee's defensiveness or anxiety but increase an interviewer's tendency to talk and opportunity for inconsistency from one interview to the next.

A directive approach (which, as we discussed in Chapter 7, can range from nonscheduled to highly scheduled, standardized) provides the interviewer with more control. A moderately scheduled approach, which allows the interviewee some discretion in responding, lets the interviewer maintain control over the interview while helping the interviewee to feel comfortable about the process.

In a highly scheduled, standardized approach, all questions are asked of all candidates in exactly the same way in the same order. This approach allows complete control by the interviewer, and consistency of responses is maintained across all interviewers. But it can produce the most nervousness for the interviewee and does not allow much room for improvisation by the interviewer.

TABLE 8-1
Employment Interview Questions

Closed questions	Would you describe yourself as a people-person or an individualist? Are you more interested in a career in marketing or in corporate communications? Did you know the salary for this job is $20,000?
Open questions	Why did you major in _____? How did college prepare you for the real world? What are your immediate and long-term career goals?
Hypothetical questions	How would you handle a hostile co-worker? What would you do if a customer demanded a refund and you were not authorized to give one? How would you resolve conflicting demands on your time by department managers?
Probing questions	Why? Could you elaborate on your decision? What happened next? Who else was involved in the project?

It is helpful to occasionally invite interviewees to ask questions about the position as they understand it. In rare instances, after hearing your orientation, the candidate may realize that the job is really not suited for her or him, and you can save yourself quite a bit of time! Asking questions allows candidates to clear up ambiguities about the position and make them more relaxed and confident for the remainder of the interview. The key to effective interviewing is to have interviewees reveal direct and honest information about themselves.

Closing the Interview

An effective closing has three parts. In the first part, allow the candidate to ask any final questions she or he may have. Asking questions gives the candidate a chance to clear up any remaining uncertainties about the position. It also gives you a chance to see how interested the candidate is in the position. Those candidates without any questions may be using the interview as a warm-up for the others they value more or may have decided during the course of the interview that the job is not for them.

The second part comprises a summary of the main issues discussed in the interview. Recap the main points about skills, responsibilities, scheduling, or other technical details, and give the candidate some indication of how the decision on the position will be made and when: for example, "I will report my findings to the personnel committee, and the final three candidates will be asked to come in for a second interview. Those will be held the week of March 20." Keep in mind that summarizing gives the candidate a sense of closure and accomplishment.

In the third part, reestablish rapport. You can do this by thanking the candidate for his or her time, shaking hands, and making sure he or she knows the way out of the office. Establishing rapport at the end of the interview creates a positive impression of you and your company.

Evaluating the Candidates

As an interviewer, you are required by law to keep an accurate record of each interview. One way to do this is to complete a standardized evaluation of each interviewee.

Once the interviews are over, list *areas of expertise* and *personal characteristics* that are most important for the position. Although your review of the job in an earlier step accomplished this, the interviewing process may have modified your expectations. Rank each candidate either quantitatively (on a scale of one to ten) or qualitatively (poor to excellent) in each area. Complete the evaluation immediately on concluding the interview — your memory is subject to unintentional distortions or revisions over time. Figure 8-1 shows a typical employment interview evaluation form.

Check to see that information gained in the interview supports information on the résumé or cover letter. For example, a candidate may have listed programming skills on her résumé but when asked about it in the interview was vague and displayed only the most basic knowledge.

When writing up comments on an evaluation form, be careful to avoid *subjective* (opinion-based) language. Include only statements that *objectively* (factually) describe the candidate's responses, appearance, or character. A good test for objectivity is to ask yourself, "If someone else reads these comments, will he or she gain clear factual knowledge of the candidate on which to base a decision?" or "Would another interviewer agree with these statements?" We also discourage interviewers from making broad personal judgments without supporting evidence. The statement "It is my view that Joseph Karn is just right for this job" fails to explain *how* and *why* the interviewer reached that conclusion. More effective are comments that emphasize job-related facts, especially those outlined in the job description. The comment "The candidate has worked as a public relations assistant for one year. Her job required numerous presentations to business groups as well as the communication skills listed on her résumé" gives an objective summary of why the applicant is a strong candidate for the job.[8]

Poor (P), Fair (F), Average (A),
Good (G), Outstanding (O)

INTERVIEW WORK SHEET

Applicant's name _____   Interviewer _____
                                                                           Last name

Internal _____ External _____ Other _____   *Type of interview*
                                               Identify   ❑ Screening
Position(s) best   1. _____   ❑ For a specific job
qualified for: 2. _____   ❑ Other

Salary discussed?   Yes _____ No _____   If so, range quoted: _____

Earliest starting date _____   Interview availability _____

Special instructions for contacting applicant (if any) _____

Was the employment application completed?   Yes _____ No _____

	P	F	A	G	O	*Interviewer's specific comments* (use back if necessary)
Communication skills						
Motivation						
Analytical skills						
Personal qualities						
Experience						
Reference and/or performance evaluation						
Other skills or impressions						

Overall evaluation of applicant: _____Outstanding (we should make extra effort to remember and place)

                                    _____Above average (probably able to do a good job)

                                    _____Below average

Referrals: (Use back if necessary)

          Unit   *Supervisor*   *Date*

FIGURE 8-1   *A standard employment interview evaluation form*

Evaluation is a difficult task. If several candidates demonstrate excellent potential as future employees, hard decisions and choices must be made during this stage. Base your final ranking of the candidates on an objective comparison of the job's priorities with the strengths and weaknesses of the interviewees.

Interviewee's Responsibilities

The interview role that you will perform most often early in your career is that of interviewee. Many of you reading this text have participated in interviews before. There are a number of proper steps, procedures, rules, and behaviors associated with the interviewee role. Indeed, much of your work in performing this role occurs before you ever shake hands with an interviewer. You have to do your homework if you want to impress wary, experienced, and professional interviewers.

Developing a Personal Biography

The first responsibility of the interviewee is to develop a personal biography, which is a compilation of information pertaining to any aspect of yourself that may be relevant or interesting to a potential employer. Working on a personal biography will make your task easier when you turn to the specifics of your résumé.

Educational experience is a basic requirement for any personal biography. Most employers are only interested in learning about more recent educational experiences (i.e., college or graduate school as opposed to high school or junior high). Compile the names and addresses of the educational institutions you attended, your grade point average and/or rank in graduating classes, dates of graduation, any honors or awards associated with academic success, and any honors or awards associated with extracurricular activity. Although you will not include all these data on your résumé, you are likely to need access to this information during the interview.

Work experience is also an essential component of any personal biography. List work experience with most recent employment first, followed in order by each prior job. The employer's name, address, and phone number; positions held; job descriptions; salary history; supervisor's name; reason for leaving; and inclusive dates of employment belong in this section of the biography. Once again, you may not include all this information on the résumé, but you will nevertheless need to have it ready.

Employers are always interested in the *organizational activities* in which you participate. Similar to extracurricular activities in school, organizational activities are those involving civic, religious, fraternal, philanthropic, or social organizations. Employers are interested in these activities for two reasons. First, participating in events where organizational and leadership skills must be exhibited helps to prepare people for work life by serving as a proving ground for similar responsibilities at work.

Second, because many businesses are involved in similar activities themselves (United Way campaigns, fund raising, and so forth), they prefer employees with this lifestyle and experience. As you compile information on organizational activities, include the name, address, and phone number of the organization; your duties and responsibilities; inclusive dates of participation or membership; names of key people in the organization who can comment on your performance; and any notable achievements with the organization.

In the next section of your personal biography include *hobbies, interests, and special skills.* Employers know how important these personal features can be to job success and usually ask about them in an interview. The key is to make definite connections to the job you seek. For example, musical skill or participation in musical events often indicates creativity, persistent practice, and even teamwork. In one case, an interviewer was particularly impressed when he learned that a job candidate traced family ancestries as a hobby because the company was about to launch new products for people older than sixty, who are generally interested in family histories. In this section list each hobby, interest, and special skill and indicate when and how you became interested in this feature and how it will help you to do your job better. Include any special training you have had in developing this feature, and include names of people who can comment on your expertise in the area.

Having comprehensive information about yourself will be a great help when you have to compose a résumé and cover letter for a job you are interested in. It may seem like a lot of work with little payoff, but we can assure you that any time spent in this area is worth the investment. Besides the fact that this information can be used for your résumé, it also serves as a memory aid for remembering personal characteristics that are likely to be probed in an interview.

Researching the Company

Once you have identified the organizations in which you are interested, learn as much about them as you can so that you can find out if your values are compatible with theirs and adapt your résumé to the positions available. In addition, researching a company will give you detailed knowledge that you can demonstrate in the interview. One job seeker we know wanted to win a job at a major fund-raising organization. He checked through business journals to find out which organizations had made large contributions recently and complimented his interviewer on those successes. There is nothing so impressive as a job candidate who cares enough about the job or organization to become familiar with it before the interview. And knowing the company can increase your self-confidence about your ability to fit its needs.

Several specific pieces of information will aid you in the interviewing process. The *company history,* which includes the length of time the company has been in business, the names of parent or branch companies, and the original business if different from the present, can give you a feel for where the organization is going. The company's *business purpose,* including the specific products or services offered by the organization, may have an influence on its corporate culture and employee demographics. The *potential for growth,* evidence that the company has stagnated, performed consistently, or grown, can give you an idea of general job security at the organization. The *location* of offices, plants, distribution points, and major retail outlets or service centers can indicate where you may be located or transferred. The *organizational structure* — whether it is a tall organization with structured policies for advancement or a flat organization with potential for team building — may complement or contradict your work style. Knowing the company's *major competitors* can alert you to sensitive topics such as recent successes by competitors. Communicating information in these areas in an interview will be impressive to the interviewer, but be careful not to overdo it. Remember, you are there to provide information about yourself, not to show off or upstage the interviewer.

Getting this information is not difficult — most of it can be learned through the following sources:

School placement offices
On-campus recruiter presentations
Brokerage offices
The company's public relations department
Macmillan's Directory of Leading Private Companies
Career Guide to Professional Organizations
American Society of Training and Development Directory
Dun & Bradstreet's Million Dollar Directory
Standard & Poor's Directory
Issues of *Forbes, Fortune, Business Week, Money, Inc.,* and the *Wall Street Journal*
Present or past employees

Informational Interviewing

There is a limit to what you can learn about a company, industry, or job by reading about it in a directory, visiting a placement office, or doing other indirect research. A critical complement to such research is to meet with people who are currently working at jobs in which you have an interest. Talking to people in the field is one of the best ways to find out if you are actually interested in the day-to-day reality of a particular job or industry.

The process of meeting and talking with people in the work force is known as *informational interviewing,* and it offers several important benefits. First, it allows you to watch people on the job (Do they seem happy? busy? stressed? involved? apathetic?) and develop contacts within a company. And as you observe and talk with the person, you get a more accurate picture of the job than most job descriptions can provide. Keeping this knowledge in mind is a great help when preparing a résumé or employment interview responses for a similar job — an employment interviewer is likely to be impressed by your "inside" knowledge of the field.

The best way to set up informational interviews is to ask around — friends, acquaintances, current or former co-workers, and especially guidance counselors or placement office workers may be able to give you names of people to call. Describe the job you are looking for and ask if they know of anyone doing that job or something similar. All you need is one or two names; after that, you can begin to network through the interviews themselves.

To prepare for an informational interview, make a list of the things you would like to know about the job — What is a typical day like? What skills or abilities are required? How many and what kinds of people do you work with? and so forth. You can also ask questions about how the person got into the job — what interested her or him about the field; where did he or she work before; what was the most important factor in being hired (if

Interact!

You may already have had some experience with job employment interviewing. If you had a summer job, worked before attending college, or currently have a part-time or full-time job, you probably went through some kind of formal interview process. At a minimum, you completed an application form and either talked with a hiring representative from a personnel department or with the person who would supervise you on the job.

In this activity, we practice the process of employment interviewing and the techniques we have introduced in this chapter. To begin the activity, each member of the class writes a one-page job description. The job description should contain the name of a company, its industry or field of service, the title of the position, basic qualifications that are needed (education, work experience, communication skills, and so forth), salary level, date that applicants must forward a resume, your (real) name, title, (real) address and phone number so the interviewee can contact you, and an Equal Employment Opportunity disclaimer. As the "interviewer" for the job you have described, you have the final say in the hiring decision.

The completed job descriptions are then placed in a binder, which students can browse through to choose the job for which they wish to apply. Thus, while you are preparing to interview for a classmate's job, a fellow student is preparing to interview for yours. Based on the job description you select, prepare a cover letter and résumé appropriate for the position, and submit it to the "interviewer." The interviewer then contacts the interviewee to arrange a time and setting for the interview.

Before interviewing the applicant for your job description, make up an interview schedule containing basic questions that you need to ask the applicant. A detailed review of the applicant's cover letter and résumé is a good source for these basic questions. Be sure to refer to the résumé and cover letter during the course of the interview.

As the interviewee, research the industry and the company to which you are applying. Prepare responses to standard questions, and be ready to elaborate on the information presented in your résumé and cover letter.

After the interview, the interviewer should use the evaluation form in Figure 8-1 to summarize the interview and decide on follow-up actions. If possible, the interviews may be videotaped and shown to the class. In this situation, the class can use the evaluation form to assess the interviewee. In order to assess the interviewer, consider the following questions.

1. Did the interviewer make the interviewee comfortable?

2. Did the interviewer follow an appropriate question sequence?

3. Was the interviewer listening? How could you tell?

4. Did the interviewer gather sufficient information to make an informed decision?

In a class discussion, share responses to the following questions.

1. What aspects of interviewing were most difficult? Why? What can be done in the future to improve your skills in these areas?

2. Were there any surprises in the interview? How did you handle unexpected occurrences as they confronted you?

3. How important were listening skills in your role as interviewer? As interviewee? Give specific examples.

4. Did you receive the information you needed to make an educated decision about the applicant? What did you decide? As an interviewee, do you think you presented a successful image? Why or why not?

---

known). Personal reactions to the job, such as what the person likes or dislikes, finds challenging, or wishes were different about the job, can also provide valuable insights for the informational interviewer.

It is important to remember, however, that the informational interview is *not* a job hunt. Do not wear out your welcome by hinting at or dwelling on job openings at the company. Also, keep the interview short (fifteen to twenty minutes should be enough).[9]

One of the most important things you can gain from an informational interview is the name or names of others to contact in your field of interest. You can do this by asking the person for referrals to others in the field or even in the company. Thus, even if you were able to locate only one or two people to interview, after those interviews are complete you should have two to four more possibilities, and so on. Remember to send a note of thanks to the person soon after talking with him or her, and keep detailed records of each interview and what you learned in it.

It is nearly impossible to overdo informational interviewing. Whether you are looking for a first job, changing jobs, or re-entering the work force, informational interviewing gives the job search a personal, human perspective that can calm your nervousness about employment interviews and help you develop communication skills that will be vitally important in your career.

Preparing a Résumé and Cover Letter

It is best to prepare the résumé and cover letter after you have conducted your research of the company. In this way you can design these documents to reveal personal strengths and genuine interest in the company. All too often, job candidates simply prepare a résumé and cover letter, save them on a computer disk, find a job they want, change the name and address on the cover letter, and send the same documents to every company they apply to. This type of generic job hunting does not demonstrate your uniqueness, which is essential in getting the job you want.

Design the résumé and cover letter based on your personal biography and the research that you have accumulated on the company. Résumés should generally be one page long and never longer than two pages. For those with more money than time, there are literally hundreds of résumé services that can provide advice about preparing résumés, but we strongly discourage using them. Doing your résumé yourself can give you the self-knowledge and self-confidence necessary to make a difference in an interview.

Most résumés include basic and essential information such as your career objective, educational background, and work experience. Although this information will not change from one job application to the next, the manner in which it is presented may vary. It is important for the résumé to be readable at a glance. Cluttered, confusing, or disorganized résumés probably will not make it past the first reader. Résumés should be concise, well organized, neat, and error free. We know organizations that will not consider a candidate whose résumé has even one typographical, grammatical, or printing error. The following are some résumé basics.

Identify your job objective. At the top of the résumé, state your goal and the skills that directly demonstrate qualifications for the job. Spell out the area in which you wish to work in short, energetic phrases. The following list compares effective and less effective job objectives.

Strong

- ◆ A position in sales that uses my ability to make persuasive presentations and demands self-motivation and enthusiasm

- ◆ A position with Hubbard Catering that emphasizes strong customer relations skills

♦ To use my management skills, creativity, and tutoring experience as Volunteer Coordinator for Central School District

Weak

♦ A position with Jenwrite company

♦ A job that will allow me to grow and develop my skills

♦ To be hired by Spark Distributors to do marketing

Specify education.   Give names of institutions, major fields of study, and dates of attendance. Begin with your most recent educational experiences, including continuing education classes or training classes if relevant. Include academic awards or honors, such as membership in an honor society.

Relate your experience to the job you seek.   Make sure *all information is relevant to the job you want.* Even if you are very proud of an achievement, such as designing the layout for a marketing brochure, if you are applying for a job as a sales representative, relate your creative ability to sales or drop the item.

Include school projects or volunteer achievements.   Especially for new graduates, the skills and responsibilities used in these contexts can substitute for a lack of formal job experience.

Cite personal characteristics.   Your experience and achievements will show relevant personal qualities such as leadership, ability to work with others, motivation, and resourcefulness. There is no need to repeat them in a separate section. Other personal characteristics, such as height, weight, or marital status, are unnecessary.

References.   Simply state, "Available on request." If the employer is interested, he or she will be sure to ask for them.

We have provided two different résumé formats that will be attractive to organizations (see Figures 8-2 and 8-3). Figure 8-2 shows a basic résumé organized according to specific jobs and activities. Figure 8-3 demonstrates a *functional* résumé, which highlights general skills and areas of strength. Functional résumés are generally used by people with extensive experience and too many jobs to list, or who are applying for a job in a new field and need to demonstrate their relevant skills. Figure 8-4 shows a variety of résumé "don'ts." Note that the placement, format, and style of some elements on the résumé are the source of most of the problems. With careful thought, the appropriate elements can be reworked into an excellent résumé. Remember that you have to determine what a company is looking for in a job candidate and provide exactly the kind of information that will interest that company.

BARBARA DOMINCO

Present address
1100 Woodbury Road
Philadelphia, PA 19235
Phone: (215) 936-1744

Permanent Address
35 Marshall Avenue
Eau Claire, WI 12345
Phone: (423) 671-5783

OBJECTIVE	Public relations or marketing position requiring strong communication skills, creativity, and computer experience
EDUCATION	Temple University, Philadelphia, Pennsylvania Bachelor of Arts degree, 1992 Major in business with emphasis on marketing, public relations, and organizational communication GPA: 3.5 cumulative; 3.7 in major Elected to Alpha Chi student honor society
EXPERIENCE	
August 1991 to present	**Public Relations Assistant,** Temple University, Philadelphia, Pennsylvania Assisted director of Public Relations in development campaign. Researched potential donors and wrote direct mail correspondence. Participated in annual fundraising telethon.
Nov. 1990 to May 1991	**Customer Service Representative,** Mellon Bank, Philadelphia, Pennsylvania Wrote a series of 15 "Answers to Common Questions" brochures for customers' questions about banking services. Used computer database to analyze customer needs and concerns.
Oct. 1989 to May 1990	**Manager/Sales Clerk,** Strawbridge and Clothier, Philadelphia, Pennsylvania Scheduled cashiers and other personnel and worked on merchandise inventories. Provided customer service and set up displays.
ACTIVITIES *1991-1992*	**Classified Editor,** *The Temple Times,* Temple University. Layout staff, 1988-1991 Used desktop publishing techniques to design and produce classified pages. Supervised five staff members.
1992	**Chair,** United Way Student Volunteer Committee. Member, 1990-1991. Organized campus-wide Volunteer Day. Participated in community rehabilitation projects.
SKILLS	Wordperfect and pfsWrite on IBM and Apple computers Lotus 1, 2, 3 Desktop publishing Typing (approximately 45 wpm) Fluent in Spanish
REFERENCES	Available on request

FIGURE 8-2   *Basic résumé format*

Cover letters should begin with a specific, impressive paragraph — it is essential to grab the reader's attention, get him or her excited about looking at your résumé, and create the impression that you are a valuable asset to his or her organization *without* actually using these words. For example, a successful opening paragraph may read, "My experience in volunteer com-

Robert Jackson
34 Waverly Street
Houston, Texas 77592
(806) 862-9913

CAREER GOAL	To obtain a sales position leading to management that utilizes strong communication and marketing skills.
SALES AND MARKETING	Managed over twenty accounts for large music club. Developed promotional campaigns for new product lines. Increased sales by $240,000 in nine month period.
ADMINISTRATION	Implemented, and supervised office records. Coordinated purchase orders and prepared contracts. Handled customer service training program for telemarketing employees.
WORK HISTORY *1989-1992*	Account Manager, SuperDisc Compact Disc Club, Houston, Texas
1988-1989	Telemarketing Coordinator, SuperDisc Compact Disc Club, Houston, Texas
1987-1988	Telemarketer, SuperDisc Compact Disc Club, Houston, Texas
EDUCATION *1992*	Certified by International Association of Business Communicators
1987	Colorado State University, Boulder, Colorado, B.A. in English
REFERENCES	Available on request

FIGURE 8-3   Functional résumé format

munity work has provided me with communication, management, and organizational skills required by the position of assistant to the public relations manager. During the past four years I have designed and organized three fund-raising campaigns for local hospitals that have brought in more than $450,000."

The body of the letter should specifically tell the reader what position you are applying for and give one or two brief accomplishments that dem-

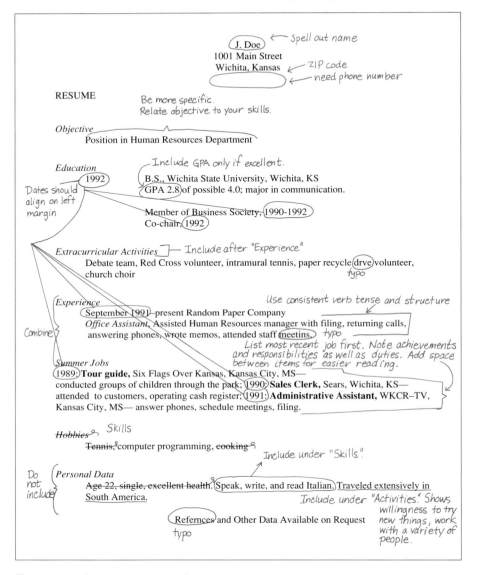

FIGURE 8-4   Beware of these common résumé mistakes

onstrate how you are qualified. Indicate how you learned of the position and who you know as a contact at the company. Close with specific language such as "I will be in Houston on November 8 and would like to arrange an appointment," or "I will call on Thursday, May 22, to set up a time for an interview." Figure 8-5 shows an effective cover letter for the résumé in Figure 8-2. The cover letter in Figure 8-6 (which accompanies the résumé

1100 Woodbury Road
Philadelphia, PA 19235
March 24, 1992

Mr. Harold Britten
Personnel Manager
195 Hennepin Ave.
Phillips-Margolis Company
Minneapolis, MN 55213

Dear Mr. Britten:

Please accept this letter and the enclosed resume as application for the position of assistant marketing manager at Phillips-Margolis. The Director of Public Relations at Temple University, George Holton, suggested that I contact you about the position as it is appropriate for someone with my background, experience, and interest in the area.

While at Temple University, I have balanced academic success in marketing and communication with real world experience. As a public relations assistant, I produced a direct mail campaign that raised over $238,000 with a response rate of 79 percent—compared with the previous year's 57 percent. As a customer service representative, I used computers for writing and producing brochures, news releases, and promotional materials as well as for research. As a sales clerk in a major department store, I shared rotating management and scheduling duties with a staff of three in my department.

My immediate goal is to apply this experience to the needs of Phillips-Margolis on my graduation this May. I would like to meet with you to discuss my qualifications for the position. I will call you the week of April 2 to arrange an appointment. If you wish to contact me before that time, please call me at (215) 936-1744.

Thank you for your consideration.

Sincerely,

Barbara Dominco

Barbara Dominco

enc: resume

FIGURE 8-5   *A strong cover letter is an important complement to your résumé.*

in 8-4) contains some of the most common weaknesses in cover letters, with suggestions for improvement.

Résumés and cover letters must be neat and printed or typed on high-quality paper (usually white, gray, or ivory bond paper with twenty-five or forty percent cotton content). Make sure the print is dark and clear with no

J. Doe
1001 Main Street
Wichita, Kansas
(513) 477-9925

Return address
Date
(Align with closing)

~~June 3, 1992~~

Ms. Pauline Renford → *title or department*
Bond Supply Company
San Francisco, CA   91803

use formal address, i.e., "Ms. Renford"

"Personnel Assistant" or "Benefits Administrator is a more appropriate entry-level position.

State your value to the business in clear, specific terms.

Dear Pauline:

I would like to apply for the job of Manager of Human Resources at your organization. I have worked very hard in school and I feel qualified to work in the field of personnel because of my background in communication and my work experience.

Not on resume; connection to job not clear.

I worked with Marilyn Garber as an intern in the personnel department at MetroWest Communications Company and learned a lot about how human resources are handled in a high-tech environment. In addition, I got a lot of "hands on" experience that you will find valuable. I have held a variety of other jobs that all show my enthusiasm for work and my willingness to take on new responsibilities.

Vague; needs direction

Add phone number; suggest a good time to call.

If you are interested in my qualifications, please call me. ~~I sincerely hope to meet with you and to work for Bond Supply Company.~~

Thank you for your consideration.

Sincerely,

J. G. Doe

write out name

J. G. Doe

FIGURE 8-6   *Cover letters should be attention-getting and well focused — or they will not be read*

smudges. Give your current address and phone number on the cover letter just in case the résumé is lost.

Dressing Appropriately

Just as your résumé should promote a competent, neat, professional image, so should your personal appearance. One of the first and most obvious impressions you will make in an interview is the way you are dressed. The general rule is that you should match the dress of the interviewer. If you have a chance to informally visit the company before your interview, take note of the general dress of the employees. If you cannot visit but know someone who works there, ask him or her what the standard attire is.

If visiting or making inquiries is impossible, you can use some general guidelines for dressing. For professional positions, dress conservatively (dark suits, white shirts/blouses, standard ties/ribbon ties, dark socks/neutral hose, dark shoes). You really cannot go wrong with this attire (see Chapter 5 for more specific information). Dress according to the professional expectations for that particular job. Some positions require more conservative attire than others. Wear clothes that fit and are relatively comfortable. Choosing colors, patterns, and matches will do little good if you look or feel uncomfortable.

Preparing to Ask and Answer Questions

Once you have been invited for an interview, prepare for your performance. The first step is devising questions that develop knowledge of the company that you were unable to ascertain through your research. Prioritize your list of questions so that the most important areas come first, because you may not get a chance to ask all your questions during the interview. When some questions are answered naturally during the course of the interview, mentally move down your list to a question that obtains information you do not have. Preparing and asking questions provide you with additional insight into the company, show your interest in the job, and demonstrate communication skills. Inquisitive interviewees appear more competent to interviewers.

Preparing to answer questions requires additional thought. You can safely assume that some of the following "boilerplate" questions will be asked. How might you respond to these sorts of questions?

1. Describe a typical day in your current (or last) job. What are (were) your major responsibilities?
2. What are some things in your job that you have done particularly well?

3. What are some problems you encounter in your job? What frustrates you the most? What do you do about it?

4. How has your present job prepared you to take on greater responsibilities?

5. What interests you about this position? What kind of position would you expect to progress to?

6. What are some of your reasons for leaving your current (last) job?

7. How would your last employer rate your job performance? What would she or he say you did well? What would be criticized?

8. How would you define an ideal work environment?

9. What are some of the things you would like to avoid in a job? Why?

10. What are your long-range goals?

11. What would you look for in an ideal supervisor?

12. How do you define "success" in your work?

13. Why do you want to work for us?

14. What did you think of your old boss?

15. What kind of salary are you looking for?

16. Do you like to work overtime?

17. Are you satisfied with your career at this point?

18. What has been the single most important professional experience of your life?

19. Why should we hire you?

This list could go on indefinitely, but essentially covers four major categories: 1) Why are you here? 2) What can you do for us? 3) What kind of person are you? 4) How much will you cost? Although interviewers may find hundreds of ways to phrase questions, these are the critical areas of interest to them. Your responses to these areas during the interview (regardless of how the specific questions are phrased) should be candid, well-organized, incisive, relevant, to the point, and positive. It is fine to volunteer some negatives, especially in the context of challenges you have met or problems you have resolved. When responding, you are wise to *avoid* making disorganized or irrelevant statements, evading or rationalizing, being overly critical of others, changing the subject or giving many unimportant details, talking only of favorable points, or making bad jokes. The excerpts below show strong versus weak responses to basic questions.

Question: Describe a typical day in your current job. What are your major responsibilities?

Answer: Well, every day is different, so it sort of depends on the whim of my supervisor . . . you know, I really think that my skill in word processing would fit your company's needs. That's something I do a lot. Most of the time, I hardly make any errors, except for spelling, but I can always use a spell-checker. In fact, I think people who can't take advantage of computer technology are out of place in today's business environment.

Question: I see. What other computer skills do you use in your job?

Answer: We use a database and spreadsheet to prepare budget reports, and the publications department produces a newsletter through desktop publishing.

Question: How often do you prepare budget reports?

Answer: Ummm . . . That isn't exactly part of my job, although I am responsible for requesting funds for my department. It's a very important responsibility.

Weaknesses. The interviewee has (intentionally or unintentionally) changed the subject, given a disorganized response, implied criticism of her or his current supervisor, given irrelevant details, and implied possession of skills not actually acquired. Starting from the same question, the following exchange illustrates strong interviewee responses.

Question: Describe a typical day in your current job. What are your major responsibilities?

Answer: Well, I am responsible for scheduling meetings in my department, so the first thing I do every morning is check the schedule to review upcoming meetings. I then prepare and distribute agendas for the meetings.

Question: How do you do that?

Answer: These agendas are based on notes given to me by the department supervisor, who generally does a good job of getting me the necessary information early enough that I can contact everyone who will attend the meeting. Recently, I have been doing a lot of the background research and preparation myself.

Question: What do you find most challenging about this responsibility?

Answer: It is difficult to get people together, and I am sometimes frustrated when others don't seem to care about meetings that I have spent a lot of time trying to organize. Overall, though, I feel that this responsibility has taught me a lot about communicating with a variety of people, following up on messages, and working out conflicting interests and goals in order to find convenient times for people to meet.

Strengths. The interviewee keeps to the questions asked, giving relevant, detailed responses. She or he has volunteered some negative information in a candid way, but in general speaks well of co-workers. The responses are well organized, describing a task and the skills necessary to accomplish it.

Listening and Utilizing Nonverbal Communication Skills

Although you may be tempted to focus on responding as the central interviewing skill, listening and nonverbal behavior can strengthen and improve your responses. During the interview, listen very carefully to the entire question before responding. Pause briefly before answering questions. This gives you a chance to formulate your response and indicates to the interviewer that you are developing a considered response. Focus on the content of the response and speak with confidence. Always look the interviewer in the eye when responding. If you are asked a question that you cannot answer, simply say so and do not act embarrassed. This happens frequently, and an interviewer has more respect for an interviewee who admits to ignorance than one who tries to fake it.

Use normal gesturing patterns, and sit erectly in your chair. The following list shows behaviors practiced by interviewees that can leave a positive or a negative impression on the interviewer.

Positive	Negative
Arriving early	Arriving late
Alertness	Inattentiveness
Responsiveness	Lethargy
Relaxed manner	Withdrawn manner
Emphatic attitude on key issues	Tenseness
Smiling	Frowns
Clear, even voice	Mumbling
Direct eye contact	Fidgeting

Handling Discriminatory Questions

At times an interviewer will ask a question, such as "What would your spouse think about relocating to the Southwest?" In their attempt to get a "complete" profile of a candidate, interviewers may purposely or unknowingly pose questions that are illegal. What do you do when asked an illegal question? You have several choices. You can answer it and hope to get the job. Or you can refuse to answer it on the ground that it is illegal and risk the chance that you will not be hired. You can simply respond, "I am sorry, but that is not a bona fide occupation qualification and I will not answer," but such a reply is not likely to promote good relations between you and the interviewer, especially if she or he was merely trying to be friendly and conversational. The best way to handle marginal or illegal questions is to politely put the ball back in the interviewer's court. For example, if asked, "Do you have any small children at home?" you can respond, "I understand your concern about identifying possible obstacles to my commitment to the job, but be assured that I am fully prepared and qualified for the tasks and responsibilities involved and have the ability to manage my time effectively." In this case, you are answering an unasked question that reflects the interviewer's real concern.

If a job applicant thinks she or he has been discriminated against during the hiring process and can provide evidence of such discrimination, the law requires the employer to prove that no discrimination took place.[10] It is often difficult for the employer to do this. If you feel that you have legitimate cause for complaint and were unsuccessful in alerting the employer to illegal interviewing or hiring practices, the courts provide a last resort.

Following Up the Interview

The employment interview does not end when the candidate walks out of the interviewer's office. If you are sincerely interested in the company and the job, take the time to follow up the interview with a letter of thanks to the interviewer. Such a letter accomplishes several purposes. It demonstrates your enthusiasm for the job and the company. It also reflects excellent communication skills, provides the interviewer with additional feedback about you and your interview, and can also serve as a reminder of your interview and set you apart from the crowd. Writing a *short* (one or two paragraphs are enough) note of appreciation never hurt an applicant and quite likely will garner some additional consideration that will benefit your chances of getting the job. The following basic guidelines apply to follow-up letters.

1. Address the interviewer as he or she introduced himself or herself to you in the interview. (Dear Ms. Markowitz:)

2. Note the date of your interview and the job in which you are interested. (Thank you for giving me the opportunity to interview for the position of Personnel Assistant at Barnes Company last Monday.)

3. Comment positively on the interview and briefly restate your interest in the job. (The interview was highly informative. Now that I know more about the job, I would like to reemphasize my interest in a career at Barnes.)

4. Restate your major qualifications. (I believe that my background in psychology, experience as a volunteer peer counselor, and strong oral and written communication skills can make a positive contribution to the Human Resources Department at Barnes.)

5. Offer to provide more information. (I look forward to hearing about the job. If you would like any additional information, please contact me at 617-983-2880.)

Appraisal Interviews

Appraisal interviews are conducted to evaluate employees for their performance over a certain period of time (generally specified by company policy). Successful and well-conducted appraisal interviews serve a number of important functions. These interviews provide feedback to employees about their performance, which is essential to achieving organizational goals. Supervisors obtain feedback from employees who prefer a confidential atmosphere in which to discuss their concerns. In some organizations the appraisal interview may be the only time that manager and employees sit down face to face to talk about job performance and responsibilities.

Appraisal interviews are often used to motivate workers. By going over performance standards and comparing these to the employee's behavior, managers can motivate workers to go beyond their normal work levels. Appraisal interviews can build morale. When workers know how they are doing and are encouraged to continue their progress, they feel better about the organization and develop more positive attitudes about the workplace.

Reviewing Performance

As a first step in the appraisal process, the manager reviews the performance of each employee being evaluated. Many organizations follow a process of performance review and development, which includes frequent appraisal interviews, so that managers and employees work consistently toward well understood goals. Files should document every noteworthy incident or behavior. A thorough analysis of all pertinent information for each employee is conducted prior to the actual evaluation, and the employee is given a chance to provide input on her or his view of the job objectives and how they have been achieved.

During the evaluation process, superiors use preestablished criteria in a standard format as a means of judging the worth of each employee. There are several standardized techniques available, but most evaluators rely on two characteristics: performance factors and rating systems.

Performance factors.   Performance factors are elements in an employee's job description that can be objectively evaluated according to some baseline measure. The employee should be told in advance of the evaluation period on the basis of what factors she or he will be judged. Following are several performance factors that are often used during performance appraisals.[11]

Punctuality	Accuracy	Communication skills
Initiative	Leadership skills	Versatility
Job knowledge	Organizational skills	Cooperation
Creativity	Responsibility	Delegation skills
Planning	Dependability	Productivity
Cost control	Neatness	Consistency

Rating systems. Rating systems show how various performance factors will be evaluated. Some rating systems are qualitative; managers simply discuss each performance factor in a descriptive and evaluative manner. They may write paragraphs using adjectives to describe how they judge the worth of each factor.

More frequently, rating systems are quantitative. Here a performance factor is rated according to some numerical ordering system to reveal the worth of performance. Some organizations use scales that range from one to five or one to ten. Other companies rank-order employees according to each relevant performance factor.

A combination of quantitative and qualitative rating systems can be used, and this approach is quite prevalent in organizations. Employees are given a quantitative rating along the performance factors with a written explanation and narrative evaluation to supplement the rating. (See Figure 8-7.)

Equal employment opportunity regulations. As with most workplace interviews, the appraisal process is strictly regulated by Title VII of the Civil Rights Act. Even though there are no laws that require appraisal interviews, equal employment opportunity guidelines require companies that conduct appraisals to do so uniformly and consistently, to measure actual work performance, and to apply evaluation criteria equally to all employees.[12] The key to staying within federal guidelines is to focus exclusively on actual job performance, use documented evidence when possible, and avoid subjective performance criteria.[13] Honesty, integrity, loyalty, and trustworthiness are risky criteria because these virtues cannot always be assessed objectively with any reasonable accuracy.

Conducting the Interview

When the interviewee arrives, quickly establish rapport with him or her, and then move directly into the interview.[14] Briefly discuss the purpose of the performance appraisal, and give an overview of what will be covered. After this orientation, present your evaluation. Go over each major area of performance, explaining how you arrived at your decision and detailing the evidence used in the evaluation. As you discuss each issue, use specific language and provide examples such as "One of your job responsibilities is

Merryhill Enterprises, Inc.

Performance Evaluation Form

This form is to be used to evaluate all employees biannually. The immediate supervisor will consider all relevant factors associated with an employee's job description and render an objective evaluation along two dimensions. A quantitative score will be given for each area covered as well as a written description stating particular details. Employees will have an opportunity to discuss their evaluations with the evaluating supervisor before the evaluation is forwarded to the personnel office for disposition.

Scoring: 1 = very poor performance;   5 = average performance;   10 = perfect performance.

Motivation 1   2   3   4   5   6   7   8   9   10
Comments:

Job knowledge 1   2   3   4   5   6   7   8   9   10
Comments:

Executive potential 1   2   3   4   5   6   7   8   9   10
Comments:

Communication skills   1   2   3   4   5   6   7   8   9   10
Comments:

Leadership skills   1   2   3   4   5   6   7   8   9   10
Comments:

Delegation skills   1   2   3   4   5   6   7   8   9   10
Comments:

Overall evaluation   1   2   3   4   5   6   7   8   9   10
Comments:

FIGURE 8-7   Appraisal interview form

to schedule quarterly meetings of the accounting staff and to distribute each meeting's minutes to the branch offices, ensuring that the data are accurate, readable, and timely. You have provided comprehensive minutes with clarity and speed, and it is my opinion that you are ready to take on some additional responsibilities in analyzing the data. I understand that the data are complex and we have to discuss methods for setting new goals in this area."

During the interview, be sure to encourage participation, feedback, and explanation. Some interviewees may not provide verbal input because of the anxiety or stress associated with evaluation, yet it is important for you to know how they feel about your evaluations. Ask for their self-evaluation for each of the performance factors. Ask them to rate themselves objectively but from their points of view. You will be surprised at how often employees overrate and underrate themselves. Such information can serve as a discussion starter for communicating about how they view their jobs.

Feedback is a critical element in an appraisal interview, and the responsibility for giving and receiving it rests with both the supervisor and the employee. The focus of feedback is not to pass judgment, but to report specific *events or behavior,* their *effects,* and what to do about them. Subjective interpretations by the supervisor or the employee should be minimized during the interview.

Two types of feedback are available during the appraisal interview. *Corrective* feedback attempts to alter negative or inappropriate behavior. In order to be effective, corrective feedback should be expressed in specific terms as much as possible. For example, "You did not prepare charts for the presentation yesterday as you were supposed to do" highlights a specific problem on the employee's part that must be addressed.

Supportive feedback encourages desirable behavior by the employee. Supportive feedback lets the employee know what he or she is doing right — and such knowledge is as important to performance as being alerted of areas that need improvement. When an appraisal interviewer concentrates not only on correcting problems or identifying new responsibilities, but on good work as well — especially behavior that goes beyond the employee's personal and work goals and contributes toward overall organizational goals — the employee is likely to strive toward outstanding rather than merely acceptable work. For example, "I'm pleased that you have learned to work on the new computer system and have helped other people to use it too" shows the employee that his or her willingness to go beyond what is expected is noticed and appreciated by the supervisor. Feedback is an opportunity for the supervisor to thank the employee for good work.

Supervisors are wise to use both supportive and corrective feedback to achieve maximum benefits from a performance review. For example, "Your work on this month's budget has been outstanding, and I would like to see that level of accuracy in the weekly updates" begins with supportive feedback and relates the praise to a situation that needs improvement, providing guidance and motivation at the same time. Corrective feedback can also be given first, for example, "In the future, you should sign up for a training course before you work with heavy machinery, but I am impressed by your interest in learning about that aspect of work at the plant." The supervisor can use the approach that best suits the employee's needs and communication style.[15]

The appraisal interview is an opportunity for employees to learn more about what is expected and valued in their work, and let their supervisors know how they are doing as well. The employee listens carefully as the supervisor discusses and gives feedback on each of the performance factors, noting areas of strength (where supportive feedback is given), weakness (a combination of supportive and corrective feedback), or special problems (where corrective feedback is given).

If you are being evaluated and disagree with the supervisor's assessment, discuss your reaction in a calm and objective manner, and offer to provide evidence of your position if necessary. If the supervisor has made general statements about your performance, ask for specifics — both of you may learn from them. Be familiar with your organization's policies on appraisal interviews. Knowing these guidelines ensures responsible communication by both parties.

Setting Revised Goals

Once each of the points has been covered and each performance factor has been discussed by both parties, set mutually derived goals for the next evaluation. As with all goal setting, both interviewer and interviewee identify elements of the job that are critical to employee and organizational productivity and determine realistic goals so that there is a good chance for their achievement. Mutual goal setting during the appraisal interview encourages employee participation in a significant decision-making process.

Finally, end the interview on a positive tone. Summarize the interview and ask for additional comments, questions, and explanations from the interviewee. At this point, the interviewer reemphasizes the importance of the performance appraisal process and encourages the employee to think positively about the next evaluation period. Appraisal interviews are meant to help employees and supervisors work better together. When receiving an evaluation, make a sincere effort to understand the supervisor's viewpoint, and to act on the mutually derived goals that are set. When employees and managers seriously and conscientiously participate in the appraisal process, it provides a valuable source of feedback that can lead to overall improvements in their work relationship.

Disciplinary Interviews

One of the most sensitive areas of business and professional communication is discipline. As evidenced by more than one million terminations per year, human nature makes it unlikely that the need for disciplinary action will disappear any time in the near future, so it is in your best interests to learn how to handle this delicate situation effectively.[16] For the most part, people do not relish the idea of having to discipline other people; having to punish those who are rebellious, unproductive, or lazy is not a pleasant activity.

When problems with employees occur, the skillfull manager or supervisor must be ready to administer a disciplinary response that will improve the problematic condition. Administering discipline can lead to productive outcomes if handled properly; others take note and recognize the goals, boundaries, protocol, and procedures that are appropriate in that particular organization. In other words, effective discipline can prevent problems from occurring in the future.

Nevertheless, disciplinary interviews must be handled with care. Official agencies such as the federal government and unions have enacted regulations for such interviews, and breaking them can get a manager into a lot of legal trouble. In addition, clumsy or mishandled disciplinary interviews can provoke controversy in the workplace and encourage employee resentment of supervisors. The most critical aspects of disciplinary interviews include notifying the employee of the problem, interviewing the employee, instituting disciplinary action, and documenting the incident.[17]

Notifying the Employee

Once misconduct has been noticed, the next step in the process of discipline involves notifying the employee so that corrective actions can be administered. Some offenses result from problems associated with the system, structure, or technology of a job rather than from misjudgment, bad faith, or carelessness on the employee's part. If you decide that the fault for an offense can be assigned to technical difficulties, you can simply inform the employee that you are aware of the problem and will work with him or her to correct it. Technical difficulties may include lapses in mail service, computer problems, equipment failure, and so forth.

If the employee is at fault, however, it is best to inform her or him of the problem calmly, directly, and quickly. Do not wait for a few weeks for the situation to "cool down." Smooth and decisive action deters other employees from similar actions. Set up a time for a disciplinary interview when you will not be disturbed and the office is relatively uncrowded.

Reviewing the Employee's Side of the Story

Interview the employee before conducting other investigations. If the particular situation requires you to interview others who may be involved in the misconduct or who know about the facts of the incident, be extremely careful to maintain the confidentiality of all employees.

Immediately get down to business, but maintain a nonhostile attitude. Ask for the employee's explanation for his or her behavior. Facts and explanations do not always coincide, so be sure to clarify any apparent contradictions between the employee's account and your understanding of the occurrence. Appropriate questioning techniques include open, mirror, and reflective questions, such as "Why do you think the equipment malfunctioned?" or "When James noticed the malfunction, you told him everything was under control. Were you distrustful of James's involvement in your project?" These are more appropriate because they allow the employee more latitude to respond and facilitate understanding between interview parties.

An accused employee may concede or accept responsibility for an act of misconduct, make an excuse, or justify her or his actions. It is your responsibility to *listen carefully* to the employee.

Instituting Disciplinary Action

Base all decisions on company policy, and provide written documentation to the employee if necessary. Be specific in your evaluation, and apply disciplinary measures consistently.

If, for example, you have recorded several occurrences of tardiness and absenteeism, you will give a stricter punishment to this employee than to a first offender. Your organization is likely to have a standard policy for warnings and repeated transgressions, a concept known as *progressive discipline*. Be sure that your employees are aware of the rules. If an employee has provided a reasonable explanation of what occurred during the offense, it may mitigate the punishment as well.

Explain the purpose of the discipline.   Base discipline on objective facts and the context of common goals. Stress the productive aspects of discipline. Put the disciplinary action in perspective of the employee's past record and future with the organization. Once you have informed the employee of the disciplinary action, discuss ways in which the situation can be improved. For example, if an employee has been disciplined for absenteeism whose root cause is alcohol-related, the supervisor might suggest counseling or a referral to an employee assistance program to give the employee the best chance of returning to full productivity. Be reasonable in your judgment of employee behavior, and ensure appropriate actions in the case of misconduct.

Document the incident and the interview.   Write an objective and detailed report of the incident, and file it with the appropriate offices (personnel, administration, etc.). Include in the report the steps that were taken with the employee and note all aspects of his or her own self-defense. Doing so ensures that the case will be reviewed accurately should disagreements or additional problems arise.

Media Interviews

As the following scenario illustrates, media interviews are a powerful communication tool.

> Isabel, a public relations assistant at a finance company, arrived at her office building one morning and was approached by a woman who asked her name and company affiliation. As Isabel responded, she noticed that the woman had a small notebook in hand and was ready to take notes. The woman introduced herself as a reporter with the local newspaper and informed Isabel that she wanted information for a story about an employee of the company who was suspected of illegal business activity. Isabel refused to comment to the reporter, but later in the day a local television station called to request an on-camera interview about the firm and its business practices. After consulting with her supervisor, Isabel agreed to a limited interview in which she would lay out the company's mission statement, its policy for ethical business behavior, and a statement on the situation. Using strong communication skills to present examples of company policy during the interview, she successfully demonstrated that her company's ongoing commitment to correct business practices was in no way diminished by the employee's behavior. She prevented an isolated incident from becoming a media event.

More frequently than you may realize, businesspeople are subjected to interview requests from the media. If the businessperson is a "public figure," such as the well-known chair of a large corporation, refusing interview requests is news in itself. Entire public relations and external communications departments work with the media daily to promote favorable images of their organizations, limit the damage done by competitors' rumors, and advertise new products and services. Given that the chances to be seen and heard via media coverage are more frequent these days, it is worthwhile to learn how to handle media interviews.

Types of Media Interviews

One of the more common types of media interviews is the *in-person press interview,* in which representatives from a press organization make personal contact, request an interview, and pose questions about a topic of interest.[18] These interviews can occur in the studio or newsroom or in the field. If the subject matter is controversial, reporters, photographers, or camerapersons are likely to arrive on the site (field) to capture the story in a natural setting.

Mediated press interviews are conducted through mass communications devices such as cameras/microphones linked via satellite or tele-conferencing. Although the stress of face-to-face contact with a reporter is less, the equipment and technology involved may be even more distracting.

You are probably very familiar with another type of media interview, *talk shows*. *Wall Street Week* is an example of this type of interview. Talk shows are planned well in advance, and the program is sometimes taped and then broadcast several days later. In most cases, the level of questioning is not as intense as in the first two interview formats. Regardless of the type of media interview you participate in, however, you are wise to understand the factors you must master to be successful. These factors can be broken down into four categories: preparation, format, practice, and performance.

Preparation

To prepare for a media interview, conduct as much research as time allows. Collect your information, including statistics, evidence, statements by employees, and a general statement of the organization's position. You may be the only voice to give your organization's side of the story, so have facts in order and clarified. Also be aware of the "big picture" — that is, how the interview can influence the situation and your organization's image in the long run.

Format

Become familiar with the location, participants, and medium of the interview. Will the interview take place on location (at your place of work) or in a studio? How long will it last? What type of questions will be posed? Who else will be interviewed for this story? Getting answers to these questions will help you to anticipate the interview's direction and focus.

If possible, collect information about the media organization and the person conducting the interview. How has he or she treated interviewees before? Should you be prepared for leading, biased, or loaded questions? If a member of a media organization has contacted you for an interview, his or her goal will be to gather newsworthy information about a specific topic. If you have made contact to get a message to the public, be sure your goal and purpose are clearly defined and can be accomplished in the amount of time allotted for the interview.

Knowing the intended medium of the story provides you with a great deal of knowledge about how to communicate your message. Printed media allow audiences more time to consume your responses, so you can elaborate, whereas television spots require briefer answers. Will the information be edited before broadcast or print? If so, request a copy of the final tape or print piece before it is aired or released.

Practice

Practice reduces anxiety and smoothes out the wrinkles in an actual interview. If possible, memorize your responses and say them out loud. Practice in front of a mirror so that you can observe your nonverbal style as you respond. Have someone else role-play the interview so that you can get into the rhythm of the anticipated interview. Tape- or video-record yourself if possible so that you can hear or see your actual responses.

Performance

The key to an effective performance is listening. Concentrate on the interviewer's message, and reduce environmental distractions (such as bystanders or equipment) to a minimum. Mentally review your research and goals before the start of the interview, and consider them as you listen to the interviewer's questions.

When you answer, pause to collect your thoughts whenever necessary. Communicate your response briefly and confidently. Saying too much is usually more risky than saying too little. Keep your emotions in check. Remaining calm and confident increases the credibility and effectiveness of your message.

Summary

You are likely to encounter various interview situations in your career. The most prevalent type is the selection interview. You can be most effective as an interviewee by writing a personal biography in advance of the interview, researching the company, preparing a résumé and a cover letter that are tailored to the specific job for which you are applying, dressing appropriately, and preparing to ask and answer questions. You must also know how to respond to illegal questions diplomatically but precisely. As you move up in your career, you will probably assume the role of interviewer at some time. The skills required in this role include developing job specifications, reviewing applicant materials, scheduling and conducting interviews, and choosing the best candidate for the job.

Another type of interview, the appraisal interview, is a common method of evaluating employee performance. Appraisal interviews can help to motivate workers, build morale, and allow an effective exchange of feedback between supervisors and workers. The appraisal process is usually based on performance factors, rating systems, or a combination of both. The appraisal that yields the greatest benefit is straightforward but considerate, nonhostile, encouraging, and specific.

Disciplinary interviews, the hardest to conduct, must be handled with care. In this case, as an interviewer you identify the problem, notify the employee, review his or her story, evaluate all evidence, and institute appropriate disciplinary action. The process must be documented carefully, and you must maintain objectivity as well as attention to federal guidelines.

Media interviews, the last category, are an increasing fact of daily work life. To use this interview to best advantage, you are wise to conduct as much research as time allows, know the format of the interview, practice answering questions aloud, listen carefully to the interviewer's questions, and respond confidently and succinctly.

Discussion

1. What are bona fide occupational qualifications? What were the BFOQs for jobs you have held?

2. What are some ways for employers to locate job candidates? Which are most effective, and why?

3. What are the two basic requirements for a legal interview question? Can you give some examples of legal and illegal questions and explain their status? How should illegal questions be answered?

4. What elements should be included in a personal biography? When this information is adapted to a résumé, what are the most important considerations in terms of the content and appearance of the résumé?

5. Why are appraisal interviews critical to healthy supervisor-employee relations? What are the major steps in conducting an appraisal interview?

6. Discuss the role of disciplinary interviews in business. How should a supervisor determine disciplinary action?

7. What are the different types of media interviews? What are the important elements in preparing for and participating in a media interview?

Activities

1. Consider the employment interview. Rank-order ten factors that you feel can make or break the opportunity to produce favorable outcomes. Share your list with your classmates.

2. Write five interview questions that are worded illegally. For each question, make the necessary corrections to convert it into a legal one.

3. In a small-group discussion, explain how much time you believe should be spent in opening "chitchat" between interviewer and interviewee. What are the advantages and disadvantages of such chitchat?

Would this vary depending on the type of interview under consideration?

4. Select any *five* of the performance factors that are important topics in an appraisal interview. For each of these factors, construct sample questions appropriate to the following business contexts:
   a. A principal appraising a teacher
   b. A production supervisor appraising a line worker
   c. A baseball manager appraising a player
   d. A minister of music appraising the church organist

Notes

1. J. Beilinson, "Workforce 2000: Already Here," *Personnel* 67 (1990): 3–4.
2. H. Z. Levin, "Supervisory Selection Systems," *Personnel* 63 (1986): 61–65.
3. L. Bowes, *No One Need Apply* (Boston: Harvard Business School Press, 1990).
4. B. E. Bostwick, *Resume Writing: A Comprehensive How-to-Do-It,* 4th ed. (New York: John Wiley & Sons, 1990).
5. E. P. Kelly and R. J. Aalberts, "Americans with Disabilities Act: Undue Hardship for Private Sector Employers?" *Labor Law Journal* 41 (1990): 675–684.
6. K. E. Buckner, H. S. Feild, and W. H. Holley, "The Relationship of Legal Case Characteristics with the Outcomes of Personnel Selection Court Cases," *Labor Law Journal* 41 (1990): 31–40.
7. C. S. Atwood and J. M. Neel, "New Lawsuits Expand Employer Liability," *HRMagazine* 35 (1990): 74–75.
8. D. Arthur, "Writing Up the Interview," in *Recruiting, Interviewing, Selecting, and Orienting New Employees* (New York: AMACOM, 1986).
9. R. N. Bolles, "Where Do You Want to Use Your Skills?" in *The 1991 What Color Is Your Parachute?* (Berkeley, Calif.: Ten Speed Press, 1991), pp. 102–149; Y. Parker, *The Resume Catalog: 200 Damn Good Examples* (Berkeley, Calif.: Ten Speed Press, 1988); D. Arthur, *Recruiting, Interviewing, Selecting, and Orienting New Employees* (New York: AMACOM, 1986).
10. M. S. Weisel, "Employer's Burden of Proof in 'Mixed Motive' Title VII Litigation and Available Remedies: *Hopkins v. Price Waterhouse* One Year Later," *Labor Law Journal* 42 (1991): 45–51.
11. C. W. Downs, G. P. Smeyak, and E. Martin, *Professional Interviewing* (New York: Harper & Row, 1980).
12. C. J. Stewart and W. B. Cash, *Interviewing: Principles and Practices,* 5th ed. (Dubuque, Iowa: William C. Brown, 1988).
13. Ibid.
14. Ibid.; Downs, Smeyak, and Martin, *Professional Interviewing*; J. P. Zima, *Interviewing: Key to Effective Management* (Chicago: Science Research Associates, 1983).
15. H. Karp, "The Lost Art of Feedback," in J. Williams Pfeiffer (ed.), *1987 Annual: Developing Human Resources* (San Diego, Calif.: University Associates, 1987), pp. 14–24; A. Gabor, "Catch a Falling Star System," *U.S. News & World Report,* June 5, 1984, pp. 43–45.

16. L. V. Imundo, *Employee Discipline: How to Do It Right* (Belmont, Calif.: Wadsworth, 1985).

17. G. H. Morris, S. C. Gaveras, W. L. Baker, and M. L. Coursey, "Aligning Actions at Work: How Managers Confront Problems of Employee Performance," *Management Communication Quarterly* 3 (1990): 303–333; M. L. McLaughlin, M. J. Cody, and H. D. O'Hair, "The Management of Failure Events: Some Contextual Determinants of Accounting Behavior," *Human Communication Research* 9 (1983): 208–224.

18. E. Blythin and L. A. Samovar, *Communicating Effectively on Television* (Belmont, Calif.: Wadsworth, 1985).

Group Communication Strategies

Groups are increasingly important to businesses because of their role in task sharing and problem solving. **Part 4** covers the principal influences in group dynamics and introduces a variety of techniques for problem solving, negotiating, and handling potentially destructive conflicts within an organization.

❑ Chapter 9 explores the effects of factors such as size, norms, and participation on group functioning and introduces some special group formats.

❑ Chapter 10 describes the process of preparing for and participating in a meeting, using a variety of critical thinking skills and problem-solving techniques.

❑ Chapter 11 presents practical and value-based approaches to handling negotiation and conflict that will be of long-term importance to you in your career.

Chapter 9

*F*undamentals of Group Communication

OBJECTIVES

After completing this chapter, you will be able to:

1. Understand why groups are important in business

2. Identify the characteristics of an effective group

3. Recognize the factors that contribute to or hinder group communication

4. Improve your participation level in groups

5. Understand the function and types of group leadership

6. Evaluate the role of special groups in business

Put this book down and take just a moment to list all the groups in which you participate. You will probably notice that you are a designated member of some group or groups. If you are a fraternity or sorority member, belong to an athletic team, or attend meetings of some professional student society on campus, you are involved in formal groups. Indeed, your enrollment in this course makes you a member of the group that meets in this classroom!

You will probably also notice that you participate in a good number of informal groups as well. You have regular friends with whom you eat daily, others with whom you study, others with whom you go to movies or games, and still others with whom you interact as you travel to campus.

In the 1950s, social psychologist Kurt Lewin suggested that group dynamics are indeed pervasive.[1] He argued that all people exist in a life space of which groups are an important part. Lewin's theory was based on the notion that a person cannot be separated from the groups with which he or she identifies. This theory has several premises: people are members of many groups at one time, a person's groups are an important part of his or her life space, groups create tensions in the life space, and therefore groups influence the movement of the person within the life space.

Groups are as prevalent in business and professional organizations as Lewin described them in humans' personal lives and as you have likely observed them on your campus. As you enter the work force, you will be asked to become part of work groups, and your participation will increase as you move up in the organization. (Researchers have estimated that executives spend as much as ten hours a week in various group meetings.[2]) You will become a member of formal work departments, such as accounting, personnel, production, or computer services, which are often further subdivided into work groups. For example, the human resources department may include groups that focus on employee benefits, training, recruitment, building maintenance, salary administration, and security. You will also serve as a member of formal committees within the organization, such as safety, credit union review board, or security. You will participate in lunch groups, after-work "happy hour" groups, car pools, or break-room groups. Indeed, the communication between and within groups is vital to the organization.

We cannot stress too much how differently businesses and professional organizations would operate without group communication. We offer the following propositions about communication in groups, all of which have a substantial research base:[3]

◆ Higher quality decisions are made by groups than by people working alone.

◆ People who participate in group decision making are more committed to the group's decisions than to those given them by a manager or supervisor.

◆ Pitfalls and hazards that may be ignored by a person working alone are regularly uncovered by groups through debate and questioning.

◆ Employee morale is higher when people are teamed with co-workers on projects and tasks.

◆ People who regularly communicate with others in the organization are more satisfied on the job than employees who are isolated from others.

◆ Employees who network with others in organizational groups are more committed to the goals and missions of their organizations than those who do not so participate.

◆ People who are teamed together in work groups take greater responsibility for the task, and the "fixing of blame" for errors is shared by all.

Can there be any wonder, then, why organizations devote a great amount of time and energy to the maintenance and perpetuation of groups? The positive outcomes can make the difference between a profitable company and a loser. People who develop strong communication skills and use them effectively in group situations regularly exhibit the best performance.

In this chapter, we introduce you to the basics of groups — what they are, how they function, and what types there are. We start with two basic questions: What do all groups have in common? Just what makes a group different from a collection of people?

What Is a Group?

According to Michael Argyle, there are five kinds of small groups in which social interaction takes place.[4] These are the family; adolescent friendship groups; work groups; committees, problem-solving groups, and creative groups; and therapy groups. We concentrate on work groups and problem-solving groups in the organizational context.

For years, one of the great debates among scholars of group communication centered around what constituted a "group" and, specifically, in what circumstances a "small" group was no longer small. Definitions of groups ranged from three persons all the way to fifteen or twenty.

Clearly, the interaction that takes place between two persons — a dyad — is different from what takes place among three or more — a group. As the size of a group increases, the interaction among the members becomes more formal, there is less chance for each member to participate, topics become less intimate, and tasks take longer to accomplish. Unlike a dyad, which has one relationship, groups have many relationships. The larger the group is, the more relationships there are to maintain (see Figure 9-1).

The best way to define a group is to look at the behavior of people

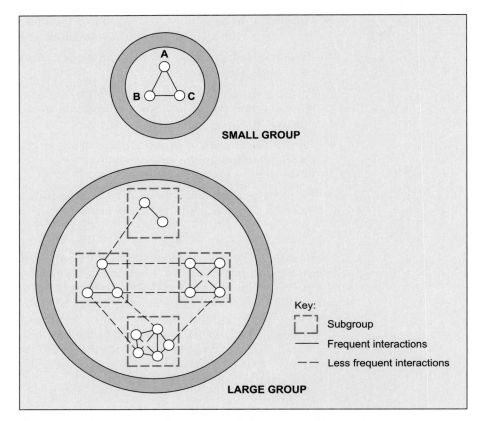

FIGURE 9-1   Size, location, and frequency of interaction are important
factors in group communication. Members of small groups have more
consistent interactions than do members of large groups.

within the group. There are several important behaviors that you can observe when a group is functioning:

◆ The participants know themselves by name or role.

◆ There is a considerable amount of interaction among the participants.

◆ Each participant has some degree of influence on each of the other
  members.

◆ Each participant defines himself or herself as a member of the group
  and is also defined by outsiders as a member.

◆ The participants share some common goal, interest, or benefit by
  holding membership in the group.

◆ There is leadership present.

Let us look at each of these behaviors a bit more closely.

Name or Role

Unlike public speaking situations, where the speaker knows the audience en masse (e.g., Los Angeles Lions Club, University of Michigan Business School faculty, Dallas Masonic Lodge, the 11:00 A.M. M-W-F general accounting class), in group situations, the members know each other as individuals. In each group you belong to, you either know the participants' names (e.g., Mr. Cooper, Diane, P. J.), their roles (e.g., boss, vice-president, discussion leader), or both.

Considerable Amount of Interaction

Communication plays an important role in every productive group. In meetings, some members request information and others provide it. There are disagreements among members. Members clarify their positions and statements.

In reality, communication seldom occurs in a uniform or consistent pattern. In some groups, dominant participants "hog the floor." In other groups, isolates contribute very little, if anything. Sometimes participants are encouraged to interact with each of the other members. In still other groups, who speaks when and for how long is controlled by the leader.

Influence

When a group gets together, each person influences and is influenced by the others to some degree. Participants who express forceful arguments that are backed by powerful documentation may strongly influence others in the group. Influence can be nonverbal as well as verbal. If one group member scowls at another, it may influence the way that he or she reacts, speaks, or even votes on an item.

Membership

Over a period of time, as groups continue to meet and interact, the participants bond together. They take pride in their work. They are proud to be members of the same group and express these feelings to others who are not members. By the same token, outsiders identify these people as members of the group as they continue to meet over time. This sense of membership is a key factor distinguishing an effective group.

Common Goals, Interests, or Benefits

In almost all cases, common goals represent the "glue" that holds the group together. They may even be the entire reason a person chooses to be part of a group. If a person does not see that working with others is a means to achieve a common goal, further a common interest, or help facilitate a common benefit, then he or she should withdraw and complete the task individually!

Leadership

Every functioning group exhibits leadership. In some cases, external sources formally designate the leader. For example, you may consider your teacher in this class to be a leader. She or he was assigned to this position by the departmental chair.

A leader can also emerge from the group interaction. Sometimes a group formally votes and selects a person to lead. At other times, because of the quality of her or his contributions to the group, a person is simply looked to by others as the group leader.

There are many groups, however, in which it is difficult to pinpoint any one person as the group leader. Yet leadership is certainly present as the group interacts. In these cases, we say that the group has *shared leadership* in that all of the functions of leadership are present, but they are provided by several members, not just one.

Factors Influencing Group Communication

We have already pointed out in previous chapters that achieving effective communication is not easy. Group communication, because of the variety of people who participate, requires additional effort. There are several factors that affect the quality and quantity of communication within a group, including cohesiveness, norms, roles, conformity, groupthink, and conflict. Some factors have a positive effect on group communication; others are barriers that must be overcome. We examine each of these, highlighting methods for achieving successful group communication.

Cohesiveness

One major goal for any group is to remain intact no matter how difficult the situation or challenging the environment. Cohesiveness refers to the degree to which a group "hangs together." There are two ways to talk about cohesiveness.

A group is cohesive when each of its participants retains her or his membership. There are many reasons group membership is desirable: attraction to other members, perceived benefits that cannot be obtained alone, or financial and social investments that cannot be abandoned.

A group is also cohesive according to the extent to which participants perceive their membership in the group. The more that the participants identify with the purposes and goals of the group, tell outsiders of the activities that the group engages in, and take pride in being a member, the more cohesive the group is.

Highly cohesive groups are much more likely to meet challenges and obstacles successfully than groups that are lower in cohesiveness. In his book on group composition and cohesiveness, Marvin Shaw suggested the following propositions:[5]

◆ The quantity and quality of communication in high-cohesive groups are much more extensive than in low-cohesive groups.

◆ High-cohesive groups exert greater influence over their members than do low-cohesive groups

◆ High-cohesive groups achieve their goals more effectively than do low-cohesive groups.

◆ Member satisfaction is greater in high-cohesive groups than in low-cohesive groups.

Maintaining cohesiveness in a group is a challenge, but strong and effective communication can help. Taking time to encourage members to feel proud of belonging, reinforce accomplishments both inside and outside of formal meetings, and allow others to express themselves freely are ways that you can promote cohesiveness in your group interactions. The following example serves to illustrate these principles.

Pat and Carol are members of a professional group that meets once a week to decide on fund-raising activities for local charities. As so many different people are members, there is a lack of cohesiveness in the group. Pat and Carol decided that nothing substantive would be accomplished unless they helped to build a sense of belonging. In their meetings they began to make comments such as "Jim, you know this area of town — what is your opinion of our efforts there?" "Danny, you always know where the big donors are in your own business — who do you think we should target for donations to our group?" and "I am so proud of how we have pulled together in the last two meetings!" "People around town are saying so many nice things about our group's accomplishments." "It is wonderful that anyone here can freely give his or her opinion without criticism." After three meetings, groups members were making similar statements, and the level of cohesiveness continued to build to productive levels.

Norms

Group norms are standards or limits that define appropriate behavior. They are rarely formally communicated to the members, and new participants in the group must learn what these are through observation or trial and error. Consider the following norms:

Negative criticism of another person is unacceptable.
Meetings are "strictly business."
First names are not to be used during meetings.
A single topic's discussion cannot exceed ten minutes.

As you can see, norms can reflect group members' preferences and can influence how the group operates. A failure to follow group norms can produce negative consequences for a member. He or she may be isolated from others, ignored, and, in some cases, not even notified of group meetings.

Groups must carefully monitor their norms to prevent members from becoming disenchanted with petty rules or policies and to facilitate interaction among different members. In the margin of this book, write out five norms that you have seen successful groups use to remain effective. Next, write at least three norms that unproductive groups possess. How can groups replace the second list with the first? In the next class period, ask your instructor about the norms she or he sees emerging in this communication class. Compare these to the first list of productive norms that you wrote in the margin.

Roles

As we mentioned earlier, every participant in a group has a role. In many groups, participants play several roles. Taking on a role produces certain expectations in others about how you will behave in the group. For example, you expect your teacher will prepare for class, take attendance, give lectures, facilitate discussions, meet with students outside of class, prepare examinations, and turn in final grades. You expect that a work group supervisor will regulate the work of employees, call staff meetings when necessary, give performance appraisal interviews, review complaints or grievances, and so forth.

In a group, we often find that people emerge in certain roles because of the way they communicate with other participants in the group. The following is a list of group roles that are often played by members:[6]

Isolate — one who sits and fails to participate
Facilitator — one who makes sure that everyone gets to talk

Dominator — one who speaks too often and too long
Harmonizer — one who keeps tensions low
Free rider — one who does not do her or his share of the work
Detractor — one who constantly criticizes and gripes
Digressor — one who takes the group on wild goose chases
Airhead — one who is never prepared for group meetings
Socializer — one who is a member of the group only for social and
    personal reasons

From the preceding list, are there some roles that you excel at? Which of these roles really irritate you? Which of these roles are incompatible with one another? Do you think that airheads and free riders get along well? What about isolates and socializers? Recognition of these roles provides the group with a means of maximizing the positive ones and minimizing the less effective ones.

Conformity

Conformity simply means agreement with or correspondence to set ideas, rules, or principles. In a group, these ideas are often the opinion of one or more dominant members. In essence, participants "give in," compromise, or abandon their individual positions to align with others in the group.

Reasons for conformity.   People conform to group ideas and opinions for many reasons, not the least of which is that no one can act with complete independence of all other group members. It is inevitable that simply interacting with others will influence how you think about the issues being discussed.

Another force for conformity is time. If a group is about to conclude its work, you may receive hostile or uncooperative treatment if you bring up another idea or try to spark debate on an issue that has already been resolved ("C'mon, Bob, we agreed a week ago that we would hire the new candidate"). Highly directive or authoritarian leadership, which suppresses individual contributions to a group, also encourages conformity (although we do not promote this process). Finally, social pressure or the need to "belong" may discourage disagreement with other group members. In highly cohesive groups, the desire to maintain the group as a unified body can influence a person's freedom to disagree with others.

Conformity and group functioning.   Conformity may be necessary for group effectiveness. Groups eventually must reach decisions, hopefully by consensus, and conformity among group members provides a means to reach decisions. Conformity to various rules, standards, and especially the goals of the group are necessary under all conditions of group decision making. Members may be encouraged to disagree about the definition of the problem, the alternatives generated, and the criteria by which to evaluate alternatives, but certain fundamental issues — such as why the group exists and how it should operate — must be agreed on by everyone.

Emergency situations, which require quick decisions, seldom afford the luxury of conflict or disagreement. Even in less tense moments, there are moments in group discussion at which any additional advocacy or dissension among group members deteriorates into useless discussion. At this point, the group should strive for conformity to avoid wasting time.[7]

Finally, groups that are naturally contentious and argumentative may benefit from promoting conformity. Getting group members to view the problem from others' perspective and to consent to a mutually agreed on decision is a monumental task for some groups. In situations in which group conflict is common, failure to promote conformity can lead to a diminished effect on morale and working relationships.[8]

Groupthink

When carried to its extreme, conformity leads to groupthink. (Figure 9-2 illustrates the relationship between conformity and groupthink.) *Groupthink* is the term for situations in which a group fails to explore alternative solutions, problems, or concerns in an effort to present a united or cohesive front to outsiders. Irving Janis outlined several conditions that lead to groupthink.[9] One is being out of touch — when a group meets for long periods of time away from its regular routines, members forget the big picture and do whatever is necessary to make the group succeed, regardless of how those actions may harm others. A second is being out of order — informal and nonstandardized decision-making procedures let a group venture into unproductive areas with no way to get back on course. A third is being overruled — when group members feel that criteria and decision-making procedures are thrust on them by a leader, they are likely to follow along without much advocacy or dissention. A fourth is being out of resources — when faced with a critical problem, a short time frame for deciding, and no reasonable alternative other than the one favored by the leader, the group falls back on groupthink.

A tragic example of groupthink was the space shuttle *Challenger* disaster in January, 1986. The contractors who helped to build the *Challenger* were uncertain about the viability of launching the shuttle on that fateful morning but deferred to (in some cases were overruled by) NASA officials because time was short, alternatives were few, and the launch for that day was deemed very important.[10] Essentially, those members of the group making the decision to launch the shuttle suffered from most of the groupthink factors just mentioned (*being out of touch* — not enough communication on the day of the launch; *being out of order* — departure from regular

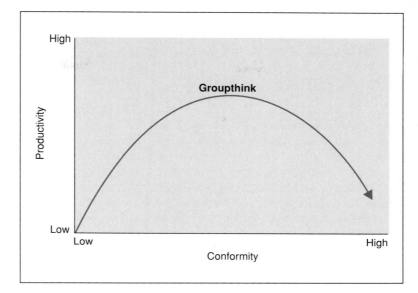

FIGURE 9-2   *As conformity increases, it becomes a disadvantage rather than an advantage to the group's communication and productivity.*

decision-making rules; *being overruled* — higher level decision maker ignoring information from lower levels; *being out of resources* — primarily time).

Symptoms of groupthink.   How can groups determine if they are victims of groupthink? Three major symptoms can be observed.[11] A first symptom is the group's tendency to view itself as powerful and omnipotent. Prior success, self-indulgence, and feelings of superiority can lead the group to this attitude. Group members may share illusions of invulnerability that encourage excessive risk taking. Furthermore, the group may feel that its behavior is beyond scrutiny and may therefore enact decisions without regard to moral consequences.

A second symptom of groupthink is closemindedness. A group experiencing groupthink tends to shut out information that does not conform to prevailing group opinion. Group members rationalize this avoidance by claiming that the contradictory information is insignificant or irrelevant to the group task or that the source of the information is ill-advised or inconsequential.

Pressure toward uniformity is a third symptom of groupthink. Uniformity of members' opinions, values, and ideas usually leads to one-sided decisions. Pressure toward uniformity comes from two sources: self and group. Self-imposed uniformity minimizes personal doubts or counterargu-

FOCUS on *Corporate Communication*

BEN & JERRY'S

What happens to communication when an organization more than doubles its work force in three years? If the company is Ben & Jerry's, the answer seems to be "Don't take things for granted — talk a lot more, and make sure everyone is listening." The Vermont ice cream manufacturer, which currently employs about 380 people, has been striving to meet the demand for its products, but the struggle has not diminished its unique culture and has increased its attention to communication issues.

Until this growth spurt, structured communication did not really exist in the company. Responsibility for companywide employee communication originally belonged to the human resources department, then was affiliated with the public relations department, and now resides with the administration department at the main Waterbury location, where a communications team assesses and plans for the growing needs of employees.

The communications team works to implement new communications systems (i.e., more structured forms of communication), show people how to use them, and find out if they are meeting people's needs throughout the company. The communications team includes the company president, the assistant to the president, and the communications coordinator, who is also editor of the company newsletter.

One major medium of communication is the employee newsletter, *The Daily Plant,* produced in-house via desktop publishing technology and assistance from the art department. The *Plant* contains updates from various locations and departments and even personal ads. Nevertheless, the *Plant* is just one element in a culture that emphasizes creativity and innovation with a strong commitment to community. The culture derives from the combined charisma of founders Ben Cohen and Jerry Greenfield and the company's mission statement: a written commitment to quality in its products, respect for individuals and communities, and the determination to seek new creative ways of addressing challenges without becoming "corporate."

One of the basic characteristics of the company is its creative use of traditional forms of communication. For example, group communication is an important component of most organizations. At Ben & Jerry's, group participation reflects employees' personal identification with their company. Committees on everything from human resource issues and employee advisory groups to the Joy Gang and Green Team (responsible for keeping people laughing and for elaborating the company's commitment to environmental causes, respectively) show the role groups play in holding the rapidly expanding company together and maintaining its sense of identity.

ments about prevailing group opinion. This may occur because members value the opinion of the group more than their own ("We know they must be right; they always are") or because they see consensus of the group as more important than the expression of contradictory viewpoints.

As the company grows, it maintains its spirit through the concerted efforts of several groups. The Joy Gang coordinates events such as Elvis Day (featuring Presley tunes and Graceland's menu). The public relations department provides cafeteria reruns of "Late Night with David Letterman" (including his "Top 10" lists of least-popular ice cream flavors, such as "Zsa Zsa Gaboreo" and "Manuel Norieggnog") and "Today" show excerpts featuring Ben and Jerry. Other groups, especially those that provide employee supports, such as the child care center and a mediation training class, give people a sense of mutual commitment to the company.

Not only are groups formed for a wide variety of unusual purposes; the way groups function also reflects the free-spirited culture at Ben & Jerry's. Staff meetings resemble pep rallies: Ben and Jerry show up to cheer people on, and music and videos add to the celebration. At theme meetings focusing on particular issues, concerns, or problems, the staff may choose tokens — plastic toys, silly hats, even wax lips for one meeting on communication — and break into problem-solving groups by identifying matching tokens.

Although most employees are from in state and reflect Vermont's ethnic and cultural demographics, there is an interesting difference between the work force at the original Waterbury plant and the work force at the newer Springfield location. The Waterbury employees are a more regionally diverse group: many commute from a radius of an hour to get to work, and three years is considered a long tenure with the nascent company. The Springfield employees, even though at a newer and younger site, have a well-established employee culture because they both live and work in the same community. (A tongue-in-cheek excerpt from the *Daily Plant*'s "Multi-site Glossary of Terms" reads, "Main Plant — elitist term used by Waterbury employees to mean *their* plant"; "Corporate — playful term used by Springfield employees to mean *Waterbury*.") The multisite structure has resulted in increased attention to communication among all parts of the company but with ongoing recognition that it is still okay to have fun, even when dealing with an issue as important as communication.

Perhaps one of the best-known characteristics of Ben & Jerry's culture is its commitment to a broad spectrum of social and environmental causes. From products like "Rainforest Crunch" ice cream, to an annual "Merry Mulching" fest to compost discarded Christmas trees, to a "Chili Cookoff" to raise food money for fourteen thousand local families, the company is characterized by commitment to community. Many people join the company because of these ideals and see in their organization a working balance of economic success and social responsibility.

Groups impose their own pressures for uniformity by exerting direct pressure on a deviant member to conform to group desires. These pressures may range from subtle tactics, such as nonverbally expressing disapproval (frowns) or ignoring nonconforming group members, to more direct behaviors, such as attacking these members or questioning their motives and loyalty. ("So, Betsy, you want to make us look as if we don't get along just because you're nervous about the decision?").

Minimizing groupthink. There are several ways to lessen the tendency toward groupthink.[12] Groups must question themselves and their actions to ensure better decision making. One specific technique for encouraging open discussion is to have the leader ask each member of the group to assume the role of critical evaluator. It should be stressed that the role is one of constructive, rather than destructive, questioning. Another technique is for the group, from time to time, to divide into several subgroups with similar tasks to determine if group composition and size affect the ability of the group to remain adversarial and objective. Sometimes splitting the group into smaller subgroups can lead to fresh perspectives.

A third technique is for each member of the group to discuss the group's discussion and actions with trusted outsiders to obtain an untainted and objective viewpoint unaffected by the group atmosphere. Even friends or spouses can serve in this role. A fourth method of avoiding groupthink is to have the group designate a special meeting where all misgivings, second-guessing, and objections are aired. Each member is encouraged to express any doubts she or he may have about any phase of the group's deliberation.

Conflict

Conflict is one of the most misunderstood facets of group communication. Many group leaders avoid conflict because they think it detracts from a group's purpose and goals. Their attitude is that when conflict is present, a group is not running smoothly.

We take the position that conflict is what group meetings are all about. Conflict can be used productively by leaders to test group-generated ideas or propositions before they are implemented. Conflict does not signal that a meeting is disorderly, raucous, or rude. It means people are actively discussing issues. We believe that if a group does not exhibit conflict by debating ideas or questioning others, there is very little reason for it to exist. The members may as well be working by themselves. Conflict, then, is the essence of group interaction. Leaders can use conflict as a means to determine what is and what is not an acceptable idea, solution, or problem. In a very real sense, conflict and advocacy are kindred spirits.

There is one word of caution, however. The conflict we are talking about refers to debate on issues, not personalities. A group will not be productive if arguments are centered on the participants, rather than on what the participants are talking about. A contribution such as "You've never known what you're talking about before, and you don't know what you're talking about now" is not the type of conflict we advocate. Group members and especially leaders must be diligent in refocusing members' attention on the issues, not on personalities, when conflicts arise. We discuss conflict management and other challenges to communication in depth in Chapter 11.

Getting Involved in Groups

Now that we have covered the basic factors (size, norms, cohesiveness, and so forth) that influence group dynamics, we turn to the study of group participation. Groups in the workplace can take several forms. You may be assigned to formal task groups, or you may elect to volunteer for special project groups. In any case, your level of involvement affects the group process and your attitudes toward the group.

One of the more important factors in group involvement is the style of participation employed by the groups. Authoritarian, laissez-faire, and participative structures allow varying degrees of member contribution and participation, with very different results.

Authoritarian Structures

An authoritarian style of decision making is one in which a leader hands down a decision to the group. The participants are not involved in the process; they simply follow what the leader tells them to do.

Two situations call for authoritarian decision making: crises and lack of knowledge. When the group faces a crisis situation, decisions must be made swiftly, and there is little time for a group discussion. When members are asked to give opinions, provide evidence, or supply details on material about which they have no knowledge or information, valuable time and effort are wasted, and other participants may be embarrassed or offended.

Apart from these circumstances, authoritative decision making has major disadvantages. Morale among participants is lessened because members want to contribute but cannot. The confidence members have in their leader is low, while the feelings of suspicion run high. The chance for a poorer decision is high because some valuable input may never surface and ideas may remain untested.

Laissez-Faire Structures

A laissez-faire style of decision making is one in which there is minimal involvement on the part of the group leader. A group operating with this type of decision making in essence makes its own decisions without guidance or direction from a leader. The group is "on its own." This type of group is difficult to deal with because some people may see themselves as fulfilling the leadership function without actually demonstrating the necessary skills. Laissez-faire groups are likely to grope aimlessly for ways of identifying problems or establishing criteria unless a concerted effort is made among various group members to do so. There are probably some people who enjoy group work without a directive leader. Nevertheless, research has indicated that valuable time and resources can be wasted in a directionless group.

Participative Structures

According to Gary Yukl, participation "usually refers to a management style or type of decision procedure through which subordinates are allowed to influence some of the manager's decisions."[13] In every group, there are degrees to which participants are allowed to demonstrate that influence. When we refer to participative decision making, we mean that the leader does not make the decision for the group (authoritarian), nor does he or she turn over the decision to the group (laissez-faire); rather, the leader makes the decision with the group.

Research has indicated that there are a number of benefits to this style of decision making. Group members who participate in decision making are more committed to the outcome or result. Participation yields a more interesting and satisfying experience for the group members. Better decisions result when group members have skills or knowledge not possessed by the leader and are willing to cooperate with him or her in meetings.

For the participative decision-making process to work, several conditions must be met. A leader must have sufficient authority to delegate and share decision making with the group. The leader must have group members who are knowledgeable about the subject matter and willing to participate in a discussion about that content. There must be enough time for the group to complete a discussion and reach consensus. And the leader must be competent in such participative methods as questioning, delegating, defining, gatekeeping, agenda setting, and others.

We would be remiss if we failed to say that there are some problems with these methods. Not only does participative decision making take more time; it can create expectations on the members' parts that they will be influential in other group affairs. Some participants may perceive their leader as deficient in confidence and expertise. Furthermore, when a decision belongs to a group as a unit rather than to individuals, assigning responsibility for failures and shortcomings is difficult. Yet on balance, participative decision making seems to be highly valued in organizations that practice it.

Group Leadership

Participation and leadership in groups are frequently interrelated processes. The degree to which group members make their own decisions affects the leadership style with which they will be most comfortable. There are many different descriptions of leadership. Some emphasize that a leader is one who influences the actions of others. A communication-specific definition is that a leader is a member of a group who speaks the most, speaks the most to the group as a whole, is spoken to the most, and directs communication in the group to productive levels.

One mistake that many casual students of group communication make is to suggest that a manager or supervisor is necessarily a group leader. This is simply not true. A person can be "in charge" of a group without exhibiting any leadership qualities. A member who leads a group may be its least experienced, lowest ranking participant. If you played organized team sports before you enrolled in college, you probably remember quite clearly teams in which the captain did not exhibit true leadership. The person who "fired up" the team, gave it direction, and assisted others when needed may have been "one of the gang," not a designated leader as such. Many training and development programs today attempt to teach managers or supervisors how to be leaders. The focus of these programs is on transforming managers from people with titles into people who exhibit true influence, direction, and motivation.

Types of Leadership

Leaders in business organizations and the professions can be viewed in four ways.[14] Each defines leadership differently and provides insight into how a person can become a leader. These four approaches are traits, style, situational leadership, and functional leadership.

Traits.   Put down this book for a moment and think of some people you believe are true leaders. Now contrast them with some people you definitely know are not leaders. What about their personalities, physical appearance, or behaviors is markedly different?

The trait approach is the oldest method by which people have attempted to measure leadership. Before the turn of the century, group and organizational scholars began to differentiate characteristics that belonged to leaders from those that belonged to nonleaders. In other words, the search was for those stable characteristics that defined a person as a leader.

Space does not allow us to fully detail every finding in these studies, and many are contradictory and inconclusive. Nevertheless, three studies do merit attention. Ralph Stogdill summarized decades of trait research and concluded that in general, leaders seem to be higher than nonleaders in intelligence, scholarship, dependability and responsibility, activity and social participation, and socioeconomic status.[15] Joseph Jaworkski's research found that leaders outdo nonleaders in presentation of a compelling vision, power, exemplification of organizational values, risk taking, and entrepreneurial imagination and transformation.[16] In one of the landmark research efforts under the trait approach, John Geier discovered negative traits that keep a person away from the leadership role.[17] These are uninformativeness, nonparticipation, extreme rigidity, authoritarian behavior, and offensive verbalization. To summarize the trait approach to leadership, leaders demonstrate intelligence, dependability, social skills, vision, power, values, risk taking, and imagination but avoid rigidity and offensive behavior toward others.

Style.   A second way to conceptualize leaders is to focus on their styles. Styles are the behaviors that leaders use when interacting with group members. A discussion of styles assumes that there is "one best style" that works best in most situations.

The most popular classification of leader styles follows that outlined for decision making: authoritarian, participative, and laissez-faire. Notice that when classifying a leader into one of these three categories, you necessarily rely on behaviors. Actions, defined by what leaders say or do, determine if a leader is one style or another.

Another way to conceptualize styles is by determining how a leader emphasizes tasks (the problem at hand) and relationships in the group through communication with the participants. According to Blake and Mouton, an emphasis on both people and production (tasks and relationships) yields the best results in most situations.[18]

Situational leadership.   A third view of leaders suggests that there is no one best style but rather that the best style is the one adapted to the situation at hand. This approach, known as the situational view, has two positions regarding how flexible leaders can be in demonstrating situation-specific behavior. One position holds that the effective leader is flexible and adapts his or her behavior to the demands of the situation. Leaders are assumed to read a situation and select the appropriate behaviors for that circumstance. Hence, as a leader, you would not always place equal emphasis on tasks and relationships because the situation in which you find yourself may well require you to emphasize one over the other.

One of the best examples of this position is the work of Paul Hersey and Ken Blanchard, whose situational leadership theory is based on a leader's ability to *adapt* to a group's maturity level.[19] According to the theory, maturity is a combination of a group's willingness and ability to do a task. The more willing and able the group is, the more mature it is. As a group progresses in maturity, it requires less direction and less socio-emotional support.

Hersey and Blanchard suggested that a group begins in a *directing* phase; here the leader must provide a great deal of guidance. As the group matures, it moves to a *coaching* phase, which allows the leader to instruct, act as a role model, and nurture group members. In the *supporting* phase, the leader is in the role of peer and gives compliments, reassures, minimizes doubts, and encourages productivity. In the most mature phase, *delegating*, the leader directly or indirectly moves responsibility for group tasks, creativity, solutions, and decisions to group members. In this phase, members shoulder more of the group's work.

The other position regarding leader flexibility assumes that the leader is a constant and that the point is to match the leader to situations that are appropriate for his or her leadership style. Research on this position was conducted by Fred Fiedler, whose work assumes that leaders cannot with any degree of effectiveness act one way with some groups and yet another way with other groups.[20] His theory calls for leaders who are competent in particular tasks and with particular types of people to be placed with groups that are similar in their task and relational orientation. For example, a communication department was composed of very young faculty members who were bright and energetic but demanded complete participation in the decision-making process. Their former chairperson did not work out because she was very experienced and somewhat dogmatic about her own views. She preferred to make decisions first and then inform the faculty. A new chairperson was hired who was young, energetic, less experienced, and certainly less "set in his ways." He sought input from the faculty to assure himself that decisions reached were correct. This appropriate match between group and leader was very successful. Figure 9-3 illustrates these two perspectives on situational leadership.

Functional leadership.   Sometimes groups contain several members who can perform many of the duties and responsibilities of a leader. When groups rise to the occasion and perform leadership functions depending on need, the group is using a functional approach to leadership. Some group members may be very task oriented and push the group toward solving the problem. These members supply the group with a task function. Other members may be adept at maintaining harmony and social relations in the group and serve the group in this way. Think about the last time you were in a group situation. Did you notice that several people were fulfilling the roles and functions of leadership? Perhaps you were successful at persuading group

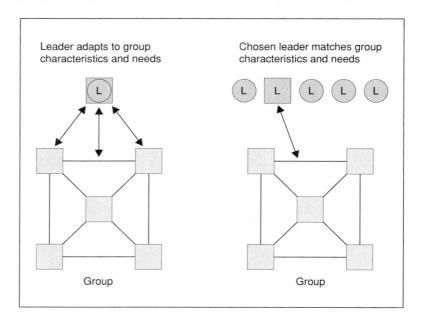

FIGURE 9-3   *Situational leadership is based on an individual's ability to be flexible. Some leaders adapt to changes in the group; in other situations, the leader is chosen because he or she matches the group's characteristics.*

members to adopt a particular viewpoint or were able to reduce conflict. If so, you were providing the group with leadership functions.

Special Groups

We now turn to some less common (but increasingly popular) formats for groups. Modern books on business and professional communication are devoting increasing space to what many consider to be the "wave of the future" for group meetings: tele-conferencing and video-conferencing. Because of increased time and financial pressures, many organizations are relying on electronic means of conducting group meetings. Efforts to increase productivity have also resulted in new kinds of groups known as quality circles and teams. These groups bring together people with different experience and perspectives to encourage mutual learning. All of these special formats have significant impacts on group communication.

Tele-conferencing and Video-conferencing

Tele-conferencing requires a hookup that enables each participant to hear the others in remote locations. Typically, one or more participants are present at each of several locations, with a speakerphone on a table in front of them. Video-conferencing requires a camera and microphone with a signal sent by satellite to a monitor at remote locations. Again, one or more group members can participate at each of several locations.

Advantages. Organizations may choose to hold a discussion using one of these two modern electronic methods for several reasons. The primary reason is cost. Once an organization has invested in the necessary equipment, the only real charge is line use, either for the telephone or satellite dish. When compared with the thousands of dollars companies spend in airline fares to get people to face-to-face meetings, the savings in tele-conferencing or video-conferencing are substantial.

Another advantage is time. Travel eats away at time. Let us look at a typical trip from Dallas, Texas, to Los Angeles, California. A businessperson leaves her home at 6:00 A.M. to catch a 7:00 A.M. flight. On arriving in

Technology adds yet another factor to the dynamics of group interaction. Video-conferencing is a rapidly growing form of communication in business because of its time- and money-saving potential.

Los Angeles at 11:00 A.M. CST (9:00 A.M. local), she takes a taxi to a building, arriving at 11:45 A.M. CST (9:45 A.M. local) for a meeting that begins fifteen minutes later. The meeting lasts an hour and a half, making it 1:30 P.M. CST (11:30 A.M. local). After lunch, she hails another taxi, leaves Los Angeles at 4:00 P.M. CST (2:00 P.M. local), and arrives back in Dallas four hours later. When she arrives home at about 10:00 P.M., the day is over. This executive spent sixteen hours attending one meeting! With tele-conferencing or video-conferencing, the meeting would have taken an hour and a half out of her day. In business, time is money, and there is no question that both can be saved through these methods.

Disadvantages.   The primary disadvantage of electronic communication stems from people's natural preference for face-to-face interaction. Many people like to meet with others face to face, shake hands with the other person, chitchat about nonwork events, smile, and so on. There is something to be said for the way that people are comfortable communicating. To many people, face-to-face interaction provides not only the greatest amount of information but the most comfort. To these people, no dollar value can be placed on communicating with others in person.

Special communication requirements.   More than in any other type of meeting, discussions that are conducted electronically require precise and well-defined rules of interaction because nonverbal communication is restricted or unavailable. In tele-conferencing, participants are limited to the voice. There is no way to judge the reactions that can usually be discerned from facial expressions. These reactions, such as confusion, anger, hesitancy, surprise, dismay, displeasure, or pain, are frequently relied on by participants in face-to-face meetings.

In video-conferencing, nonverbal reactions are available to participants but on a limited basis. Members do not feel the sense that the group is "in a meeting." Furthermore, there is a great loss of control over who takes the floor when.

As a result, there is no naturally identified way of deciding "who speaks when on what." In an ordinary meeting, speakers change with signals such as pointing, leaning forward, sitting back, taking the floor by starting with "but . . ." or "well. . . ." These signals are not available in tele-conferencing and video-conferencing. Therefore, the group must establish rules and procedures for changing speakers. Without these, there will be offensive interruptions, "floor hogging," several people speaking at once, and shouting, among other possibilities.

The group leader can control the flow of communication by stating that "to obtain the floor, you must be recognized by me." Another may say, "No one may speak longer than three minutes at a time." Controlling the flow of communication through these or other means is a major challenge in tele-conferencing and video-conferencing.

Quality Circles

Quality circles are groups of employees who meet on a regular basis during work time to improve quality control and job methods. These groups have increased in prominence in many different kinds of organizations and saved countless numbers of businesses thousands of dollars. Although extremely popular in the 1970s and 1980s, the impact and presence of quality circles are still being felt today.[21]

The benefits of quality circles have been reported by a number of different organizations, and we will only summarize their findings here.[22] As we mentioned earlier, quality circles produce high-quality solutions to work-related problems. Enhanced work productivity results from the implementation of these solutions. Substantial improvement in horizontal and vertical communication patterns within the organization occurs after quality-circle work. This benefit seems to derive from the increased diversity of communication among participants who would otherwise not interact. Participants in quality circles demonstrate an increased commitment to the organization and its goals. A related advantage is enhanced job satisfaction and lower absenteeism among employees involved with quality circles. Finally, members of quality circles claim that their participation in these groups provides both information and emotional support for dealing with the complexities and uncertainties of the organization. Although considered by some as a passing fad, quality circles as a form of group communication yield benefits that are difficult to deny. Perhaps that is why many organizations continue to enjoy their advantages.

Quality circles are based on the belief that the people who know the work the best are those who do it. In today's exceedingly specialized working world, many managers or supervisors are not as skilled or as knowledgeable about tasks as subordinates are. Quality circles invite these workers to attend meetings and actively participate in making their work better and more productive. Quality circles are commonly employed throughout the company. A quality circle whose focus is improved customer relations may include a vice-president, a receptionist, a public relations manager, an accountant, and a dock worker. In this way, the diversity of the group creates a climate of uniqueness and unfamiliarity that leads to creative solutions.

Self-Managing Teams

Self-managing teams, which are similar to quality circles, are small groups of employees who share the responsibility for a significant task. These employees work together to solve day-to-day problems and are involved in planning and coordinating activities.

Self-managing teams are consistent with many of today's changes in the work force. We find that more and more organizations are eliminating or thinning middle managers. Because these teams manage themselves, they do not need to report directly to a supervisor. This is the primary difference between quality circles and self-managing teams, as quality circles still have the authority figure (manager or supervisor), whereas self-managing teams have autonomy. These teams also speak to a trend in the marketplace to lower the vertical hierarchy by chunking the system into smaller, lateral units and flattening the organization. In addition, organizations are increasingly relying on employees to be heavily involved in decision making and problem solving. Brian Dumaine reported that in a 1990 survey of 476 Fortune 1,000 companies, only 7 percent of the work force was organized into self-managing teams but that more than 50 percent of these firms indicated that they would rely on these in significant ways in the near future.[23]

Research has indicated that people who participate in these teams report higher job satisfaction, increased self-esteem, greater employee development, and increased job security. Organizations benefit by having increased flexibility, increased productivity, leaner staffs, less bureaucracy, lower turnover, and decreased absenteeism. Major companies in the United States — such as Xerox, Proctor and Gamble, Volvo, and General Electric — have introduced self-managing teams and have reported a 25–40 percent gain in productivity with a lowering of production costs by as much as 25 percent.[24]

Self-managing teams have demonstrated that it can be a major mistake to underestimate the value of involving lower level workers. When given the opportunity, these workers manage themselves quite well and accept high levels of responsibility. Workers who have participated in self-managing teams have discovered a sense of ownership in their jobs that they would not have experienced otherwise.

Dumaine illustrated this well when he reported that during one of their weekly meetings, a team of Federal Express clerks spotted and solved a billing problem that saved the company more than $2.1 million each year. Their self-managing teams reduced problems in billing and lost packages by as much as 13 percent in 1989.[25]

Teams perform four major activities: they uncover and analyze problems, complete tasks, establish and maintain personal relationships, and facilitate group and organizational processes. In accomplishing these tasks, each member of the group is considered a credible resource, and the team is committed to making maximum use of individual contributions. Thus, team members tend to be committed and motivated to implement team decisions.

Team building entails attention to both tasks and relationships. When a team is charged with the responsibility of performing tasks, it must identify and diagnose problems, implement action to provide a workable solution, and follow up with a strong and thorough evaluation of any action that has been taken.

Work teams take groups a step beyond quality circles. They are self-managing, have autonomy in solving day-to-day problems, and provide a great lift to employee morale.

The relationship dimension shapes the climate in which the team operates. Teams operating in a favorable climate exhibit a strong degree of participation in group decision making, demonstrate productive and managed conflict, and use feedback effectively. There are substantial advantages for a group that can work as a team. Participants are motivated to pull together, decisions are made with high levels of commitment and motivation, and a spirit of camaraderie develops within the group.

Comparisons and Contrasts Among Special Groups

Many scholars have compared and contrasted self-managing teams, quality circles, and traditional work groups. Tables 9-1 and 9-2 on page 302 illustrate some of these differences.

Summary

This is the first of two chapters on group communication. The focus in this chapter is on fundamental issues associated with group communication in business and professional settings. Groups are necessary because decisions reached by groups are usually superior to those generated by individuals.

TABLE 9-1
Comparison of Traditional Work Groups and Self-Managing Teams

Traditional Work Groups	Self-Managing Teams
Organized around job functions	Organized around observable, completed outputs
Employees focused on performing specified tasks	Teams accountable for producing specific end results
Many different job categories	A few very broad job categories
Classic chain of command	Flat, informal structure
Daily operational decisions referred up the organizational chart	On-the-line responsibility for daily operational decisions
Reward systems tied to individual performance, seniority, and type of job	Reward systems tied to individual performance, breadth of skills, team performance, and profitability
Supervisory management	Peer influence and personal commitment

Chart courtesy of Zenger-Miller, Inc. © 1990.

TABLE 9-2
Comparison of Quality Circles and Self-Managing Teams

Quality Circles	Self-Managing Teams
Implemented in mature plants	Implemented in newer sites
Usually voluntary participation	Participation usually not voluntary but variation in individual participation levels
Members: subset of a work group	Members: the entire work group
Initial leader usually a supervisor elected or appointed by senior management	Initial internal leader is elected by the group; external leader appointed by senior management
Deal with one problem at a time, usually a large problem over a long period	Deal with many different problems, including small day-to-day issues
Moderate to strong motivational impact	Strong motivational impact
An overlay to existing organizational structure	Largely replace existing organizational structure

Reprinted, by permission of publisher, from *Personnel* January 1985. © 1985. American Management Association, New York. All rights reserved.

The nature of group communication grows out of what groups do, what purposes they serve, and what constitutes a group. The various elements of group behavior include roles, interaction, influence, membership, common goals, and leadership.

A number of factors influence group communication. Cohesiveness refers to how connected group members are with one another; research demonstrates that cohesive groups are more successful than noncohesive groups. Norms, the standards or limits for defining acceptable behavior, also shape groups in obvious and less obvious ways. Group members who do not conform to norms may be sanctioned by others. Another factor influencing groups is the roles that group members play. Roles can be positive or negative, and recognizing the differences among them is important. Conformity and groupthink are critical factors in group work. Groups must be able to conform to various procedures and methods of discussion to reach consensus on issues, but at the same time they must be wary of groupthink, or failing to discuss critical issues so as to maintain agreement and positive relations in the group. Groupthink can lead to poor decision making. Conflict, the most problematic aspect of group communication, can be the essence of group vitality and creativity. A six-step approach to conflict can yield beneficial resolutions.

The extent of a group member's involvement depends on the nature of the group's decision making — is it authoritarian, laissez-faire, or participative? — and on how much team building occurs. The success of a team depends on the climate — does it facilitate considerable participation, lead to productive conflict, and employ feedback?

Another important dimension of group communication is leadership. Leaders can be classified according to the traits they exhibit, their behavioral styles, their adaptability to the situation at hand, or their ability to perform the duties and responsibilities of a leader.

Group communication changes in the case of special groups. Tele- and video-conferencing, which are used in companies to reduce costs, can rob participants of the benefits of face-to-face interaction, so appropriate adjustments have to be made to keep communication flowing. Quality circles and self-managed teams can enhance productivity and increase communicative effectiveness.

Discussion

1. What are some of the organizational benefits of working in small groups? What characteristics of a small group distinguish it from a collection of unrelated people?

2. What is the relationship among cohesiveness, conformity, and groupthink? How does each dimension affect the quantity and quality of small-group communication?

3. Why is group conflict important?

4. How does the group's participation level and decision-making style affect its results?

5. Discuss the four approaches to group leadership. How do group members and the group's task affect which approach is the most appropriate?

6. What special communications issues are raised by tele- and video-conferencing?

7. Discuss some of the differences between quality circles and self-managing teams. What are the advantages and disadvantages of each?

Activities

1. What types of tasks do you believe are best suited for groups? For dyads? For individuals? Compare your lists with others in class.

2. Think of some groups you have been a member of that had the following characteristics. Explain how effective and efficient each group was.
   a. High degree of cohesion
   b. Participative group leader
   c. One dominant member
   d. Interpersonal conflict during discussion
   e. Unprepared, uninformed group members

3. Do you believe that there is a single leadership style that is effective in most situations? If so, explain in an essay what that style is and why. If not, use your essay to explain your position.

Notes

1. K. Lewin, *Field Theory in Social Science* (New York: Harper & Row, 1951).
2. R. Y. Hirokawa and D. S. Gouran, "Facilitation of Group Communication: A Critique of Prior Research and an Agenda for Future Research," *Management Communication Quarterly* 3 (1989): 71–92.
3. G. A. Yukl, *Leadership in Organizations,* 2nd ed. (Englewood Cliffs, N.J.: Prentice-Hall, 1989).
4. M. Argyle, "Five Kinds of Small Social Groups," in R. S. Cathcart and L. A. Samovar (eds.), *Small Group Communication: A Reader,* 5th ed. (Dubuque, Iowa: William C. Brown, 1988), pp. 33–41.
5. M. E. Shaw, *Group Dynamics: The Psychology of Small Group Behavior,* 2nd ed. (New York: McGraw-Hill, 1976).
6. L. B. Rosenfeld, *Human Interaction in the Small Group Setting* (Columbus, Ohio: Merrill, 1973).

7. J. Longley and D. G. Pruitt, "Groupthink: A Critique of Janis's Theory," in L. Wheeler (ed.), *Review of Personality and Social Psychology,* vol. 1 (Beverly Hills, Calif.: Sage, 1980), pp. 74–93.

8. I. L. Janis, *Victims of Groupthink: Psychological Studies of Foreign Policy Decisions and Fiascoes* (Boston: Houghton Mifflin, 1972); D. M. Schweiger, W. R. Sandberg, and R. J. Ragan, "Group Approaches for Improving Strategic Decision Making: A Comparative Analysis of Dialectical Inquiry, Devil's Advocacy, and Consensus," *Academy of Management Journal* 29 (1986): 51–71.

9. I. L. Janis, *Groupthink: Psychological Studies of Policy Decisions and Fiascoes,* 2nd ed. (Boston: Houghton Mifflin, 1982).

10. R. Y. Hirokawa, D. S. Gouran, and A. E. Martz, "Understanding the Sources of Faulty Group Decision Making," *Small Group Behavior* 19 (1988): 411–433.

11. Janis, *Groupthink.*

12. Ibid.

13. G. A. Yukl, *Leadership in Organizations* (Englewood Cliffs, N.J.: Prentice-Hall, 1981), p. 203.

14. K. Barge and R. Hirokawa, "Toward a Communication Competency Model of Group Leadership," *Small Group Behavior* 20 (1989): 167–189.

15. R. M. Stogdill, "Personal Factors Associated with Leadership: A Survey of the Literature," *Journal of Psychology* 25 (1948): 35–71.

16. J. Jaworkski, "The Attitude and Capacities Required of the Successful Leader," *Vital Speeches of the Day* (August 1982): 68–70.

17. J. G. Geier, "A Trait Approach to the Study of Leadership in Small Groups," *Journal of Communication* 17 (1967): 316–323.

18. R. Blake and J. S. Mouton, *The Managerial Grid* (Houston: Gulf Publishing, 1964).

19. P. Hersey and K. H. Blanchard, *Management of Organizational Behavior: Utilizing Human Resources,* 5th ed. (Englewood Cliffs, N.J.: Prentice-Hall, 1988).

20. F. E. Fiedler, "The Leadership Game: Matching the Man to the Situation," *Organizational Dynamics* 4 (1976): 6–16.

21. F. G. Elias, M. E. Johnson, and J. B. Fortman, "Task-Focused Self-Disclosure: Effects on Group Cohesiveness, Commitment to Task, and Productivity," *Small Group Behavior* 20 (1986): 87–96.

22. M. L. Marks, P. H. Mirvis, E. J. Hackett, and J. F. Grady, "Employee Participation in a Quality Circle Program: Impact on Quality of Work Life, Productivity, and Absenteeism," *Journal of Applied Psychology* 71 (1986): 61–69; Elias, Johnson, and Fortman, "Task-Focused Self-Disclosure."

23. B. Dumaine, "Who Needs a Boss?" *Fortune,* May 7, 1990, pp. 52–60.

24. Ibid.

25. Ibid., p. 52.

Chapter 10

Meetings: Forums for Problem Solving

OBJECTIVES

After completing this chapter, you will be able to:

1. Evaluate how individual, group, and organizational goals influence a meeting

2. Create an agenda and adapt it to a variety of meeting formats

3. Use situational knowledge to prepare for a meeting

4. Develop and employ critical thinking skills to improve communication during a meeting

5. Choose appropriate problem-solving methods to achieve goals

6. Engage in effective decision making

7. Recognize what triggers anxiety in group situations and improve your handling of it

8. Evaluate group performance thoroughly and objectively

In Chapter 9, we introduced you to the basic characteristics of groups, group leaders, and special group formats. Now we focus on the group *process* — the meeting — to show how groups use meetings to identify and achieve goals, share information, make decisions, and solve problems. As a functioning member of a business or professional organization, sooner or later you will have the opportunity to plan, participate in, or lead a meeting, and an understanding of the basic process of communication in this context can improve your ability to contribute to meetings in your career.

Several types of meetings are common to most organizations. Planning meetings, staff meetings, and annual meetings bring together groups of employees or stakeholders to share information and update the group on the direction it and the organization are taking. Typically, these meetings are scheduled regularly and have set agendas, that is, the same basic issues are discussed in every meeting. For example, production schedules, budget control, and artwork might be discussed at every weekly editorial staff meeting at a publishing company, but each week the group will have new developments and information to share and learn. Annual meetings present a similar situation. The basic activities — election of officers, a state-of-the-company address, voting on various referenda, and so forth — take place every year, but each year the nominees are different, the company's performance varies to some degree, and new referenda are proposed.

Because information-sharing meetings are relatively planned and routine, we choose not to cover them in great detail in this chapter. Instead, we focus on problem-solving meetings, which add to the basic function of information sharing the task of finding solutions and making decisions about events or situations that have the potential to affect the organization's performance. Problem-solving groups may be referred to as task forces, troubleshooting teams, or strategic communication committees, but their basic function is to identify and resolve specific problems by applying strong communication skills and problem-solving techniques. We structure our discussion of this process around the four components of strategic communication to show you how to maximize your effectiveness in problem-solving meetings.

Goal Setting: The Agenda

You can think of an agenda as a road map. Have you ever gone on a vacation and just taken off? You might have, but if you did, there was probably an awful lot you missed seeing along the way because you did not think in advance about what you wanted to experience. You also probably wasted quite a bit of time as you went on your way.

The same principle applies to meetings. A meeting that is not well planned can neglect issues that need to be resolved, waste time, and produce frustration among members. An agenda is a guide that specifies what is to be discussed, when, in what order, and for how long.

The degree to which each of these considerations is detailed, and the format in which they are presented, varies widely due to differences in organizational policy and the nature of the meeting itself. We begin by presenting a formal agenda because it contains the basic components that are adapted to suit other types of meetings. Figure 10-1 shows two alternative formats for agendas. A formal agenda for a meeting may read as follows:

- Roll call of participants
- Reading of minutes from previous meetings
- Presentation of topics
- Requests for additional topics
- Communications to be read
- Reports of special committees
- Reports of standing committees
- Unfinished business
- New business
- Closing concerns
- Adjournment

You may be familiar with this format, but let us take a moment to clarify the purpose of each step. Roll call is simply an attendance check — is everyone present and ready to begin? Reading the minutes summarizes what took place in earlier meetings of the group. If this is the first (or only) meeting, this step is not necessary.

After the minutes, the leader reviews the topics to be discussed. If a group member wishes to add a topic to the list, it is done at this point, not later. Communications to be read include any messages from people not present at the meeting that have to be considered during discussions. Many agendas present this information as an "overview" given at the start of a meeting.

Committee reports often form the bulk of formal meetings. *Special committees* are temporary subgroups created to look into short-term or specific problems. *Standing committees* are permanent subgroups that concentrate on long-term developments in broad areas such as budgeting, personnel, or purchasing. These committees meet on their own time and regularly report back to the complete group. In less formal meetings, individual members may report on findings or update the group on developments in a particular area.

Managers' Meeting Agenda
March 25-29
25th Floor-Auditorium

Monday, March 25	8:15-8:30	Overview of marketing	
	8:30-12:00	Feedback/estimates on 1992 products	*Sales Managers* Paul McAllister Sam Kaplan Karen Friedman Ray Daley Bill Russell Joan Webster
	12:00-1:30	Working lunch: marketing plans	
	1:30-4:30	Introduction of new sales training plan for 1992	*Sales Managers* Paul McAllister Sam Kaplan Bill Russell Joan Webster
	4:30-5:00	Wrapup	*Sales Managers* Ray Daley Susan Ellis

Unfinished business and new business include topics that were not agreed on at earlier meetings and new issues that have to be addressed. Committees may be formed to look into these areas. In problem-solving meetings, addressing such issues takes the bulk of the meeting time. The agenda may include a "working lunch," periods of time set aside for small group work on sub-parts of the problem, training sessions, or time allotted for brainstorming possible solutions.

Closing concerns and adjournment round out the meeting, giving a summation of what has been accomplished and where the group may go next. Informal agendas may simply include a "wrap-up" or "summary" to provide closure to the meeting.

The group leader takes the agenda and fills in any details about the business that are known in advance. For example, one section of an agenda can look like this:

AGENDA FOR TRAINING SESSION

Thursday, January 4, 1992

7:30 AM	Buffet breakfast		Conference Room
8:30 AM—	REGIONAL OFFICE TRAINING	GROUP LEADER	
4:30 PM	Chicago Office	*Thomas Ryderson*	Room 120
	Miami Office	*Magaret Brown*	Suite 3
	Detroit Office	*George Owens*	Suite 4
	San Francisco Office	*Jim Robertson*	Room 110
	New York Office	*Susan DeKooning*	Suite 2
	Seattle Office	*Cathy Atwater*	Suite 1
10:00 AM	Break		
3:00 PM	Break		

FIGURE *10-1*   *Variations on the formal agenda: The managers' meeting agenda shows an excerpt from a multi-day conference held to plan the sales campaign of a small regional company. The training session agenda shows the framework for a meeting in which employees from branch offices of a large national organization meet at company headquarters to participate in training activities.*

Reports of Standing Committees
Finance (M. Jackson — 5 minutes)
Suspensions and reinstatements (D. Holloway — 10 minutes)
Unfinished Business
Permanent meeting location (10 minutes)

You may wonder why we have included time limits on the agenda. Time limits are not rigid boundaries that cut off discussion. Rather, they provide the group with a guide to the importance and depth of the discussion intended for topics in a meeting.

If possible, all participants receive a copy of the agenda before the meeting. The agenda can be mailed or hand-delivered to the participants, or they can pick up a copy. In this way, everyone can have the opportunity to prepare for the meeting and bring whatever materials may be necessary to have a productive discussion.

The agenda serves as the framework within which the group leader organizes time and topics. But leaders are not the only contributors to a group's direction. Effective group members must consider three additional levels of goals that exist within small groups: organizational, group, and individual goals.

Organizational Goals

Organizational goals are set at upper levels of the organization and describe pathways to excellence. Recall our discussion in Chapter 2 on how organizational goals are set, monitored, and evaluated. Groups are directly and indirectly affected by organizational goals because the ultimate purpose of groups is to solve problems that may prevent the attainment of organizational goals. To work effectively, serve the purpose of the organization, and avoid conflicts between group agendas and organizational goals, groups are wise to keep in mind the overarching goals of the organization.

Group Goals

Group goals serve the mission and purpose of the group itself. Often a higher authority will form a group and specify a "charge." The charge serves as the fundamental goal of the group. For example, a chief executive officer may appoint a group to recommend a change in the distribution system of wholesale products. The group's general goal may be "to develop a new and more effective wholesale distribution system." More specific goals can be established within the fundamental goal, such as "to develop a computerized tracking system for wholesale customers" or "to establish a new method for routing trucks to final destinations." Each of these goals may require a series of meetings in which to devise strategies for achieving it.

Ongoing groups that meet periodically without a specific charge from higher authority develop their own goals. These goals depend on the nature of the group's tasks and the reason for its existence. For instance, ongoing groups devoted to improving productivity on the job may designate a general goal of "determining methods of increasing productivity." Specific goals such as "monitoring productivity in the tool shop" and "evaluating quality control techniques" can then be set for individual meetings.

Groups may also set process goals. Process goals attempt to improve the working of the group itself. If, after a series of meetings, group members feel they are not working together as well as they could, they may set goals to improve their internal harmony, research skills, decision-making methods, or ability to deal with time pressures. Because group goals may change as groups mature or as new information becomes available that affects original plans, groups must continually monitor their goals to ensure that their actions are serving the best interests of both the groups and organization.

Individual Goals

Individual goals, or goals that group members have in addition to the group's stated goals, also play a role in the group process. Your motives for joining a group may reflect an individual goal, such as the decision to meet new people at work. Some people join groups to satisfy their need for achievement. Still others set goals for gaining recognition, knowledge, power, information, or skills.[1] You probably belong to some groups now for personal reasons; it is very likely you will be involved in some work groups for personal reasons.

Setting and maintaining individual goals are key ingredients in group effectiveness. Group members will be unhappy and therefore less effective if they are unable to accomplish their own individual goals. All three types of goals — organizational, group, and individual — should be considered when participating in a meeting. As Figure 10-2 shows, they can reinforce or contradict each other. Groups function more effectively when members set effective and appropriate goals in each area.

Situational Knowledge: Preparing for the Meeting

Proper advance planning for a meeting is important to its success. Location, participants, scheduling, and other environmental issues can affect the outcome of the meeting.

Think for a moment about a meeting you have attended that took place in a very cold room. Were you eager to participate or pay attention to the discussion? No! Your mind was on the temperature of the room, the sweater you left at the dorm, or the weather forecast for the next day. Or consider a meeting in an "auditorium"-style arrangement in which the leader wants full group participation. How frequently will people need to turn around to see who behind them is talking in the discussion? Finally, consider meetings in which you were thirsty and there were no refreshments. All you could think about was the soft drink or beer you were going to get afterward. Knowing the conditions of the meeting beforehand will allow you to be a much more effective planner and participant.

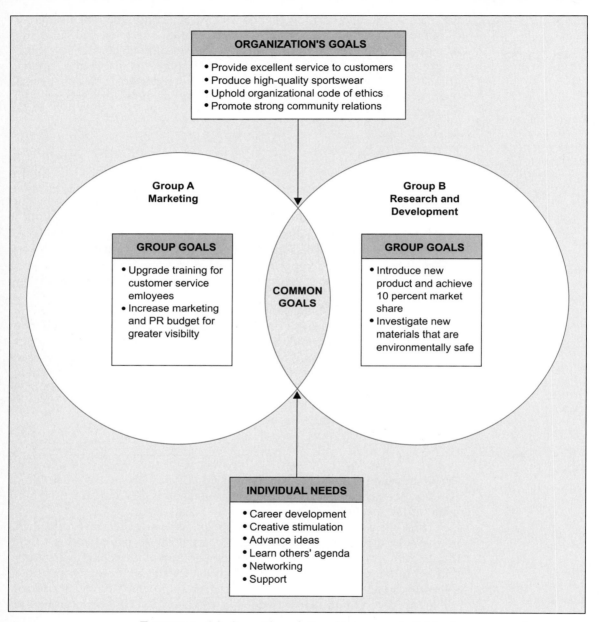

ORGANIZATION'S GOALS
- Provide excellent service to customers
- Produce high-quality sportswear
- Uphold organizational code of ethics
- Promote strong community relations

Group A
Marketing

Group B
Research and
Development

GROUP GOALS
- Upgrade training for customer service emloyees
- Increase marketing and PR budget for greater visibilty

COMMON GOALS

GROUP GOALS
- Introduce new product and achieve 10 percent market share
- Investigate new materials that are environmentally safe

INDIVIDUAL NEEDS
- Career development
- Creative stimulation
- Advance ideas
- Learn others' agenda
- Networking
- Support

FIGURE **10-2** *The relationship among individual, group, and organizational goals affects group performance.*

Meeting Facilities

There are several issues to consider when you are deciding where to hold a meeting. The primary concern is that the physical dimensions of the room are comfortable for the people planning to attend. You are smart to visit the facility before scheduling your first meeting there so that you can see for yourself what advantages and disadvantages the room will have for your meeting.

Does the room you are considering have enough space for all the people in your group? Are there large picture windows that may be distracting? Does the room have plenty of electrical outlets, proper storage space, adjustable lighting switches, and adjustable temperature controls? Are there other meetings booked at the same time that yours is planned? If so, is the room soundproof so that noise from an adjacent room does not "bleed" through the walls? How far away from the room are restrooms, soft drink machines, water fountains, and telephones? Is the room large enough to provide for whatever seating arrangement you think is best?

There are several different options for arranging the room for a meeting, and it is important that the one you choose is appropriate for the type of meeting to be held. For example, an auditorium-style arrangement is not conducive to full-room participation. A "U-shape" can distract participants' attention from the leader because they can easily look at each other.

An *auditorium* setup includes chairs but no tables. The chairs are lined up in straight rows with a center aisle between them. All eyes are to the front, where the leader conducts the meeting. A *classroom* arrangement uses tables and chairs. Tables are typically lined up in straight rows with a center aisle separating them. Two or three participants sit at a table. As with the auditorium setup, everyone looks straight ahead. The *U-shape* is designed for full-room interaction. Tables and chairs are arranged so that participants sit adjacent to or directly across from one another. This arrangement is good for meetings that require discussion as well as presentation. The *conference* arrangement seats all members around the same table. The leader typically occupies the seat at the end. This arrangement is used for discussions only; a presentation, especially with visual aids, is quite awkward for leaders using this setup. *Satellite tables* are an innovative arrangement that gives considerable room for the leader to roam around the room while still conducting a discussion. Participants sit around individual tables, and each table occupies its own independent space and arrangement in the room. This setup is excellent for subgroup meetings or breakouts when participants separate into teams to work on specific problems. Figure 10-3 illustrates several of these setups.

If you are responsible for renting a meeting area outside your company, do not overlook the need for a clear, signed contract specifying exactly what you expect to be furnished and how much you expect to pay for meeting items. Do not assume that a slide projector is always available or

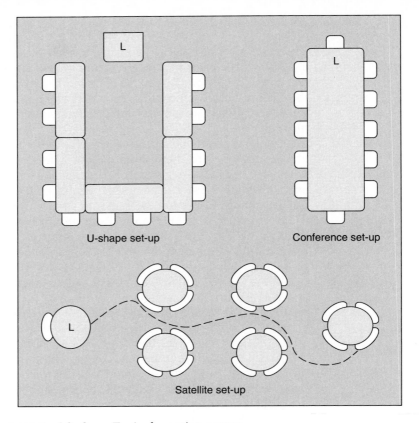

U-shape set-up

Conference set-up

Satellite set-up

FIGURE 10-3   Typical meeting setups

that pitchers of water are furnished free of charge. Find out in advance and save yourself much grief later!

Audiovisual Requirements

If you are meeting on-site or are bringing your own portable equipment with you to an off-site meeting, your primary concern is to ensure that the audiovisual equipment you plan to use works! Testing bulbs in slide projectors, checking for adequate paper in a flip chart, and making sure that marking pens have not dried up are routine activities.

Often you will find it more convenient to use or rent equipment provided by the facility in which you will hold the meeting. Many hotels and convention centers have equipment such as slide projectors, microphones, projection screens, and lighting that can be controlled from a podium. Ask yourself, "Given the requirements of this meeting, what equipment is necessary to be effective and productive?" Items you may consider include:

Microphone and speakers
Podium
Slide projector
Overhead projector
Film projector
Projection screen
Flip charts and marking pens
Display easels
Extension cords and electrical adapters

Setting Rules of Order

Meetings run more smoothly when conducted according to an orderly procedure and established rules. The most well-known set of rules is *Robert's Rules of Order,* which gives precise standards of parliamentary procedure to follow in specific situations.[2]

How much you depend on rules of order for your meetings is determined by how formal the interaction is and the nature of past participation. If you have a group that is very boisterous and "disorderly," falling back on rules such as these can be very effective for proceeding through an agenda. If, however, your group has always worked well informally, the introduction of rigid rules for voting and points of order can have a really chilling effect.

One major advantage to the use of established rules of order is that the group leader is less likely to use or be accused of personal bias in decision making. The leader's credibility increases when she or he states that "according to the rules, we must have a two-thirds majority to pass the amendment; as we do not, the motion fails."

Knowing the Group

Recall our discussion in Chapter 9 of group roles, norms, and tendencies toward conformity, cohesiveness, or conflict. When preparing for a meeting or group activity, you are wise to find out who the other members of the group are and how the group is likely to interact. For example, you may find that the group consists of several dominators but also includes a person known as an excellent facilitator. You can thus hope that any problems of groupthink caused by the dominators will be lessened. We encourage you to collect as much information as possible about how the meeting will be conducted, the topics to be discussed, and who will be present. The more prepared you are, the greater your opportunity will be to contribute to the group.

Developing Critical Thinking Skills

There are many skills necessary for effective communication, participation, and problem solving in meetings. The foundation of these skills is the ability to think critically about the subject or issue under discussion in a meeting. Doing so allows group members to formulate and express ideas that move the group toward achieving its goals. In this section, we discuss the basic skills of critical thinking — analysis, reasoning, interpretation, and evaluation — and how to incorporate them into your communication.

Analysis

Analysis is the process of tearing apart an issue and examining its component parts and how they relate to the whole. This skill is particularly important when group members are exploring the characteristics of a problem. To develop strong analytic skills for use in a group meeting, participants must exhibit the following:

◆ Patience with alternative viewpoints and methods

◆ An ability to clearly define terms and a willingness to demand the same from other participants

◆ A broad, openminded approach to the problem

◆ A search for commonalities and differences

◆ A comparison and contrast of the problem under discussion with others that have been previously discussed

◆ A summary of what the group has discussed up to a certain point

As you can see from this list of skills, group members must demonstrate a wide range of competencies for effective group communication, including the ability to hear a number of competing viewpoints. This is healthy for decision making. Furthermore, it is essential that group members stay on track with a focused purpose so as to reduce inefficiency. Comparing and contrasting viewpoints are two of the more important communication behaviors in a group context. And when group members summarize previous statements, they have an easier time recognizing where they have been and where they hope to go.

Problem-solving meetings are held in many kinds of organizations, from large multi-national businesses to local school systems. Here, teachers work in small groups during a conference in Milwaukee, Wisconsin.

Reasoning

Reasoning is the ability to pull a variety of data together and draw sound conclusions from them. There are two broad categories of reasoning: deductive and inductive. *Deductive reasoning* moves from general truths to specific conclusions. The most popular form of deductive reasoning is the *syllogism,* a three-part argument containing a general truth, a related claim, and a conclusion. The most famous example is "All men are mortal; Socrates is a man; therefore, Socrates must be mortal."

You can use deductive reasoning when others make general statements in a meeting. By relating general truths to specific experiences, you can draw valid conclusions. For instance, consider the following dialogue in a recent meeting of corporate managers:

Dave: "Our company reputation is built on keeping our regular customers happy."
Amanda: "The last reports showed customer complaints are rising."
Chris: (drawing conclusion) "I think we should put that trial program to attract new customers on the back burner."

In this case, Chris listened to two general premises. She then drew a convincing conclusion based on what had been presented in the first two premises.

Inductive reasoning moves from specific statements to general conclusions. There are four forms of inductive reasoning that you can use in a group meeting: example, sign, comparative, and causal.

Example reasoning.   Reasoning by example is the most popular form of inductive reasoning. You will probably notice instances of it during most people's communication, whether in group, interpersonal, or public speaking situations. Reasoning by example involves collecting specific cases and then making a generalization based on them. The following excerpt from a problem-solving meeting of staff members shows the effect of reasoning by example:

Roger: "Mary has been out for three days straight, Tim went to the doctor yesterday, and Bill should have stayed home today. We need to have a temporary who can fill in during the winter months when lots of people get sick."

Interact!

In this chapter, we introduce a five-step process for group decision making. The steps include (1) introducing the problem, (2) defining and analyzing the problem, (3) establishing criteria for the solution, (4) generating possible solutions, and (5) evaluating possible solutions. A group leader must be able to drive the process, summarizing positions and assertions, mediating conflicts, and so forth, although the group's "leader" may not necessarily be the member with the highest ranking title.

This simulation gives you the opportunity to practice problem solving and decision making in a small group. Divide the class into groups of five people each. The groups represent corporate safety councils in a large plant where heavy machinery is manufactured. One person in each group, the group leader, is responsible for enforcing all safety requirements at the plant and must report all violations to government regulators. The remaining group members are supervisors in various divisions of the plant. The groups are newly formed; this is the first meeting for all of them.

The first problem the councils wish to tackle is the increasing number of employees in the plant who refuse to wear the required safety helmets while they are not engaged in active work. When they are busy performing their jobs, they wear them. When they are on break, chatting with another employee, or walking from one part of the plant to another, some of the workers remove their helmets and expose themselves to possible injury and the company to possible liability. Each of the group participants has been asked to research why the helmets are not worn all the time that the worker is clocked in, and the following reasons have been uncovered:

1. The helmets are uncomfortable.

2. There isn't really any danger to employees when they are not actively working.

3. Wearing the helmet off duty should be the employee's decision.

4. Visitors to the plant rarely wear helmets, and no one minds.

5. Helmets wouldn't help much if a major accident occurred anyway.

The safety councils have been given the responsibility of ensuring that workers wear their safety helmets at *all* times they are in the plant, whether or not they are actually working, without causing extreme disaffection or conflict. Use the five-step problem-solving process to work through the problem and evaluate your solutions. After completing the exercise, share your results and decision with the other groups. In a full class discussion, consider the following questions:

1. How did the steps flow as the meeting progressed? Did the leader ever feel tempted to skip or transpose steps? What kind of patience or assertiveness was necessary to enforce each step? Was it provided by just one leader, or by others in the group as well?

2. Do you think the process of reaching a solution was more efficient and effective with these steps than without them?

3. What barriers or obstacles did the group experience within each step? What was done to overcome them?

4. Assess the decisions reached by the safety councils. Were they significantly different? Is it possible that there is more than one good solution to the problem? How confident is each group with its decision?

Because it is based on true, observable situations, Roger's conclusion is very persuasive to the rest of the group. Effective group communication frequently depends on the ability to persuade others in the group to adopt a common point of view.

The best way to argue against this kind of reasoning in a meeting (if you do not agree with the conclusion being expressed) is to show that the examples cited are not typical, representative, or timely. If a flaw can be proven to exist in the examples, the resulting generalization will also be flawed. Consider the following possible response to Roger's argument:

Josh: "It's true that there has been quite a bit of absenteeism this winter. But that is only because of the unusual flu epidemic we have been experiencing. Last year we didn't need to consider a temporary."

Josh shows that Roger's examples may not be the only way of looking at the absenteeism problem.

Sign reasoning. Sign reasoning involves drawing conclusions from simple observations. Consider how often you use sign reasoning. You wake up in the morning, pull up the window shades, see heavy clouds, and assume that it will rain. You notice someone on the sidewalk wearing jewelry and furs and conclude that he or she is wealthy. You hear the bell clanging from the fire station and suppose that there must be a fire somewhere. You pass a government building with the flag at half-mast and conclude that an important person has passed away.

These examples point out the drawback of sign reasoning: it encourages *hasty generalization,* or conclusions based on small or nonrepresentative samples of data. Basing your conclusions on a single observation, you have no way of knowing if the jewelry is stolen goods; the bell is a false alarm; the worker who runs the flag up and down the pole has been called inside to get a telephone call in mid-job! You cannot assume that a sign has only one meaning (the one you are thinking of) in all cases. Your perceptions have a strong influence on how you use sign reasoning in communication. It is important to remember that your view of the world may be different than others', and that the assumptions underlying sign reasoning can easily communicate misunderstanding, bias, or stereotypes detrimental to effective group interaction.

Comparative reasoning. Comparative reasoning occurs when a participant in a meeting pulls together two examples and reasons that what is true in the first case must be true in the second. Consider the following example. Rosa, a plant safety supervisor at Delmore Co., remarks, "Over at Bennzoil, a six-week course in new safety techniques cut work accidents more than 17 percent in just one year. We really need a program like that here. We could probably cut our accident rate 25 percent."

Rosa is reasoning by comparison. After comparing safety measures at Bennzoil and Delmore, she concludes that what worked at Bennzoil can work at her firm as well. She assumes that the two firms are similar enough to make the comparison valid. If, however, the two firms are not similar or Rosa's conclusion is based on inaccurate information, the comparison is *fallacious,* or unsound.

If you think that fallacious reasoning is being introduced in a group discussion, you will have to disconnect the two cases being compared and demonstrate the major differences that invalidate the comparison. For example, in response to Rosa's position, Loretta, an engineer, says, "I know someone at Bennzoil. He told me their original accident rate was so high that even with a 17 percent reduction, they still have more accidents than we do. We don't need a program like that because we don't have a problem like theirs."

Another form of comparative reasoning is *analogic reasoning*. An analogy compares two situations or processes that are essentially different, so that one may be understood more clearly. Analogies explain and clarify but generally are not the basis for decision making. For example, in one meeting Paula wants to make sure that everyone in the group understands how a new assembly technique will work. She says, "The technique is like food preparation at a fast-food restaurant: we keep a minimum of extra supplies, simplify the production process, and increase our ability to speed up service when necessary." The words *like* and *as* frequently signal analogic reasoning. Comparative reasoning is important to communication because it works to clarify the issue under discussion. A clear understanding by all group members is essential for reaching a decision on an issue.

Causal reasoning.   Causal reasoning tries to answer the question "Why did that happen?" When using causal reasoning, you assert that one factor is strong enough to produce an effect in another factor. If you had a few accidents last winter, you may consider the question "Why?" and then decide to put snow tires on your car. If you have had several unsuccessful job interviews, you may purchase a more conservative or professional-looking outfit to improve your appearance when you interview for jobs.

During group meetings in businesses and professional organizations, the search for causes takes up a considerable amount of time and communication effort. Let us eavesdrop on a meeting in which several military officers are discussing low levels of morale in their division:

Lt. Coffey: "The enlistees hardly ever get a chance to get out of here. They need some time away from the same old routine."

Cpt. Johnson: "Maybe. But I think that what's really bothering them is the poor quality of food they get here."

[Notice that both Johnson and Coffey assert causes for low morale. But because the officers are engaged in a discussion, their ideas are open for rebuttal, which comes quickly from two others.]

Lt. Betts: "That's rubbish. You spend the money to make elaborate meals for them, and they might feel better for about five minutes. They won't work one bit harder, and you know it."

Cpt. Gonzalez: "Yeah, and we're really talking about the wrong stuff here anyway. Lack of off-base activity and bad food may hurt morale, but the real cause of the problem includes lack of recognition, lack of pride, and lack of motivation."

The example shows two ways to counter causal reasoning. Lt. Betts claims that Cpt. Johnson has identified the wrong cause of the low morale — food could not possibly have that much effect. Cpt. Gonzalez argues that there are multiple causes, not just one cause, of the problem. Strong communicators can evaluate and discuss multiple causes without losing sight of the need for a solution. When a group becomes enmeshed in a search for causes, it may lose sight of its original goals. For this reason, group members also need the ability to interpret causes.

Interpretation

Interpretation is an extension of causal reasoning in which you ask not only "Why did that happen?" but also "What does it mean?" Simply listening to facts, arguments, data, or opinions in a group meeting will not improve your decision-making ability. You must be able to take all this information, interpret it, and use it to draw valid conclusions.

What do you do when you interpret information? In essence, you are saying, "What this means is . . ." When you interpret, you apply your own knowledge and experience to the data to figure out what they mean, especially for the other group members. Persuasive and effective interpretations typically stress the relevance, importance, or impact of data on the group. Interpretations also clarify information for the group. The key to interpreting information for others is to have a clear understanding of *why* the data look like they do. This understanding allows you to communicate a strategy for change.

In one group sales meeting Bill, a manager, wants to make sure that all of the sales representatives understand what three consecutive months of downward numbers mean to them and the business:

Bill: "Mary, please put the graph of our three-month sales plan and results up on the board." [She does.] "As you see, we were down 3 percent in June, 4 percent in July, and 6 percent in August."
Tim: "Doesn't look too good."
Bill: "No, it doesn't. These figures mean that we have fallen short of our goals three consecutive months. I believe the shortfalls result from slow sales in our new mall outlets. We need to improve our relationships with the mall vendors."

How many of the salespeople would have been able to draw that conclusion without Bill's interpretation? Furthermore, would the numbers have meant much to them without this input? Probably not. Interpretations are very important because they tie information and ideas together, helping to create shared meaning for group members.

Evaluation

Evaluation is the making of judgments about information or data. In most cases, judgments are made in categories such as positive/negative, favorable/unfavorable, valuable/worthless, workable/unworkable, expensive/cheap, or good/bad. Of course, evaluations are rarely clear-cut. People usually make evaluations in degrees, using qualifiers such as "fairly," "moderately," "basically," "ordinarily," and "partially."

Some scholars advocate avoiding evaluation whenever possible and suggest that placing a value label on another person's contribution to a group produces poor feelings and disharmony in the group, and undermines the group's ability to communicate freely and openly. We feel that before a group member casts a vote or conforms to a group consensus, he or she must evaluate the information that has been presented.

Even if you try to avoid evaluation, you may frequently be asked for your reactions to ideas or proposals during meetings. Participants in a group expect you to assess information you have heard. If evaluation is an inevitable part of individual involvement in group decision making, then why not share your evaluation with all the participants? Evaluations are an important part of feedback in meetings, and feedback is essential to the group's success.

Communication Competence: Problem Solving and Decision Making

In addition to improving communication, critical thinking allows problem-solving meetings to succeed. Problem-solving groups are very prevalent in organizations; they exist in more than 90 percent of the Fortune 500 companies.[3] Entire volumes have discussed the advantages and disadvantages of various problem-solving techniques. These techniques have much to offer groups that meet to make decisions in response to organizational and group goals. Three qualities are necessary for competent problem solving: *variety* — when group members' perspectives differ, many aspects of the problem can be suggested and discussed; *simplicity* — ideas generated during group deliberations should be arranged logically and checked for repetition and relevance; and *usefulness* — because ideas have varying degrees of usefulness to the group, members must be able to focus their energies on those that will most likely result in the right decision.[4] Communication competence is vital to ensure that group members are able to understand the problem and share their ideas with each other appropriately and effectively.

Selecting the most appropriate problem-solving technique and then adhering to its format enable groups to recommend effective decisions. We focus here on some of the most popular and proven problem-solving methods: reflective thinking, the nominal group technique, the Delphi technique, and advocacy. We then present options for decision making.

Reflective Thinking

Reflective thinking is a five-step process whose success depends on each participant's willingness to contribute to the process. One of the chief advantages of the reflective thinking technique is its efficiency. Rather than having a group ramble and flounder about with a problem, reflective thinking provides a clear and concise road map that can save both time and energy.

Step one: introduce the problem.   Group members state their perceptions of the problem and the general goals the group is striving to achieve. The statements should be brief, with no discussion, questions, or debate allowed. At the conclusion of step one, the group knows the dimensions of the problem as perceived by the members. A variety of perspectives is essential in this stage.

Step two: define and analyze the problem.   Members try to agree on the problem and objectives. In this step, the group discusses qualities, characteristics, and elements of the problem. The leader squashes any attempt to talk about solutions! Members may present personal philosophies, evidence, opinions, statistics, or other relevant information and compare and contrast the present problem with any related problems. Group members probe and challenge each other's perceptions of the problem.

The following substeps can increase the group's ability to define the problem:[5]

1. *Problem recognition* involves clarifying the extent of the problem, presenting evidence supporting the claims, and even challenging the problem's existence.

2. *Development of the problem statement* identifies those who have a stake in the problem, specifies values or goals associated with the problem, elicits various viewpoints and attitudes on the problem, and proposes a workable definition of the problem.

3. *Exploration* illuminates possible directions for the solution phase by breaking the problem into smaller parts for subsequent analysis, identifying related or associated problems, and suggesting possible causes for the problem's existence.

4. *Internal summary* builds consensus before moving to the next step. The leader may say, "We have decided the problem is _____, and _____ are related issues and probable causes."

As you can see, the critical thinking skills discussed earlier play a vital role in defining the problem. With the problem identified, defined, and analyzed, it is time to move to step three.

Step three: establish criteria.   The group decides what elements the solution to the problem should achieve or include. These *criteria* will be used later in the discussion to judge potential solutions. For example, if you and your friends are deciding how to spend a Saturday night and there are several activities to choose from, establishing criteria can help you to decide which is the best for the group. One person may suggest that money is a factor, thereby giving the criteria "Whatever we do, it can't cost more than $10 per person." Another may have to get up early the next morning, thereby giving the criteria "We have to be back at the dorm by 12:30 A.M. at the latest." Still another may request that the activity be something new — for example, "Let's not go to a movie; we always do that." These criteria can help your group narrow the options and make the best decision for all concerned.

The criteria must be relevant to the problem at hand. The following general rules can ensure the choice of relevant criteria. *Overall strength* — the criteria address the effectiveness and efficiency of proposed solutions, including the extent of the solution, possible future consequences, and realistic chances of carrying out the plan. *Resources* — the criteria assess the time, money, effort, or employee morale necessary to implement each of the possible solutions. *Ethics* — ethical criteria prevent possible infringements on the rights of other people or organizations. These criteria should address the legality, morality, honesty, and decency of each possible solution. Ethical criteria may focus on the employees of the organization ("Eliminating fifty jobs right before Christmas is simply not acceptable"), other organizations ("We can't tell our competition we are going out of business when we are not"), the environment ("Dumping waste into the river is cheap but would have serious consequences for the river ecosystem"), or the community ("Building an adjacent plant would displace a lot of residents"). Ethical criteria should address each of the groups affected by the solution.

The best solutions are those that suit the criteria established in this stage. Keep in mind that criteria must be established *before* the group tries to come up with solutions. Doing so keeps group members from changing their minds about what they are trying to accomplish during the course of the meeting.

Establishing and adhering to criteria are essential for effective decision making and save the group countless hours of directionless deliberation. In sum, group members should probe and challenge each other to ensure they have worthy criteria against which to judge a solution. Selecting a solution will then be much easier.

Step four: generate possible solutions.   In this step, group members present logical and workable solutions to the problem. Often referred to as *brainstorming,* the goal is to generate a list of creative solutions but not to evaluate their worth. No solution is dismissed or even criticized at this stage. Although some ideas may seem bizarre when first presented, they can be modified to be effective and ingenious. Before moving to the next step, the leader reviews the list of possible solutions to make sure that all have been recorded correctly and to ensure that they do not repeat each other.

Step five: evaluate possible solutions.   Using the criteria established in step three, group members discuss the worth of each of the solutions generated in step four. The leader introduces each proposed solution and asks the group to evaluate it by the criteria agreed on in step three. The goal of this step is for the group to make a final decision by selecting the most viable solution — the one that best satisfies the criteria.

You may wonder, "What if more than one proposed solution meets all the criteria?" or "What if no solution can meet all the criteria?" In the first instance, the group must decide if the two solutions are mutually exclusive. If not, then the group may implement both. In the second instance, the group selects the solution that fulfills the most criteria. Before adjourning the meeting, moving on to another problem, or continuing to another point on the agenda, the leader restates the problem and the solution so that all group members understand them.

The example on page 330 shows how reflective thinking works.[6] To help you understand the example, the term *cup* refers to the size of soft drinks sold in fast-food restaurants. The profits for a restaurant are higher when large cup sizes are sold. This meeting has been called to discuss how restaurant owners can be persuaded to increase the size of the drinks they offer in their restaurants. The group includes some of the top sales managers in the division and the meeting is led by a vice-president (VP).

Reflective thinking is a powerful tool for finding solutions to particular problems. After working through the example, you can understand the importance of taking each stage in its proper order and systematically working through the various steps.

The Nominal Group Technique

The nominal group technique, or NGT, allows groups to discuss problems and solutions in a relatively structured setting. This technique has been found especially useful in newly formed groups and in groups with large differences in status and communication dominance among members.

NGT has five steps: preparation, silent generation of ideas, round-robin recording of ideas, discussion, and voting. Let us cover how each of these steps is accomplished, starting with preparation.

Preparation.   The group leader or *facilitator* prepares a question for discussion. The question must be succinct, simple to understand, and cover only one topic. A very poor question is "What are our safety problems and objectives, and what specific projects and programs can we undertake to ensure greater safety and efficiency in our plant?" The question is vague, wordy, and contains at least three different topics. A far better question clearly addresses one issue: "What objectives must our plant safety program accomplish?"

Before the meeting starts, the facilitator gathers flip charts on which to record members' responses, tape to attach the charts to the wall, and index cards on which participants can write ideas. At the outset of the meeting, the facilitator explains the four-step process and emphasizes the meeting's importance for the group and organization.

Silent generation of ideas.   After the question is posed and understood by all participants, the leader announces a specific period of time in which the group members may write down ideas related to the question. These ideas are best stated as phrases or brief sentences. Carl Moore suggested that the time period be restricted to four to eight minutes.[7] A short time period limits the number of items that the participants produce so that the group will be able to manage all or most of them. During this time, participants work independently and silently.

Round-robin recording.   The leader calls on each participant and asks for one idea. The leader writes each contribution on a flip chart as it is given. No discussion or elaboration is allowed. The leader then moves to another member and takes an idea, to another, to another, and so forth until all ideas written by the participants have been given. As a page of the flip chart is filled, the leader tapes it to the wall, where it is visible to all participants. To save time, the leader asks participants not to contribute any ideas that have already been recorded. Each idea is numbered to simplify voting on the ideas.

Discussion.   This step clarifies any confusion group members have about ideas. The leader reads each idea and invites comments and questions. The leader encourages members to discuss any items they wish, not simply those they contributed to the group. No voting, expression of opinion, or other type of debate takes place at this point.

Voting.   In the final step, group members decide on the ideas they have generated. The leader distributes five index cards to each participant, and each participant reviews the list, selects the five best ideas, and writes the number of one idea in the center of each card. The participant ranks the five ideas by placing a number from one to five in the upper right-hand corner of the card, with number one the best of the five ideas. When the

PROBLEM SOLVING ON THE JOB

GOAL: *To convince food service operators to increase the size of their fountain drinks.*

PROBLEM: *Operators do not want to sell large drinks.*

I. Introduce the Problem

VP: "Let's start off by having each of you give a brief summary of the problem as you see it: why are restaurants reluctant to increase their drink sizes?"

Linda: "Operators don't understand that larger sizes are more profitable."

Robert: "Operators are afraid consumers won't buy the larger drinks."

Ingrid: "Large drinks jeopardize our other promotions."

Jack: "We just don't have the marketing materials we need to sell them."

II. Define and Analyze the Problem

VP: "Now that we've seen everyone's perception of the problem, let's dig into these ideas and find out exactly what we're trying to solve here. I want you to elaborate on what you've just said. Everyone should feel free to disagree, ask questions, add comments or experiences, or say whatever. I want to make sure we really know what we're dealing with, so let's analyze it in detail. Just as a springboard for discussion, Linda, let's start with your observation that the operators don't understand our strategy very well."

Linda: "Operators don't really understand why selling large sizes helps their business. We need to educate them about what kind of a gold mine they're sitting on."

Robert: "I think they're just scared to put a large cup in front of the consumer. They're afraid it won't sell."

Ingrid: "I think we've made our free refill promotion so successful that we can't sell the big cup idea. No one will want to offer refills on forty-four-ounce cups. If they can't offer the large size cup *and* the refill, they're going to stick with what's worked in the past — the refill."

Jack: "Our promotional materials are really good on the forty-four-ounce cup, but they don't show the benefits of increasing the other drink sizes as well. Our salespeople don't have pre-packaged information that they can use to push the larger drink sizes."

VP: "So, if I could try to summarize what we've said here the last few minutes, it seems that although our sales force has been very effective in selling the forty-four-ounce cup, we have not been pushing the complete set of larger cup sizes. We do not have promotional brochures outlining the advantages of the larger cup sizes, and restaurant owners need to be told about them. We've also said that many operators see refill promotions and larger cup sizes as a contradiction."

III. Establish Criteria

VP: "Okay, we've got a handle on the problem! Before we start to look for specific solutions, let's try to figure out what we want the solution to do. Remember, we will judge our suggested solutions by these criteria, so make sure you consider effectiveness, resources, and ethical questions when devising them! I'll be listing them on a flip chart as we go."

Linda: "I think the solution has to include a written explanation of why the larger sizes are better. Operators will trust us if we put it in writing."

Robert: "We need to have the solution ready as soon as possible."

Ingrid: "The solution must consider the customers — we can't expect operators to sell larger size drinks if customers end up getting less for their money."

Jack: "The solution has to include some kind of financial bonus that equals the selling power of free refills."

VP: "So, we've decided on criteria that our solution has to meet: the solution has to include written material that the field sales force can use with the trade, it has to be efficiently implemented, it has to include some sort of financial incentive for the food-service operator, and it has to be acceptable to the consumers."

IV. Generate Possible Solutions

VP: "Now, let's think of as many possible solutions as we can. We are not going to evaluate any of these right now; I'll just make a list as you call them out. Now, it's okay to ask a question for clarification or to get more information, but we won't challenge or debate any of these solutions while they are being given. I'll list these for us."

Linda: "Let's talk to marketing about making a glossy brochure for our field sales force that begins with information about profitability of soft drinks, moves to our brand, and then shows the value of increasing the cup sizes for the operator."

Jack: "I think we should offer a free tank of syrup to any operator who goes to the larger cup sizes and stays with them for three months."

Robert: "We could just work with our bottlers in phasing out small cups. If the small cups weren't made, the restaurants couldn't sell them!"

Ingrid: "We can use a coupon incentive to get operators to try the larger cup sizes."

VP: "So, these are the solutions we've come up with. Anything else? Okay, let's move on to evaluating these solutions."

V. Evaluate Possible Solutions

VP: "Now we'll take the solutions in this chart one by one and match them against our criteria. We'll rule out or modify any solution that doesn't match up and see what happens. Okay, our first solution was to have a brochure made focused on upgraded cup sizes. Now, does this satisfy our requirement for written material? Yes! Does it touch on some kind of financial incentive for the operator? No, but we might be able to modify it. . . ."

[Matching of solutions to criteria continues.]

VP: "So, as a result of this discussion, we've decided to produce a marketing brochure that our sales force can use to show operators why they should increase their cup sizes. The brochure will include an incentive coupon for a free tank of syrup if operators increase their cup sizes for a minimum of three months. The solution meets our criteria of providing written information and financial incentive to operators, and because consumers can still purchase a twenty-four-ounce drink at the same price they have always paid for it, we are not proposing anything unacceptable to them."

participants have finished, the leader collects the cards and assembles a tally in front of the group. Figure 10-4 shows the results of applying the Nominal Group Technique to the "fountain-drink" problem presented in the last section.

In many cases, a clear winning idea emerges. In others, there may be a "dead heat" between two or more, requiring the group to rank the tied alternatives.

The Delphi Technique

The Delphi technique uses questionnaires to collect opinions and judgments from experts, who usually remain anonymous. Typically, questionnaires are done by mail, although they can be distributed through computer modems or tele-conferences as well. A strength of the Delphi technique is making projections and forecasts for the future when it is desirable to have pooled judgment.

The Delphi technique is not a survey or a one-time poll. The questionnaire is repeated over several rounds to collect progressively more specific information. The results from one round of questions dictate the questions for the second round and so forth. You would select this method of decision making in circumstances in which subjective judgments are desirable, face-to-face exchange is not possible because of time or cost restraints, or participants disagree to the extent that anonymity must be ensured to achieve results.

The Delphi technique includes four steps: decide to administer a questionnaire and select a group to respond, formulate the questions and produce the questionnaire, note a deadline date for return in the mailing, and receive and analyze the questionnaires. When using this technique, you must take into consideration several matters. The people to whom you address the questionnaire must be experts — you are gathering information from them. Response rates increase when you produce a personalized cover letter (or in the case of a tele-conference, personalized instructions), when you guarantee anonymity, and when you promise to provide all respondents with a copy of the results.

Keep the questionnaire very brief and to the point. It is far better to increase the number of rounds in the Delphi than to complicate the questionnaire or overburden respondents. The questionnaire will be easier to respond to if it includes closed questions (such as true-false and multiple choice) rather than open questions that require the respondents to write. Anticipate approximately a ten-week time frame for the process to be completed.

Here is an example of the Delphi technique in action. A large company's personnel department wanted to improve its minority recruiting. Personnel directors from similar-size corporations throughout a three-state region were

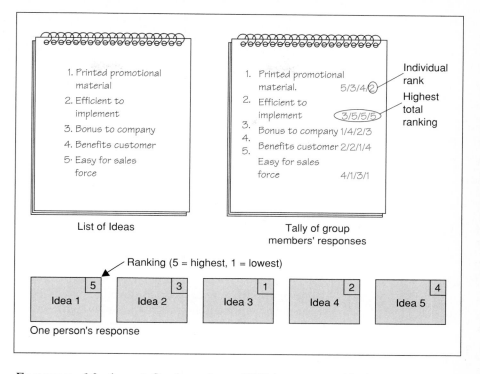

FIGURE 10-4   *A flipchart shows NGT in progress. Each group member has considered the list of ideas on the left and ranked each one on a separate card. The completed tally for each idea is shown on the right. Idea 2 emerges as the highest-ranked idea.*

surveyed for ideas. The first-round question addressed by the Delphi technique was "What problems inhibit recruitment in large corporations?" Based on the results of the questionnaire, the second-round questionnaire asked respondents to rank the top five problems and invited them to list others. Finally, based on those results, the third round solicited solutions for the problems.

The outcome of the study allowed the firm to determine which problems it had in common with others and several means by which they could be corrected. The results of the study were sent to all personnel directors who participated.

Advocacy

Advocacy, or presenting competing views on a controversial issue, greatly increases a group's insight into the issue. Advocacy improves group problem solving by identifying alternative positions and promoting a greater awareness of the important issues that must be resolved. Advocacy also forces group members to consider the strengths and weaknesses, pros and cons, and advantages and disadvantages of various viewpoints.

Without advocacy, groups have a tendency to become closeminded, often choosing solutions that are personal favorites or are easier to implement or sell to upper management. Advocacy in group problem solving can take two forms: devil's advocacy or dialectical inquiry. Both are attempts to encourage groups to compare the relative values of competing viewpoints.

Devil's advocacy.   You are probably familiar with the term *devil's advocate.* You may have even been accused of playing this role. Charles Schwenk described devil's advocacy as "structured conflict in business decisions. . . . The [devil's advocate] role should involve the formal introduction of dissent into decision-making processes in which premature consensus inhibits the challenging of assumptions and the consideration of a range of alternatives."[8] In other words, devil's advocacy is a good way to fight groupthink or excessive conformity.

Some group members may enjoy playing devil's advocate and challenging the assumptions and ideas of other group members. Although sometimes called detractors because of their apparently negative attitude, "volunteer" devil's advocates provide the group with a valuable service if their arguments are constructive. You may recall the scene in the film *Big* in which twelve-year-old Josh (in adult form) responds to a slickly packaged, jargon-filled marketing report about a less-than-exciting new toy with "I don't get it." His remark broke the group's conformist attitude and sparked inquiry and brainstorming.

If a devil's advocate does not emerge naturally from a group, the role may be assigned to a group member. Assuming the role can be both fun and challenging if the advocate is prepared. By playing this role properly, you can command the attention of important decision makers and enhance your stature within the group and organization.

Devil's advocacy is actually a sequential process beginning with formal or informal commitment from the group.[9] Group members must recognize the value of advocacy during problem solving and commit themselves to an objective and openminded attitude toward the arguments presented against prevailing opinion.

Selection of the devil's advocate (if not assumed voluntarily) must involve group members who are competent and credible. Group members must feel that the advocate knows what she or he is talking about and has a track record of effectiveness. In other words, the advocate must be credible enough to be taken seriously.

The devil's advocate has to decide which part of the problem-solving process to focus on. Advocacy can be advanced in the problem identification stage through challenges to the assumptions on which the problem is based. It can also be employed in the problem definition and analysis phase through questioning of the evidence of data presented in support of particular arguments. And it is often used during the phase of problem solving when possible solutions are being evaluated and promoted by group members. The devil's advocate may even decide to engage in all of these phases, although strategic selection is advised to avoid being labeled a detractor.

The next step is preparation. The devil's advocate must do her or his homework so that the case presented against differing viewpoints is solid and persuasive. While other group members may focus their attention on information and ideas that lead to solutions, your job as an advocate is to present information and opinions that contradict these viewpoints. When you conduct research in preparation for group meetings, concentrate on information that weakens, denies, or threatens positions that are likely to be taken by group members.

The final step in this process is issuing the challenge. Challenging others' viewpoints, opinions, ideas, or information can be accomplished in different ways. A devil's advocate can point out the inconsistencies, irrelevancies, or inaccuracies in the data or the logic being used to present arguments. In addition, a devil's advocate can use previously established criteria to refute the viability of positions being taken by group members. Of course, the most competent method of refutation or advocacy relies on critical thinking skills and effective argumentativeness techniques. By way of example, consider the following group meeting where John has decided to assume a devil's advocate role during the problem identification phase.

The group was formed to determine what could be done about poor customer service. The group has concluded that the fault lies with customers being uninformed about the services offered by the company. Their expectations are too high about what the company can deliver. John remarks, "It seems that if we want to increase our share of the market, we should not be blaming customers for their lack of knowledge of our services. That would simply cause them to look elsewhere for what they want. Rather, we should be responding to their needs by providing new services that they do want. Let me give some evidence that proves my point. Research and development has mentioned on several occasions that they can develop new products if they know the market is there."

See how John was able to move the discussion into a new light by playing devil's advocate through effective argumentation skills. What other alternatives might John be able to argue?

Dialectical inquiry. The second type of advocacy, dialectical inquiry, is similar to devil's advocacy in that the advocate opposes prevailing opinion but goes one step farther in proposing another opinion or plan of action.[10]

The sequence of stages for this process were outlined by Charles Schwenk and Richard Cosier.[11] In stage one, a prevailing or recommended strategic plan and the data used to derive it are identified. In stage two, an attempt is made to identify the assumptions underlying the plan. In stage three, a counterplan is identified that is feasible, politically viable, and generally credible but that rests on assumptions opposite those supporting the plan. In stage four, a structured debate is conducted in which those responsible for formulating strategy hear arguments in support of both the plan and the counterplan. In the last stage, this debate, in contrast to a traditional management briefing, consists of a forceful presentation of two opposing plans that rest on different interpretations of the same organizational data bank. The following example illustrates key elements of this process.

> During the testing of a new hypertension drug, a pharmaceutical company learns that the drug induces hair to grow in places where none existed before. A meeting of researchers and marketers is held to discuss the problem. One team of researchers is concerned that this side effect may prevent the introduction of the drug into the hypertension market ("People will search for something else that doesn't grow hair on their necks and backs. We should just shelve the product until we can eliminate this side effect"). Marketing people argue that the drug should be refined to capture the market of people going bald who are trying to grow their hair back. The research team retorts that the idea is impossible — there is no way to stop unwanted hair growth on other parts of the body. After a pause, one person responds, "Why can't you formulate the drug as a topical treatment that grows hair only where it is applied?" Research members look at one another and agree that it may just be possible.

This new interpretation of the problem and its potential solution opened the way for a different product to be developed and marketed — preventing the loss of time, effort, and resources that had gone into developing the original drug.

Advocacy in the form of dialectical inquiry must attack and defend, whereas the devil's advocacy approach only has to attack. Some researchers rate dialectical inquiry superior to devil's advocacy because advancing a counterplan leads to the generation of constructive alternative positions.[12] In addition, some people may not appreciate someone who attacks their position without offering one of her or his own ("If you're so sure this won't work, what can you suggest that's better?").

When group members are faced with competing plans, however, they may tend to focus myopically on the relative advantages of the plan and ignore the underlying assumptions supporting their positions.[13] Devil's advocacy can prevent this myopia. Groups may decide to employ both techniques, enacting them strategically. Regardless of which approach is taken, advocacy is an essential part of the problem-solving process.

Decision Making

There are many ways groups can engage in the decision-making process during meetings. Yet the entire reason they engage in that process is to produce a result or a final decision. Leaders can use two techniques to bring about effective decisions: consensus and voting.

Consensus.   Consensus is unanimous agreement among group members concerning a particular decision. Reaching consensus is the goal of many decision-making groups. In most groups, consensus is reached through the correct application of issue-specific conflict. As we discussed earlier, proper conflict management permits participants in a group to debate, test ideas, question evidence, and so forth. In essence, in those groups in which conflict is used properly, a consensus can be reached because all participants are testing ideas in a systematic manner. Conflict as a means for discussion allows members to resolve their differences with a resulting single, best solution to a given problem.

The major advantage of reaching a consensus is that all group members exit the meeting committed to the same outcome. This is not true of methods that rely primarily on voting. In many cases in which voting is employed, members remain committed to the positions they supported in the discussion but that the group voted down. As a result, they remain uncommitted to the decision that was made, and they are resentful in their attitude toward the group and the solution.

How do you achieve consensus in a group discussion? Several rules are useful: (1) Drop your personal position when it is shown to be unworkable or illogical. (2) Maintain an open mind concerning conflict and differences of opinion. Remember that conflict is a means by which the group can achieve its goals. If the group does not argue and exhibit conflict, why does it need to meet in the first place? (3) Unless pressed for time, do not substitute majority votes, trading, compromising, or averaging for reaching a consensus decision. Continue to work through the problem until all members agree with and are committed to a solution. (4) In cases in which discussion has stalemated, try to identify those issues that are agreeable to all members present so as to isolate the issue(s) on which there is disagreement. This is called the "most common denominator" rule. Participants in a group have to know on what issue the focus of the differences of opinion is based. Otherwise, arguments occur on several different issues at once!

Voting.   One of the most frequent methods used to resolve problems is voting. In most cases, voting is a "majority rule" means of making decisions.

We are biased against voting and urge that this method be avoided if at all possible. With this method, a decision is forced on some of the participants. The risk of having group members uncommitted to a decision and holding a negative attitude toward the group and the decision is, in our opinion, not desirable. Nevertheless, there are two circumstances in which voting is useful: if the group is under time constraints that do not allow the group to proceed through a normal discussion and reach consensus and if the group is too large to hold a consensus discussion.

If at all possible, use voting to narrow down options on which a consensus decision can be reached. For example, imagine that a group has five disparate, mutually exclusive solutions that all seem reasonable and workable. The size of the group and time constraints prevent it from working through the proposed solution in a consensus-building fashion. The group can take a vote on each of the options and determine which two of the five solutions the majority of the members seems to favor. Having narrowed the solutions down to two, the group can then hold a consensus discussion and work through to a single desired option. Notice that when the members finish this type of discussion, they have actively participated in the decision-making process and will be committed to the decision reached.

Anxiety Management

There are several causes of anxiety in meeting situations. In some instances, the meeting is not an opportunity for open discussion; rather, it is a closed forum in which powerful members monopolize communication or coerce others into agreement on issues. If you are of lower status or simply uncomfortable with an authoritarian style, such a meeting may upset you and result in communication apprehension. To address your nervousness, you can suggest that the group take a break from the discussion and allow everyone a turn to summarize the group's progress to that point. In this way, others who may also be apprehensive will gain mutual support.

Another example is a meeting in which everyone else knows one another but in which you are a newcomer. You may feel shy, anxious, and nervous about speaking up or stating a position. It may be difficult to become friendly with group members before the initial meeting of the group. Nevertheless, once you know people's names and position in the organization, you will have some basic information with which to work. By approaching the relationship with a goal of improving group communication as well as lessening your own anxiety, you will be able to shift the focus from yourself and your nervousness and concentrate on becoming comfortable with group members.

In companies that have diverse work forces — people of many different educational or cultural backgrounds or even different ages — differences in communication styles may cause apprehension in a group meeting. For example, many companies cite instances in which a woman's input is ignored by the men in the meetings, but when the same suggestion is advanced by a male colleague, it is accepted for discussion. Conflicting cultural norms

Who's in favor of breaking for lunch? Voting is a useful tool for rapid decision-making or getting a sense of a group's position on an issue.

in areas such as boastfulness, dominance, or even use of nonverbal gestures such as touching, eye contact, or facial expressions may make group meetings anxious events if you fail to prepare for such differences by becoming familiar with different norms and styles.

Finally, meetings held to resolve a group conflict or to mediate serious arguments can cause apprehension because of the sensitivity of issues involved. You can use a variety of methods to contain anxiety that stems from conflict (see Chapter 11).

Evaluating Group Effectiveness

Modern business and professional organizations are rarely satisfied with the way they are. This is true no matter how successful, productive, or effective the organization is. Unless there is a strong and clearly articulated vision for the future, today's successes are tomorrow's busts.

One key method by which organizations may prepare for the future is by evaluating the present. To define what we mean by evaluation, we must contrast it with description. Description focuses on what a group or person is doing; evaluation focuses on how well the group or person is doing it. Evaluation, then, requires a judgment or an assessment.

As John Brilhart noted, "Unless practice is constantly evaluated, it may result in bad habits. The means to learning is practice with analysis and evaluation leading to change in future discussions."[14] You are probably aware of the cliché "Practice makes perfect." Unfortunately, this is true only if the practice itself is perfect! Therefore, you must monitor and evaluate the effectiveness of the groups in which you participate if you intend to join the future.

Many different students of group communication have provided categories, rating forms, evaluation instruments, or questionnaires designed to assess the strength of different units. In the next sections, we discuss the dimensions of group evaluations and techniques for conducting them successfully.

Dimensions of Group Evaluation

A very effective evaluation system was devised by Albert Kowitz and Thomas Knutson, who divided group evaluation into three dimensions: informational, procedural, and interpersonal.[15]

Informational. According to Kowitz and Knutson, the informational dimension is concerned with the task that the group is working on. Evaluation of that task can be broken down into several components. One is whether the task before the group lends itself to discussion. If not, the group may have to expand the scope and nature of its topic. If the task is suitable, a second component presents itself: How prepared is the group for discussion? Was needed research or necessary advance planning done by the members before the meeting? Is there a need to get more information before the group can make an adequate decision?

As for a third component, how well does the group "tear apart" the problem? You will recall from the previous chapter that analysis depends on reducing an issue to its component parts. Is there evidence of high-quality information giving, opinion giving, evaluation and criticism, elaboration and integration?

Note that of these factors, evaluation and criticism are extremely important to the success of the group. The group meets to test ideas. If there is early agreement and signs that certain participants are reluctant to express reservations, the meeting is headed toward groupthink. Does anyone state, "Let me play devil's advocate for a moment"? In evaluating a group, you should see evidence of productive conflict with debate, questioning, and exploration of alternatives.

Procedural. Evaluation of procedural functions looks at how well the group's activities and communication are coordinated. We have specified earlier in this chapter that most of these functions are performed by the leader. Yet in groups where the leadership function is a shared one, each participant has a responsibility to exhibit some essential leadership behaviors.

The key functions to be evaluated include eliciting communication, delegating and directing action, summarizing group activity, managing conflict, evaluating process, and releasing tension. Let us highlight a few problems that you may see in these areas.

One behavior that occurs with regularity in groups is some members talking too much and others talking too little. To counteract this behavior, an astute leader and others attempt to keep the lines of communication open among all group members, a function known as gatekeeping. A line such as "Tim, I think you've covered that issue pretty well. Bob, do you have anything to add?" is a tactful way to suppress and elicit contributions.

Another recurring behavior is a return to issues that have seemingly been decided on or worked through. When this happens, many members get frustrated and tense. You will hear, "We never get anything done in here," or "We're just spinning our wheels." There are two possibilities for corrective action. One is the use of summaries. Does the leader or do other members continually keep the group posted of its progress with remarks such as "What we've been talking about is . . ." or "So, what we seem to be saying is . . ."? A second possibility is to determine if the group has lost sight of its objectives. What is the group trying to accomplish, and how well does the present discussion help to accomplish these objectives?

Finally, there is a need for members to release tension at certain points of interaction. This can be done through a joke, sharing of feelings, and so on. Kowitz and Knutson stressed that participants may need to be reminded of their individual responsibilities and importance in the overall group function. Once members are aware of what is expected of them, tension can decrease and the group can resume making progress.

Interpersonal. In this portion of the evaluation, the emphasis is on the way that the members work with each other, which includes the climate or atmosphere in which the task is accomplished. There can be little doubt that when the circumstances in which the group operates are uncomfortable or unpleasant, productivity and results will be affected in negative ways. There are four areas that can be assessed in this dimension: positive reinforcement, solidarity, cooperativeness, and respect toward others.

We have already noted that one of the most dangerous things that can happen in a meeting is when the conflict shifts from tasks to individuals. Personality conflicts can distract the group from its primary task and responsibility. The group leader and each member should attempt to convince the group to "stick to the facts" or "get back on the problem" whenever an outburst such as "You've never known anything about this before, and who the hell are you to talk about it now?" occurs.

If the atmosphere is negative or unpleasant, the leader or any group member can use rewards to emphasize the positive aspects of the meeting. There may, however, be some issue-based reasons behind the negative statements being made. If this is the case, the reason for the derogatory comments merits exploration.

Individual Evaluation

Apart from the group as a whole, each individual participant can be assessed. The focus of such an evaluation is on how well members helped the group accomplish its task and how well they performed functions in the process.

An excellent instrument for evaluating individual participants and leaders was created by Larry Samovar and Steven King.[16] Each of the factors on their instrument has been previously defined and discussed in these chapters. We simply list the factors that can be assessed.

Participants.   Eleven factors make up the individual member evaluation form. The form may be completed either by another group member or the group leader. The following is an example of a participant evaluation form.

PARTICIPANT EVALUATION FORM

Name of group member _____

Name of rater _____

Date _____

For each characteristic, fill in a rating from 1 (excellent) to 7 (poor). Write any comments in the space below the rating list.

Participant Characteristics

1. _____   Preparation
2. _____   Speaking
3. _____   Listening
4. _____   Openmindedness
5. _____   Sensitivity to others
6. _____   Worth of information
7. _____   Critical thinking skills
8. _____   Group orientation
9. _____   Procedural contribution
10. _____   Assistance in leadership
11. _____   Overall evaluation

Comments:

Leaders.   There are also eleven factors on the leadership evaluation form. Note that this form operates best when the group has an assigned or designated leader. In this way, the evaluator can focus on one individual and how well he or she performs the role. The following is a sample leadership evaluation form.

LEADER EVALUATION FORM

Name of leader _____
Name of rater _____
Date _____

For each characteristic, fill in a rating from 1 (excellent) to 7 (poor). Write any comments in the space below the rating list.

Leadership Functions

1. _____   Open discussion
2. _____   Asked appropriate questions
3. _____   Offered reviews
4. _____   Clarified ideas
5. _____   Encouraged critical thinking
6. _____   Limited irrelevancies
7. _____   Protected minority viewpoints
8. _____   Remained impartial
9. _____   Kept accurate records
10. _____ Concluded discussion
11. _____ Overall leadership

Comments:

For both the individual and leadership evaluation factors, assessments can be made about the relative strengths and weaknesses for each group member. Evaluating these areas contributes to improvement in group work.

The Group Behavior Inventory

One of the more reliable methods of group evaluation is the Group Behavior Inventory (GBI).[17] It is a long instrument consisting of seventy-one items. The following evaluation form includes items from the GBI that conform to the dimensions discussed in this and the previous chapter.

GROUP EVALUATION MEASURE

Rate the following items according to how you feel about the group or its members in the following way: 1 = strongly agree, 2 = agree, 3 = neither agree nor disagree, 4 = disagree, and 5 = strongly disagree.

1. _1_ The group is an effective problem-solving team.
2. _2_ Divergent ideas are encouraged at group meetings.
3. _5_ Members are more intent on satisfying the leader than on optimizing the potential output of the group.
4. _3_ The goals of the group are clear-cut.
5. _2_ It is important to be on friendly terms with other group members.
6. _5_ Conflict within the group is submerged rather than used constructively.
7. _1_ There is an open examination of relationships among group members.
8. _3_ The group should be achieving more than it is.
9. _4_ There is a destructive competitiveness among members of the group.
10. _1_ Group meetings result in creative solutions to problems.
11. _5_ There is no point in raising critical problems at group meetings.
12. _1_ There is open examination of issues and problems at group meetings.
13. _3_ Group members are willing to listen to and to understand me.
14. _1_ Group meetings should be continued.
15. _3_ The policies under which the group works are clear-cut.
16. _5_ Meetings are not effective in discussing mutual problems.
17. _4_ The chairman should give the members guidance.
18. _3_ Meetings are trivial.
19. _5_ The criterion for evaluating ideas in the group is "who said it" rather than "what was said."
20. _3_ The chairman is oriented toward production and efficiency.

To score this measure reverse scoring for items 3, 6, 8, 9, 11, 16, 17, 18, 19 (i.e., if you scored these items with a 5, replace it with a 1, replace 4 with a 2, keep 3 the same, replace 2 with a 4, and replace 1 with a 5). Add up all 20 items using the replaced scores for the above items. A low score (20–50) suggests a very effective group. A high score (70–100) reveals group problems. A mid-range score (51–69) represents a group that could rapidly improve with a few changes in how it operates.

This evaluation measure can come in handy after meeting with a group several times to determine areas of strength and weakness. All group members should score the measure and discuss their individual results with the group. In this way, everyone will understand the relative perceptions of their counterparts, and weaknesses can be healed and strengths can be maintained. Look for specific areas that need improvement, and work together to strengthen these.

Summary

Meetings are a prevalent form of communication in organizations. This chapter discussed how to conduct effective meetings, including how to set the agenda and keep the focus on goals. Groups must develop strong and realistic goals to effectively solve problems. Such goals can be specified according to organizational, group, and individual goals. The situational aspects of meetings include obtaining proper meeting facilities, setting up audiovisual equipment, maintaining rules of order, and getting to know the other participants in the group.

The communication competencies for strategic problem solving in groups rest on the ability to think critically. This skill is made up of analysis, reasoning, interpretation, and evaluation. In terms of daily practice, groups must select a problem-solving technique that best suits their needs. The three techniques available to them are reflective thinking, the nominal group technique, and the Delphi method. To further refine their problem solving, groups engage in advocacy; this ensures that possible assumptions and alternatives have been identified and discussed. Devil's advocacy and dialectical inquiry are available for this purpose. To make effective decisions, groups can either vote or reach a consensus among groups members (the preferred method). Decision making is not difficult if the previous steps have been completed properly.

Meetings are not without anxiety-provoking circumstances, particularly when meetings are closed forums, when they are composed of people with diverse backgrounds, or when they are called to mediate serious arguments. Containing anxiety takes skill and inventiveness but is neither complicated nor impossible.

No matter how successful a group's communication is, it cannot be maintained without monitoring. Groups can improve their performance only when they appraise their skills, methods, techniques, and behaviors. Evaluation can be made of the group itself or of the specific individuals involved in the group. The group evaluation measure provided in the chapter can be adapted and used for the group to which you belong.

Discussion

1. Why is an agenda a useful starting point for a meeting? How might a standard formal agenda be adapted for the following meetings: coworkers meeting with a human resources representative to discuss benefits issues; an ongoing employee support group; a self-managing team assessing its progress?

2. Discuss the various possibilities given for meeting setups. In what circumstances would each be most appropriate?

3. Why are critical thinking skills vital to communication? In what ways are you using critical thinking skills now in school or on the job?

4. Discuss reflective thinking, the nominal group technique, and the Delphi technique. What seem to be the strengths and weaknesses of each method?

5. Why are devil's advocacy and dialectical inquiry techniques useful in group problem solving? What communication failures can they prevent?

6. What are some advantages and disadvantages of consensus and voting as decision-making processes?

7. What are some causes of communication anxiety that can be amplified in a group situation? Which of these have you experienced, and how did you react to them?

8. Discuss a variety of approaches to group evaluation. How does evaluation provide direction and suggest areas for improvement?

Activities

1. Construct sample agendas for each of the following group meetings. Note the modifications you make from the agenda listed in this chapter.
   a. Disciplinary committee meeting
   b. Corporate safety board meeting
   c. Company credit union committee meeting to approve loan requests
   d. Fraternity's annual election of officers

2. When is interpreting information appropriate or inappropriate for a leader and a group? Consider the difference between "telling" and "discussing" in your answer.

3. Why are some people reluctant to be a "devil's advocate" in group meetings? In your class discussion, find out if other classmates feel the same way.

4. If you were a group leader of a decision-making body and consensus was difficult to achieve, what steps would you take to effect a decision? Compare your list with other members of your small discussion group.

Notes

1. C. S. Palazzolo, "The Social Group: Definitions," in R. S. Cathcart and L. A. Samovar (eds), *Small Group Communication: A Reader,* 4th ed. (Dubuque, Iowa: William C. Brown, 1984), pp. 1–23.
2. H. M. Robert, *Robert's Rules of Order* (Glenview, Ill.: Scott, Foresman, 1990).

3. R. Y. Hirokawa and D. S. Gouran, "Facilitation of Group Communication: A Critique of Prior Research and an Agenda for Future Research," *Management Communication Quarterly* 3 (1989): 71–92.

4. B. J. Broome and D. B. Deever, "Next Generation Group Facilitation," *Management Communication Quarterly* 3 (1989): 107–127.

5. F. G. Smith, "Defining Managerial Problems: A Framework for Prescriptive Theorizing," *Management Science* 35 (1989): 963–981.

6. The following discussion is typical of problem-solving meetings held in the fountain food service division of Dr. Pepper/Seven-Up Co., Dallas, Texas.

7. C. H. Moore, *Group Techniques for Idea Building* (Newbury Park, Calif.: Sage, 1987).

8. C. R. Schwenk, *The Essence of Strategic Decision Making* (Lexington, Mass.: Lexington Books, 1988), p. 87.

9. Ibid.

10. Ibid.

11. C. R. Schwenk and R. A. Cosier, "Effects of the Expert, Devil's Advocate, and Dialectical Inquiry Methods on Prediction Performance," *Organizational Behavior and Human Performance* 26 (1980): 409–424.

12. R. A. Mason, "A Dialectical Approach to Strategic Planning," *Management Science* 15 (1969): 403–414; Schwenk, *The Essence of Strategic Decision Making;* Schwenk and Cosier, "Effects of the Expert, Devil's Advocate, and Dialectical Inquiry Methods."

13. Schwenk and Cosier, "Effects of the Expert, Devil's Advocate, and Dialectical Inquiry Methods."

14. J. K. Brilhart, "Observing and Evaluating Discussion," in Cathcart and Samovar (eds.), *Small Group Communication,* p. 559.

15. A. C. Kowitz and T. J. Knutson, *Decision Making in Small Groups: The Search for Alternatives* (Boston: Allyn Bacon, 1980).

16. L. A. Samovar and S. W. King, *Communication and Discussion in Small Groups* (Scottsdale, Ariz.: Gorsuch-Scarisbrick, 1981).

17. The complete Group Behavior Inventory can be obtained from the Library of Congress, Photoduplication Service, Washington, D.C. 20540 (request document ADI-8787). For further reference on the use of group evaluations, see F. Friedlander, "Performance and Interactional Dimensions of Organizational Work Groups," *Journal of Applied Psychology* 50 (1969): 257–265, and I. T. Kaplan and H. H. Greenbaum, "Measuring Work Group Effectiveness: A Comparison of Three Instruments," *Management Communication Quarterly* 2 (1989): 424–448.

Chapter 11

*N*egotiation and Conflict Management

OBJECTIVES

After working through this chapter, you will be able to:

1. Explain the difference between argumentation and verbal aggressiveness and evaluate yourself in each area

2. Identify the three dimensions of every bargaining session

3. Employ bargaining strategies appropriate to the situation

4. Define conflict and differentiate it from other competitive situations

5. Recognize conflicting goals and how to deal with them

6. Take steps to manage conflict productively

In addition to their function as forums for problem solving and decision making, groups are a frequent source of "competitive" communication in organizations. Competitive communication is characterized by interdependent, yet conflicting, goals, and it can occur at all levels of an organization. Commitment to organizational values and ethical standards, strong verbal and listening skills, interpersonal communication ability, and understanding of group roles, norms, and dynamics are all essential to the handling of competitive communication successfully. In a sense, the material in this chapter draws on every aspect of strategic communication that we have discussed.

People may avoid negotiation and conflict because of their apparent difficulty and stressfulness. People may also avoid these situations because they dislike arguing or have been the target of attacks by verbally aggressive communicators. Certainly, failing to reach a resolution in any of these situations can produce negative results for individuals and the organization. Nevertheless, negotiation and conflict are vital to the long-term growth and health of a company and its employees. Tensions resulting from unredressed needs or conflicts can undermine employee morale, motivation, and trust in the organization. By learning productive methods of negotiation and conflict management, you can contribute a great deal to the groups, organizations, and people with whom you work.

And that is the true focus of this chapter — helping you to apply the skills necessary to communicate successfully and effectively in difficult, even competitive, circumstances. We begin with a brief summary of the difference between argumentation and verbal aggressiveness, address the unique skills and demands of bargaining and negotiation sessions, and conclude with one of the more complex situations in communication: conflict management.

Argumentativeness and Verbal Aggressiveness

What makes one person more likely than someone else to engage in arguments? What happens when people who are arguing about issues refocus their attention on each other? Although we briefly touched on the subject of group conflict in Chapter 9, here we show you how to evaluate your own tendencies in this area and their implications for communication in your career.

The tendency to view argumentation positively is called *argumentativeness*. More specifically, Dominique Infante contends that "argumentativeness includes the ability to recognize controversial issues in communication situations, to present and defend positions on the issues, and to attack the positions which other people take."[1]

Generally speaking, argumentativeness in the workplace is a positive and constructive strategy. Arguing for causes, positions, and ideas within organizations is often viewed favorably because people who are effective arguers achieve their goals more often. Research has shown that subordinates prefer superiors who are high in argumentativeness because they feel their bosses will be more successful with their superiors and the entire unit or department will benefit from effective argumentation skills.[2] The review of critical thinking skills in Chapter 10 is designed to improve your ability to argue constructively.

The tendency to attack other people instead of arguments is termed *verbal aggressiveness*. Dominique Infante and Charles Wigely provided the following definition: "Verbal aggressiveness . . . denotes attacking the self-concept of another person instead of, or in addition to, the person's position on a topic of communication."[3]

When comparing argumentativeness with verbal aggressiveness, you discover that the difference between these two traits is the *focus* of the attack. Argumentative people concentrate on positions, issues, reasoning, and evidence. Verbally aggressive people concentrate on attacking others personally.

The difference is very important in how others view the arguer/aggressor and in how the trait affects career relationships, productivity in groups, and ability to achieve organizational goals. According to Infante, people can possess both traits, although interestingly, people with a high degree of argumentativeness are less likely to use verbally aggressive strategies.[4]

Determining Your Argumentativeness and Verbal Aggressiveness

Now that we have discussed argumentativeness and verbal aggressiveness, you are probably wondering how you rate along these dimensions. One way to find out is to score yourself on scales designed to measure these traits.[5] The scale on page 351 measures argumentativeness. It identifies your reactions to controversy. The scale on page 352 measures verbal aggressiveness. It reveals how you usually try to get people to comply with your wishes. When responding to each statement, think of specific examples that confirm your assessment to ensure honest and accurate results.

How do you feel about the results of these tests? Do you wish that your level of argumentativeness was higher and your level of verbal aggressiveness lower? The following suggestions can help.

Controlling Verbal Aggressiveness

Uncontrolled verbal aggressiveness can lead to interpersonal difficulties. Attacking the personalities or self-concepts of others demonstrates poor

ARGUMENTATIVENESS SCALE

This scale contains statements about arguing controversial issues. Indicate how often each statement is true for you by placing the appropriate number in the blank to the left of the statement. If the statement is almost never true for you, place a 1 in the blank. If the statement is rarely true for you, place a 2 in the blank. If the statement is occasionally true for you, place a 3 in the blank. If the statement is often true for you, place a 4 in the blank. If the statement is almost always true for you, place a 5 in the blank.

1. _5_   While in an argument, I worry that the person I am arguing with will form a negative opinion of me.
2. _4_   Arguing over controversial issues improves my intelligence.
3. _2_   I enjoy avoiding arguments.
4. _3_   I am energetic and enthusiastic when I argue.
5. _3_   Once I finish an argument, I promise myself that I will not get into another.
6. _4_   Arguing with a person creates more problems than it solves.
7. _3_   I have a pleasant, good feeling when I win a point in an argument.
8. _5_   When I finish arguing with someone, I feel nervous and upset.
9. _2_   I enjoy a good argument over a controversial issue.
10. _4_   I get an unpleasant feeling when I realize I am about to get into an argument.
11. _3_   I enjoy defending my point of view on an issue.
12. _5_   I am happy when I keep an argument from happening.
13. _2_   I do not like to miss the opportunity to argue a controversial issue.
14. _4_   I prefer being with people who rarely disagree with me.
15. _3_   I consider an argument an exciting intellectual challenge.
16. _4_   I find myself unable to think of effective points during an argument.
17. _2_   I feel refreshed and satisfied after an argument on a controversial issue.
18. _2_   I have the ability to do well in an argument.
19. _4_   I try to avoid getting into arguments.
20. _2_   I feel excitement when I expect that a conversation I am in is leading to an argument.

Tendency to approach argumentative situations: add scores on items 2, 4, 7, 9, 11, 13, 15, 17, 18, and 20. _26_
Tendency to avoid argumentative situations: add scores on items 1, 3, 5, 6, 8, 10, 12, 14, 16, and 19. _40_   _— 14_
Argumentativeness trait: subtract the total of the ten tendency-to-avoid items from the total of the ten tendency-to-approach items.

What does the final # mean?

sensitivities to feelings and usually hurts those who are targets of this aggression. Controlling verbal aggressiveness is a multistage process that begins with an identification of the various forms of this communication strategy. Types of verbal aggressiveness include character attacks, competence attacks, insults, threats, nonverbal signs, ethnic or gender slurs, teasing, ridicule, profanity, and physical appearance attacks.[6] When you notice yourself using any of these tactics, reformulate your strategy so that you focus on the issues instead.

The next stage in reducing verbal aggressiveness is to understand how and why it occurs. There are at least four reasons for this behavior.[7] *Psychopathy,* or mental disorder, can stimulate attacks on people (clinical counseling is recommended in this case). *Dislike of others* can cause verbal aggressiveness, especially if you are put off by the appearance or personality of the person with whom you are communicating. *Social learning,* or observing and imitating parents, siblings, peers, and significant others who

VERBAL AGGRESSIVENESS SCALE

If the statement is almost never true for you, place a 1 in the blank. If the statement is rarely true for you, place a 2 in the blank. If the statement is occasionally true for you, place a 3 in the blank. If the statement is often true for you, place a 4 in the blank. If the statement is almost always true for you, place a 5 in the blank.

1. _4_ I am extremely careful to avoid attacking a person's intelligence when I attack her or his ideas.
2. _2_ I use insults to "soften" stubborn people.
3. _4_ I try very hard to avoid influencing people by making them feel bad about themselves.
4. _2_ If someone refuses to do a task I know is important for a reason that does not seem valid to me, I accuse him or her of being unreasonable.
5. _5_ When others do things I think are misguided, I try to be extremely gentle with them.
6. _2_ If someone I am trying to influence really deserves it, I attack her or his character.
7. _1_ When people demonstrate poor taste, I insult them to shock them into proper behavior.
8. _4_ I try to make people feel good about themselves even when I think their ideas are useless.
9. _3_ When people simply will not budge on a matter of great importance, I lose my temper and make strong emotional outbursts.
10. _4_ When people criticize my shortcomings, I take it in good humor and do not try to get back at them.

11. _3_   When people insult me, I get a lot of pleasure out of overreacting.
12. _4_   When I dislike someone strongly, I try not to show it in what I say or how I say it.
13. _2_   I like poking fun at people who do or say careless things to "wake them up."
14. _4_   When I attack a person's ideas, I try not to damage his or her self-concept.
15. _4_   When I try to influence people, I make a great effort not to offend them.
16. _4_   If I see someone act cruelly, I tell everyone else how terrible he or she is in hopes of changing his or her behavior.
17. _4_   I refuse to participate in arguments when they involve personal attacks.
18. _2_   When I am unable to influence others through conventional tactics, I resort to yelling or screaming at them.
19. _2_   When I am not able to refute others' positions, I try to make them feel defensive to weaken their positions.
20. _3_   When an argument shifts to personal attacks, I try very hard to change the subject.

42

25
17

Add your scores on numbers 1, 3, 5, 8, 10, 12, 14, 15, 17, and 20. Call this Total A. Add your scores on numbers 2, 4, 6, 7, 9, 11, 13, 16, 18, and 19. Call this Total B. Subtract Total B from Total A. If the result is between twenty-five and forty, you have a low tendency toward verbal aggressiveness. If your score is between ten and twenty-five, you have a moderate tendency toward verbal aggressiveness. If your score is below ten (especially a negative number), you probably use verbal aggression frequently.

use verbal aggressiveness with you or in your presence, can encourage verbal aggressiveness. *Desperation* can lead to verbal aggressiveness in a final effort to win an argument. Desperation as a motive is particularly common if the aggressor possesses deficient critical thinking skills. She or he may be unable to express clear and objective dissenting opinions and may feel there is no alternative than attacking the self-concept of others involved in the discussion. Understanding and being aware of these causes of verbal aggressiveness can help you to control the urge to attack people personally.

The best method for controlling verbal aggressiveness is by becoming a better communicator. The critical thinking skills discussed in Chapter 10 are intended to make you more proficient at formulating and expressing your ideas for constructive discussions with others. Learn these skills and practice them on a regular basis. You will find that engaging in constructive argumentation decreases the urge to attack others personally.

Bargaining and Negotiation

We now turn to situations that frequently involve argumentation and verbal aggressiveness. The first, negotiation (also referred to in this chapter as bargaining), generally occurs when communicators take opposing roles (such as buyer and seller, union leader and company representative, or supervisor and employee).[8] Because of their different affiliations, participants in a negotiation session are likely to have very different goals, needs, and communication styles compared to problem-solving groups that work toward one goal. Or, they may have a common goal but disagree on the means and methods to achieve it.

Negotiation is usually a planned and structured process of communication. Although arguments may occur spontaneously based on something said in the discussion, negotiators frequently plan tactics to be used and topics to be covered before the encounter.

In a bargaining session, two or more people with different goals exchange communication to produce a mutually desirable outcome.[9] Parties involved in the bargaining relationship must recognize that they are mutually dependent — seldom can an acceptable outcome occur unless all parties recognize this fact.[10] Most bargaining scenarios require give-and-take in the form of *concessions,* or acknowledgments of an opponent's truth, right, or privilege in a specific instance. Communicators must bargain forcefully and strategically by using effective argumentation skills while at the same time remaining aware that some concessions must be made so that all parties feel satisfied with the outcome.

Formal versus Informal Bargaining

The bargaining process can be observed in both formal and informal situations. Formal bargaining situations develop when recurring issues require deliberation and confrontation over time. There are a number of situations in professional organizations that require periodic bargaining.

One of the most important examples of formal bargaining is labor-management negotiations. Labor contracts are usually specified for a certain length of time, thus requiring bargaining sessions when the contract expires. Other examples of formal bargaining include negotiation between representatives of government and industry over disputed laws or policies, bargaining with subcontractors or law firms over services to be rendered, bargaining with financial institutions over credit or credit ratings, and negotiation with suppliers over prices. Formal bargaining is recurring, anticipated, planned, and structured.

Informal bargaining is also quite prevalent in the workplace and usually involves spontaneous situations that are seldom repeated. Informal bargaining may occur any time two or more parties must depend on one another to resolve divergent goals. For example, managers and employees often bargain over job description, salary, roles, and performance standards. Each is interested in having the other accommodate her or his goals. Peers bargain with each other to resolve issues such as turf or territory disputes, recognition for accomplishments, work schedules, and even personality differences.

Informal bargaining may even occur across organizational boundaries. Asking for discounts from vendors, negotiating with airlines about how frequent flier miles are counted, and bargaining with hotels about corporate rates constitute informal bargaining situations. Regardless of whether the situation is formal or informal, similar strategies are used to effectively negotiate with others.

Basic Skills for Presenting a Position

The first step in a negotiation session is advancing an offer within limits acceptable to the other bargaining party. Many bargaining positions are first expressed as broad statements that lay out a general goal. An offer that appears to be unreasonable on first hearing may in fact become persuasive as the negotiator takes it through the subsequent steps in the bargaining process.

Of course, it is better for the negotiator to begin with an offer that is clearly reasonable. Reasonable offers, which seem to make sense and correspond to known facts and standard beliefs, show that the negotiator is bargaining in good faith. Regardless of the quality of your initial offer, you will usually need to persuade others that your position is worthy of their support. Strong use of evidence gives credibility to your position more effectively than any other tactic. *Evidence* usually includes some form of information — published documentation, statistics, expert opinion, examples and illustrations, or testimony. We discuss information management in detail in the next section. *Summarizing* is another key element in expressing a bargaining position because it demonstrates consistency and steadfastness during negotiation. Others may be looking for signs of *equivocation* or inconsistency. Summarizing the elements of your argument may help to clear up any confusion about the position you have taken and why you have taken it. Negotiation is more effective when everyone involved understands one another's positions on the issue.

Finally, look at the position taken by the other side in the negotiation. In what ways is the position realistic or unrealistic? If any elements of the opposing position are weak or irrelevant, identify them as such and try to avoid having them become the focus of the negotiation. In the long run, it is better to address the major strengths of the opposing position, mindful of opportunities to use such arguments to support your own position. Throughout the negotiation, use critical thinking skills to analyze, evaluate, and interpret the opposing position. Doing so allows you to formulate effective counterarguments.

Dimensions of Bargaining and Negotiating

According to bargaining and negotiating experts, there are three dimensions to this process: information management, making concessions, and positioning.[11] Each of these dimensions represents a category of strategies, tactics, and behaviors that are used by negotiators to advance their goals.

Information management.   When engaging in bargaining with others, you are wise to have at hand as much research and information as possible, but you must also manage the information effectively — use it to promote your goals for the negotiation session. Information can be managed in a number of ways that lead to a stronger bargaining position.

You can seek explanations from your opponents in an effort to clarify the issues, realign their position according to prevailing evidence, or reduce ambiguity that can be used against you. You can manage information in a

Buying a car is a common example of negotiation. You are likely to get the best bargain by setting goals and ensuring that you are well informed about all aspects of the market before entering negotiations with the dealer.

bargaining session by requesting that your adversaries assign priorities to their goals and objectives. Sometimes bargainers enter a negotiation session with a "grocery list" of objectives they hope to achieve, knowing they will have to compromise on some. Ask the opposing party to rank its objectives in order of importance.

You can use questioning techniques to better understand others' motives and goals. Asking direct questions such as "Why do you feel this way?" "What does your group hope to get out of this?" or "How do you expect us to compromise that much?" can encourage your adversaries to put the major issues on the table.

Finally, you can refocus the discussion on your own agenda. In bargaining sessions, abundant information favoring the opposition's position may be introduced. For example, if one of the two negotiating parties has access to greater resources, such as time, money, special research, or legal services, that party may attempt to overwhelm the negotiation with excess data. Nevertheless, such information does not decrease the importance of your evidence and your group's position on the issue. If you feel you are being overwhelmed by the quantity of your opponents' information (regardless of its relevance), redirect the focus of the discussion toward your own objectives so you can move the negotiation toward a settlement that supports your position. For example, saying, "I can see your point, but if you look at our data, you will see that the statistical trends point to a strategy in line with what we are offering" can prevent sheer quantity of information from overriding a fair negotiation.

Making concessions.　　As we have mentioned, negotiators have to come to the bargaining table expecting to give up, or *concede,* some of their goals to obtain some in return. Concession is useful in several ways. Making concessions demonstrates cooperativeness, which usually gives a positive impression to others and may encourage them to reciprocate. Providing concessions is a good way to maintain interest in the negotiation. Lags or lapses in the bargaining process can occur as participants become bogged down by old issues and stale ideas. Providing a minor concession from time to time can open new windows of opportunity, stimulate fresh approaches to the negotiation, and revitalize communication among the bargaining parties. Concessions early in the bargaining process communicate a conciliatory tone. You can avoid accusations of rigidity and closed-mindedness through concessions that demonstrate a belief in cooperative discussion.

When you have decided to make a concession, objectively evaluate the opposing argument's strengths to determine an appropriate concession. Concessions can take the form of time, money, resources, responsibilities, autonomy, and even changes in job descriptions. After you make a concession, show how both your own and your opponent's needs and goals are served by the concession, and clearly redefine your position so the negotiation can continue.

Positioning.   *Positioning* means moving the focus of the negotiation to issues important to you. This technique must be used carefully to remain ethical. Ask yourself if the issues that interest you are the central issues in the discussion. If not, refrain from emphasizing them at the expense of more important organizational goals. Many negotiators use positioning to show their side in its most favorable light. Be very careful that in highlighting the positive aspects of your group's agenda, you do not distort or misrepresent your actual position.

Positioning can result from preestablished rules and procedures. Many formal bargaining situations prescribe certain methods of discussion, pro-

Interact!

Negotiation is a skill that you will need throughout your career whether you work in a corporate setting, a volunteer or nonprofit organization, an academic field, a profession such as law or medicine, or a service industry. In all cases, your proficiency and effectiveness as a negotiator can influence the quality of work life for you and your organization.

In addition to tangible outcomes such as saving time and money, successful negotiation allows participants to feel satisfied that they have bargained the best deal they could possibly work out. Within the context of a win-win negotiating stance, the ability to drive a hard but fair bargain is the mark of a good negotiator.

For this activity, divide the class into groups of three. In each group, one person takes the role of a buyer for a large organization, who is responsible for purchasing quality goods and services at the best possible price. Another person portrays a sales representative for a company that supplies an essential service to the organization. The third person is an evaluator. This person decides the budget for both the buyer and the seller; that is, the evaluator tells the buyer the top limit on how much money she or he is allowed to spend and the seller the lowest possible price she or he can accept. The evaluator then observes how each negotiator works within the assigned budgets. The buyer and seller know only their own (not each other's) budgets.

Each group should choose one of the companies and one of the services listed below and think about the unique needs and challenges the combination presents to the buyer and seller. It is also possible to create your own bargaining scenario using companies and services you may be familiar with in your own experience.

Company	**Service**
Manufacturer	Packing/shipping
Small retailer	Software/computer support service
Department store	Office services
Bank	Advertising

Fund-raising organization	Insurance
Telecommunications company	Accounting services
University	Legal services
Publishing company	Distribution/transportation
Television or radio station	Security services
Airline	Property lease
City agency	Maintenance/janitorial service
Hotel or restaurant	Printing
	Raw materials broker
	Food service
	Equipment or furniture rental

As the company buyer, your role is to get the best possible service at the best possible price. As the sales representative, your objective is to get the buyer's business in an agreement that is mutually satisfying to both parties but profitable for your firm as well. As the observer, your role is to assess the strategies taken, the results obtained, and the skill with which each participant communicates her or his position.

The simulation should take about twenty minutes. If an agreement (or even a tentative agreement) is not reached, both parties must be prepared to explain to the evaluator why an agreement could not be reached, giving their own view and the other person's view. The participants should then discuss the following questions.

1. What attempts were made by the negotiators to ensure that each party obtained some needed or desired goal from the interaction? If such attempts were not made, what were the consequences?

2. The negotiators should discuss how they arrived at their initial bargaining positions. Were their bids and offers extremely high or low? If so, what were the consequences?

3. Consider the concessions made during the bargaining sessions. Who made the first one? Was it difficult? If you proposed a concession, did you expect one in return?

4. How well did the participants use strong listening skills? What other communication skills were demonstrated?

cedures for decision making, or an agenda of topics to be discussed. The following is an example of a set of preestablished rules:

◆ Each side must allow the other to take a turn talking.

◆ All parties must agree on each major issue.

◆ We will determine relevant topics before beginning the negotiation.

If during a negotiation session, the other group's representatives have prevented your side from having a turn to speak, you can remind them that the negotiation is to follow a pattern of alternating turns and can request an opportunity to speak. In this way, you will be able to bring up your side's concerns within the agreed-on rules. You can then go on to discuss your side of the issues under negotiation.

Finally, positioning can be accomplished by appealing to the right to a balanced negotiation. If you sense that the discussion has concentrated on the others' goals and objectives, calling the imbalance to the attention of the entire group may bring the discussion back to a more balanced level of deliberation. Negotiators also have ethical obligations to bargain in good faith, respect the rights of other negotiators, and encourage fair and open discussion of issues.

Strategic Bargaining

The bulk of research literature on bargaining and negotiation points to two basic patterns of communication strategies: cooperative and competitive. Often termed integrative because they frame the bargaining session with the potential for mutual gain and multiple goals, *cooperative strategies* are open, honest, and upfront attempts at objective and productive problem solving.[12]

With cooperative strategies, bargainers are interested in fully understanding the respective positions of all parties. Information is exchanged in a frank and disclosive manner so that everyone has a clear picture of all the issues. Effective listening and responding skills aid in minimizing misunderstandings. The primary objective of cooperative strategies is to use communication in a way that maximizes the goals of the bargaining participants. The following list presents a variety of cooperative tactics:

Expressing agreement with, assistance to, or approval of opponent's position
Offering information
Offering concessions
Offering promises/commitments
Summarizing arguments
Indicating conciliation
Providing clarification
Seeking a problem-solving approach
Facilitating discussion through adherence to proper procedure

Cooperative tactics can be used to achieve a "win-win" outcome, in which both sides benefit from the bargaining session.

Competitive strategies, often referred to as distributive, seek to maximize one's own position at the expense of the adversary. The term "distributive" refers to the bargainer's assumption that a gain for her or his side equals a loss for the other side, i.e., limited benefits are redistributed through bargaining. Competitive bargaining strategies do not consider problem solving and cooperation as valid tactics. Rather, the goal of these strategies is to win at all costs. In fact, these strategies tend to result in a "lose-lose" outcome — neither party leaves the negotiation satisfied.

Competitive strategies use information in self-serving ways, giving only enough information to create the impression of disclosure while eliciting maximum information from the opponent. Competitive bargainers see each other as combatants whose side must either prevail or perish. These tactics may even involve deception or diversionary maneuvers to gain a competitive edge. Competitive tactics, such as the following, rarely involve concessions or compromise.

> Challenging, disagreeing with, or rejecting the opponent's position
> Changing the topic to refocus the discussion to one's advantage
> Asking for concessions
> Accusing an opponent of incompetence, negligence, and/or bad faith
> Requesting information
> Making threats or demands
> Issuing ultimatums
> Making personal attacks against an opponent
> Advancing arguments against an opponent

Using bargaining tactics effectively. As you look at the respective lists of bargaining tactics, you quickly notice that the cooperative tactics appear positive, while the competitive tactics seem negative. This is true in a general sense, but remember that bargaining situations are demanding, complex, and argumentative and usually require a combination of tactics for effective negotiation. Cooperative tactics promote rationality and reasonableness; only in extreme cases should competitive tactics be called on to ensure that your side is not taken advantage of.

How are bargaining tactics to be used? It depends on the situation, although there are some general guidelines to follow.[13]

1. Initial strategies should include firm but cooperative messages. Adversaries should get the idea that you are serious about the negotiation but are not so inflexible that you will refuse to yield on any issues.

2. Opening bids (such as offers or proposals) should be high because you value your proposals. By asking for more than you really expect to get, you allow concessions to be made later while at the same time communicating your desire to obtain your highest goals.

3. Cooperative tactics (such as promises and concessions) can be used to clear roadblocks in negotiations. When you sense that the discussion is going nowhere, it is often helpful to give in a little to get the bargaining back on track.

4. Competitive tactics may be introduced (although they are not encouraged) if you perceive that the opposition is taking advantage of the situation.

5. Maintain a high level of enthusiasm during bargaining. An upbeat and energetic attitude during bargaining sessions communicates commitment and perseverance to achieve goals.

6. Rely on a variety of information to maintain a strong position during sessions. Remembering what has been said and approved in previous sessions as well as keeping track of information during the current session ensures a high degree of bargaining competence.

7. Issuing threats, ultimatums, or demands against adversaries is rarely useful. Negative tactics such as these usually lead to resentment and conflict.

8. Maintain a professional demeanor throughout the bargaining sessions. Avoid resorting to underhanded or unethical tactics during bargaining. Be sure your conduct is beyond reproach.

9. Acknowledge the equality of bargaining parties.

10. Use effective critical thinking skills. Strong use of evidence, reasoning, and analysis can improve your position in the bargaining situation.

Bargaining and negotiation are common communication strategies in business and professional settings. Recognizing and utilizing the various dimensions and tactics of bargaining provide communicators with skills that promote goal achievement. Those who can bargain effectively are more likely to attain positions of enhanced responsibility and authority because they can be trusted to get the best deal for their group. In the example on page 364, identify the positive and negative actions taken by each group.

Conflict Management

When bargainers come to the table with serious purposes, strong negotiation skills, and mutual dependency, they can attain productive outcomes. But there are many examples of bargaining sessions that lead to serious conflict among parties. A variation on the case of Treecorp (see page 366) shows a less-successful scenario in the bargaining process.

In this example, the bargaining session escalated into a full-blown conflict that was unproductive and out of control. How did this happen? How does conflict differ from the other types of communication we discuss in this chapter?

What Is Conflict?

Conflict can take many shapes in the workplace. It can occur between people representing organizational units, much like the preceding example, it can occur between organizational levels such as labor and management, or it can even manifest in personal relationships between people who work together. Conflict is a dynamic process that is precipitated, developed, and governed by the joint communication strategies of the parties involved.

Joyce Hocker and William Wilmot defined conflict as "an expressed struggle between at least two interdependent parties who perceive incompatible goals, scarce rewards, and interference from the other party in achieving their goals."[14] Notice that parties must be interdependent. Conflict results when people view other people — people on whom they depend — as the reason they cannot attain their goals. Interdependency forces the conflict: if a person could accomplish her or his goals without the interfering others, conflict would not arise. The same dynamic properties that make group and organizational communication valuable are also the spark for potential conflict.

The relationship between negotiation and conflict is displayed dramatically when breakdowns in the former lead to outbreaks of the latter.

WINNING A BARGAIN AT TREECORP

Treecorp is a paper manufacturing company in the Northwest that is expanding its corporate headquarters by moving into a new multistory complex in a large downtown area. The executive vice-president (VP) for planning and facilities has told the public relations (PR) and training and development (TD) departments that they are to be housed on the same floor because their departments report to the same vice-president and have some functional overlap.

She tells the departments in a combined meeting that the furnishing/equipment budget for the combined department is limited. The two departments will be expected to compromise and work out an arrangement for spending the $2 million allocated for office space and computer support. She concludes by saying that the $2 million is theirs to spend as they wish as long as there is agreement between the departments. The departments are given one month to reach their decision and report back to the executive VP.

The department members gather in their respective areas to formulate strategy for the upcoming bargaining sessions. Members of TD are strongly in favor of fully enclosed standard offices for private counseling sessions with clients and trainees. Equipment and computer support are important to them but not as important as private offices.

The PR people believe they *must* have a sophisticated new computer system so that they can network with each other, enjoy graphics support, and print documents at high speed and quality levels. Although they really want standard offices, they are willing to live with "cubicle" offices if they can get the computer system. Both PR and TD plan to bargain for maximum benefits (i.e., computers *and* offices) for their respective sides.

There are some other issues that are likely to be discussed but that are not directly relevant to the office/computer problem. Some members of the PR department are jealous of the attention focused on TD at this time. The previous vice-president in charge of the departments was originally from PR and favored the PR department. The new vice-president is from TD and seems to favor it.

Some members of PR used to be in TD and vice versa. There is considerable gossip between departments, and some personal feuds have developed between employees. The departments compete with each other for new positions, salaries, travel budgets, and operating expenses.

The following scenario is an excerpt from

Prevalence of conflict.   The ability to recognize, engage in, and manage conflict is an important skill for anyone but especially so for those who aspire to succeed in organizations because conflict is widespread in organizational life. It has been estimated that managers spend 20 percent of their time managing conflict.[15] Conflict occurs between peers, between superiors and subordinates, and among people in different organizational units. It would not be overstating the case to say that conflict is one of the most troublesome communication activities in organizations.

Conflict in organizations.   Conflict in organizations may vary from disputes over territorial encroachment to personal disharmony. One of the largest sources of conflict stems from misunderstandings and communica-

the final bargaining session to decide on the new office setup. It shows an effective use of information management, concessions, and positioning that leads to a mutually acceptable "win-win" outcome. As you read through the discussion, note where negotiators have used these strategies effectively.

TD: "Now let's see. You want the computer system as well as fully enclosed offices, and you think we should make do with a less sophisticated system. Right?"

PR: "Well, in principle that may sound like an unfair exchange. But if you look at the last three annual budgets, you will notice that your operating expenses and travel budget have exceeded ours by 28 percent. Don't you think it is unfair for us to have to split the $2 million down the middle when we have been getting fewer funds all along?"

TD: "I thought we had already resolved that issue. In a paper company, training costs more money than public relations do. Besides, we *must* have private offices to do our job; it's a separate issue from computers that will make us more efficient."

PR: "Now wait a minute! You can't be serious that you want more than 50 percent of the construction budget."

TD: "Our department has increased productivity in every quarter over the last four years, whereas your department has only done so in three quarters. Your department has also expanded by three employees, while we have not been allowed to expand."

PR: "Hold on now. You know that it is difficult to gauge the actual productivity of a public relations department. Nevertheless, those new positions are critical to maintaining our public awareness campaign."

TD: "All I am saying is that from a bottom-line perspective we are one of the most productive departments in the company, yet we receive little reward in return."

PR: "What if we were to give up one position now and one new position in the next budget? In return you would allow us to get the new computer system."

TD: "We still want the regular offices, but we might be willing to share some of our operating expenses with you."

PR: "Would it be possible for you to give up some travel money so we can expand our public awareness campaign into the Southwest?"

TD: "Perhaps, if the positions that you are giving up are people with a training background."

PR: "I think we have a deal."

TD: "Fine."

tion failures. According to Mark Knapp, Linda Putnam, and Lillian Davis, conflict may also erupt from differences in goals or values, diverse economic or financial interests, role conflict, environmental changes, or even contradictory group loyalties.[16] Any time people perceive that a person, group, or even a difficult situation is preventing them from accomplishing a goal, conflict is possible.

Causes of Conflict: Competing Goals

The primary cause of conflict is competing goals. Even though people usually enter into a conflict situation with established goals, they may

NEGOTIATIONS BREAKDOWN . . .

TD: "Now let's see. You want the computer system as well as fully enclosed offices, and you think we should make do with a less sophisticated system. Right?"

PR: "Now hold on a minute! You people in TD always seem to be in a rush to get things settled. Let's clarify some issues first."

TD: "What issues? You get either offices or computers. PR is always trying to distract us from the real issues. Our deadline for making the decision on the budget is approaching quickly, and we don't seem to be making much progress."

PR: "Of course, wait until the last minute to make important decisions. I can't believe you people! What about travel budgets and operating expenses? Those are issues that ought to come into play here."

change as the conflict situation develops and understanding of the conflict partner increases.[17] As goals shift, so does the communication of the conflict. Essentially, there are two types of goals in most conflict situations: content and relational.

Content goals.   *Content goals* are those involving the apparent issues or obvious reasons for a dispute. These goals are characterized by issues of competing resources (computers versus offices), decision making (participation in decisions), and rights (maintaining fairness), among others. Examples of competing content goals include:

Jim: "If Joe gets the new service vehicle, I'll have to wait."
Joe: "Jim's new service route lets him get home earlier."

Mary: "Tanika is taking over this project without much input from me."
Tanika: "Mary hasn't shown much initiative with special projects in the last six months."

Roberto: "Cicely never consults me on the important decisions made around here."
Cicely: "Roberto always seems too busy to ask about the new emerging issues in the company."

In each of these examples, the conflicting parties believe they understand the real content goals in the situation, yet each has a perspective that is different and unknown to the other. They understand their own goals, but it is obvious that they have few ideas about the goals of their conflict partner. Failure to communicate differing goals usually leads to conflict, while understanding the respective goals of conflict partners is one of the keys to conflict management.

TD: "Why? Those are fixed costs. If the CEO thought you needed more funds, he would give them to you. You have to prove yourself worthy first."

PR: "Give me a break! When you were in PR, we were really unproductive but had a bigger budget. Now that you're in TD, you think you own the company."

TD: "How dare you attack me personally! Why, I ought to . . ."

PR: "Forget it. You're no negotiator. Send someone in next time who can at least pretend to be objective."

TD: "Right. And next time why don't you bring your baby-sitter with you?"

Relational goals. In every conflict situation there is a second level of goals being pursued by the conflicting parties that is frequently less obvious than content goals. *Relational goals* comprise how each party views the nature and importance of its relationship with the conflict partner. According to Hocker and Wilmot, "Relationship goals define each party's importance to the other, the emotional distance they wish to maintain, the influence each is willing to grant the other, the degree to which the parties are seen as a unit, or the rights each party is willing to grant to the others."[18]

Relational goals are not openly discussed as often as content goals because doing so draws attention to personal differences. They are, however, no less important than content goals. Indeed, conflict may not be managed until relational goals are managed. In the Treecorp example, the relationship between the two bargainers emerges as a clear cause of additional conflict, despite the focus on content goals (new computers and offices) expressed by the communicators. Many people are willing to acknowledge only content goals when involved in the conflict, but it is rarely the case that relational goals do not also exist.

Now look back to the three examples of conflicting content goals. If you were to manage these conflict situations, it would help you to know that Jim and Joe have been competing for a promotion for the past few months, that Tanika and Mary have different personalities and work styles that do not mesh, and that Roberto and Cicely formerly were intimate friends but had a traumatic breakup. Relationship goals are always present in conflict and have to be brought out for effective management to occur. Submerging or denying their existence can postpone a resolution.

Managing Conflicting Goals

In order to be manageable, goals must be clarified so that parties can accurately understand the respective positions of their counterparts. Both content and relational goals must be brought out into the open and honestly discussed to prevent confusion and misunderstanding. The only way that people in a conflict can share the perspective of their adversaries is by understanding their goals. The following steps can help you to clarify goals:

◆ State your goals in clear, unambiguous language — use language that the other party will understand.

◆ Elicit clearly stated goals from the other party.

◆ Openly discuss the difference between your content and relational goals.

◆ Make sure that you and your opponent have a shared understanding of each other's goals.

◆ Show that upholding your goals will not prevent productive management of the conflict.

The next step is to assemble collaborative goals. The key to managing any conflict is working toward an interdependent solution. If you consider only your own goals, without regard to the other party's interests, you will delay the productive resolution of differences. Adversaries probably will not want to work toward achieving your goals unless you show a willingness to do the same for them.

Collaboration begins by clarifying each party's goals. Next, conflicting parties strive to promote collaboration by actively rejecting selfish or incompatible goals. Here are some ways to encourage goal collaboration:

◆ Search for commonalities among the competing goals.

◆ Recognize that some of your opponents' goals may not have long-term implications — you will be able to live with them more easily.

◆ Remember that "every defeat is a victory and every victory is a defeat" because people who always get their way may be disliked for it.

◆ Give some concessions while asking for some.

◆ Develop new goals that incorporate and complement the competing goals of all parties.

Conflict Styles and Tactics

A useful tool for discussing conflict styles is the conflict grid. The conflict grid juxtaposes content and relational goals. Because every conflict includes some level of concern for content goals and some level of concern for relational goals, we can characterize a particular conflict style by the relative importance it places on each of these goals.

The grid contains a vertical dimension that represents concern for content goals and a horizontal dimension that depicts concern for relational goals. Figure 11-1 graphically represents the grid.

Using 1 to indicate low concern and 9 to indicate high concern, you can plot coordinates on the grid to represent particular conflict styles. Each strategy employs specific tactics, which you may recognize and be familiar with.[19]

Competing. A (9,1) style represents a high concern for personal goals and a low concern for the relationship. This is termed a *competing* style. Tactics related to a competing strategy demonstrate more concern for personal goal achievement than for relational stability. They include denial, hostility, confrontation, and verbal aggressiveness. Examples of competing messages are as follows:

◆ "That is simply not the case."

◆ "It is obvious that you do not pull your weight around here."

◆ "How can you argue for a position as groundless as this?"

◆ "If you ever bothered to look at the data, you might be able to see a trend in the direction I am describing."

Accommodating. At the opposite side of the grid is a (1,9) style, which represents low concern for personal goals but high concern for relational maintenance. The style is known as *accommodating* because the person using it places a high priority on the relationship with the conflict partner and in all likelihood will give in to his or her wishes to preserve it. Accommodating tactics show eagerness to satisfy the goals of the other party even if it means giving up personal goals in the process. They are unassertive, cooperative, yielding, and obliging. Examples of accommodating messages are:

◆ "If it's important to you, then let's do it."

◆ "I see your point of view."

◆ "Let's do it your way this time."

Avoiding. A (1,1) style is termed *avoiding*. It represents low concern for both personal goals and relationships. This style is represented by people who simply do not care if the job gets done or if they have satisfactory relationships with those they compete with. Tactics falling under the avoiding category include passive and uncooperative messages or postponements of conflict. Avoiding tactics can also represent complete apathy or denial that a conflict situation even exists. Examples of avoiding messages are:

◆ "I don't really care if we work this out."

◆ "Why don't we wait until there is a real problem before we argue over this?"

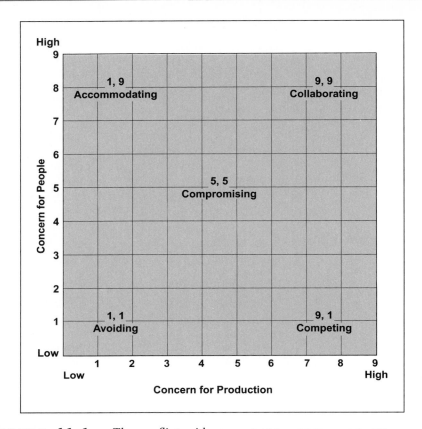

FIGURE 11-1   *The conflict grid*   *Source:* R. Blake and J. Mouton, "The Fifth Achievement," *The Journal of Applied Behavioral Science* 6 (1970), p. 418. © 1970 by NTL Institute. © 1974 by Xycom, Inc., Sterling Forest, Tuxedo, NY 10987. Reprint permission granted.

◆ "This is really a nonissue for me."

◆ "I don't know what you are talking about; I feel fine about our relationship."

Compromising.   Moderate concern for both dimensions (5,5) results in a *compromising* style. For example, Paul and Wendy both want the newly vacated office with a window, but Paul wants to upgrade the furniture in his office, whereas Wendy wants a new computer. In addition, even though they are not friends or colleagues, they do respect one another. Their conflict over the vacated office is likely to be one of compromise. Compromising usually indicates only moderate concern for the goals and the relationship. Tactics depicting this category include vagueness, conciliation, and concessions. Examples of compromising messages are:

- "I am not certain that we should be discussing this."
- "Perhaps I ought to reconsider my initial position."
- "Maybe we both ought to give a little."

Collaborating.   Finally, extreme concern for both goals and relationships (9,9) promotes a style known as *collaborating*. In the previous section, we explained how collaborative goals can help parties realize their goals in a conflict and at the same time maintain their relationship. As an ideal strategy that promotes both personal and relational goal attainment, collaborating tactics emphasize problem solving, qualified support, and integration. Examples of collaborating messages include:

- "Let's take a look at our respective positions and determine their strengths and weaknesses."
- "If the data are correct, I can back your plan."
- "If you combine our two requests, the end results will actually resemble our initial plans."

A Strategic Approach to Conflict

The conflict grid is useful for demonstrating the various communication possibilities for people engaging in conflict. But it is limited in the sense that identifying one style for a particular conflict situation oversimplifies and probably obscures what happens in real conflict. It is quite unlikely that there is one best style for any conflict situation.

Communicators must remain flexible when approaching conflict situations so that the selection of a strategy is suitable for the people concerned, the goals to be achieved, and the situational constraints involved. Multiple strategies may be necessary to productive conflict engagement. This is especially true when the conflict changes course and reveals new patterns of communication, goals, or motives for participants. Communicators must be able to respond to the changing conditions of the conflict situation. There are a number of factors that can influence the selection of a conflict strategy.

Throughout this book we stress a strategic approach to communication. Goal setting, situational knowledge, communication competence, and anxiety management are no less important to productive conflict management than to any other communication situation. Let us discuss each one of these factors in turn to determine how they can lead to successful conflict resolutions.

Goal Setting

One of the most important considerations in any conflict situation is that the goals of communicators can change over the course of the conflict. Acknowledging valid arguments from opposition members, recognizing the importance of their goals to them, and understanding how they communicate in a conflict can modify your initial content goals. You should be ready to respond with an alternative conflict style if the goals of the conflict appear to be changing.

A second consideration for selecting a conflict style is the likelihood of multiple goals.[20] You decide on a particular style (such as competing or avoiding) based on your main goal and your perception of your opponent's primary goal. But be flexible enough to shift to a more compromising position if it shows promise of promoting additional goals for both parties. It is extremely risky to boil down discussion to just one issue; then little room exists for negotiation.

Relational goals also influence the choice of a conflict style. Your decision on conflict style can be affected by the cohesion you feel with your conflict partner. If you feel connected to him or her in some personal way, you are less likely to use competing or avoiding strategies and more likely to employ more positive strategies.

Also consider the professional relationship you have with your conflict partner. You will probably select different styles depending on her or his status, influence, and organizational position. For example, research has shown that managers tend to be accommodating with superiors, collaborative with subordinates, and compromising with peers.[21]

Finally, when you decide on a conflict style, consider the long-term relational consequences of your actions. If your adversary is someone with whom you hope to carry on a long-term relationship, employing avoiding or competitive tactics throughout the conflict may destroy your relationship. The destruction of a long-term relationship may not be worth the short-term gains you make with such tactics.

Situational Factors

Similar to situational knowledge in other communication contexts, situational factors refer to elements in the conflict that affect the nature of conflict and the styles you select to deal with it. For example, the physical environment (where the conflict takes place, such as in a private office, in the cafeteria, or in a meeting) will affect how you communicate during a conflict. Aggressive tactics are particularly risky when the conflict occurs in public view.

Time constraints can also affect how you use conflict tactics. For example, if you are expected to settle your differences with someone in a limited time frame, you may feel unable to develop a successful, positive style and may resort to tactics such as avoiding or competing. If you have a lot of time in which to work out the conflict, more elaborate styles such as collaborating and compromising may be possible.

Communication Competence

In conflict situations, you are smart to be aware of your strengths and weaknesses — your communication competence. Competencies include argumentation skills, control of verbal aggressiveness, listening skills, and verbal and nonverbal skills.

If you think back to our discussion of critical thinking skills in Chapter 10, you can easily understand how important the ability to analyze, evaluate, and communicate these ideas is to the management of conflict. The better you understand the situation, the better chance you have of realizing your goals.

Controlling verbal aggressiveness is important in conflict situations as well. Allowing (or encouraging) the discussion to drop to the level of personality attacks accomplishes nothing in the way of conflict management — it only escalates the conflict.

Listening skills are essential to the choice of a conflict style — knowing what your opponents are saying and why they are saying it can tell you a lot about what style will work best in resolving conflict with them. Poor listening is one of the most frequent causes of conflict as well as one of the largest obstacles to conflict resolution.

In addition to these skills, a sincere effort to remain flexible aids in resolving disputes. Flexibility during a conflict allows you to adapt to the changing dynamics of conflict patterns. For example, you may decide that an accommodating strategy is effective in the initial stages of a conflict, but as the conflict progresses the opponent's stubbornness or hostile reaction to you may make competitive tactics more useful. By remaining flexible, you will be able to make a change in your conflict style to counter the shift. In general, successful conflict managers are highly sensitive to shifts in conflict strategies by their opponents.

Anxiety Management

Conflict can be a major cause of anxiety in the workplace. Particular situations, such as an argument with a superior, hostility in a group meeting, or even a sensitive bargaining session, may be dreaded or avoided if you are uneasy with the possibility of conflicts arising. But conflict can have productive outcomes, and there are occasions in which it is better to engage in conflict than to avoid it. The following example illustrates a common form of conflict in the workplace.

> Katrina and George have never liked one another, primarily because of contrasting personalities and competition for company resources. Their usual method of handling disagreement or competitions has been to work behind the scenes to achieve their goals (gossip, grapevine, coalitions, and so forth). One day their manager invited the two of them to a private meeting to discuss the problems that were arising from their conflict — tension, lowered morale and productivity, and less attention to their work, to name just a few. After controlling their anxiety at being confronted with the fact of their difficulties, both opened up and related why they did not appreciate the way the other operated. Each was surprised at how honest the other was and that the conflict had grown to such proportions, simply because they had never faced it.

To lessen your anxiety in a conflict, focus on its goals and outcomes. Consider the relief you will feel after working through a conflict situation rather than avoiding the conflict and allowing distrust, resentment, or other negative feelings to simmer. You can also manage conflict-related anxiety by viewing your conflict partner in positive, human terms rather than as an enemy who means to undermine you or your career.

Seeking the support of others who share your goals and position in a conflict can be reassuring. If you dread conflict because you feel isolated by it, discovering that others support your side can lessen anxiety considerably.

Finally, taking a break to collect your thoughts and clear your head is an effective way to manage anxiety in conflict situations. Often the tension of a conflict continues to build as the conflict progresses, and you may find that you are becoming too anxious to use your communication skills effectively. If it is possible to call a "time out" to take a deep breath and relax, doing so can help you to calm your nerves and regain your composure. All these tactics for managing anxiety can increase your chances of resolving the conflict in a successful and positive manner.

Summary

The nature of any conflict situation derives from how the adversaries deal with argumentativeness and verbal aggression. Argumentativeness is a willingness to stand up for and promote ideas despite opposition. Verbal aggressiveness is the tendency to attack the personal characteristics or self-concept of an opponent instead of the issues under discussion. Verbal aggressiveness is a negative trait that often results from poor critical thinking skills and that prevents conflict resolution.

Most competitive communication situations can be addressed through bargaining and negotiation, which can occur formally or informally. Bargaining includes three dimensions: information management (being able to acquire, retrieve, and use information in a bargaining session), concessions (knowing when, where, and how much to give to opponents), and positioning (refocusing attention on issues of your concern or advantage). Strategic bargaining consists of cooperative (problem solving) and competitive (maximizing one's own position at the expense of the other) tactics. The selection of the most appropriate bargaining strategy depends on the situation, although general guidelines can be applied.

Conflict, the struggle between interdependent parties who perceive incompatible goals, may exist at all levels, situations, and relationships in an organization. The primary cause of conflict is competing goals, which can be managed through clarification of opposing or conflicting goals so that collaborative goals can be worked out. At the same time, content as well as relational goals have to be specified so that a comprehensive resolution can be achieved.

Conflict styles can be demonstrated through the use of a conflict grid. The grid identifies five different styles often used in conflicts: collaborating, competing, avoiding, compromising, and accommodating. Each style gives rise to particular tactics.

Despite its usefulness, the conflict grid does not take into account the complexity and uniqueness of any particular conflict. To do so requires application of the four parts of strategic communication — goal setting, situational knowledge, communication competence, and anxiety management — as a way of successfully resolving conflict.

Discussion

1. What is the difference between argumentativeness and verbal aggressiveness? What are the implications of each for organizational communication?

2. How do information management, making concessions, and positioning affect the progress of a negotiation and the agenda of issues to be discussed?

3. Describe the general guidelines for bargaining. When, if ever, might competitive tactics be used?

4. Discuss possible causes of and participants in conflict at work. Have you experienced work-related conflict? What were the causes and results?

5. What is the difference between content goals and relational goals? How can each contribute to conflict?

6. Discuss the conflict styles represented in Figure 11-1. What are some benefits and drawbacks of each style? (Remember to consider both short-term and long-term possibilities.)

7. How are communication skills essential to managing conflict strategically? Be sure to discuss the role of setting goals and managing anxiety in successful conflict resolutions.

Activities

1. As a manager, you will be confronted with verbal aggressiveness by employees, peers, and superiors. What strategies can you employ to maintain high standards of communication effectiveness and professionalism in such circumstances?

2. Select two classmates as partners. The three of you round-robin the roles of manager, employee, and observer. The observer assesses how well each participant presents and then defends his or her position on these topics:
   a. Pay raise
   b. Time off to attend to personal activities without having to make up the time
   c. Travel on personal, instead of company, time

3. What strategies do you believe are most effective in "positioning," in which you move the focus of the negotiation to issues important to you? Your instructor will list these on the board until all strategies in the class have been recorded. Then rank-order these as a class.

4. In an essay, discuss the consequences of competitive negotiating to a long-term relationship with the other party.

Notes

1. D. A. Infante, *Arguing Constructively* (Prospect Heights, Ill.: Waveland Press, 1988), p. 7.
2. D. A. Infante and W. I. Gorden, "Superiors' Argumentativeness and Verbal Aggressiveness as Predictors of Subordinates' Satisfaction," *Human Communication Research* 12 (1985): 117–125.
3. D. A. Infante and C. J. Wigley, "Verbal Aggressiveness: An Interpersonal Model and Measure," *Communication Monographs* 53 (1986): 61.
4. Infante, *Arguing Constructively*.
5. These scales were developed by D. A. Infante and A. S. Rancer, "A Conceptualization and Measure of Argumentativeness," *Journal of Personality Assessment* 46 (1982): 72–80. This version was reported in D. De Wine, A. M. Nicotera, and D. Parry, "Argumentativeness and Aggressiveness: The Flip Side of Gentle Persuasion," *Management Communication Quarterly* 4 (1991): 386–411.

6. Infante, *Arguing Constructively*, p. 21.

7. Ibid.

8. The distinction between bargaining and negotiation is not enough to quibble with. Others have made similar arguments. See L. L. Putnam and M. S. Poole, "Conflict and Negotiation," in F. Jablin, L. Putnam, K. Roberts, and L. Porter (eds.), *Handbook of Organizational Communication* (Beverly Hills, Calif.: Sage, 1987), pp. 549–599; D. F. Womack, "Assessing the Thomas-Kilmann Conflict MODE Survey," *Management Communication Quarterly* 1 (1988): 321–349.

9. L. L. Putnam and T. S. Jones, "Reciprocity in Negotiations: An Analysis of Bargaining Interaction," *Communication Monographs* 49 (1982): 171–191.

10. Putnam and Poole, "Conflict and Negotiation."

11. W. A. Donahue, M. E. Deiz, and M. Hamilton, "Coding Naturalistic Interaction," *Human Communication Research* 10 (1984): 403–426.

12. R. E. Walton and R. E. McKersie, *A Behavior Theory of Labor Negotiations: An Analysis of a Social Interaction System* (New York: McGraw-Hill, 1965); Putnam and Jones, "Reciprocity in Negotiations"; Putnam and Poole, "Conflict and Negotiation."

13. W. A. Donahue, "An Empirical Framework for Examining Negotiation Processes and Outcomes," *Communication Monographs* 45 (1978): 247–257; L. L. Putnam and T. S. Jones, "The Role of Communication in Bargaining," *Human Communication Research* 8 (1982): 262–280.

14. J. L. Hocker and W. W. Wilmot, *Interpersonal Conflict*, 3rd ed. (Dubuque, Iowa: William C. Brown, 1991), p. 12.

15. K. W. Thomas and W. H. Schmidt, "A Survey of Managerial Interests with Respect to Conflict," *Academy of Management Journal* 19 (1976): 315–318.

16. M. L. Knapp, L. L. Putnam, and L. J. Davis, "Measuring Interpersonal Conflict in Organizations: Where Do We Go from Here?" *Management Communication Quarterly* 1 (1988): 414–429.

17. Hocker and Wilmot, *Interpersonal Conflict*.

18. Ibid., p. 48.

19. R. R. Blake and J. S. Mouton, *The Managerial Grid* (Houston: Gulf Publishing, 1964); K. W. Thomas and R. H. Kilmann, *Thomas-Kilmann Conflict MODE Instrument* (Tuxedo, N.Y.: Xicom, 1974); Womack, "Assessing the Thomas-Kilmann."

20. Knapp, Putnam, and Davis, "Measuring Interpersonal Conflict."

21. M. A. Rahim, "A Measure of Styles of Handling Interpersonal Conflict," *Academy of Management Journal* 26 (1983): 368–376; M. A. Rahim, *Managing Conflict in Organizations* (New York: Praeger, 1986).

*P*resentation Strategies

Presentations play an important role in sharing information and guiding actions within organizations. **Part 5** introduces the skills necessary to speak effectively and without apprehension during a presentation. Regardless of your position in a company, you can benefit from knowing and practicing these skills.

❏ Chapter 12 uses the components of strategic communication to explain the principles of successful presentations.

❏ Chapter 13 focuses on the specific demands (on speakers and listeners) of a variety of informative presentation strategies

❏ Chapter 14 explores the process of persuasion and the goals that persuasive presentations can facilitate within an organization

❏ Chapter 15 completes the study of presentational speaking by introducing special presentation formats, such as impromptu speaking, televised speaking, and symposiums.

Chapter 12

*D*eveloping and Delivering Effective Presentations

OBJECTIVES

After completing this chapter, you will be able to:

1. Identify goals, including topic and purpose, for your presentation

2. Assess the audience's needs and potential responses to your message by gathering situational knowledge

3. Identify the main points to be included in your presentation and research them thoroughly

4. Use supporting materials, an introduction, and a conclusion to enhance the credibility of your message

5. Put the pieces of the presentation together in the form of an outline

6. Demonstrate communication competence by choosing an appropriate and effective delivery style

7. Manage speaking anxiety by understanding its causes and anticipating and rehearsing the delivery of your message

Opportunities to speak publicly are multiplying rapidly in this age of information. Although many people hold the assumption that new information technology such as electronic mail, video-conferencing, cellular phones, and fax machines have replaced some of the functions of business presentations, in truth, increasing dependence on technology means that many business decisions are being made more quickly and that more diverse groups of people are participating in decision making than ever before. A presentation is the most effective way to reach these audiences.

Successful presentations demonstrate that the speaker is confident and sincerely believes in the message being delivered. In a successful presentation, the speaker and audience establish a mutual understanding of or commitment to goals that is not possible with written or electronic channels. Even interpersonal and small group communication are less powerful because fewer people are touched by the message.

In general, presentational speaking does share some similarities with other forms of oral communication. All depend on the components of strategic communication — goal setting, situational knowledge, communication competence, and anxiety management — which ensure adequate preparation and effective performance in presentational speaking, as they do in the other communication contexts we have discussed. In addition, speaking to a group shares a problem common to all forms of oral communication. Unlike visual or written communication, which can be reread or reviewed, any form of spoken communication must be clear and convincing the *first* time it is given.

Nevertheless, making a presentation is quite different from speaking with others in dyadic or small group contexts. Ensuring audience comprehension is more difficult because feedback is less direct and less spontaneous. During a presentation, the speaker must read the audience's nonverbal behavior to infer members' moods and reactions to the message.

In the business world, public speaking takes the form of making presentations either to fellow employees, managers, and supervisors or to an audience of people outside the speaker's organization. The following scenarios illustrate two examples of such presentations.

Nancy is a communication major working as an intern in the human resources division of a local computer software firm. The firm is experiencing strained management-employee relationships and a high turnover rate in its staff. Mark, the vice president of human resources, believes that the company will be severely hurt by the situation. He assigns Nancy the job of researching the employees to determine how their needs can be better met. Two weeks into her research, Mark asks her to make a preliminary report of her findings to a group composed of Mark, the chief executive officer, the chief financial officer, and the three members of the company's communication department. Nancy realizes that she may not get another chance to speak directly to these people, and she wants to give them a clear and comprehensive understanding of her findings, their importance, and what each of her listeners can do about the situation. She knows this will be the most significant presentation she has yet made.

Akbar is an entrepreneurial student who has been involved in a university-sponsored program to collect leftover or unused food supplies from hotels and distribute them to shelters. He would like to start up a similar program in his hometown. To do this, he must persuade a group of hotel managers and administrators that this is an opportunity to greatly benefit the community and reduce operating costs at the same time. He uses contacts at a variety of hotels and has received replies from twelve interested managers. His final challenge is preparing the presentation, which includes targeting the hidden costs of wasted supplies, anticipating and overcoming legal or regulatory obstacles, and demonstrating how to get a program started with minimum time and resources. He needs the managers to agree with him and implement the program he believes in. He understands how crucial this presentation will be.

These scenarios show the potential range of presentations and audiences you will encounter in your career. For many people, speaking before a group is the most fearsome activity imaginable. Yet some basic guidelines can help you understand the fundamentals of presentational speaking and make connections to skills discussed in earlier chapters, thus lessening your anxiety.

The focus of this chapter is on preparing for a presentation using the model of strategic communication. We begin by explaining how to select and narrow a topic. Then we discuss the significance of situational knowledge and the importance of performing an audience analysis to understand the relationship between the topic and the audience. Building on that preparation, we discuss communication competence as demonstrated in the creation, structure, and delivery of a message. Finally, we devote attention to the phenomenon of public speaking apprehension and methods of handling it.

Our focus in this chapter is on basic principles; in Chapters 13 and 14, we discuss special considerations for preparation and delivery of informative and persuasive presentations. In Chapter 15, we apply this knowledge to a variety of special presentational formats.

Goal Setting: Identifying the Topic and Purpose

The starting point for the development of a message is the selection of a topic. Making this decision in a work setting is usually quite easy; topics emerge naturally from the interplay of your job, your audience, and the organization's needs. For example, as a business manager you may be asked to talk to new employees about the benefits package provided by your organization.

Nevertheless, you are also likely to encounter occasions on which the topic is relatively unclear, you must choose among several possible topics, or you have been assigned an inappropriate topic and need to suggest an alternative. In these situations, you can use several techniques to identify a topic. Although there are no fail-safe formulas, the following methods can assist you with the task:

1. Engage in personal brainstorming. Sit down and think about special knowledge you already possess, things you have done, experiences you have had, or issues that are important to you. Then map out this information so you can visualize relationships among ideas. You can list headings for experiences, interests, and hobbies and then identify potential subtopics under them. Mapping also helps you organize information, evidence, and data that relate to your topic (see Figure 12-1).

2. Brainstorm with others. When you use this option, you not only gain additional ideas that result from group synergy; you also get a preview of how relevant a topic is to others. Thus, it can be helpful to use classmates, co-workers, friends, or colleagues to assist you in generating potential topics.

3. Use the reference room of your library. If necessary, ask the reference librarian for help in using general reference works. The following works may be particularly useful in preparing business presentations:

    The Reader's Guide to Periodical Literature
    Business Periodicals Index
    Business Information Sources
    Encyclopedia of Business Information Sources
    The Executive's Sourcebook to Marketing, Company, and Demographic Data
    Databasics: Guide to On-line Business Information
    The Business Week Almanac

After you have generated several potential topics, you select the actual topic for your presentation. As you do so, consider three criteria:

1. Are you knowledgeable and/or interested in this topic? Because you will speak most authoritatively on topics you know best, choose a familiar topic whenever possible. When circumstances prevent such a choice, look for topics that you have always wanted to know more about. An active interest in the subject will make your research more exciting.

2. Is the topic relevant to your audience? Consider what you know about the audience. Will this group of people find your topic informative, useful, or interesting? While most, if not all, topics can be made

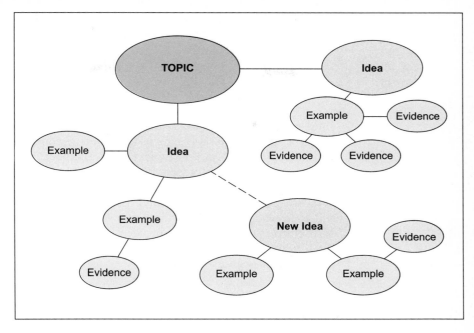

FIGURE 12-1   *Mapping is a technique for generating and organizing ideas. It can also be used to visualize links between ideas and supporting materials.*

interesting, starting with a topic that your listeners need and want to hear about will make your task much easier.

3. Is the topic a good one for this assignment? Presentations are given for many reasons, and an effective topic may be inappropriate if it does not support or correspond to the reason for the presentation. For example, a company seminar on health care benefits would appropriately include presentations on employees' health insurance choices, how the company's wellness and nutrition program has improved work quality, or changes in workers' compensation policy. All these topics relate directly to health care as it is mediated by the company.

    Less appropriate would be a presentation on how an employee trained for and participated in a marathon, a call for a national health insurance program, or an explanation of a new treatment for diabetes. Although these topics are health related, they do not have a direct connection to the company's health care policies.

When you are in doubt about either the assignment or the relevance of a particular topic, ask the person who is organizing the presentation (or your instructor for an in-class presentation). Be sure to have your questions answered far enough in advance so that you can change your topic if necessary.

General Purpose

Once you have selected a topic, the process of refining it begins. The first *filter,* or question to ask yourself, is that of general purpose — why will you give a speech on this topic to this audience? This question identifies the basic goal of your presentation.

The goal is usually motivated by one of four general purposes: to inform, persuade, motivate, or celebrate. That is, you may want to enlighten your audience on a topic by providing new information or ideas (inform), change or reaffirm the audience's attitudes (persuade), urge audience action for your cause (motivate), or help your audience acknowledge an individual achievement or event (celebrate).

To inform.   Informative presentations provide ideas, alternatives, data, or even opinions, but most importantly they provide credible, reliable information to back up the major points. When giving an informative presentation, you function as your audience's teacher. It is not always easy, however, to know the audience's level of background knowledge on the topic, nor is it easy to narrow the topic so that you are working with a manageable and teachable amount of information.

Expanded sources of information, such as on-line databases and computer networks, make the selection of material for informative presentations more important and challenging than ever before. We discuss the issue of developing and structuring an informative presentation in greater detail in Chapter 13.

An informative presentation must be accurate, reliable, and credible. For example, if you are asked to give a report in your communication class on the problems with financial aid disbursement at your school, check and double-check your statistical information, the conclusions you draw, and any other elements of the presentation that may contain inaccuracies. Cite your sources to increase both your credibility and the significance of the data. Remember that to teach your audience effectively, you are wise to be an expert, not simply a layperson with a few statistics to present.

To persuade.   Persuasive presentations can work at three levels: they can change or reaffirm existing attitudes about important topics, strive to gain audience commitment, and motivate action. For example, if you are somewhat concerned about the environment, you may decide to attend a presentation on your company's recycling program. As you listen to a manager speak about recycling and conservation, you suddenly realize the importance of these issues. You leave the session determined to recycle cans and avoid styrofoam coffee cups. If you actually follow through with these intentions, the manager's presentation was effective at all three levels.

In persuasive presentations, you are asking the audience to make a commitment to your viewpoint, and to act in ways that you advocate. As with informative speaking, persuasive presentations require conscientious research to uncover the best available data on the topic. In addition, persuaders must present a course of action that can be accepted by a group of people who might choose otherwise. We discuss persuasive formats and techniques in detail in Chapter 14.

To motivate. Presentations designed to motivate audience members are a special type of persuasive speech. Motivational speeches employ persuasion but rely more extensively on stimulating the emotions and feelings of listeners as a method of inducing action. Members of the clergy may use biblical images and the subconscious fears and hopes of their audiences to encourage spiritual action. Drill sergeants may use highly charged, emotional language to push "raw" recruits to new levels of physical exertion. Although drill sergeants and clerics employ different motivational strategies, the emotional intensity they can inspire is often very similar.

To celebrate. Ceremonial presentations often share many of the elements found in informative, persuasive, and motivational speaking, as we discuss in Chapter 15. Included among this group are the following presentations:

◆ Introduction — introducing other speakers

◆ Acceptance — welcoming an honor or reward

◆ Tribute — making toasts

◆ Good will — remembering and honoring the past

◆ Inspiration — presenting a memorial or eulogy

◆ Celebration — rejoicing in achievements

Ceremonial presentations demonstrate your commitment to organizational ideals or your organization's commitment to its valued ideals. For example, many organizations hold "roasts," or comic tributes, to retiring employees who have been vital elements of the organization throughout the years. Ceremonial presentations require you to consider the common ties that bind participants together as a group.

Whereas in this course you may be given a general purpose and asked to select a topic, in business you are frequently assigned a topic and must then choose the general purpose (approach) that will be most successful. As a result, general purpose normally takes a purer form within the classroom — an assignment for an informative presentation will largely avoid persuasive, motivational, or celebratory goals — whereas in the workplace it is not at all unusual for a manager to use one message to inform, persuade, motivate, and celebrate. In this book we focus on each of these goals separately, an approach that introduces beginning speakers to the unique characteristics and demands of each purpose and better prepares them to combine or adapt goals for presentations later in their speaking careers.

Specific Purpose

The second filter for refining your topic is the specific purpose. The specific purpose of a presentation is derived from the general purpose and identifies what you as the presenter want the audience to think, believe, feel, or do as a result of listening to your presentation. As we have discussed throughout this book, specific goals are far more effective in directing communication to achieve shared meaning and desired results. Public speaking requires deliberate and specific goals, just as interpersonal, group, and organizational communication does.

The specific purpose should contain a single idea. Some basic considerations for the specific purpose are, Is the idea manageable in the time allowed for the presentation? Is the idea challenging to the audience? Is the idea important to the organizational values and/or career goals of the audience? The specific purpose is then translated into a *thesis statement* — a single declarative sentence that summarizes the main ideas to be presented to the audience.

The thesis statement may emerge as the speaker researches and develops the message. For example, a specific purpose may be: "I want my audience to know about the role of personal computers in an advertising agency." After the speaker researches the topic, a more specific (and useful) thesis statement may be: "Within an advertising agency, major uses for personal computers include word processing, business management, and graphic design." A well-considered thesis statement is crucial in the delivering of an effective message.

Successful communication results from the achievement of a series of interrelated goals, each flowing from the one before it. This element of continuity means that goals must be set at every stage of the presentation process, from selecting a topic and doing research to practicing your delivery. Goals prompt you to monitor your work continually, thereby ensuring that you attend carefully to each phase of your presentation's development.

Situational Knowledge: Analyzing the Audience

In presentation speaking, the process of finding out about those to whom you will be speaking is termed *audience analysis,* and it corresponds to the second component of strategic communication: gathering situational knowledge. When preparing for a presentation, you can research individual members of the audience, organizational factors that affect the audience, and even location, time, or other physical influences. Audience analysis helps you to understand the speaking situation as it unfolds as well as how best to prepare for the audience's needs and likely response to your message. In other words, effective speakers continue to gather information and monitor the situation throughout the presentation.[1]

Demographic information — the audience's size, age, social class, educational level, gender, cultural background, and occupational status — is fundamental to any audience analysis. Demography (the collection and study of such information) is a necessary first step toward establishing more specific and complex analyses of a target audience. The target audience — the key decision makers who are members of the general audience — are an important focus for your analysis. You are more likely to succeed by tailoring your ideas, information, and appeals to these audience members.[2]

Audience attitudes toward many social and economic issues can be predicted through careful demographic analysis. For example, if you learn that your audience will be composed of employees in the manufacturing division of your company — mostly blue-collar males aged forty to sixty, with union membership — you can conclude that a presentation on why the the company should deunionize to encourage new hiring policies will have to be approached with careful preparation and an understanding of possible negative audience response.

This is not to say that audience analysis encourages stereotyping or can be ignored if you think you already know, for example, what a typical clerical worker is like. It is vital to approach audience analysis with an open mind because you are likely to discover unexpected characteristics of audience members that may provide the key to connecting with them. By analyzing and understanding the implications of the audience analysis, you will have a good sense of how to aim your presentation and what language and imagery to employ.

Remember also that it is important to know whether you are speaking to accountants, engineers, marketers, janitors, or a combination of different employee groups. They may all work for your company, but each group has a different perspective on the organization and is likely to be different from your own. Be sure to modify your presentation to accommodate each group because the most successful presentations are those that address every member of the audience and make each person feel involved and important.

Three categories of audience analysis can be considered when doing a profile. Each of the three categories provides a different starting point for thinking about your audience's needs.

◆ Audience type — why have these people decided to attend your presentation?

♦ Audience characteristics — what are the religion, education, race, age, and gender of audience members?

♦ Environmental characteristics — how will the setting and surroundings affect the speaking situation?

Interact!

One of the most important aspects of making a presentation is knowing the audience. This simulation gives you the chance to conduct an analysis on the members of your class, to whom you will be making presentations during the course of the semester. As a result of your analysis, you will be more aware of the background, interests, and needs of your audience and far more likely to deliver a successful presentation.

First, decide what kind of and how much information you need about your audience. Review the categories of audience analysis information, and select those you believe are relevant to your situation.

Next, decide the method by which you will collect the information you want. Some possibilities are interviews (either one to one or in groups), observation techniques, or a printed questionnaire. Consider your options carefully in terms of how much time, effort, money, and other resources each option requires to obtain quality information. The following is a sample questionnaire you can use in conducting audience analysis:

Audience Profile Questionnaire

1. Name _____ 2. Age _____ 3. Sex _____ 4. Race _____
5. Religious affiliation _____ 6. Place of birth or longest residence _____
7. Marital status _____ 8. Years of school completed _____
9. College major _____ 10. Current job _____
11. Hours/week _____ 12. Career goals (list three) _____
13. Values. List three responses to the following: In a perfect world, I would be _____.
14. Values. List three responses to the following: I am happiest when I am

_____.
15. Three most important group memberships _____.
16. Hobbies _____ 17. I travel _____ days/year.
18. Hearing or reading about _____
makes me angry, skeptical, sad, afraid.
19. Hearing or reading about _____
makes me happy, confident, secure, enthusiastic.
20. Political affiliation _____
21. In one sentence, describe the importance of your work (or studies) in your life. _____

_____

Before you begin collecting data, consider some of the barriers to gathering information that you may encounter, such as contacting audience members, distributing and collecting surveys, or choosing a representative sample to profile. Once you have anticipated these problems, what can you do to overcome them if they occur?

Be sure to allow enough time not only to collect but also to analyze this information and its significance for your presentations. What information do you have — surveys, interview notes, questionnaires, a journal of observations? How can you organize the information? Consider calculating percentages (twenty-two of thirty class members are communication majors), creating categories (values held by this audience include freedom and having fun), cross-tabulating (categorizing by two or more specific characteristics such as women who are older than thirty and are working fifteen or more hours per week), and identifying trends and patterns (people in this class are concerned with environmental issues and tend to participate in many outdoor activities).

Finally, use this information when preparing class presentations. Think of ways to include specific evidence from the analysis in your speech — for example, open a presentation with an anecdote about a topic that you have found of interest to a majority of your classmates.

After you have completed your analysis and before you present any speeches to the class, share your audience analysis experience with other members of the class. You may find that many of them had the same frustrations and experiences you had! The following questions can help guide your discussion:

1. Did you collect enough information? Too much? In hindsight, what adjustments would you make to the method you chose so as to achieve an appropriate quantity of information?

2. What quality of information did you collect? Was any of the information not useful? What can be done in the future to improve the quality of information you gather?

3. What was the most difficult part of the analytic process? Was any part particularly time consuming or error prone?

4. In what specific ways can your speech be stronger as a result of your analysis? Has your attitude changed or your confidence increased as a result of knowledge of your audience?

Presentations made to familiar co-workers may require less investigative work than do presentations made to people you do not know; nevertheless, do not underestimate the importance of any category of demographic information just because it is easy to collect. For example, you will make presentations in this class, and you can simply look around the room to determine the gender ratio, racial make-up, approximate age bracket, and educational level of your audience members. Obtaining other demographic information may be more difficult, but not impossible. One excellent method is to ask questions of people who are knowledgeable about the audience — friends, supervisors, co-workers, or even people who have presented to the group before. Less obvious categories, such as sociopolitical status, religious affiliations, and economic status, can often be discovered through research, which can be done in the library with the assistance of a librarian. The environmental characteristics of the speaking situation, such as time limit, size of the audience, and location, can be ascertained in a visit to the site ahead of time and in talks with the people who asked you to speak.

In some instances you may have opportunities to ask questions of potential audience members (such as in this class). The questionnaire provided in the *Interact!* box is a starting point for such question sessions. You can begin now to practice for presentations in your business career.

Identifying and Researching Main Ideas

Once you have narrowed a topic to a specific purpose and thesis statement and identified the outstanding characteristics of your audience, the next step is to identify and research your main points. Ask yourself, "What does the audience need to know and accept to accomplish the specific purpose I have selected for the presentation?" If, for example, you are an account executive for an advertising agency and your goal is to persuade a local restaurant owner to select your agency to handle the restaurant's advertising campaign, what are the main ideas you need to stress to show her or him the benefits of selecting your agency?

Generating Potential Main Ideas

A good method of locating main ideas is to think systematically about the topic. Doing so reminds you of what you already know about the topic and suggests areas that require additional research.

Although there are many ways ways to generate main ideas, we recommend a *topical* system based on the methods of such famous speakers as Aristotle, Cicero, and Francis Bacon.[3] The topical system uses a small set of headings or topics to identify standard ways of thinking and talking about any subject. The basic premise of the approach is that the infinite number of possible topics contain a finite number of themes — a result of our shared ways of thinking about human affairs. The following sixteen topics can be used to describe any subject on which a presenter might choose to speak.

A. Attributes
  1. Existence or nonexistence of things
  2. Degree or quantity of things, forces, and so on

3. Spatial attributes, including location, distribution, and position of things, especially in relation to other things
4. Time — when an event took place, how long it lasted, and so forth
5. Motion or activity — type, degree
6. Form, or the physical or abstract shape of a thing
7. Substance, or the physical or abstract content of a thing
8. Capacity to change — whether an event or situation is predictable or unpredictable
9. Potency — power or energy, including the ability to further or hinder something else
10. Desirability — whether the thing results in rewards or punishments
11. Feasibility — how well the thing works, how practical it is

B. Basic relationships

1. Causality — the relation of causes to effects, effects to causes, and so forth
2. Correlation — correspondence between, coexistence of, coordination of things or forces
3. Genus-species relationships — common charactistics or distinguishing characteristics of a thing or group of things
4. Similarity or dissimilarity in appearance, content, form, shape, and so forth
5. Possibility or impossibility of an event happening

Let us return to our hypothetical account executive preparing to pitch the restaurant owner and managers for an account. How can she or he stress any of the sixteen themes? To answer this question, consider that after some thought the account executive comes up with the following points:

1. The ad agency has been serving the community for more than thirty years (existence).
2. The agency handles more than twenty restaurant accounts and gains more every year (degree of experience/expertise).
3. The agency is located conveniently in the downtown business district (spatial attribute).
4. The agency can put together a trial campaign in two weeks (time).
5. Restaurants that have used the ad agency have reported substantial increases in customers (activity).
6. The agency can provide several choices for the look of the campaign and specializes in the latest design and graphics (form).

7. The agency will work with the restaurant owner to articulate a precise message for the campaign (substance).

8. The agency will modify the campaign if it is not bringing the desired results (capacity to change).

9. The agency projects a 32 percent increase in the restaurant's business based on campaigns done for similar restaurants in the past (potency).

10. The agency can promote increased business that will allow the restaurant owner to open another restaurant and enjoy greater profits (desirability).

11. The agency is a practical choice because of its expertise in the area of restaurant advertising and the competitive rates being offered (feasibility).

Of course, it would be an overwhelming task to stress all these themes in the course of one presentation. Nevertheless, the account executive now has a wealth of main ideas and can select the two or three most suited to the needs of this restaurant owner.

Doing Research

The topical system, although useful for generating potential main points, must be supplemented by additional research for information to support your ideas, especially if the topic is an area in which you are not an expert. A good starting point for such research is consultation with experts and specialists on your topic through the process of informational interviewing described in Chapter 8. Questions to be asked in such an interview include "What books and articles do you recommend I read?" "What resources have proven especially useful to you?" and "Do you know other people who might provide additional help?"

Following up leads provided by experts and filling in missing details often means visiting a library. The card catalogue, reference room, and periodicals section are all good starting points for research, as are the reference works cited earlier in this chapter. If you are in doubt about the location of materials in the library, ask for help; reference librarians are trained to find relevant information quickly and efficiently. Not only will the reference librarian be familiar with special indexes and guides to materials; he or she will be able to assist you with on-line computerized indexes, databases, and abstracts that provide the most up-to-date information.

One of of the most useful tools for organizing your research and taking notes is the index card. You can use these cards to create a bibliography and take comprehensive notes. A bibliography is a detailed list of all the

The Reader's Guide to Periodical Literature *is an excellent reference to resources on a wide range of presentation topics. Other sources, such as the* Business Periodicals Index *and the* Encyclopedia of Associations *target more specific topics related to businesses and organizations.*

books, articles, interviews, and abstracts you review in the course of your research. For each publication, write the complete title and reference information on the card in case you need to find it again later. On the back of the card, write a brief summary of the content.

Then take specific notes on each of the sources. You can code the sources by letter; write the letter of the source on one side of the card and the detailed information, and the page number on which you found it, on the other. If you are taking down a direct quote, be painstakingly careful to copy it exactly, including spelling and punctuation. Include information related to one main idea per card — that way, you can easily organize your finished research into main ideas. These notes are the basis for developing supporting materials for your presentation.

You are likely to generate dozens of viable main ideas. Although you may believe that the more ideas and research you include, the stronger the resulting presentation will be, using a large number of main ideas will test the audience's attention span and tolerance for fatigue and require you to exceed the normal time limit for a presentation (from five to thirty minutes). No strict definition exists for the "correct" number of main points, but for most messages it is wise to keep the number within the range of three to five.

Providing Support for Ideas

Regardless of the purpose of your presentation, you will use some form of supporting materials to give credibility to your main ideas and make the message more informative, interesting, relevant, clear, and acceptable — all the better to reach the audience. Supporting materials facilitate learning. Although teaching the audience is a fundamental goal of most presentations, learning can be uncomfortable or frightening and can therefore be resisted. Indeed, people tend to resist attempts by a speaker to change them or provoke some action. Supporting materials can greatly help the speaker to overcome these barriers to complete a successful presentation. These materials include explanations, examples, statistics, testimony, and visual aids.

Explanations

Explanation is the act or process of making plain or comprehensible. This is often accomplished by a simple statement of the relationship of a whole and its parts — for example, "The executive committee is one of many committees created to deal with specific problems in our organization." Other methods include:

◆ Providing a definition ("The executive committee is a group of people responsible for maintaining up-to-date guidelines for disposal of hazardous waste")

◆ Using synonyms (words with approximately the same meanings) or antonyms (words with opposite meainings)

◆ Using comparisons (showing listeners the similarities between something familiar and something unfamiliar)

◆ Showing contrasts (supporting an idea by emphasizing differences between it and something else)

◆ Giving a brief history

◆ Providing an operational definition (defining the term *logging off* by describing the steps involved in exiting a particular program on a computer)

Explanations should be framed within the experiences of audience members. The presenter must also be careful not to make such explanations too long or abstract.

Examples

Examples connect the main ideas of a presentation with a real or an ideal state envisioned by the speaker. Examples take a variety of forms, including extended detailed illustrations and brief specific instances. Illustrations can be either hypothetical (a story that could, yet did not, happen) or factual (a story that did happen). A presenter may involve the listeners in a hypothetical illustration by suggesting, "Imagine yourself in an employment interview. You want this job, and for the first ten minutes or so everything has been going smoothly. Then the interviewer starts to ask a series of personal, and in your view, illegal questions."

When using hypothetical or factual illustrations, the speaker is smart to consider whether the story is relevant and appropriate to the audience; whether it is typical, rather than exceptional; and whether it is vivid and impressive in detail. If the illustration fails to fulfill any of these criteria, the speaker is wise to find a more suitable alternative.

A specific instance is an undeveloped, very brief illustration — more a reference than an example. Using specific instances successfully requires that the audience recognize the names or events to which the speaker is referring. For example, a reference to "GATT" in a presentation on foreign trade will be ineffective if the audience is not familiar with the role of the General Agreement on Tariffs and Trade in the post–World War II international economy. Nevertheless, citing specific instances with which the audience is familiar can foster an audience's belief in and identification with the speaker as "one of us."

Statistics

As a form of supporting material, statistics describe the result of collecting, organizing, and interpreting numerical data. They are especially useful when you wish to reduce large masses of information to general categories ("The average score for college students on the Personal Report of Communication Apprehension is 75"), emphasize the size of something ("Business and industry currently spend more than $200 billion annually for training and development — more than is spent for education at primary, secondary, and college levels"), or indicate trends ("In 1973, African Americans made up 27 percent of military infantry, gun crews, and seamanship specialists; in 1989, the figure was 19 percent").

When using statistics, you must concern yourself with their accuracy and bias and with their clarity and meaningfulness. Addressing the first issue involves answering such questions as, Were correct data-collecting techniques used to obtain the statistics? Do the statistics cover sufficient cases and lengths of time? Are the statistics taken from competent sources? The second issue includes pragmatic considerations such as: Can you translate these difficult-to-understand numbers into more immediately under-standable terms? How can you provide adequate background for the data? Would a graph or visual aid clarify the data or statistical trends you are presenting?

Testimony

Testimony is a statement by a credible person (source) that lends weight and authority to the speaker's presentation. Credibility is based on whether the source is an acknowledged expert on the specific subject and is free of bias and self-interest. The audience's perception of the source is important as well. Is the source well known to the audience? If not, the speaker must tell the audience why the source is a good authority. If the source is known, does the audience accept her or his opinion as knowledgeable and unbiased in any way? To lend support to a message, the testimony of a source must *be credible* and *perceived as credible* by the audience.

Visual Aids

Like all forms of supporting material, visual aids enhance the clarity and credibility of the message. And, by using multiple channels of communi-cation, they appeal to multiple senses and so increase listeners' retention of significant points. They also help the presenter control apprehension by providing a point of familiarity in an uncertain situation.

These advantages are especially important for business and professional settings. As Tom Cothran pointed out:*

> Numerous studies lend tangible support to the argument for using visuals. . . . At the University of Wisconsin, for example, researchers determined that learning improved up to 200 percent when visual aids were used in teaching vocabulary. Studies at Harvard and Columbia have found audiovisuals improve retention by from 14 to 38 percent over pres-entations where no visuals were used. Research at both the University of Pennsylvania's Wharton School of Business and the University of Minne-sota report that the time required to present a concept can be reduced up to 40 percent when visuals complement a verbal presentation. . . .
>
> Wharton's research considered presenters as well as their presentations. . . . Among its findings: Presenters who used visuals were perceived more favorably overall than those who did not use visuals. Specifically, presenters who used visuals were "perceived as significantly better prepared, more professional, more persuasive, and more interest-ing" than those using no visual support. In meetings where a decision was required, a larger percentage of decisions agreed with presentations made with visual support than without.

The Minnesota study's most startling finding was this one: "Presentations using computer-generated graphics are 43 percent more persuasive than unaided presentations." In addition . . . "a typical presenter using presentation support has nothing to lose and can be as effective as a better presenter using no visuals," the researchers reported. "The better a presenter is, however, the more one needs to use high-quality visual support."[4]

Types of visual aids.   Obtaining these advantages requires skill in selecting appropriate aids and using them well. There are three basic categories of aids: the actual object or a model of it, pictorial reproductions, and pictorial symbols. In the first category, for example, a Macintosh computer may be introduced during a presentation on how to create computer-generated graphics. Also consider logistics in using a visual from this category. Actual objects should be used only if they can be easily handled during the presentation. Likewise, a model built in painstaking detail may lose its impact if the audience is too far away to see it clearly.

Photographs, slides, sketches, videotapes, cartoons, and drawings are included in the category of pictorial reproductions. In keeping with the old saying "A picture is worth a thousand words," pictorial reproductions show the main ideas of a presentation in new, exciting, and interesting ways.

Abstract concepts and statistical data are often represented through pictorial symbols such as graphs, charts, and diagrams. These may be prepared on a variety of media, including flip charts, blackboards, overhead projections, or handouts.

Selecting visuals.   When considering a visual aid for your presentation, you are wise to keep several criteria in mind.

1. *Use aids that are large enough to be seen.* In addition to checking the size of the visual itself, you should ensure that all writing included on the visual is large enough to be easily readable. When possible, take the visual aid to the room where it will be used and test for visibility from all sections the audience will occupy during the presentation. If doing so is not possible, ask advice from people who know the setting, and then make informed guesses about the potential number of listeners and average viewing distances.

2. *Keep the content of visual aids simple and focused.* Pictures and words should be as uncrowded and simple as possible and should avoid unnecessary details that may distract the audience. Rather than trying to include too much information on one visual, you are smart to use multiple visuals, each containing only those features and details essential to clarify and highlight the specific point being made.

3. *Prepare visual materials carefully.* Audience members interpret the design and form of the visual aid as a reflection of your attitude toward them and toward the message. Thus, the form of the aid has

great potential to enhance or detract from your credibility regardless of the visual's content. Professionals may be hired to prepare visuals for particularly important presentations, although for the most part, understanding the basic design and format rules described above can help you to create visuals for your own presentations.

Developing an Introduction and a Conclusion

To this point, we have worked through basic principles for creating the body of a message — clarifying and focusing the purpose, identifying and researching main ideas, and using supporting materials. We now turn to the front and back sections of the message — the introduction and the conclusion.

The Introduction

As you think about how to begin a presentation, consider a similar situation: the first meeting of a class. When you took your seat on the first day of this class, for example, what was it that you wanted to know? If you are at all like students we have asked, there were at least three categories of information you sought to acquire: course coverage (what will be the content and focus of the course?), course requirements (what is required to complete this course?), and course instructor (what kind of person will this teacher turn out to be?). These questions fall into three general categories: issues of *orientation* (what's happening?), *motivation* (what's in it for me?), and *rapport* (will I like and respect this instructor?). Although you may already have obtained partial answers to these questions before the first class session (from friends, former class members, and so forth), the questions still remained, and you and the instructor probably spent at least a portion of the first meeting answering them.

The introduction to a presentation serves similar functions. It informs the listener what the message is about (orientation), why the listener should attend to it (motivation), and why the speaker is a credible source for the message (rapport). As the speaker thinks through the introduction, he or she should consider which of these issues requires attention and what kind.

Orientation.   One method of orienting the audience is to state the topic to be discussed, articulate the thesis statement, explain the presentation's title, or review the purpose of the presentation. A speaker at a business fund-raiser for local arts groups may begin: "Some of you may wonder why this presentation is titled 'Give; Don't Give Up.' I'm here today to tell you why it's more important now, in the face of difficult economic times, than ever before to contribute to cultural organizations."

Another method of orienting the audience is to preview the structure of the message: "Cultural organizations provide three vital services to our community: they expand our view of the world and each other, they raise issues that we need to discuss, and they enrich our lives and our children's lives."

The speaker may also explain why the topic was narrowed as it was: "When I was asked to give a fund-raising presentation to you, who are business leaders in the community, my first question was 'What can you do for us?' I soon realized that I needed to tell you what *we* are doing, and hope to continue to do, for *you*."

Motivation. Motivational strategies include linking the topic and thesis statement to listeners' lives: "How many of you have attended a cultural event in our community in the recent past? Think how our city would be diminished if these events were no longer held."

Showing how the topic has affected or will affect the audience's past, present, or future is another motivational strategy. A speaker may begin a presentation by saying: "You may not have realized it, but tourism generated $34 million for our city last year. Surveys showed that many of these visitors came to participate in our numerous cultural events, and in the process they bolstered the profits of your businesses."

Demonstrating how the topic is linked to a basic need or goal of the audience is a third method of motivating an audience to listen. This can be done by saying: "Cultural events are an important part of making our community vital and prosperous, and I'm sure that all of us want to keep it that way."

Rapport. Building rapport can take several forms. Language that demonstrates competence, such as citing important and respected people, noting relevant events, or describing your expertise on the topic, increases the audience's receptivity to your message.

Trustworthiness, another important factor in building rapport, can be demonstrated by showing that your present behavior is consistent with past behavior on the topic under discussion, giving time to opposing points of view, and being consistent with verbal and nonverbal behavior. Nonverbal behavior that shows confidence and enthusiasm for the topic, such as a strong voice, direct eye contact with members of the audience, and a measured delivery, promotes an image of trustworthiness.

Complimenting the audience and using humor are additional techniques for developing rapport. Doing so shows that you identify with people in the audience, respect them, and can laugh with them.

In considering introductory strategies, you are wise to remember that many of the most effective strategies contribute to multiple functions. For example, a story can provide both orientation and motivation, and humor can enhance both motivation and rapport. Thus, when you are developing an introduction, make it as compact as possible and as effective as possible in fulfilling the audience's needs for orientation, motivation, and rapport.

The Conclusion

The conclusion seeks to provide a sense of completeness and closure. It is often signaled by the phrases "in conclusion" or "in summary" and is accomplished by reminding the audience of the highlights of the presentation and reemphasizing their significance. This not only helps the audience remember what you have said (people ofen remember best what they heard last); it allows you to reinforce the cohesion and importance of the message.

In addition to summarizing the main ideas of the message, you can use the conclusion to reestablish the connection of the topic to the larger context and to provide psychological closure by reminding audience members how the topic affects their lives. Both functions can be achieved by tying the conclusion of the speech to the introduction — bringing both together by reference to and elaboration of quotations, illustrations, or questions that were used in the beginning.

Because the conclusion serves as a summary and an ending, it should be brief and decisive; it should not trail off. When the audience hears a concluding phrase, it will — and is entitled to — believe that the presentation has reached a close. Thus, use your conclusion to reinforce the thesis for your audience, to place that thesis in the larger context known to your audience, and to provide, if possible, a "clincher" (a telling quotation, illustration, or question). Then sit down.

The Outline: Basic Considerations

Now that we have identified all pieces of the presentation — main ideas, supporting materials, introduction, and conclusion — the time has come to put it together. The *outline,* a visual, schematic summary of the message, shows the order of the ideas and the general relationship among them.

Types of Outlines

There are basically three types of outlines: a *complete-sentence outline,* which lists each head and subhead in complete-sentence form; a *topic outline,* which reduces the sentences to brief phrases or single words; and a *speaker's outline,* which includes only key words and important quotations/statistics written on small index cards.

All three forms are useful for different purposes. The complete-sentence outline allows others to study the organizational structure and give feedback on its strengths and weaknesses. For this reason, teachers who ask students to hand in outlines usually ask for this format. The topic outline allows the speaker to consider and reconsider organizational choices while working on the presentation. Once those choices are final, the speaker creates a speaker's outline to aid or trigger her or his memory during the actual presentation. As a result of these different advantages, the speaker is wise to start with a complete-sentence outline and later reduce it to a speaker's outline for the actual presentation.

Basic Principles

For both complete-sentence and topic outlines, there are four major conventions for writing the outline.

Appropriate numbering systems. The most widely used numbering system alternates letters and numbers, as shown in the following outline. The main heads are placed at the left margin and subheads are indented, forming a clearly identifiable column. Heads or subheads that run more than a single line are further indented so that the content portion of the entry aligns with the content above it.

Introduction (methods for establishing orientation, motivation, rapport)

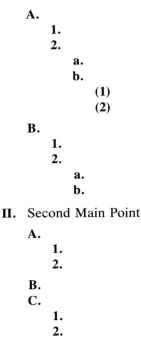

I. First Main Point
  A.
    1.
    2.
       a.
       b.
         (1)
         (2)
  B.
    1.
    2.
       a.
       b.

II. Second Main Point
  A.
    1.
    2.
  B.
  C.
    1.
    2.

III. Third Main Point

  A.
  B.

Conclusion (methods for summarizing, linking, and clinching)

Heads of equal importance.   The main points (Roman numerals I, II, and III) are the main divisions of the presentation and should be of equal importance to the topic. Similarly, the first subdivision of these heads (capital letters A and B) designates logical and equally important divisions of the first main point. This principle also applies to the other subdivisions represented by Arabic numerals and lower-case letters.

Consistency in form.   A complete-sentence outline uses complete sentences throughout and does not lapse into topic heads; a topic outline uses topic heads, not sentences. In the sentence outline, the punctuation follows written conventions (e.g., use of periods); no punctuation is needed at the end of lines in a topic outline.

Balance in form.   Because a topic is not "divided" unless there are at least two parts, an outline normally has at least two subheads under any main head. Even though exceptions are possible, normally for every heading marked I there is at least a II, and for every A there is at least a B.

Transitions

When an audience member listens to the presentation you have outlined, he or she lacks the advantages possessed by the reader of a book or the viewer of a videotape. That is, the audience member can neither reread a selection — using punctuation as a clue to meaning — nor rewind the tape to discover what was missed. If the listener misses your point, he or she has missed it completely. Thus, you must do what you can to guide your listeners through a presentation by providing clear transitions.

Transitions link the various elements of the outline, showing why and how each element relates to the other elements. Transitions help the audience understand the logical relationships among the main points and their subpoints, and they explain how the introduction, body, and conclusion fit together. In short, transitions serve as "signposts" that help listeners understand where you are going, where you are, and where you have been.

Transitions need not be elaborate, although they should be frequent and well spaced throughout the message. You may, for example, start with a preliminary forecast of the main points in the introduction ("Today I will talk about three dimensions of . . .") and end with a final summary as part of the conclusion ("I have talked about the three dimensions . . .").

As you develop the message, transitions take the form of internal previews that anticipate or summaries that review a main point, subtopic, or supporting material ("Having explained what I mean by . . . , I would like to turn next to . . ."). The transition from one point to the next should be smooth and obvious. When listeners find it difficult to follow your organizational structure, they rapidly lose interest and will neither remember nor accept the thesis of your message.

Communication Competence: Presenting the Message

Having generated a message and put it into a standard presentation format, a presenter is now in a position to think about effective methods for delivering the message to listeners. This stage of the presentation relates to the third component of strategic communication, communication competence. The speaker must be able to identify and employ a delivery that is both effective and appropriate to the message, audience, and occasion.

Support for a balanced emphasis on content and delivery is provided in the research literature on nonverbal communication. Judee Burgoon, David Buller, and Gill Woodall summarized approximately one hundred studies on channel reliance — which channels or codes most influence listeners as they assign meaning to communication events.[5] They concluded that adults place greater reliance on nonverbal cues (which include issues of delivery) than on verbal cues (issues of content) in determining meaning. They also concluded that 60 to 65 percent of the meaning in a communication exchange is conveyed nonverbally.

This general pattern, the authors suggested, has several qualifiers: (a) young children place greater reliance on verbal cues (the words) than adults do; (b) reliance on nonverbal cues is greatest when there is a conflict between the verbal and nonverbal channels; (c) "verbal content is more important for factual, cognitive, abstract, and persuasive interpretations, while nonverbal context is more important for judging emotional and attitudinal expressions, relational communication, and impression formation"; and (d) there are individual differences in channel dependence (some people rely on nonverbal channels, some typically rely on verbal content, and others adapt their channel choice to the situation).[6]

Types of Delivery

Given these findings on channel reliance, a presenter must carefully consider the choices available for the presentation of a message. The presenter must make an early choice of an appropriate method of delivery. To do this, he or she decides if the presentation will be developed on the spot (impromptu), given from brief notes (extemporaneous), written out and read (manuscript), or memorized word for word and recited (memorized).

Impromptu.   Impromptu speaking is best avoided whenever possible. If the presenter knows or anticipates being called on to make some remarks, the message should be prepared in advance. This will increase the likelihood that the message is not weak in terms of organization, forms of support, quality of word choice, or effectiveness of delivery. Nevertheless, there will be times when the presenter is given little, if any, chance to prepare; for example, when the presenter is told to make a brief presentation to a committee at work, asked to say a few words on a topic about which she or he is knowledgeable, or asked on the spot to answer a question or describe a policy or procedure. (We discuss techniques for successfully handling impromptu presentation in Chapter 15.)

Extemporaneous.   Extemporaneous delivery encourages thorough preparation and adaptability to the contingencies of the situation. The presenter starts with a full-sentence outline and then reduces that outline to a speaker's outline for rehearsal and actual presentation. Rehearsal helps the presenter to become conversational in delivery, but because she or he is working from ideas and key words, rather than from complete sentences, the message is never delivered exactly the same way twice. The wording of the ideas remains flexible to allow the presenter to better adapt the message to the audience. With extemporaneous speaking, segments of the message can be expanded or reduced depending on audience response.

Manuscript.   When the situation requires precise wording (e.g., a technical or research report where exact wording is crucial) or exact timing (e.g., a television presentation of exactly nine minutes), the appropriate mode of presentation may be manuscript speaking. In this mode, the speaker prepares an organized and easily readable manuscript that has an oral, conversational style. Starting with a full-sentence outline, the speaker writes out the whole message. To ensure that the final product is conversational, the speech is orally rehearsed (perhaps with a tape recorder) before it is committed to paper. Once the message has been developed into final form, the manuscript is prepared for reading (e.g., triple spaced and marked for special emphases, etc.), and the speaker rehearses until she or he feels very comfortable with the delivery. A successful manuscript delivery looks and sounds as if the speech were being delivered extemporaneously — that is, the delivery is conversational and unforced, and includes eye contact with audience members.

Memorized.   Except for a lack of something to place on the lectern, podium, or teleprompter, a memorized speech is really no different from a manuscript speech. Thus, approaches to preparation and use overlap for these two modes of delivery.

The memorized speech is frequently used in situations in which reading a manuscript appears inappropriate. (In Chapter 15, for example, we describe forms of ceremonial speaking where a memorized speech is the appropriate choice.) In creating such a presentation, the speaker's goal is to make the speech sound as if it were being delivered extemporaneously.

Memorized presentations lack the security of a manuscript to which the speaker can refer, so the speaker anticipates and rehearses for the possibility of a memory block. If a block occurs, the speaker focuses on key words until able to click back into the memorized phrases of the presentation.

Characteristics of Effective Delivery

Regardless of the delivery method you choose, its function remains the same — to aid listeners in understanding, accepting, and retaining what you have said. Although there are multiple ways to achieve this goal, they all involve the application of four general criteria.[7]

Effective delivery is intelligible. Before audience members will accept a message, they must hear it. Thus, the presenter has to practice speaking with adequate volume and appropriate rate. In the case of a microphone, this means keeping the proper distance. With a standard podium mike, this is about six inches or a little closer. If the speaker gets too close to the mike, however, some sounds (e.g., the letter *p*) become overemphasized and create an annoying sound for audiences.

In addition to volume and rate, intelligibility also requires attention to articulation and pronunciation. Not only will mispronunciation inhibit clarity; it will lead to negative judgments concerning the credibility of the speaker. Thus, whenever there is the slightest doubt about proper pronunciation, it is worth the effort to consult a dictionary. Tape-recording a rehearsal version of the presentation or having a friend listen and comment is useful for enhancing the intelligibility of a message.

Effective delivery is conversational. In ordinary conversation participants use a great deal of variation in the pitch and volume of their voices. They also indicate their involvement in and commitment to the dialogue via body orientation and eye contact, and they reinforce the points they make with gestures and physical movement.

In short, variations in voice and physical action are used naturally and unconsciously to focus attention on and reinforce the content of a conversation. These variations provide an excellent model for a public presentation. The presenter should strive to talk with, rather than at, a group of listeners. Good delivery can be characterized as a conversation with an audience.

Effective delivery is direct. Good delivery signals to listeners that the speaker truly cares about communicating with them. In our culture, respect for and interest in an audience are communicated primarily with eye contact. Sustaining appropriate eye contact with listeners also helps the presenter discover how the message is being received.

Achieving these goals requires eye contact with all segments of the audience. A practical strategy for achieving this is to start the presentation by locating a small number of listeners in different parts of the room who are responding positively with smiles and head nods. Establishing eye contact with these people can help a speaker gain confidence during the first moments of a speech. As the presentation proceeds, the speaker can then widen eye contact to include the total audience by moving her or his gaze randomly and smoothly, rather than systematically, throughout the room and looking directly into the eyes of individual listeners.

Effective delivery is unobtrusive.   Good delivery focuses attention on the speaker's message, not on the speaker. The three principles we have just discussed — being intelligible, conversational, and direct — promote this goal. You can also take steps to eliminate distracting mannerisms such as playing with note cards, rocking back and forth while standing in one place, locking both hands on the lectern or in pants pockets, or excessive use of pauses such as "uh" or "you know."

You may not even be aware of your tendencies to practice these or similar mannerisms. One way to recognize them is to videotape yourself or to watch others. Simply identifying distracting behaviors is often the greatest part of eliminating them. You can also engage in *negative practice* — consciously overemphasize the distracting mannerism while rehearsing the delivery of the presentation. This allows you to become hyperaware of the behaviors while you are speaking.

Other Considerations

In addition to the four general principles of effective delivery, there are several additional considerations worthy of comment.

Appearance.   As you recall from Chapters 7 and 8, first impressions of another person are to a large degree the result of physical appearance cues. In a presentation, this means that audiences use natural elements such as the speaker's height, weight, and body shape and planned cues such as clothing, accessories, or cosmetics as bases for credibility judgments that affect the development of subsequent impressions.

You are wise to analyze your appearance in terms of how you will be viewed by a particular audience. Ask yourself how the audience may react to your dress, accessories, neatness, degree of formality in your clothing choice, and general attractiveness. What are audience members likely to conclude on the basis of this assessment? What judgments are they likely to form about you? An awareness of such issues increases your sensitivity to audience perceptions. Many speakers, for example, choose to dress slightly more formally when speaking than they normally do. This can boost your confidence and suggest to the audience that you care about the speech and the speaking situation.

Your appearance and delivery, however, must be comfortable for you. Efforts to completely change your natural style of speaking, dress, appearance, or even gesturing are likely to result in audience perceptions of incongruity and inconsistency. Although you can improve your style, an all-out attempt to "be someone else" during a presentation will decrease your rapport with the audience.

Use of visual aids.   Visual aids should be prepared early enough to allow you to practice with them until you can use them quickly and smoothly. Important points to remember during both practice and the actual presentation are as follows.

1. *Visual aids must be easily seen by every member of the audience.* In many rooms, there are hooks and clips at the front of the room on which visual aids can be hung. When this is not the case, it is usually possible to place them on an easel. Wherever they are placed, the goal is to locate them high enough so that every member of the audience can see them quickly and smoothly. This requires both advanced thought about placement and rehearsal of actual placement.

2. *Talk to the audience, rather than to the visual aid.* Listeners want your attention, and you have to be able to discern their reaction to your message. Neither is possible if you are talking to the visual aid. Thus, help listeners to understand your visual by telling them what you want them to see, hear, and understand. At the same time, maintain eye contact with them to determine whether this understanding is taking place.

3. *Display the visual aid only when it is being used.* Visual aids are intended to enhance understanding, not compete for the audience's attention. Keep aids from being seen until you are ready to use them, and remove them when you have finished. For this reason, avoid passing visual aids (such as handouts) through the audience while you are speaking. There is no surer way to lose the attention of portions of your audience!

Fielding Audience Questions

In most situations, questions are postponed until the end of the presentation. This need not be the case, however, and you are wise to decide in advance whether questions will be handled during or after the speech. In either case, a small number of guidelines can contribute to a smooth and effective questioning period.

Anticipate likely questions.   As you think about your topic and audience, anticipate potential questions. Are there points that may be confusing? Are there points that may produce disagreement? Just as students must anticipate and prepare for teachers' questions at examination time, speakers can and should prepare responses to the questions they anticipate receiving from the audience.

Repeat questions from the audience.   This helps everyone hear the questions from the audience and is essential if the session is being recorded on audiotape or videotape. Repetition also allows you to buy time when hit with a surprise question for which there is no ready answer or to clarify confusing or unclear questions.

Use answers to reinforce the goal of the presentation.   Do not let questioners pull you away from the thesis of the message. Instead, use questions as an opportunity to frame responses that contribute to your goal. When questioners persist in pursuing irrelevant questions, say that you will talk with them individually at the close of the meeting or send them some additional information.

Treat all questions with respect.   Many speakers dread the possibility of a hostile question or critical remark during the question-and-answer session. This need not be the case. David Burns suggested a simple, yet effective, method for coping with such situations without getting into arguments or being locked into a defensive position: compliment the questioner on her or his insight and respond to any points of truth or areas of agreement that you can find.[8]

Give the questioner a genuine compliment.   Say something positive about the ideas being expressed. People who attack speakers in an aggressive, critical way are frequently insecure and looking for recognition. They want to feel important, and they may be jealous of your central position in the situation. If somebody asks an intimidating, hostile question, you can simply say, "That's a very important question. Thank you for asking it." If you say this with sincerity, you can avoid an awkward debate that will make everyone tense. Complimenting people who ask questions encourages others in the audience to do the same because it creates a safe environment for them to share their ideas.

Look for a point of agreement or truth.   Although doing so may contradict your natural desire to argue and defend yourself, it is very effective to be flexible and openminded. In this way, you can come to a deeper understanding of the issue and increase your credibility with the audience. Consider the following example.

Audience member: "Your ideas about this new business proposal sound far-fetched to me. I think that we need to solidify our regional market before we try to expand abroad."

Speaker: "You have a good point — our regional sales have traditionally been the backbone of this company. But we need to expand so that we can avoid slumps if the regional economy takes a downturn."

When you do not have an answer, punt.   Occasionally, you will receive a question for which you have no ready answer. When you are not able to answer, choose an alternative approach to the question so as not to lose control of the questioning period. There are several ways to do this.

◆ Rephrase the question into one that you can answer — for example, by narrowing it to an area of your expertise or relating it to the main idea of the presentation.

◆ Redirect the question by saying, "That's a good point. What do *you* think we should do?" or "We just happen to have an expert on that topic in our audience. Dr. Stone, what do you think we should do?"

◆ Acknowledge that you do not have an answer at this time and promise to get back to the questioner at a later date. Whatever the choice, implement it smoothly and confidently, just as you delivered the main body of your presentation.

Anxiety Management

We now turn to the fourth component of strategic communication, anxiety management, which has particular importance for presentational speaking. Consider the following example.

A popular Washington hostess, entering a room in one of the capital's finest hotels, recognized a well-known government official. Hands clasped behind his back, head bowed, he was pacing up and down the length of the room.
"I'm going to deliver a speech," he told her.
"Do you usually get this nervous before addressing a large gathering?" asked the woman.
"Why no," he answered. "I never get nervous."
"In that case," demanded the woman, "what are you doing in the ladies' room?"[9]

The experience of this governmental official is one with which many people can identify. Although there are many symptoms besides disorientation, the sense of panic that frequently accompanies speaking before a group is quite unlike any other fear. When Americans are asked to answer the question "What are you most afraid of?" they report one of their worst fears to be speaking before a group.[10] Fear of public speaking ranks with fear of the dentist, heights, insects or bugs, snakes, death, and flying as a widespread phenomenon.

Given this fear's widespread nature, you are likely to encounter communication apprehension, which has also been termed *reticence, shyness,* and *unwillingness to communicate,* sooner, rather than later, in your career as a speaker. Based on our discussion of apprehension in other contexts, you know that many conditions can cause communication anxiety even in informal situations and that anxiety may be a trait to which some people are more predisposed than others. There are also some additional causes of anxiety about public speaking and ways to deal with them effectively.

Why Is Public Speaking Frightening?

To answer that question, let us review the origins of anxiety about communicating in public and specific suggestions for countering them. Scholars have proposed three ways of explaining how apprehension develops, is maintained, and can be treated: skills deficit, conditioned anxiety, and negative cognitive appraisal.

Skills deficit.   One explanation for anxiety is that the speaker lacks adequate skills for making a successful presentation, and so he or she fears or even avoids doing it. A real lack of presentation skills results in embarrassment, failure to reach the audience, and a sense of frustration and helplessness for the speaker. In a business setting, it may also result in loss of sales, fewer chances to participate in major projects that may lead to promotions, and a perception that the speaker is not a particularly talented or qualified employee. These are serious problems, so a speaker who feels she or he lacks adequate skills should do everything possible to bring them up to speed by targeting the points we have made in this chapter about choosing a topic, analyzing an audience, and so forth. Most important of all is *practice.* We cannot overemphasize the role of experience in calming anxiety — even if you are never completely comfortable with speaking before a group, you can learn exactly what you are capable of and what to expect from yourself through experience. Once you have mastered the skills of public speaking, you no longer need to fear threatened by personal failure.

Conditioned anxiety.   Conditioned anxiety results when neutral communication situations collect negative connotations, images, and memories

A presentation workshop like the one shown here can help you identify the strengths and weaknesses of your speaking style and provides helpful feedback from other workshop participants.

over time. The speaker is informally "taught" to be anxious about speaking through a succession of negative events, such as a teacher punishing her or him for speaking up in class or a parent telling her or him to be quiet around adults. Being punished for early attempts to communicate can lead to fear of communication situations, especially public speaking, later in life.

One method for reducing conditioned anxiety is *systematic desensitization* (SD).[11] SD is based on the theory that a person cannot be relaxed and anxious at the same time, and so the process attempts to overlay pleasant, relaxing images and experiences on the anxiety-causing situation. SD also uses deep muscle relaxation techniques that help the speaker to identify a real physical sense of relaxation, for which he or she can strive while speaking. The following list illustrates a typical step-by-step process for using SD:

1. Before you begin, make a list of situations that cause varying degrees of anxiety, from lowest to highest. For example, one list may include lying in bed just before going to sleep, discussing the upcoming speech a week before it is scheduled, getting dressed the morning of the speech, entering the room on the day of the speech, walking up to the podium, and giving the speech.

2. Then assume a relaxed position, take several deep breaths, and become as relaxed as possible.

3. Move from hands through feet and systematically tense muscle groups, hold the contraction for several seconds, relax the muscles, and concentrate on the relaxed state you experience. For example, make a fist and tense the muscles of your right hand and forearm for five seconds; then relax and note how these muscles feel as relaxation flows through them.

4. After you relax all the muscle groups, envision a pleasant scene, and associate the feeling of relaxation with the image.

5. Stay relaxed and think about the situation with the lowest anxiety level on your list.

6. Move down the list of progressively anxious situations. Stay relaxed and consciously link the physical feeling of relaxation with the scene you are envisioning.

7. If you feel a twinge of anxiety at any point, leave the list of situations, and envision the original pleasant scene. Take deep breaths and tense and relax muscle groups to bring back the sensation of relaxation.

8. When you have gone through every item on the list, return to the original relaxed state by breathing deeply and envisioning pleasant scenes.

Although SD may not work for every person, it is one of the most successful techniques for reducing conditioned anxiety. For those who find it effective, SD's conscious efforts to promote relaxation inhibit anxiety, thus weakening the link between communication and nervousness.

Negative cognitive appraisal.   Negative cognitive appraisal is a process of unrealistic negative self-evaluations, in which communicators assume that they are going to fail and then worry about failure and its consequences. Negative cognitive appraisal is best handled by reducing negative self-statements (such as "I know I'm going to lose my train of thought") so that you are able to concentrate on your skills and the message and are able to speak more confidently and competently. This is done through the process of *cognitive restructuring* (CR).

CR attempts to change or modify the thought process by identifying the impact of negative self-statements on the speaking situation. Once you see how the negative statements result in discomfort and behavior during a presentation, you can then focus on reducing negative thoughts by substituting more positive, coping statements.

Keeping a log is important to using CR successfully. In the log, you note the negative self-statements that you use frequently. When writing these statements, you also cultivate awareness of what these statements really are: irrational. For example, if you find yourself thinking, "I'm going to sound stupid," consider your skill and experience and the preparation you have put into the presentation. In reality, you will undoubtedly be among the most knowledgeable people on the topic in the room. Write down these positive coping statements in your log.

There are two types of coping statements. *Context statements* emphasize the nonstressful aspects of the situation. *Task statements* emphasize what you can do to ensure a successful presentation. To be most effective, confront negative self-statements that occur before, during, and after the presentation. The following is a sample entry in a CR log.

Situation: I have been asked to give a thirty minute presentation at a monthly breakfast meeting.

Description: My presentation will deal with financial projections and strategic planning; my audience consists of colleagues as well as upper management.

Negative Self-Statements	Coping Statements
Before: I will forget some of the data for my financial projections.	*Context:* I have not forgotten important information in previous speeches.
	Task: I will have all the important data on both my outline and my slides.
During: I'll sound amateur.	*Context:* I know everyone in the audience and we respect each other's knowledge.
	Task: I am well prepared and have excellent visual aids.
After: Upper management won't find my projections credible.	*Context:* I have an established track record with upper management.
	Task: My charts are based on data provided by the company treasurer.

These techniques for managing anxiety are not independent — they work best together. If you wish to manage anxiety, you will find it useful to practice all three: learn and practice the skills of public speaking, use relaxation and deep breathing to achieve physical comfort when speaking, and learn to identify irrational negative statements that increase anxiety and replace them with positive task and context coping statements.

Summary

Presentations are vital to successful communication in business. If they are not assigned or determined by the context, their topic and purpose can be generated through brainstorming, mapping, or library research. The topic and specific purpose correspond to the communication goals for the presentation. After these goals are set, a thorough audience analysis, which covers several categories, provides the presenter with situational knowledge and insight into how to target the message to best achieve her or his goals.

In regard to the body of the presentation, main ideas can be identified by the topical system, which includes sixteen themes common to most subjects. The speaker should generally limit the presentation to three to five of the themes that best suit the audience and the occasion. These main ideas can then be researched through a variety of resources, including informational interviews, reference books, databases, and queries to a reference librarian.

Supporting materials are drawn from research on the topic and can include explanations, examples, statistics, testimony, and visual aids. The purpose of supporting materials is to make the presentation varied and exciting for the audience and to increase the speaker's credibility. For these reasons, it is wise to choose supporting materials with care.

The introduction and the conclusion are prepared after the bulk of the presentation is complete. The introduction serves to orient, motivate, and build rapport between the audience and the speaker. The conclusion provides a summary and a sense of the significance of the presentation so that listeners will leave with a clear understanding and memory of the main ideas discussed.

An outline is the standard format for organizing the three parts (introduction, body, and conclusion) of a presentation. A full-sentence outline, topic outline, and speaker's outline serve different purposes but follow the same basic principles. These principles include using a correct numbering system for outline entries, choosing headings of equal importance, maintaining consistency in form of outline entries, and striving for balance in entries so that every heading has at least two subheadings.

When it comes to delivery of the presentation, the speaker can choose from several delivery styles — impromptu, extemporaneous, manuscript, and memorized — depending on the circumstances. The choice of a delivery style should be considered early in the process of preparing the presentation as each makes different demands on the speaker's level of preparation, skill, and choice of material. Effective delivery focuses attention on the speaker's message, rather than the speaker, and should be comfortable and natural, rather than formal or forced.

Presentations can be rendered less successful by the intrusion of communication apprehension — the fear of speaking in public. This apprehension can be caused by skills deficit, conditioned anxiety, and/or negative cognitive appraisal. Management of anxiety can be achieved through practice of public speaking, use of relaxation and deep breathing techniques, and cognitive restructuring of irrational negative self-statements.

Discussion

1. What are some of the benefits of presentations in business and professional settings? What are some of the challenges to a successful presentation?

2. Discuss the methods for generating a topic covered in the chapter. Which have you used, and how effective were they?

3. What are the four general purposes for presentations? How does the speaker narrow the general purpose to a specific purpose and thesis statement?

4. Why is audience analysis important? How can it help the speaker in a business presentation? What are its limitations?

5. How can the topical system help a speaker to generate main ideas? According to this system, what are some of the themes common to all topics?

6. Describe the types of supporting materials that can be used during a presentation. What is their function? Give an example of when each would be appropriate.

7. What are the functions of an introduction? A conclusion? What are some techniques for accomplishing these functions?

8. What are the four types of delivery? When should each be used?

9. What role does delivery play in the overall success of a presentation?

10. Describe the three techniques for managing communication apprehension discussed in the chapter. Why should all three be used to obtain the best results in decreasing anxiety? How have you handled your own anxiety in past speaking situations?

Activities

1. In business settings, the general purpose of a presentation does not usually represent a single goal. Think of situations in which you may wish to combine several goals in one presentation. What are some of

the possibilities you worked out? Discuss your ideas with other class members, and compare results.

2. How would you narrow and research the following topics: employment trends for college graduates, advertising budgets at major corporations, the "glass ceiling" and promotions for women and members of minority groups, and communication networks in multinational companies?

3. Describe the demographic characteristics that can be considered in an audience analysis. What adaptations can be made for the following audiences: college graduates versus high school graduates, senior citizens versus young adults, clerical workers versus manufacturing workers, and employees at a for-profit corporation versus volunteers at a nonprofit organization?

4. Make a list of visual aids that can enhance your presentation of the topics in question 2. Explain how each may be created and used.

5. Unscramble the following outline of a presentation describing a job description. Put the entries into standard outline form using the principles of outlining discussed in the chapter. Hint: The outline contains two main points.

Benefits	Group plan
Analyze reports	Summarize data
Collect completed reports	File reports
Mid-range salary	Prepare forecast
Health insurance	One report from production
Bonus possible	Yearly raise
One report from marketing	Use file cabinets in main office
Responsibilities	Monthly premium
Three weeks' vacation	Files should be alphabetized

6. Keep a CR log for your next in-class presentation. What were your most common negative self-statements? How did you respond to them?

Notes

1. S. E. Berry and R. J. Garnston, "Become a State-of-the-Art Presenter," *Training and Development Journal* 41 (1987): 19–26.
2. G. A. Market, "Many Executives Must Learn How to Speak," *Marketing News* 22 (1988): 8–10.
3. J. F. Wilson, C. C. Arnold, and M. M. Wertheimer, *Public Speaking as a Liberal Art,* 6th ed. (Boston: Allyn and Bacon, 1990), pp. 112–113.
4. T. Cothran, "The Value of Visuals," *Presentation Technologies* (July 1989): 6–7.

5. J. Burgoon, D. Buller, and W. G. Woodall, *Nonverbal Communication: The Unspoken Dialogue* (New York: Harper & Row, 1989), pp. 154–161.

6. Ibid., p. 158.

7. R. P. Hart, G. W. Friedrich, and B. Brummett, *Public Communication,* 2nd ed. (New York: Harper & Row, 1983), pp. 183–185.

8. Based on D. Burns, *The Feeling Good Handbook* (New York: William Morrow, 1989), pp. 311–312.

9. P. R. Evans, "'Tense' Is Good for You!" *This Week Magazine,* July 9, 1967, p. 4.

10. "The 14 Worst Human Fears," *Detroit Free Press,* June 7, 1977.

11. G. Friedrich and B. Goss, "Systematic Desensitization," in J. A. Daly and J. C. McCroskey (eds.), *Avoiding Communication: Shyness, Reticence, and Communication Apprehension* (Beverly Hills, Calif.: Sage, 1984), pp. 173–187.

Chapter 13

*I*nformative Presentations

OBJECTIVES

After working through this chapter, you will be able to:

1. Describe the importance and difficulty of making informative presentations in today's business world

2. Understand how changes in organization life since World War II have shaped the nature of presentations

3. Identify informative presentations in terms of function, type, and format

4. Utilize four basic principles for the successful creation and presentation of an informative message

In the last chapter, our focus was on the key elements involved in developing effective presentations. In it we explored such components as (a) identifying the main points to be shared with an audience and researching them; (b) developing supporting materials to make those main points believable and credible; (c) organizing and outlining the total message, including introduction, body, transitions, and conclusion; and (d) selecting an appropriate type of delivery and developing a strategy for rehearsal that will make the delivery of the presentation both comfortable and effective. In this and the next chapter, we build on this analysis and elaborate it in terms of the two basic kinds of presentations: informative and persuasive.

Every time you give a presentation in a business or professional context, you have a general purpose and a specific purpose. Whereas specific purposes vary widely, general purposes can usually be classified as either informative or persuasive. This means that the dominant purpose of some presentations is to share adequate, accurate information with an audience in ways that are interesting and understandable and that the dominant purpose of other presentations is to persuade an audience. In this chapter, we discuss the importance of the former presentations, along with guidelines and resources for you as a speaker. The next chapter takes up the latter presentations.

The Range of Informative Presentations

Organizational life is filled with informative presentations, and the range of possible uses for informative presentations in a corporate office is a wide one. Just consider the following situations:

◆ Reviewing quarterly sales figures

◆ Introducing a new policy for recruiting personnel

◆ Explaining market research findings on the feasibility of introducing a new product line

◆ Briefing executives on departmental performance goals

◆ Training people to use new computer software

◆ Reviewing a feasibility study for the purchase of new equipment

◆ Demonstrating new machinery or equipment

What do all of these presentations have in common? They are informative! Their purpose is to tell listeners something they do not already know or to supplement or reinforce their existing knowledge.

That informative presentations are a regular part of organizational life in business and the professions alone justifies their study and importance.

Nevertheless, there are many additional reasons that exhibiting skill in informative speaking is critical to your professional success.

Information-Based Society

Since the end of World War II, many aspects of organizational life have changed drastically. The composition and size of the work force, the type of work performed, the attitude and rights of employees, and the importance of pay and benefits as motivational are just some of the factors that have seen changes. Taken together, they reveal that we live and work in an information-based society. Let us consider how a few of these factors affect the informative presentations given in today's organizations.

Composition and size.   More people are working today than ever before. Whereas yesterday's work force was predominantly high school–educated men between the ages of twenty-four and sixty-five, today's work force is composed of representatives from every nationality and ethnic group, culture, age, gender, and educational background.[1] And projections indicate that ethnic and racial minorities will compose one-third of the U.S. population by the year 2000 and 45 percent by 2050. Particularly prevalent today are workers who are classified as DINKs (dual income; no kids) and OIWKs (one income; with kids). The result is that in modern organizations anyone can be making a presentation to you at any time and that when you are making presentations, the audience is likely to be a very diverse group. Analyzing and adapting to audiences are far more of a challenge than they were even ten years ago.

Type of work.   Yesterday's work force was primarily industrial. The focus was on manufacturing and producing consumer goods for sale. Today, service organizations have overtaken manufacturing firms in number of organizations and employees. Health care, insurance, counseling services, financial savings and loan, repair and maintenance organizations, and training and development firms are far more important today than ever before.[2] As one college president pointed out: "Information workers today constitute the fastest growing and most highly compensated sector of employment in the leading industrial countries; they account for nearly 50 percent of all persons employed. The industrial sector on the other hand, the actual production, extraction, and growing of goods, now employs less than one-fourth of the American work force."[3] From the point of view of informative speaking, interests among audience members are quite different today than ever before.

Attitudes and rights.   Unlike yesteryear, today's workers are more independent and less subservient. With the demise of the middle manager in many businesses and the resulting flattening of the organization's hierarchy, employees are increasingly governing and managing their own work affairs.[4] They are also more concerned with safety, security, and benefits than workers were in the past. With the number of lawsuits against companies running at an all-time high, we know that employees are aware of their rights *and* are exercising them. This means that speakers can be held responsible for what they say and companies can be held liable!

Motivational factors. For years, pay was the major factor motivating employees in businesses. Workers "smoothed over" problems caused by poor working conditions, improper supervision, and unfair labor practices by glorifying their paychecks. This is no longer the case. The majority of workers today are still interested in pay, but personal and professional development, a feeling of accomplishment and belonging, and a desire to be productive are also prime motivators. The implication of this shift in focus is that speakers have more topics and techniques to use as motivating material in a presentation.

Accumulation of Information

In today's modern organizations, more information and more sources of information are available than at any previous time. People have access to more information than they can possibly digest. There is no indication that this trend will do anything but continue to accelerate.

According to the *World List of Scientific Journals*, 59,961 journals are published throughout the world (in sixty-five languages), in which about 1 million articles appear a year; in addition, some 300,000 scientific monographs are published each year, plus 15,000 conference proceedings. According to Louis Martin, associate editor of the Association of Research Libraries, "If an average reader tried to catch up with one year's output of learned publications in the sciences, it would take about 50 years of reading at 24 hours a day for seven days a week."[5] You are certainly aware that almost every product you buy at the store has a scanning bar on the packaging that when read with an optical light automatically rings the price for the cash register and updates the inventory. The February 1991 edition of *Prepared Foods* suggested that since the arrival of scanners in the early 1980s, food companies have received 500 to 32,000 times more data than they did before.[6]

People receive information through newspapers, televisions, radios, telephones, computer retrieval sources, satellite transmission sources, interactive video terminals, and electronic mail and fax machines, to name a few. Some of these now common methods by which we send and receive information did not even exist ten yers ago.

These immense changes and developments all lead to the conclusion that the presentation of information is both important and challenging for people in modern organizations. To meet this challenge, a speaker must be knowledgeable about what informative presentations are and how best to give them.

Functions of Informative Presentations

The presentation's *function* is the answer to the question "What does this presentation do?" A successful informative presentation answers the question by sharing information, shaping perceptions, and setting agendas.

Sharing Information and Ideas

One of the goals of many informative presentations is to share information and ideas. Speakers throughout organizations are called on to share with groups of co-workers ideas about new methods, new directions, and proposed changes. Other presentations share the latest information on status quo affairs in the organization, such as sales figures, employee absenteeism, results from market research studies, and budgeting procedures.

Shaping Perceptions

Most people who listen to informative presentations are not simply taking in what the speaker says at face value. As the speaker talks, they constantly react to the material in their own minds. What the speaker says may produce questions, new thoughts, alternative ideas, and disagreement, among other responses. Many informative presentations shape listeners' perceptions by narrowing down possibilities or by defining an issue in a particular way, even though standard persuasion techniques are not used.

Even though from a speaker's viewpoint a presentation may be intended as strictly informative, what a listener does with the information is another matter entirely. Information, then, can be persuasive when the listener acts on it in ways that alter perceptions.

Setting Agendas

In addition to sharing information and ideas and shaping perceptions, informative presentations set agendas for the organization or for subdivisions of it. An informative presentation gives listeners the knowledge they need to set priorities, order their goals, and put ideas in context.

Organizing the Presentation

The pattern by which an informative presentation is organized can help the audience members grasp its content much more readily. The speaker's goal is to choose a method of organization that corresponds to the function of the presentation and content of the material to be presented.

Informative speeches generally fall into one of three major categories: descriptive presentations, demonstrative presentations, or explanatory presentations. In the next sections, we provide suggestions and examples for preparing each type.

Description

Informative presentations that focus on description satisfy the audience members' need for facts, figures, or other data. They answer "what" questions such as:

◆ What government regulations currently affect our operations?

◆ What are the demographics of our membership?

◆ What company library resources are checked out most frequently by our employees?

◆ What types of company-sponsored programs do employees want to participate in?

When a speaker has researched the topic and collected the necessary data for the presentation, he or she must choose a pattern of organization that will enhance the audience members' comprehension and retention of the message. Although there are many ways that one might organize descriptive information, two structural patterns that work especially well for such presentations are the topical pattern and the chronological pattern.

With a *topical* pattern, the main points of the message are organized as parallel elements of the topic itself. Perhaps the most common pattern for organizing presentations, it is useful when describing components of persons, places, things, or processes. Thus, for example, a speaker might use a topical pattern in a presentation on the various departments (such as sales, production, and human resources) that comprise a business organization, the characteristics of an effective supervisor, or reasons for giving a charitable contribution to the United Way.

When using a topical pattern, the sequence of topics is quite important. Presentations that begin with the most important topic and end with the least important topic may lose some audience members' interest along the way. On the other hand, a presentation that begins with the least important topic will have an exceedingly slow start and may fail to catch the audience's interest at all. The most successful topical arrangement is to choose the two most important topics and begin and end with them — doing so creates immediate interest and provides a sense of closure and significance as well.

To illustrate the application of the topical pattern to the task of presenting descriptive information, consider the following outline of a presentation responding to the question "What types of company-sponsored programs do our employees want to participate in?"

Introduction: Briefly orient audience by describing the employee survey, motivate their interest by noting that we plan to act on the information gathered, and achieve rapport by telling a story about various difficulties I encountered while conducting the survey.

I. First main point: The survey results showed that many of you would like programs on the history and current status of the organization.

  A. These topics were ranked highest by survey respondents.
    1. Visual aid: use an overhead to display the survey results (see Figure 13-1).
    2. Your answers have alerted us to the need to keep all lines of communication open.

  B. In response, we are planning exhibits, discussion groups, and more coverage of these issues in company publications.
    1. Our goal is to increase your understanding of where the organization has been and where it is going.
    2. We also hope to provide an open environment in which to discuss issues of importance to all of us.

II. Second main point: You also said you wanted programs on educational topics.

  A. One possibility is a symposium featuring the managers of various departments.
    1. Some topics for symposiums might include a) conducting performance reviews; b) determining when new employees should be hired; c) improving quality control.
    2. Symposiums will allow you to compare how routine tasks are accomplished in other departments.

  B. Another suggestion is to have outside experts speak on such topics as health, safety, nutrition, and eldercare.

III. Third main point: Finally, many of you are interested in getting to know our CEO better.

  A. We would like George Smith to give more frequent presentations to the employees, especially in a small group format.

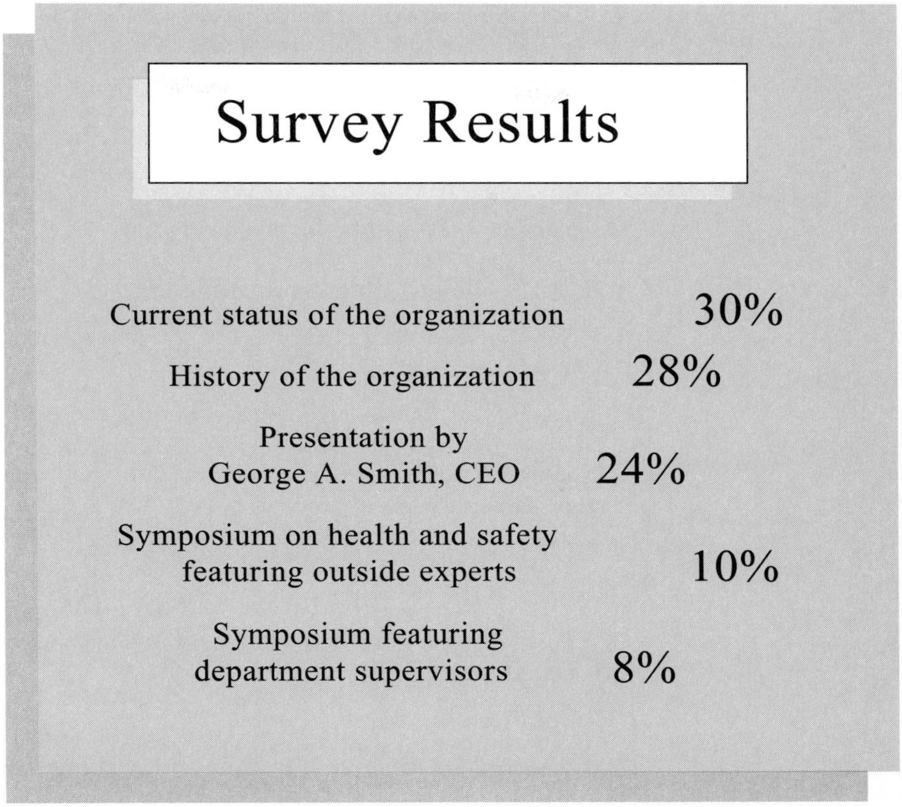

Survey Results

Current status of the organization	30%
History of the organization	28%
Presentation by George A. Smith, CEO	24%
Symposium on health and safety featuring outside experts	10%
Symposium featuring department supervisors	8%

FIGURE 13-1   When using visual aids to present statistics during informative presentations, ensure that percentages add to 100 and that numbers and categories are easily readable. The visual shown here supports the presentation on new employee programs.   Source: Examples of visual aids in Chapters 13 and 14 were created by Erena Rae of Communication Design, Norman, Oklahoma.

B. We are looking into other activities, such as a "Breakfast with the Boss," to promote this interaction.

Conclusion: Briefly summarize survey results and describe the next step in the process of implementing such programs. State the significance of the programs for the company as well as for individual employees.

A second organizational pattern that is well suited to providing description is known as a *chronological* pattern. When using this construction, the presenter organizes the main points of the message in a time-related sequence. The sequence could be highly generalized, for example:

    I. Describe the organization's past use of management by objectives as an approach to conducting appraisal interviews.

   II. Describe the present method of conducting appraisal interviews.

  III. Describe the future plans for revising the organization's approach to appraisal interviews.

The sequence may also be highly specific:

    I. On December 1, the reports came in.

   II. The alterations detailed in the reports were completed by December 4.

  III. We sent out the replacement parts on December 5.

     The chronological pattern is also useful when analyzing a process step by step. Thus, a presentation on how to use a new fax machine might be organized using a chronological pattern, as the following outline shows:

    I. First, place the papers face down onto the feeder.

   II. Second, type in the fax number to which you are sending the material.

  III. Third, press "start."

  IV. Wait for the message "On Line — Receiving" to be displayed.

   V. The pages should begin to move through the feeder.

  VI. Check to be sure that all pages were transmitted.

 VII. Call the receiver if you have doubts about the transmission.

     To illustrate how the chronological pattern may be used for a descriptive informative presentation, consider the following outline of a presentation that compares company sales performance over the last five years.

Introduction: Orient the audience by briefly summarizing the time period to be covered in the presentation, and build motivation and rapport by complimenting the audience members on their hard work and demonstrated success.

    I. First main point: In 1988, we held only 13 percent of the market for specialized testing equipment.

       A. Our major market entry was a portable unit to measure air quality.

       B. We sold an average of 23,000 units per year.

II. Second main point: In 1989, we expanded our product line to include water testing equipment and a new unit to test auto emissions.

   A. Our market share increased to 18 percent.
   B. We opened a regional office in the Northwest.

III. Third main point: In 1990, we began to phase out all harmful chemicals used in our equipment and manufacturing processes as well as to search for environmentally safe alternatives.

   A. At the same time, we maintained our strong sales by benefitting from an increased interest in home water testing.
   B. We sold over 30,000 home testing units.

IV. Fourth main point: In 1991, we had a record $56 million in sales.

   A. Our profit margin increased 8 percent.
   B. We were named one of the top ten small businesses in the region by a major business journal.
   C. We predict even better results for 1992 based on a new unit to test for chemicals in the ground water supply that will be purchased by municipalities.

Conclusion: State the significance of the presentation by summarizing that the company has built its success on developing new products to meet emerging needs, and provide closure by reviewing the outlook for the next year.

In preparing a descriptive presentation, the speaker's purpose is not to persuade, motivate, or change the audience members' minds. The task is to tell the audience "the way it is," allowing listeners to interpret the information as good, bad, neutral, or of crisis potential. The speaker may wish to provide her or his own opinions and comments in a question and answer session following the presentation.

An informative presentation generally does not extrapolate beyond the information being described. Tempting as it may be to interject statements such as "This suggests that . . ." or "When you add this new data to the information you received last week, you will find . . ." or "Although the survey was returned by fewer than 40 percent of the employees, the general trend is . . ." try to refrain from doing so. The purpose of an informative presentation is to do just that: inform! The speaker should present the data at hand in as straightforward a manner as possible.

Demonstration

A demonstration answers "how" questions, such as "How does this work?" or "How does someone or something move from point A to point B?"

Consider the following example of a demonstrative presentation given by a member of the U.S. Postal Service to a group of business leaders who had made complaints about the quality of local mail delivery and handling.

In his presentation, the postal worker demonstrated the numerous checkpoints and distribution centers through which a piece of mail travels before it reaches its destination. He supplemented the demonstration with maps, flow charts, and even photographs of the various locations. He followed the presentation with a question and answer session.

A demonstrative presentation has the potential to work in persuasive ways in the minds of listeners. You can probably see how this presentation, although technically informative, may have shaped the perspective of the audience. The speaker did not announce that he intended to vindicate the postal service, but by demonstrating the many quality checks, special distribution centers, and trained personnel staffing the post offices, he may well have changed some of the audience members' minds about their postal service.

When planning and organizing a demonstrative presentation, a *spatial* or *geographical* pattern of organizing ideas works well. A geographical pattern organizes main points in terms of their physical location, especially in relation to each other. For example, the terms "north," "south," "east," and "west" might be used in a presentation showing the physical layout of a business or the location of famous landmarks, such as the Mall in Washington, D.C.

A spatial pattern shows the physical layout of an object's parts, frequently through such directional cues as "top," "bottom," "outside," "inside," "left," or "right." When presenting a demonstration to an audience, the speaker is often involved in a range of communication from "tell" to "show," as he or she describes where the part is located and then shows the location through a visual aid. Successful spatial demonstrations are often "hands on."

The following excerpt from a presentation given to a computer workshop uses a spatial pattern to demonstrate how to start a computer. The emphasis is on showing the audience members *where* each part of the computer is located.

Introduction: Orient the audience by briefly describing the nature of the computer training workshop. Build audience rapport and motivation by describing my experience in conducting such workshops at many businesses throughout the city.

I. First main point: Start the computer.

    A. Locate the power switch on the left side at the back of the computer.

    B. Move the switch to the "on" position by flicking it down.

    C. Locate the brightness control at the right side of the computer screen (monitor).

    D. Twist the dial to the right or left to obtain a comfortable brightness.

II. Second main point: Use a program disk.

    A. The disk drive is located at the lower right side of the computer.

    B. Insert the disk labeled "Tutorial" into the disk drive (see Figure 13-2).

        1. Be sure to insert the metal end first.

        2. Be sure to insert the label side up.

    C. Read the instructions on the screen.

Although spatial and geographical patterns are most useful when showing how things or places relate to each other in physical space, the pattern of organization for a presentation should be chosen based on the goal of the speech. For example, if the speaker at the computer workshop wanted to inform the audience of possible uses for computers, he or she might choose a topical pattern rather than a geographical pattern. If the goal of the presentation was to inform the audience of the technological advances in a particular component that have occurred over the last three years, he or she might choose a chronological pattern.

Explanation

The third type of informative presentation addresses "why" questions, such as:

◆ Why is our market share declining?

◆ Why are we restructuring the department?

◆ Why do we need to raise membership dues 15 percent by the end of the year?

Each of these topics challenges the speaker to inform the audience and to justify the actions or decisions in question. "Why" questions frequently address controversial issues, and the audience may be predisposed to hostility, anger, or skepticism. Thus, one benefit of an explanatory presentation is to calm the audience. Once the audience members know why a condition exists or an action is being taken, they are more likely to consider it in a rational and calm manner. If an audience is informed, for example, of the specific factors that led to a 15 percent increase in membership dues, they are more likely to accept the increase.

Two patterns of organization are especially well suited to the goal of providing explanation: the cause/effect pattern and the comparison/contrast pattern. Once again, however, we emphasize that the pattern chosen should reflect the speaker's goal, the audience, and the occasion.

FIGURE 13-2   Pictorial representations of components or processes can be used to enhance a demonstration, for example, of how to insert a disk into a computer disk drive. Be careful to avoid overly complex drawings, though.

With a *cause/effect* pattern of organization, the presenter organizes the message around the origins and the results of a series of events. For example, a presentation on the cost of air travel might employ a cause/effect pattern by first noting the rapid rise in the cost of fuel over the winter, resulting in higher operating costs for airlines, and thus causing higher ticket prices.

The presenter might also choose to begin with a description of present conditions (the effects) and then identify and explore the possible causes of the effects. The choice between these approaches can be made based on which element (the cause or the effect) is most familiar to the audience. To illustrate how a cause/effect pattern might be used to explain an event, consider the following excerpt from an outline of a presentation on why membership dues for an organization must be raised 15 percent by the end of the year.

Introduction: Orient the audience by giving a brief overview of the problem, and build rapport by explaining your long involvement with and belief in the organization.

I. First main point (cause): The costs of running the organization continue to rise, and we have had no dues increases for the past two years.

    A. The costs of producing our journal have risen dramatically.

    B. Administrative costs of the office have also increased.

    C. We estimate that our total costs have increased by more than 50 percent (see Figure 13-3).

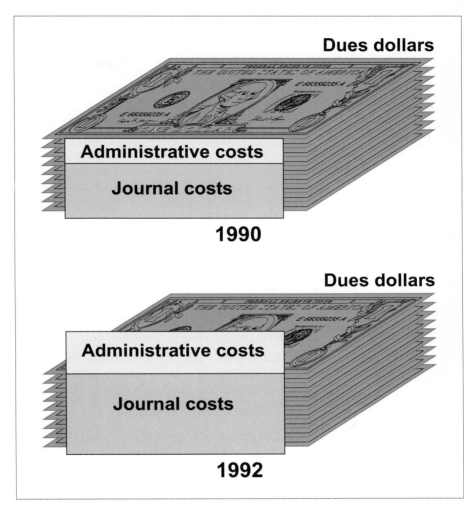

FIGURE 13-3 Comparative statistics are most effective when presented graphically, as this bar graph illustrates. Graph headings should be simple and eye-catching. This visual accompanies the explanatory presentation on dues increases.

II. Second main point (additional cause): We have implemented as many cost-cutting measures as possible during the last two years, allowing us to keep dues at the same amount.

    A. Budgets have been strictly monitored.

    B. We have also eliminated unnecessary spending.

III. Third main point (effect): In light of our increased costs, and having reduced expenditures and eliminated unnecessary spending, it is necessary to find other ways to keep the organization out of debt.

    A. A 15 percent increase in dues will cover our outstanding costs.

    B. We will begin a membership drive to increase our total dues revenue.

    C. We will look into fund-raising ideas to increase the amount of money in our operating budget.

A second way to organize an explanatory presentation is the *comparison/contrast* pattern, which identifies a familiar situation and then relates it to an unfamiliar situation that is either similar (for comparison) or different (for contrast). Consider the following outline of a presentation given to a group of management trainees in a large retail store.

Introduction: Orient the audience by briefly describing my role in the training process; provide rapport by noting that I went through the training program four years ago.

I. First main point (familiar situation): Many of you are recent college graduates. Think back to your first few weeks as freshmen.

    A. You probably didn't know many other students.

    B. You probably got lost on campus more than a few times.

    C. Slowly you learned how to get around, study, organize your time, and set priorities.

II. Second main point (comparison): You will find many similarities as new employees here at Martingale Company.

    A. As the training program progresses, you will learn skills.

        1. Seminars on public speaking and interviewing are offered.

        2. Specialized training programs for the international department will be given.

    B. You will also get to know the other trainees and supervisors.

        1. Do not hesitate to ask questions.

        2. You can learn a lot by informal communication in addition to the training program.

Conclusion: Emphasize significance of the training program and provide closure by thanking the audience for attending.

As you can see, the organization of an informative speech is an important tool to ensure that the audience members understand and remember your presentation. A logical and appropriate pattern boosts the impact of any informative presentation.

Typical Formats

Formats are the structures or settings in which informative presentations are given. The format may reflect the setting, the audience's needs, the speaker's goal, or a combination of the three. Formats for informational presentations are meant to maximize the efficient transmission of information to audience members.

Briefings are relatively short presentations that inform an audience about a particular event. General Norman Schwarzkopf was known for his incisive and humorous briefings during the 1991 war against Iraq.

Reports simply give an account of the status quo. Presentations that provide data such as the amount of money remaining in the budget and profit and loss figures are good examples of reports.

Training presentations educate listeners to help them improve specific skills. Presentations that train as a format typically provide listeners with background information, introduce specific principles, and then follow through with skill practice, which the listeners perform.

For each of these formats, the presentation is only as good as the preparation that precedes it. A strong presentation depends on the "inside" (an appropriate pattern and effective supporting materials, introduction, and conclusion) as well as the "outside" (the format).

Training presentations, like this "dress for success" seminar, rely on visual aids to increase audience understanding of the message.

Guidelines for a Successful Presentation

Now that you have an understanding of patterns and formats for informative presentations, it is important to attend to situational details.

Advance planning and preparation are the greatest defense against elements in the situation that can adversely affect your presentation. Put this book down for a moment, and think about some of the *worst* possible things that could happen to you during a presentation. Next to each of these, jot down what you could do in advance to prevent them from ruining your presentation. You probably came up with as good a list as we can. Nevertheless, here are some guidelines for ensuring successful presentations that we think are particularly worthy of consideration.

Analyze Potential Sources of Noise

Noise is anything that interferes with the communication process. Noise can occur at any time in the process. For purposes of illustration, let us look at three potential levels on which noise can occur: in the transmission of information from speaker to listener (i.e., does the listener even receive or hear the information?), in the comprehension of information (i.e., once the information is received and heard, does the listener understand the information the same way the speaker intended?), and in the pragmatics of information (i.e., once the information is heard and understood, does the listener do what the speaker wants?).

Note that these three levels of noise are hierarchical. Success on a lower level must be achieved before a higher level can even be an issue. A listener must hear information before he or she can understand it! Similarly, a listener must understand the information before acting on it.

A speaking setting actually has three potential sources of noise — physical, physiological, and psychological. Physical noise refers to distractions in the environment of the presentation. Does the room in which you will speak require a microphone for you to be heard clearly? Are there windows that will invite listeners to daydream or not pay attention to you? These are just two possible sources of physical noise.

There is no reason to find out about these problems in the midst of your presentation. Scouting out the room before you start and making appropriate adjustments are well worth your time.

Physiological noise comes from competing personal needs the listener may have. For example, is the listener too hot or too cold? Thirsty? Tired? Think of times when you have been uncomfortable as an audience member. Did you really pay attention to the speaker? All you probably thought about was when the next break was scheduled.

By satisfying listeners' physiological needs as much as possible, the speaker can increase listeners' attention. Adjusting the temperature in the room the night before you are to present can be helpful. Arranging for pitchers of water and snacks such as fresh fruit or candy can alleviate thirst or hunger. Planning breaks at strategic times can enable listeners to digest what they have just heard and ready themselves for the information to come.

Psychological noise includes internal distractions within the mind of the listener. For example, if the listener is concerned about what he is wearing tonight, what she may say when she has to speak tomorrow, or whether the spouse picked up the kids from school on time, that listener is not listening to you!

The best way to overcome psychological noise is to make sure that your presentation is more interesting and captivating than anything else the listener may prefer to think about. This is no easy task. But by using a range of voice inflections and pacing, providing a variety of supporting materials, and incorporating visual aids, you will have a much better chance of obtaining and maintaining the audience's attention.

The general point is that you as the presenter can and should control the circumstances in which you speak. Planning in advance and overcoming barriers that can create noise are crucial for your success as a speaker.

Adapt to Your Listeners

One common mistake made by beginning speakers is to assume that the *same speech* can be given to different audiences. Although the same *topic* can be presented to an infinite number of audiences, without adapting the material from group to group, speakers can quite easily fail because the audience will not perceive their presentation as relevant.

Adaptation does not mean starting over. The same main points, basic premises, and even data or evidence may be quite applicable in every group you talk with. But examples, illustrations, case studies, or incidents usually require adaptation to the particular group.

Consider: an example that employees in an accounting department may find relevant and understandable may make no sense to employees in personnel. A brief reference to an incident (such as the Korean War) that is relevant to a group whose ages coincide with that conflict may be meaningless to an audience composed of younger people. Discussing the merits of investing in company stocks and bonds may be exciting to a group of executives but depressing to a group of hourly workers whose every dollar is spent even before it is made.

The successful speaker adapts the material of the presentation according to the audience's needs and requirements. There are actually three levels of adaptation: knowledge, interest, and acceptance. In terms of *knowledge* level, the two basic extremes are audiences whose members are well informed versus those whose members are entirely uninformed. The differences in adaptation between these two audiences may be obvious to you. With an uninformed audience, you are obliged to provide more background material, define terms carefully, and link the material in the presentation to already known material. With an informed audience, you can assume more and deemphasize the three preceding factors. Indeed, if you emphasize background material, term definition, and linkage of material with an informed audience, the participants may feel insulted or bored!

The *interest* level ranges from high initial interest to no interest at all. Some listeners, for example, may find any topic related to microcomputers fascinating but be completely uninterested in topics related to plant safety. Uninterested listeners will not meet any of your objectives for the presentation, whether they are to discover, learn, laugh, or review. If audience members are not interested, they will not listen; if they do not listen, they will not understand; and if they do not understand, your objective will not be met.

What are some ways that you can facilitate audience interest? Look at some of these lines from actual speeches given in businesses and organi-

Interact!

In large businesses, informative presentations are rarely given without visual aids. This exercise is designed to give you practice in constructing visual aids for an informative presentation.

A company is relocating its headquarters to a new building in the city in about six months and will occupy five floors of the building. Planning committees have been assigned to each of the floors to decide how they should be organized. Each floor has two restrooms, two break rooms, fifteen cubicle offices and ten enclosed offices, two large conference rooms, four small conference rooms, two storerooms, and eight closets. Senior managers are willing to spend money on renovations if they understand that the changes will result in increased productivity, morale, and effective communication. The following departments have been assigned to each floor:

1. First floor — personnel (ten employees), information services (ten employees responsible for maintaining the computer network and training employees on new computer applications), mail room (five employees)

2. Second floor — office services (three employees responsible for purchasing supplies and supervising maintenance), senior management (seven employees), chief executive officer and staff (three employees), internal communication (five employees who produce the company newsletter, magazine, and plan events), planning and finance (seven employees responsible for developing long-term organizational goals)

3. Third floor — public relations (ten employees), marketing (ten employees)

4. Fourth floor — research and development (twenty-five employees)

5. Fifth floor — research and development (ten employees), accounting (five employees), payroll (three employees), legal services (four employees), inventory (five employees)

(Production, manufacturing, and distribution are done at regional branches)

The class can work on the project in groups of three to five people. Each group plays the role of a planning committee, which must decide "who goes where and why" and present the information to management. In your presentation, you may need diagrams, drawings, tables, floor plans, and so on. Use your imagination. Each committee member delivers one portion of the presentation to senior management (the other class members). You must construct appropriate visual aids to back up all decisions. Do not limit yourself to only one type of visual aid; select the methods that best meet the objective of your presentation. The actual team presentation should take approximately twenty minutes.

After each team's presentation, discuss these questions with the class.

1. Given the team's objective and specific proposals, were effective visual aids employed? If not, what are some other alternatives?

2. Did each visual aid support the point for which it was intended? Was it truly an "aid," or did it become the presentation itself?

3. Were the design and substance of each visual aid effective? What were some of the strengths and shortcomings of each?

4. How well did each team member follow the presentation techniques outlined in Chapter 12 for using visual aids? What suggestions can you make to help each participant to improve?

zations. Would they capture your interest? (If not, what are some that would?)

◆ "Have you ever wondered how successful people choose which stocks and bonds to buy?"

◆ "If I could tell you how to get a day's worth of work finished in half a day, would you be interested?"

◆ "In the next ten minutes, I will outline a new program that will significantly increase almost all the benefits that you as an employee of this company can receive."

Successful informative presentations have one characteristic in common. They all give audience members a reason to listen. They connect with needs or values of audience members and motivate their curiosity.

The *acceptance* level comprises the audience members' preset attitudes toward the topic, which may range from favorable (they are likely to agree or react positively) to unfavorable (they are likely to disagree or react negatively). Audiences that you suspect will be unfavorably disposed toward your topic must be treated more carefully than those that are favorably disposed. For example, when the director of personnel for a large corporation called the division managers together and showed them the compensation levels that would be used to set raises for the next year, she realized she needed to prepare for a negative reaction from her audience. Although the presentation was informative, the topic was unlikely to be viewed favorably by the audience, as raises had been quite low over the last several years.

In this case, the personnel director began by giving an overview of the company's pay position for the previous five years, emphasizing that compared with others, the company had kept pace with similar firms. She then noted the company's loss in market share, profit, and volume for the previous year. Following the presentation of this background information, she showed the managers the new compensation levels. Even though the news was no different after the introductory material than it would have been without it, the background information set the stage and provided a rationale for the rates. To have simply dived in and said, "Here are the rates for next year," would have produced a considerable amount of hostility.

Shared Perspectives

In every informative presentation, the data come from somewhere! Sharing with your listeners the origins of these data and providing a perspective on them are good ways to reduce unanswered questions in listeners' minds. Specific ways of doing this vary with topic and context, but they include sharing with your audience how certain numbers were figured, the source from which information was derived, how certain conclusions were drawn, where some possible problems are, and so forth.

A shared perspective benefits from including listeners' experiences and viewpoints as well. The more you link your message with what the audience already knows, the more successful you will be.

Shared perspective benefits from frequent use of *analogies*. Analogies compare two items and in essence argue that what is true in one case is also true in the other. You have heard speakers draw analogies between two time periods, two states, two presidential administrations, and even two families.

Analogies are quite useful in an informative presentation. If the audience is knowledgeable in one subject area and you are introducing new material, you can use an analogy from that area to explain how the new information is "just like what you have already heard before" or "very similar to the way we have discussed this in the past."

Shared perspective also is increased by avoiding jargon as much as possible. For example, communication specialists call a student who has a great deal of anxiety about giving a public presentation "high comm app's." To those who have not taken a communication course, communication specialists' use of this term may conjure up any number of confusing images. Confusion, misunderstanding, and resentment can result when jargon is introduced to listeners. If you must use jargon, define it so that you ensure audience understanding. A shared perspective facilitates the transfer and acceptance of information between speaker and listener.

Additional Hints

Translating ideas into clear and attractive forms is an increasingly important challenge for members of the business community. In addition to the techniques already presented, here are some additional, general hints for increasing your confidence and skill level as a speaker.[7]

1. When you are speaking informatively, think of how you became interested in your topic, and build your audience's motivation to listen by recapturing for them your own initial experience.

2. Oral rehearsal is especially important in an informative speech because you can never be really sure that you understand a concept until you hear yourself explain it.

3. Do not become overly specific too early in an informative speech because listeners forget foreign details easily; concentrate on explaining one central feature of your concept.

4. Try to recall the specific sequence of events that caused you suddenly to understand the topic you will be discussing; try leading listeners down the same path you took.

5. Dictionary definitions of key terms are rarely helpful in an informative speech because listeners need more fully amplified and more colorful explanations of a concept.

6. Long quotations from expert sources may be lacking in flair and clarity; oftentimes, you will have to supplement such remarks with your own better adapted paraphrases.

7. Each major section of a speech outline should contain a minimum of one extended example and two or more brief examples if a concept is to be truly clarified for others.

8. We strongly advise preparing a sentence outline for every speech you make, although you may choose to use a shorter version of this outline when actually delivering your speech.

9. Put the burden of proof on the use of visual aids (that is, carefully assess their potential to enhance your presentation) because their distracting capacities can outweigh their helpfulness in clarifying ideas.

10. Remember this proposition above all others: if there is any chance that listeners can misunderstand you, they will.

Summary

Informative speaking is an increasingly common form of presentation and one that most businesspeople will have to engage in at one time or another. The successful informative presentation shares traits with other kinds of presentations: it identifies the main points to be shared with an audience, it uses supporting materials to elaborate these points and increase their credibility, it presents a total message, and it is delivered in a style appropriate to the audience and its concerns.

Although informative presentations have always been a part of business life, the shift in our society away from a manufacturing base and toward an information base has changed the nature of informative presentations. Where once they were addressed to a homogeneous audience with fairly narrow concerns, they now find audiences whose compositions, and corresponding interests and needs, run the gamut of ethnic, economic, age, and cultural possibilities. At the same time, workers in general are more independent than their predecessors and expect work to provide them with more than just a paycheck. The end result of these changes is that speakers have more topics to choose from, more techniques at their command, and more need of comprehensive knowledge about the make-up of any particular audience to be successful.

An informative presentation usually has one (or more) of three functions: to share information, shape perception, or set agendas. Likewise, the pattern of a presentation reflects its function: is the presentation designed to describe, demonstrate, or explain? Possible patterns include topical, chronological, spatial/geographical, cause/effect, and comparison/contrast. Presentations also take different formats; among these are briefings, reports, and training sessions.

Once a speaker has decided on the appropriate function, organization, and format of the presentation, the work of ensuring the success of the presentation begins. To do so, the speaker is wise to follow several principles. First, analyze and prepare for potential sources of noise (physical, physiological, and psychological). Second, adapt to the listeners. Successful adaptation requires discovery of each audience's knowledge, interest, and acceptance levels. Third, work toward a shared perspective with audience members by disclosing where information came from and using analogies to reach the listeners.

A speaker can also increase his or her confidence and skill level by rehearsing the speech, avoiding simplistic dictionary definitions that are neither colorful nor broad enough, giving sufficient examples of major points, and using visual aids so as to minimize their capacity to distract the audience. Although these techniques do not guarantee that every speaker will finally come to public speaking with ease and self-assurance, they can help all potential public speakers realize the extent of their own resources and how to use them.

Discussion

1. How has the changing nature of society and the business environment affected the purpose and effectiveness of informative presentations?

2. Why are informative prsentations useful? Describe and give examples of three major functions of informative presentations.

3. What is a topical pattern of organization? What types of messages would work well with this pattern?

4. How is a demonstrative presentation organized? What are its strengths and possible weaknesses?

5. What kinds of questions are addressed in an explanatory presentation? What additional demands are made on the speaker in an explanatory presentation?

6. What are the three categories of audience adaptation that the informative presentation should take into account? Describe how each might affect the success of the presentation.

7. How does shared perspective (including both the presenter's and the audience's perspective) contribute to increased audience understanding and acceptance of the message? What are some techniques to encourage a shared perspective?

Activities

1. Pick a topic and outline suitable main points for each of the following organizational patterns:
   a. chronological
   b. topical
   c. spatial/geographical
   d. cause/effect
   e. comparison/contrast

2. Use one of the outlines you prepared for question 1, and be prepared to share some appropriate transitions from one point to another.

3. Prepare an outline for a briefing (on a topic of your choice) to be presented to members of the press.

4. Analyze an informative presentation you have heard recently. How did the speaker organize the information, adapt to the audience, and share perspectives to make the speech a success?

Notes _____

1. P. Galagan, "Tapping the Power of a Diverse Workforce," *Training and Development Journal* 45 (1991): 38–44.

2. G. P. Huber and R. L. Daft, "The Information Environments of Organizations," in F. M. Jablin, L. L. Putnam, K. H. Robert, and L. M. Porter (eds.), *Handbook of Organizational Communication: An Interdisciplinary Perspective* (Newbury Park, Calif.: Sage, 1987), pp. 130–164.

3. F. W. Wallin, "Universities for a Small Planet—A Time to Reconceptualize Our Role," *Change* (March 1983): 7–8.

4. J. D. Osborn, L. Moran, E. Musselwhite, J. H. Zenger, and C. Perrin, *Self-Directed Work Teams: The New American Challenge* (Homewood, Ill.: Business One Irwin, 1990).

5. J. Fiala, "Citation Analysis Controls the Information Flood," *Thermochimica Acta* 110 (1987): 11.

6. A. Otto, "Getting Ahead in the Paper Chase," *Prepared Foods* 160 (1991): 30–32.

7. R. P. Hart, G. W. Friedrich, and B. Brummett, *Public Communication,* 2nd ed. (New York: Harper & Row, 1983), p. 141.

Chapter 14

*P*ersuasive Presentations

OBJECTIVES

After working through this chapter, you will be able to:

1. Describe the importance of persuasive presentations in business

2. Identify the major functions of persuasive presentations

3. Select and organize supporting materials for persuasive presentations

4. Choose an appropriate format for the presentation

5. Understand the process by which persuasion occurs

6. Use a variety of resources to ensure a successful persuasive presentation

As important as informative presentations are in the business world, persuasive presentations are even more prevalent. Persuasive presentations identify and promote ideas and options to guide listeners toward the course of action desired by the speaker.

One reason for their frequency is that many persuasive presentations occur informally. Employees further their views, ideas, or suggestions in meetings, in one-to-one discussions with a supervisor, or even in social groups in addition to making formal presentations. Nevertheless, the basic resources for persuasion remain constant, although they must be adapted to the particular audience or setting.

Persuasive presentations incorporate the skills needed to prepare an informative presentation. Although the goal of a persuasive presentation may be to reinforce (or change) the audience members' beliefs or to act on the speaker's suggestions, informing the audience is one component of that process. Thus, this chapter builds on the skills introduced in Chapters 12 and 13.

Functions of Persuasive Presentations

Persuasive presentations perform one or more of the following functions: 1) to *reinforce* the listeners' beliefs, attitudes; or values; 2) to *refute* or disprove an idea or belief held by the listeners; 3) to *change* the listeners' beliefs, actions, or values; and 4) to *move* the listeners to action. As with informative presentations, the pattern used to organize the information in a persuasive presentation is itself a tool for achieving the presenter's goal. Thus, we look at both functions and patterns for persuasive presentations in the next sections.

Reinforcement

Many persuasive presentations are designed to maintain the status quo by reinforcing audience members' decisions, actions, or opinions, especially if the presenter believes that they are under attack or are in danger of being changed or rendered obsolete. To make such a presentation persuasive, the speaker must show that existing favorable conditions are in danger of becoming nonexistent or unfavorable.

This approach can be used to achieve a variety of goals: alerting a sales force to the need to reverse a trend toward providing less personalized service to clients; recommending to a planning committee to "get back to basics" and concentrate on core markets; or even petitioning a school board to back away from a proposed change in the process of textbook selection. When organizing the presentation, the speaker must first show the benefits of the present condition, then describe the threat to the status quo, and finally reemphasize the worth and viability of the present condition.

The following example shows how these steps are accomplished. It is an outline of a presentation made by a teacher to a school board that was considering legislation allowing parents and community officials to join the process of selecting books for the school system. [*Note:* After each main point in the outline (and in other outlines in the chapter), we suggest options for locating and incorporating appropriate supporting materials.[1]]

Introduction: Motivate the audience to listen by recounting a similar situation in Fargo, North Dakota; orient the audience by stating my opinion that book selection should be the responsibility of teachers and school officials; build rapport by describing my experience as a teacher in the school system.

I. First main point: Although selecting textbooks has always been the duty of school officials, parental and community intervention in book selection is gradually increasing.

   A. Testimony: a quotation from an urban history or history of education textbook can be used to describe the historical role of teachers and school officials in textbook selection.

   B. Statistics: statistics from a contemporary newspaper or journal such as *USA Today* can provide evidence that intervention in the selection process is increasing.

II. Second main point: The problem with such intervention is that parents and community leaders often cannot agree (with each other or with the school board) on the proper curricula and objectives for students.

   A. Example: use an illustration from a newsmagazine, newspaper, or education journal to highlight a similar situation in another city.

   B. Example: provide a contrasting example of a city that has successfully avoided the problem.

III. Third main point: Parental and community interference in the selection process may potentially limit learning.

   A. Statistics: cite research done in this area, which may be found in an academic journal such as *Educational Psychologist* or *American Educational Research Journal*.

   B. Visual: use an overhead or large chart to represent graphically the effect of interference on the student (Figure 14-1).

IV. Fourth main point: Parental input into textbook selection restricts student exposure to a variety of viewpoints.

   A. Explanation: explain what "restriction" means in terms of a well-rounded education.

   B. Testimony: quote a well-known and well-respected educational leader who disagrees with restrictions on learning.

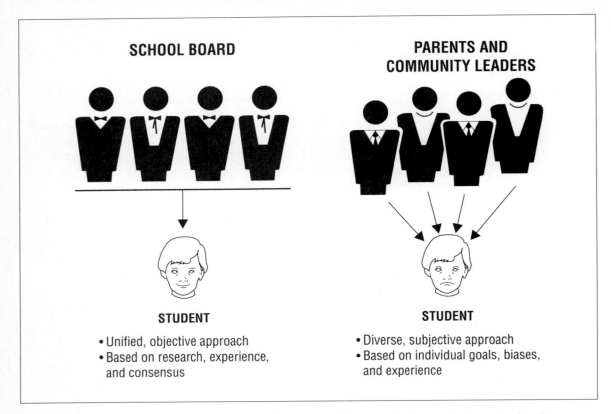

FIGURE 14-1   *This visual enhances the impact of the speaker's words by using familiar images to represent the negative effect of a change in the status quo.*

Conclusion: Ask for the school board to reject legislation (keep the status quo) based on these arguments. State the significance of doing so by noting that one role of education is to give students the means and information to decide among a variety of divergent perspectives. Close with testimony: quote students from my classes who are eager to learn and explore.

Refutation

A second type of persuasive presentation works to show listeners that a belief, event, or situation is misunderstood or misconceptualized so that the audience will accept a new or different interpretation of it. By effectively *refuting*, or arguing against, the existing perception, the speaker can correct or clarify the audience members' thinking on the subject and persuade them to accept her or his interpretation of it.

A refutative presentation generally begins by exposing the misunder-standing or incorrect assumption, then provides several points that disprove it or show that it is at best a partial truth. The following outline of a presentation given by a financial analyst to a consumer group shows an example of how this can be achieved.

Introduction: Orient the audience members by welcoming them to the presentation; motivate the audience by reading a quote about inflation from a newsmagazine; build rapport by explaining that the purpose of the presentation is to help audience members understand that many interrelated factors cause inflation.

I. First main point: Many Americans blame the government for spiraling inflation.

    A. Statistics: use statistics (which can be located through indexes such as the *Gallup Index*) to show that the public sees government responsibility for causing inflation.

    B. Example: give an account of government spending on seemingly obscure or wasteful projects, such as studying methane production in cows.

II. Second main point: In reality, one of the major causes of inflation is consumers' erratic spending patterns.

    A. Testimony: quote a respected economist on the subject.

    B. Visual: use a graph or chart to show the relationship between consumer spending and inflation during the past ten years.

III. Third main point: Demands for higher wages without strong growth in the gross national product (GNP) may contribute to inflation as well.

    A. Statistics: cite the recent slowdown in growth of the GNP. A newspaper such as the *Wall Street Journal* can provide statistics on the GNP.

    B. Example: journals such as the *Journal of Human Resources* and the *Industrial and Labor Relations Review* may provide examples of wage negotiations in a range of industries.

IV. Fourth main point: Unwise investment, both by individuals and by banking institutions, is another problem.

    A. Testimony: quote from noted financial analysts to show that many investments offering quick, high returns are deceptive and possibly fraudulent.

    B. Explanation: provide a brief explanation of investment practices in the savings and loan industry and their results.

Conclusion: Summarize the complex nature of inflation; state the significance by noting that understanding is the first step toward tackling the problem; ask for questions.

Promoting Change

Persuasive presentations that call for a change in audience members' beliefs, attitudes, actions, or values go one step farther than those that refute existing beliefs or values. The speaker attempts to *redirect* the course of the listeners' thought or behavior.

When organizing the presentation, the presenter first shows the prevalent belief or action. The successive main points provide reasons audience members should adopt a new belief or change their behavior. The presenter does this by citing the advantages of the new belief/behavior or the disadvantages that will occur by holding to the old belief/behavior. The following example is excerpted from an outline of a presentation given to several groups of executives at a small department store.

Introduction: Orient the audience to the reason for the presentation by citing declining sales figures; motivate the audience to listen by telling the story of a customer who was surprised to find an item *not* on sale; build rapport by noting my recent participation in a national promotional convention where alternative techniques for sales were discussed.

I.   First main point: We currently hold sales in practically every department of our stores on a monthly basis.

A.   Explanation: describe the practice of monthly sales.
B.   Explanation: use an article from the company newsletter to summarize why we have adhered to the policy.

II. Second main point: We need to change our policy, for several reasons. One is that sales do not necessarily increase customer traffic.

A.   Statistics: specialized periodicals such as *Sales Promotion Monitor* and *Shopper Report* may contain research data in this area.
B.   Example: describe an informal study I did over the last three months that showed nearly constant traffic, regardless of the sales.

III. Third main point: Frequent sales generally do not increase a store's volume of sales.

A.   Visual: display a key quote from a professional journal such as *Advertising Age* that supports this position (Figure 14-2).
B.   Statistics: note that statistics provided by our accounting department show that volume varies seasonally, but the pattern is not influenced by our sales.

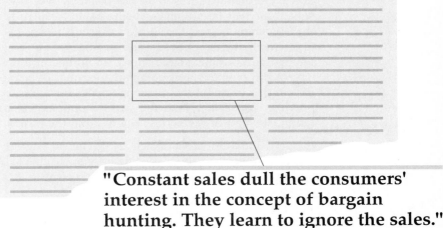

AD REVIEW

Study: Customer Traffic Not Increased by Frequent Sales

"Constant sales dull the consumers' interest in the concept of bargain hunting. They learn to ignore the sales."

FIGURE 14-2   The testimony of a well respected individual can persuade listeners to accept a change in their beliefs or actions. A visual that displays testimony as the presenter speaks it reinforces its effect by using multiple channels.

IV. Fourth main point: We should consider changes in our sales policy that will help us achieve the goal of sales — more customers making more purchases.

  A. We need to take advantage of natural trends in buying (such as seasonal trends).

  B. We need to hold less frequent, better advertised sales at strategic points throughout the year.

Note that the fourth main point *restates the need for change* while *providing suggestions* to accomplish the change. Such an ending is more effective than simply giving the listeners several reasons why their current belief or practice is not the best one. By providing an alternate belief or plan of action, the speaker primes the audience to act on her or his suggestion, as we discuss in the next section.

Call to Action

The main purpose of many persuasive presentations is to get listeners to act on the advice or direction of the speaker. This type of presentation differs slightly from one in which the speaker's goal is to bring about a change in the audience members' actions — an effective approach for *initiating* audience action differs from one meant to *modify* it.

The first main point of a presentation that calls listeners to action identifies the problem or shortcoming that exists. The second main point, however, demonstrates that the problem will not be solved, cannot be solved, or that no attempt is being made to solve it at the current time. In the remaining points, the speaker presents her or his proposed solution and urges the audience to act on the suggestion.

The following example shows an outline of a presentation made by the payroll director at a large company to groups of employees who had enrolled in a series of seminars on investment. Because the employees had little previous experience with the various options for investment, this presentation, the first of the series, begins from the basics.

Introduction: Orient audience by giving a brief overview of what each lecture will contain and a specific preview of this first lecture; motivate and build rapport by giving some examples of how listeners will benefit from acting on what they learn in this presentation.

I. First main point: The number of savings bonds purchased has steadily declined, costing the country billions of dollars in liquid capital.

   A. Explanation: describe what a savings bond is and how it works.
   B. Explanation: give a definition of "liquid capital" in mainstream terms.

II. Second main point: Due to widespread misconceptions about the nature of savings bonds, they are often overlooked by beginning investors.

   A. Example: illustrate the misconceptions of our own work force by giving several brief examples of employees' attitudes toward savings bonds.
   B. Testimony: cite an expert, such as a federal banking official, on reasons for the declining interest in savings bonds and the potential negative results for the economy.

III. Third main point: Savings bonds provide a good yield at low risk, contribute to national growth and stability, and have always been an excellent way to start investing.

   A. Explanation: define the terms "yield" and "risk" in mainstream terms.

      B. Visual: show an old advertisement for savings bonds to demonstrate their role in building the country (Figure 14-3).

      C. Statistics: a financial journal or periodical such as the *Wall Street Journal* may be a source for statistics on comparing yields and calculating risks.

IV. Fourth main point: Buying savings bonds is very simple to do — act now to prepare for the future!

      A. Pick up one of the forms I've provided explaining how to buy savings bonds.

      B. Make an appointment with me to discuss options for similar investments.

Conclusion: Reemphasize the significance of starting a savings plan now and the ease of starting with savings bonds; provide closure by thanking the audience for their attention and offering to make appointments to answer specific questions.

    The last point in the presentations gives listeners directions for taking the action by the speaker. This tactic is very effective, because by providing listeners with the direct means to act on your suggestions, you greatly increase the chances that they will do so.

Typical Formats

Persuasive presentations in a business or organization context can take a number of forms. Any of the purposes we have just discussed can be realized through these forms. Three of the most commonly used formats include sales, proposals, and motivational sessions.

Sales

Selling products, services, or ideas occupies a great deal of time in organizational life. In addition to one-on-one selling opportunities, in many cases sales presentations are formal events in which a speaker in the front of a room gives a presentation utilizing visual aids and the audience is seated in an organized fashion.

    Note that in sales presentations the speaker may be required to reinforce a belief in his or her product if the organization is about to discontinue using it. The speaker may need to change the attitude of a group of buyers toward the product line. Or the speaker may attempt to close a sale at the time of the presentation by convincing the audience to purchase the product. Thus, a sales presentation frequently will incorporate several major functions of persuasion.

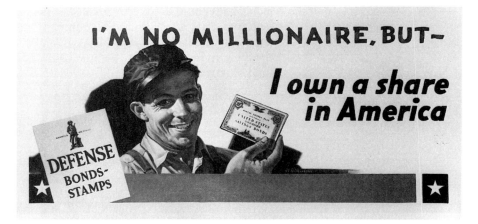

FIGURE 14-3   *Visual aids may use highly symbolic images to appeal to audience members' deeply held values and beliefs. This visual lends credibility to the speaker's call to buy savings bonds by showing the historical importance of that action.*

Proposals

Businesses and professional organizations are frequently inundated with proposals that must be acted on. The choice of action often depends on the persuasiveness with which a proposal's backer presents it. Even when the speaker succeeds, proposals are often modified from their original form before they are accepted.

Here are a few examples of proposals that might be presented to business and professional audiences:

◆ A plan to upgrade all personal computers in the corporate headquarters office

◆ A budget for a ten-day "outward bound" training program for corporate executives at a remote site

◆ A schedule for moving the home office of a company from one building to another

◆ A method by which an employee's grievance may be settled without incurring costly court proceedings

◆ A plan to employ a work force representing greater multicultural diversity

Proposals can be designed to reinforce beliefs, change beliefs, or induce action. For example, a presentation by a marketing manager may be designed to reinforce a plan to print new brochures despite some disagreement or criticism of the plan. A presentation by a personnel administrator may attempt to persuade audience members to reverse their decision on allocating funding for professional travel. Or a presentation may call for the listeners to sign their benefits contracts or return borrowed equipment.

Motivational Sessions

Persuasive presentations can certainly be motivational. You may be familiar with some of the great motivational speakers of our time, including Tom Peters, author of *In Search of Excellence;* Zig Ziglar, from *See You at the Top* fame; and Lou Holtz of Notre Dame football.[2] Each of these speakers is enthusiastic and has a strong delivery, as demonstrated by the ways they vary inflection, emphasis, rate, volume, and gestures. Furthermore, their messages are typically upbeat, filled with inspiring words that breed confidence in the listener.

Many motivational speakers use persuasion to convince an audience to change its attitude so that each person becomes better, healthier, or happier.

Many persuasive presentations take place informally, even on a one-to-one basis. How many resources and strategies for persuasion can you identify in this photo of a recruiting officer's presentation to a potential enlistee?

Some attempt to convince listeners to lose weight, invest money, perform a task better, manage employees differently, or be more enthusiastic communicators.

Basic Resources for Persuasion

Persuasion is not just form and content; successful presentations in businesses and professional organizations take advantage of resources. We now turn our attention to some of the resources that are available to you as a persuasive speaker.

Formal and informal persuasive presentations depend heavily on the audience's perception of the speaker's credibility. Here, a sales representative uses a variety of supporting materials to persuade potential customers to try the product she is promoting.

The Listeners' Perspective

As in informative presentations, audience analysis and adaptation are the key to success in a persuasive presentation. Nevertheless, the audience is considered from a slightly different angle. The power in a persuasive presentation resides in an analysis of what makes the listeners "tick" — knowing what triggers the listeners is crucial. Table 14-1 shows a variety of methods for connecting with listeners, as opposed to focusing on the speaker's needs and personal interests.

More than just sharing perspective as in an informative presentation, a persuasive presenter must take a listener's perspective because he or she is asking more of the audience, be it a change in beliefs or a call to action. Consider Martin Luther King's famous address in 1963, in which he repeatedly chanted before each point, "I have a dream."

> I say to you today, my friends, so even though we face the difficulties of today and tomorrow, I still have a dream. It is a dream deeply rooted in the American dream.

TABLE 14-1
Speaker versus Listener Perspective

Speaker Perspective	Listener Perspective
Speaker uses arguments and appeals that are pleasing to him or her.	Speaker uses arguments and appeals that are pleasing to the audience.
Speaker uses style and delivery that are natural for him or her.	Speaker uses style and delivery that will be effective and liked by the audience.
Speaker says what makes him or her feel better.	Speaker says what will bring the desired response from the audience.
Speaker views the situation from his or her point of view.	Speaker views the situation from the audience's point of view.
Speaker selects sources and authorities that are his or her favorites.	Speaker selects sources and authorities that are likely to be acceptable to the listeners.
Speaker dresses to please himself or herself.	Speaker dresses in accordance with the tastes and preferences of the audience.
Speaker assumes others share his or her beliefs, attitudes, and values.	Speaker searches for the beliefs, attitudes, and values that are held by the audience.

> I have a dream that one day this nation will rise up and live out the true meaning of its creed: "We hold these truths to be self-evident; that all men are created equal."
>
> I have a dream that one day on the red hills of Georgia the sons of former slaves and the sons of former slaveowners will be able to sit down together at the table of brotherhood; I have a dream —
>
> That one day even the state of Mississippi, a state sweltering with the heat of injustice, sweltering with the heat of oppression, will be transformed into an oasis of freedom and justice; I have a dream —
>
> That my four little children will one day live in a nation where they will not be judged by the color of their skin but by the content of their character; I have a dream today.
>
> I have a dream that one day down in Alabama, with its vicious racists, with its governor having his lips dripping with the words of interposition and nullification, one day right there in Alabama little black boys and black girls will be able to join hands with little white boys and white girls as sisters and brothers; I have a dream today.
>
> I have a dream that one day every valley shall be exalted; every hill and mountain shall be made low, and rough places will be made plain and crooked places will be made straight, and the glory of the Lord shall be revealed, and all flesh shall see it together.[3]

When a speaker encounters an unsympathetic, or even hostile, audience, other adaptations are necessary. Some of the actions a speaker can take are (a) appeal to the audience for a chance to explain his or her side of the story; (b) begin the presentation with points that reflect shared values, attitudes, and beliefs on which to base later points of disagreement; (c) minimize the differences and maximize the similarities in opinion between speaker and audience; and (d) shorten the gap between points, thus rendering it more difficult for the audience to interrupt or react in unfavorable ways. When Anson Mount, manager of public relations for *Playboy*, agreed to speak on the merits of the "Playboy philosophy" as part of a seminar sponsored by the Christian Life Commission of the Southern Baptist Convention at its meeting in Atlanta, Georgia, in 1970, he certainly needed to go farther than merely sharing his perspective with the conventioneers. Note how Mount started his speech:

> I am sure we are all aware of the seeming incongruity of a representative of *Playboy* magazine speaking to an assemblage of representatives of the Southern Baptist Convention. I was intrigued by the invitation when it came last fall, though I was not surprised. I am grateful for your genuine and warm hospitality, and I am flattered (though again not surprised) by the implication that I would have something to say that could have meaning to you people. Both *Playboy* and the Baptists have indeed been considering many of the same issues and ethical problems; and even if we have not arrived at the same conclusions, I am impressed and gratified by your openness and willingness to listen to our views.[4]

Motivators

Motivators are a second valuable resource for persuasion. Discovering what motivates people is a topic that has been discussed since the beginning of time. The classic work on motivation and persuasion was written by Abraham Maslow, who established five levels of human needs.[5] He ranked the needs by their importance:

1. *Basic needs* include access to air, food, water, sex, sleep, and elimination of waste.
2. *Security needs* comprise freedom from threats to one's physical well-being.
3. *Love and belonging needs* include sympathy, friendship, and acceptance.
4. *Esteem needs* are needs for pride, honor, duty, reputation, recognition, loyalty, and competition.
5. *Self-actualization needs* include adventure and fulfillment of one's potential.

Maslow's system of needs is based on the argument that lower level needs must be satisfied before higher level needs can be motivating factors. According to Maslow, once a lower level need has been satisfied, it no longer serves as a motivating force. When this scheme is applied to persuasion, the speaker's task becomes to identify audience needs and then phrase appeals that will fulfill those needs.

Let us look at an example of how this works in a presentation. A developer is planning a strategy to persuade a community group to invest funds to build a marina in their town. The appeal that the developer uses in his presentation is determined by his assessment of the listeners' needs.

First, the developer decides to provide refreshments such as hors d'œuvres and cocktails to the participants to satisfy their physiological needs for food and water. According to Maslow, once these are satisfied, they will no longer be motivating, and the developer can target higher-level needs.

The developer then must decide what appeals to make. Suppose he decides to appeal to the club's self-actualization need by arguing that "this is the best contribution to the community your group can make; with this marina, your town will gain visibility and prestige." The appeal will be successful if the community group members have fulfilled their belonging, safety, and esteem needs. But suppose that the group has not contributed to community safety or that the group is having financial difficulties. The self-actualization appeal will not be motivating for the group because lower level needs are still wanting.

If the developer argues that the "marina will bring your town a lot of money" and the town is running budget surpluses, the appeal will not be successful. To be persuasive, the developer will have to pitch an appeal to a need that is still unfulfilled.

The key to motivational resources is identifying the threshold level at which audience needs are fulfilled. Having identified that point, the speaker may then phrase an appeal that targets those needs that are still lacking.

Opinion Leaders

Opinion leaders are people who are capable of influencing your decisions, attitudes, and behavior. You respect their judgments, taste, and background. They are credible sources for you on a wide range of topics. As such, they are a powerful resource for persuasive presentations.

Practically every organized group has at least one opinion leader; some have several. Importantly, opinion leaders are not necessarily those who are high in rank within a business or organization; some very knowledgeable and respected individuals can be found within the "ranks." In the House of Representatives, for example, there are influential opinion leaders who will never be the Speaker of the House or even chairperson of a committee. Yet their years of service and loyal constituent base make them influential. The

Interact!

This chapter makes the case that source credibility is a major factor in audience acceptance of a persuasive message. We suggest that you attempt to enhance your credibility and that of your evidence whenever possible. Sources held in esteem by audiences are more likely to produce a positive, persuasive effect than are sources not viewed as credible.

This exercise requires you to apply the principles of source credibility to an actual speech given to a business, professional, nonprofit, or service organization. You may attend the speech in person or view it on television or videotape. Simply reading the text of a speech will not provide the details that you need to complete this exercise.

Take detailed notes during the presentation, and try to obtain other information by talking with audience members or participants after the event has concluded. If possible, interview the speaker, and, if appropriate, review any news coverage or press releases about the speech. Consider each of the following factors in your investigation.

1. Who was the speaker? Where and when was the speech given?
2. What do you believe the speaker's purpose was? What kind of audience was there? Could you discern the attitude of the audience toward the

speaker, the purpose, or the event? Were there any physical features about the facility that played a role in the speech?

3. What was the speaker's reputation? Did the audience know the speaker? If another person introduced the speaker, what effect did the introduction play in building the speaker's credibility? Did the speaker's approach to the podium, physical appearance, or nonverbal behavior affect perceptions of credibility?

4. How did the content and style of the speech's introduction affect credibility?

5. Did the speaker seem well informed and competent? How did you assess these qualities? Did the speaker use credible sources? What were they? Did the speaker appear interested in the audience and the event? How did you evaluate the speaker's dynamism? Were there any direct and obvious qualities of delivery, style, or content that affected perceptions of credibility?

6. What role did the speech's conclusion play in enhancing the credibility apparent in the speech up to that point?

7. What was the overall effect of the speech? How well did the speaker achieve her or his purposes and move the audience to action? Assess the role that source credibility played in light of these results and effects.

same is true of business settings. Influence in an organization does not always follow the patterns outlined on an organizational chart. In many offices, for example, a key secretary may be the most influential opinion leader for many important issues.

Identifying opinion leaders in an audience can be an important resource for effective persuasion. Linking your message to a person whom the audience respects is capable of bringing about instant acceptance. Aligning your ideas to coincide with those that the listeners already believe in or admire can be critical to persuasion as well.

If you want to use the influence of opinion leaders for your presentations, you cannot be shy about doing so. Remember that audience members rarely draw links for themselves. You must do this for them. Listeners will probably not think, "That sounds just like what Mr. Peters would say." If Mr. Peters is an opinion leader for this audience, overtly claim his support of the idea you wish your listeners to accept. To make effective use of opinion leaders, reference their names clearly and frequently, demonstrate ways in which your ideas are similar to their ideas, and give credit to their accomplishments through liberal use of examples, incidents, illustrations, or case studies.

Critical Thinking and Persuasion

The critical thinking skills — analysis, reasoning, interpretation, and evaluation — introduced in Chapter 10 play a vital role in persuasive presentations. Strong use of evidence (supporting materials) and reasoning enable the speaker to create a message that is logically sound and well-argued, and can withstand questions or attacks. A presentation that incorporates logical reasoning, analysis, and interpretation works persuasively in the minds of listeners as they apply their own critical thinking skills to it. We strongly encourage you to review the section on critical thinking in Chapter 10, and to seek opportunities to apply these skills to your presentations.

Source Credibility

That a speaker can be persuasive because he or she is credible was recognized in ancient times by Greek and Roman scholars, who labeled this concept *ethos*. In *Rhetoric*, Aristotle wrote:

> Persuasion is achieved by the speaker's personal character when the speech is so spoken as to make us think him credible. We believe good men more fully and more readily than others: this is true generally whatever the question is, and absolutely true where exact certainty is impossible and opinions are divided. . . . His character may almost be called the most effective means of persuasion he possesses.[6]

In essence, when we talk about credibility we mean that an audience can be persuaded on the basis of who the speaker is or what he or she has to say. There are two sources that yield credibility in a presentational context and are thus important for persuasion: the speaker and his or her supporting materials. The audience perceives credibility in the speaker by what it knows about him or her before the presentation or learns about him or her during the presentation. The speaker, in turn, derives credibility from sources, whether they are quotations, testimonies, statistics from studies, or other evidence.

In American society, people are very influenced by source credibility. Why do people buy a name-brand can of green beans instead of a store-label version? What is so magic about a car with "Ltd." after its name? Is a professor with a Ph.D. more credible than one with an M.S. or M.A.?

Put this book down for a moment. Who is the most credible source that you can think of? This person is instantly believable to you: if he or she says something, it must be right! We all have someone who is credible to us, whether it be our father or mother, a physician, a minister, an instructor we have taken several times for courses, or a writer or broadcaster from the media.

Note, however, that credibility is based solely on the audience's perception; it does not exist in any absolute or real sense. As a speaker in a business or professional organization, you have control over the information you allow an audience to have, and you therefore can shape how the audience evaluates your character and grants you credibility.

Early studies on source credibility demonstrated its significance. In this research, investigators typically varied the credibility of the source, while holding the message constant and using equivalent audiences. In one such study,[7] two audiences heard an audiotaped persuasive speech on zero population growth. The two audiences had been pretested for their attitudes about family planning, and they were roughly equivalent before the speech was given.

Both audiences heard the same presentation. One was told that the speaker was a "nationally famous expert on family planning." The other audience was told that the speaker was a "student at the University of Michigan." Posttesting revealed that the people who thought they were hearing a national expert changed their minds significantly more than the other audience did. Given that the speaker's background was the only variant, credibility obviously produced the difference.

There is no sensible reason not to enhance credibility during a presentation wherever possible. Wayne Thompson suggested that "if no other reason exists for seeking high credibility, being liked and respected is more pleasant than suffering the opposites."[8]

Components of credibility.   Three primary components make up source credibility: trustworthiness, competence, and dynamism.[9] These factors are what audiences consider when they label a speaker or a source as either credible or not credible.

Trustworthiness refers to the way that a source is perceived as being honest, friendly, warm, agreeable, or safe, instead of dangerous or threatening. In his final White House days, Richard Nixon was no longer perceived as trustworthy by the American people and was forced to resign. In the world of business, Ivan Boesky and Michael Milken lost the trust of their clients and the American public. Lee Iacocca, in contrast, is perceived as one of the most trustworthy business leaders in America — a hardheaded businessman who knows how to run a company and a potential political leader.

The second dimension, *competence*, is based on the source's expertise, training, experience, skill, ability, authoritativeness, and intelligence. Many people believe that competence is the single most important factor in determining the degree to which a source has credibility. Thus, when a speaker's competence to speak on a topic is suspect, a major effort is required to remedy this perceived defect. Consider the case of James Michener, author of many best-selling novels, who addressed the U.S. Senate Subcommittee on Science, Technology, and Space in Washington, D.C., on February 1, 1975. Because an author, even a Pulitzer Prize–winning one, is not an expert on space, Michener began his speech by raising the question of his competence and offering a plausible defense of his right to testify:

The only justification for allowing me to appear before your Committee is that for some years I have been studying the rise and fall of nations and in so doing have reached certain conclusions governing that process.

There seem to be great tides which operate in the history of civilization, and nations are prudent if they estimate the force of those tides, their genesis and the extent to which they can be utilized. A nation which guesses wrong on all its estimates is apt to be in serious trouble if not on the brink of decline. Toward the middle of the Fifteenth Century the minds of sensible men were filled with speculations about the nature of their world and, although not much solid evidence was available, clever minds could piece together the fragments and achieve quite remarkable deductions.[10]

Finally, *dynamism* is composed of a speaker's energy, liveliness, boldness, activity, forcefulness, and frankness. Many competent speakers who would otherwise be perceived as quite credible damage this assessment because of their failure to be dynamic. Some research has shown that speakers who demonstrate high levels of dynamism are likely to be perceived as more competent and believable than speakers who fail to do this.

Occurrences of credibility.   You may ask, "Where does credibility come into play during a presentation?" The answer is that it comes into play at all stages of the process. Audiences are more likely to attend presentations by and pay attention to speakers they consider to be credible, making credibility an important pre-presentation concern. Credibility is also an important factor during the presentation, as audience members are more likely to accept what they hear from someone they consider credible. Finally, audience members are more willing to carry out a commitment urged by a credible speaker.

Audiences can learn about a speaker's credibility before he or she even utters a word. Because this learning occurs outside of the presentation the speaker gives, it is called extrinsic credibility. There are many ways that extrinsic credibility can be built. Some word about how "good" or "bad" a speaker is can float down from other people who have heard the speaker. A listener can read about a speaker in the newspaper or company newsletter. And prior experience with the speaker lets audience members know what they can expect in the presentation to follow.

One of the most important ways that extrinsic credibility is communicated to an audience is through the introduction of the speaker immediately preceding the presentation. Items such as the speaker's qualifications, memberships in groups, past or present positions, and recent accomplishments can be given to build up the speaker's credibility with the audience. Remember, however, that the audience decides whether credibility exists. If listeners do not understand a speaker's qualifications or do not have any admiration for the groups in which the speaker holds membership, her or his credibility will not be enhanced.

Credibility plays an intrinsic role within the presentation itself. Here the audience learns about a speaker from listening, observing, and inferring. Factors such as the speaker's preparedness, seriousness, sincerity, poise, evenhandedness, firmness, dress, and appearance all give information to listeners that can affect their judgments of her or his credibility.

Extrinsic and intrinsic credibility can work well together. What a listener has heard about a speaker extrinsically can either be strengthened or weakened when intrinsic credibility assessments are made. If a listener has heard that a speaker is "wonderful" (extrinsic), and he or she falls short on some of the factors just discussed (intrinsic), the listener's judgment of the speaker's credibility will be worsened. If, however, the listener has heard that a speaker is "not worth hearing" (extrinsic), but he or she does well in the speech (intrinsic), the listener's assessment will be changed favorably.

As a speaker, you can build your own credibility as well as the credibility of your sources by providing their qualifications, accomplishments, company or university affiliations, or academic degrees wherever necessary. If you are citing a research study as part of your evidence, build up the quality of the study by explaining the circumstances in which it was done, the methodology, the timeliness, or any other information that will lend credence to the findings.

The Persuasion Process

We now turn to the process by which persuasion occurs and some strategies you may be called on to use when speaking to, for, or within your business or professional organization.[11]

The process of persuasion has five distinct stages: awareness, interest, evaluation, trial, and adoption. If anywhere along the line the listener "withdraws" from the process, persuasion will not result. Listeners must first be aware that a proposal exists. They then have to be interested in hearing more. After learning more about the topic, they then evaluate the feelings or reactions they have formed. In many cases, there is a trial period to assess the feasibility of the proposal. If the outcome of the trial is favorable, they then adopt the proposal and put it into practice or action.

Here is an example of how these five stages work, as applied to a presentation in which junior executives are proposing to senior management that they be allowed to travel on sales incentive trips. In this company, the trips are reserved only for top management.

Awareness: "Junior executives should be permitted to travel on sales incentive trips." (The management group may not have even known that they were interested in taking the trips!)

Interest: "The long-term results of sending junior executives on these trips are beneficial to the company." (The management group may want to know what these results are.)

Evaluation: "Think of the large return on such a small investment."
(The management group may ponder this benefit.)
Trial: "Give this plan a chance for one year to see how it works."
(The management group may consider a shorter period to assess results.)
Adoption: "If the trial period yields results that meet or exceed expectations, the activity will become permanent policy."

Of course, the process is not infallible. Think about how many times you have listened to a persuasive presentation and have "withdrawn" at some point in the process. It happens with great regularity. You may be made aware of an issue, become convinced of its logic, and even think it is a good idea, but you just do not want to implement it! As a result, you are not persuaded. The following strategies can help speakers prevent such persuasion "dropouts."

Ego Involvement

Ego involvement refers to how important a particular topic or issue is to a listener. For the most part, ego involvement is determined by the listener's commitment to the topic, in terms of time, money, prestige, or even "ownership," or possession, of the topic.

Ego involvement is reflected by the *latitudes of acceptance and rejection* held by the listener. Latitudes of acceptance are determined by asking, "Given a person's commitment to an issue, how likely is the person to accept a particular persuasive message related to that issue?" Latitudes of rejection are determined by asking, "Given a person's commitment to an issue, how likely is the person to reject a particular persuasive message?" It follows that the higher the listener's ego involvement is, the smaller are the latitudes of acceptance, and the greater are the latitudes of rejection. The lower the listener's ego involvement is, the greater are the latitudes of acceptance, and the lower are the latitudes of rejection.

Suppose you are speaking to three co-authors of a book who have worked diligently on it for several years. Their ego involvement in the project is quite high. Correspondingly, there are very few changes to the book that they will accept, and many suggestions they will reject. The chance that you can convince them to restructure the book from start to finish is low. But you may persuade them to modify the cover design or to add an extra chapter.

Order Effects

Every persuasive presentation has some arguments that are stronger than others. The question frequently facing a speaker is, "In what order should

I present my arguments?"[12] The speaker can usually choose from one of three options.

In a *climax* order, the weakest argument is presented first and the strongest last; this organization provides a recency effect, meaning that the audience will most likely remember the last (and strongest) argument. In an *anticlimax* order, the strongest argument is presented first, and weaker arguments follow; this plan gives a primacy effect (audience members are immediately struck by the strength of the argument). In a *pyramidal* order, the speaker places the strongest argument between two weaker ones.

The decision of which to employ is up to you. If you are planning to give the presentation more than once, you may wish to experiment until you are comfortable with the ordering of your ideas. Research shows that arguments presented early and late are more effective than those presented in the middle. If you have high credibility in the mind of the audience, you will find it better to present strong arguments early in the speech.

One-Sided versus Two-Sided Presentations

In what circumstances should you bring up the other side's position in your presentation? If you present only your position, the presentation is one-sided; if you bring up the other side's arguments and then refute them, the presentation is two-sided. Research shows the following:

◆ Two-sided presentations are best if the weight of evidence is on your side.

◆ Two-sided presentations are best for higher educated listeners.

◆ Two-sided presentations are best when the listeners initially disagree with your position.

◆ Two-sided presentations are preferable when you believe the listeners will be exposed to the other side following your own presentation.

◆ One-sided presentations are best when the listeners already agree with you, provided that they are not likely to be influenced by later opposing arguments.

Additional Hints

Some of your most challenging presentations in the business world will be persuasive in nature. When you combine the resources specified in this chapter with the material in Chapters 12 and 13, you should be prepared to face persuasive challenges in a confident and effective way. When facing such a challenge, you can also consider the following hints:[13]

1. In persuasion, try to give listeners the feeling that the proposal you are advocating is a natural extension of directions in which they are tending.

2. Because people agree more readily about abstract matters than about concrete matters, be especially choosy about the specific examples you use early in your speech.

3. Even though all of us identify with certain reference groups, few of us like to admit such "dependence"; therefore, do not make careless attributions about your listeners in their presence.

4. Do not be glib when presenting large-scale statistical information; always try to show the "local consequences" of such data.

5. Even though it is good to have several reasons to support your thesis, using too many will cause your audience to be suspicious of your selectivity.

6. Never underestimate candor; looking at your audience directly and admitting that you disagree with them on some issue can be a prudent course of action.

7. When you speak to a hostile audience, never save your proposal until the conclusion lest you be viewed as a coward.

8. Do not underestimate the power of careful phrasing; language has great power to color ideas. Sometimes, the elimination of bothersome bits of jargon or hackneyed expressions can open up listeners' minds.

9. When you are dealing with a hostile audience, do not allow your voice to become shrill, even though your frustration at audience resistance will push you in that direction.

Summary

Persuasive presentations, regardless of their setting and audience, usually have one of four functions: to reinforce listeners' beliefs or values, to refute these beliefs or values, to change these beliefs or values, or to move the listeners to action. Reinforcement and refutative presentations can be used to rebuild listeners' original beliefs or prove that these beliefs are untrue. From the latter use it follows that change presentations seek to go one step further and convince listeners to change a particular attitude, value, or belief. A call to action intends to get listeners to do something, such as sign a petition or donate money to a charitable cause, that they would not have done had they not heard the presentation.

Persuasive presentations take a variety of formats, which reflect the speaker's approach and use of supporting materials. Sales presentations, proposals, and motivational sessions are three of the most common formats for persuasive presentations.

To deliver a successful persuasive presentation, a speaker is wise to concentrate on the particular demands made on the audience. The effective presentation takes a listeners' perspective, discovering what makes listeners tick and whether they are likely to be favorably disposed toward a particular message. Presentational strategies differ, of course, depending on whether the audience is sympathetic or suspicious.

A persuasive speaker benefits from addressing his or her appeals to the appropriate need level of the audience. An audience whose basic needs (for food, water, shelter) are not met is not likely to respond to a message geared toward self-actualization needs. To work, persuasive messages have to be pitched to the needs that are wanting, not the ones that are satisfied.

The successful presentation also takes into account the opinion leaders in the audience and directs its appeals to or references them. The importance of opinion leaders also suggests the larger issue of credibility. A speaker who is not credible, or who uses sources that are not credible, is not likely to get very far in his or her persuasive efforts. Because credibility is in the eye of the beholder — it resides with the audience — the speaker is wise to present himself or herself in such a way as to signal trustworthiness, competence, and dynamism. The credibility gained in the process is called intrinsic credibility. Extrinsic credibility, however, is communicated through the introduction of the speaker and through other external sources of information about the speaker.

Apart from the foregoing components, persuasion is also a process, and the effective speaker knows how to use each stage in the process to advantage. In the first phase, listeners become aware that a message exists. In the second phase, they become interested in hearing more. In the third phase, they evaluate what they have heard and what they feel about what they have heard. In the fourth phase, they set aside a trial period to judge the feasibility of the message. In the fifth phase, they adopt the message and put it into practice.

Not all persuasive presentations work out quite so neatly. A speaker may have to deal with highly ego-involved listeners, with the necessity of choosing among several options for ordering arguments (arguments presented early or late get audience attention more than do those presented in the middle), and with deciding whether to give both sides of the argument. But if the speaker employs candor, careful phrasing, respect for the audience, and equanimity, he or she is much more likely to achieve the objectives of the persuasive presentation.

Discussion

1. Why are many persuasive presentations made informally? What are the basic goals of a persuasive presentation?

2. What are the functions of persuasive presentations? Can you think of situations in which a presentation might perform several of these functions simultaneously?

3. Describe the typical formats for persuasive presentations. What are the strengths of each?

4. What is a listener's perspective? Why is it crucial to take a listener's perspective when making a persuasive presentation?

5. According to Maslow, what are the five levels of human need? How do they influence the preparation and delivery of a persuasive presentation?

6. How can opinion leaders be used to boost a persuasive presentation?

7. What are the components of source credibility? How does extrinsic credibility differ from intrinsic credibility?

8. Describe the process of persuasion. What strategies can you employ to prevent listeners from dropping out during the persuasion process?

Activities

1. How do you use persuasion in informal presentations? Describe an informal occasion in which you persuaded (or did not persuade) others to choose an option or idea you favored.

2. Select a topic and construct main points for each of the presentation types discussed in this chapter: reinforcing the listeners' beliefs, attitudes, or values; changing the listeners' beliefs, attitudes, or values; and moving the listeners to action.

3. Apply the process of persuasion to outlining a presentation on the following topics: a) persuading the company cafeteria to stop using styrofoam plates and cups; b) persuading a client to sample a higher-quality brand of office paper than he plans to buy; c) persuading a personnel manager to hire several college interns for your department this summer.

4. Analyze a speaker you have heard recently according to the three components of credibility: trustworthiness, competence, and dynamism. Did all three aspects play an equal role in affecting your perception of the speaker's credibility?

Notes

1. This outline and others in this chapter are adapted from K. J. Krayer, *Basic Speech Communications Workbook* (Dallas: Bellwether Press, 1987).

2. T. J. Peters and R. H. Waterman, Jr., *In Search of Excellence: Lessons from America's Best-Run Companies* (New York: Harper & Row, 1982); Z. Ziglar, *See You at the Top* (Gretna, La.: Pelican, 1975).

3. W. A. Linkugel, R. R. Allen, and R. L. Johannesen, *Contemporary American Speeches*, 5th ed. (Dubuque, Iowa: Kendall/Hunt, 1982), p. 369.

4. Ibid., p. 178.

5. A. H. Maslow, *Motivation and Personality* (New York: Harper & Row, 1954).

6. Aristotle, *Rhetoric* (New York: Modern Library, 1954).

7. E. P. Bettinghaus, *Persuasive Communication*, 2nd ed. (New York: Holt, Rinehart & Winston, 1973).

8. W. N. Thompson, *The Process of Persuasion: Principles and Readings* (New York: Harper & Row, 1975), p. 72.

9. J. L. Whitehead, Jr., "Factors of Source Credibility," *Quarterly Journal of Speech* 54 (1968): 59–63.

10. Linkugel, Allen, and Johannesen, *Contemporary American Speeches*, p. 272.

11. E. P. Bettinghaus, *Persuasive Communication,* pp. 248–272.

12. H. Gulley and D. K. Berlo, "Effects of Intercellular and Intracellular Speech Structure on Attitude Change and Learning," *Speech Monographs* 23 (1956): 288–297.

13. R. P. Hart, G. W. Friedrich, and B. Brummett, *Public Communication*, 2nd ed. (New York: Harper & Row, 1983), p. 286.

Chapter 15

*S*pecial Presentational Formats

OBJECTIVES

After working through this chapter, you will be able to:

1. Organize and deliver a successful impromptu presentation

2. Understand the symposium format and select a topic that will be interesting and important to your audience

3. Assess how a speaker's presentation and delivery are affected by being televised

4. Practice effectively for televised presentations

5. Prepare a variety of ceremonial speeches, including speeches to entertain, introduce another speaker, and accept an award or honor

As you have seen, modern businesses and organizations present many opportunities for speaking. Up to this point, we have focused on the basic formats and styles for common speaking situations and on preparation for standard informative and persuasive presentations. You are very likely to encounter the opportunity to speak in a variety of other contexts in your career as well. Consider the following scenarios:

Your company is planning a seminar on budgeting to bring together members of the design, marketing, production, and administrative staffs. One representative from each department is needed to make a presentation on its approach to budgeting concerns, solutions, questions, and techniques. You would like to participate; as a management trainee in the marketing department, you would gain visibility outside of your group of co-workers, contribute to an important organizational goal (developing better budgeting practices), and demonstrate your enthusiasm for your job. But, you are unsure of how to prepare a presentation in the symposium format that will be used for the seminar.

You are a benefits manager for a small retail clothing chain. During a contract and benefits negotiation session between the employees' union and management, you are unexpectedly called on to summarize the progress of negotiations and to comment on the differences still to be settled. You have followed the progress of the negotiations very carefully, and you wonder if the audience will feel overwhelmed by the amount of information you have to present; you are also nervous that you have not been given a chance to prepare.

Your organization has successfully completed a major effort to increase its employees' involvement in community action and volunteer programs. A banquet has been planned to celebrate this goal and to honor individual employees who have contributed to the effort. As one of the organizers of an adult literacy tutoring program, you will be presented with a community commitment award. In your acceptance speech you would like to acknowledge the patience and effort of the students enrolled in the program as one of the major reasons for its success.

You work in the communication department of a large multinational organization that has recently decided to produce videos to supplement its standard printed publications. You have been asked to develop and tape a short presentation on quality control techniques in different parts of the corporation. Although in print form this would be a standard assignment for you, you have never worked with televised speaking. You wonder what special preparations you will have to make.

Each of these situations requires the ability to adapt your speaking skills to the unique challenges of the setting, the audience, and even the technology. In this chapter, we will show you how to prepare and structure presentations in a variety of special formats, including impromptu speaking, symposiums, televised speaking, and ceremonial speaking. We begin with impromptu speaking.

Impromptu Speaking

Business and professional settings offer many occasions on which speakers are called on to address an audience without having a chance to do any advance planning. This type of delivery, called *impromptu,* is difficult even in the best of circumstances. By way of example, consider this: a friend of ours was attending an awards banquet recently and was asked by the master of ceremonies to close the affair. Rather startled, our friend got out of his chair very slowly, rose to his feet, and said, "When someone is called on to speak without any advance notice, one of two things happens. Either he says something significant or he is brief. I will be brief."

Having something to say is just as important a goal in a speech delivered impromptu as in a planned and rehearsed informative or persuasive presentation. Skilled impromptu delivery sounds so confident that the audience might not suspect the speaker has not prepared in advance. It is organized, assured, and makes an important point. Impromptu delivery is often used when providing concluding remarks to a meeting or putting a meeting in perspective for an audience. Ceremonial speeches, which we discuss later in the chapter, frequently employ an impromptu style of delivery.

Organizing an Impromptu Speech

One of the advantages of being well organized is that even if the speaker does not have a lot to say, he or she can sound authoritative, because in short presentations (which impromptu speeches generally are) the audience is likely to remember the points made rather than how they are extended or elaborated. The following guidelines will help you to quickly organize a presentation to be delivered impromptu.

Give a pleasantry.   Begin your speech with a short line that sets the tone for the rest of your comments. This line also buys you some time to think of where you are going next. Sample opening lines include:

◆ "I appreciate the chance to comment . . ."
◆ "Thank you for the opportunity to . . ."
◆ "I am pleased to be able to . . ."

Give a preview line.   The preview line organizes your message by telling the audience what points you will cover. The preview is very simple, yet very important — it alerts the audience to the progression of main points as you speak. The following examples of preview lines are used frequently by speakers:

◆ "I want to make three points today: First, . . . ; Second, . . . ; Third, . . ."
◆ "I'd like to touch briefly on the advantages of the program and then on some of the disadvantages."
◆ "There are two basic areas of concern: _____ and _____ ."

Give a transition line.   Before you discuss your first point, give a transition to signal that you are moving into the body of the speech. In an impromptu speech, transitions are very simple. They preview the main point that follows. Here are two examples:

◆ "I'll start with the advantages."
◆ "Let's look first at _____ "

Discuss the main points.   After you have given the transition, elaborate on the first point. Unless you are particularly expert on the topic, you probably will not have many "hard" research facts, such as statistics, to present. You more than likely will have opinions, examples, case studies, incidents, "ballpark" figures, trends, or personal observations to offer. Give another transition before moving to the next point. Sharply limit the number of points — one rule of thumb is to discuss three or fewer ideas.

Conclude.   Complete your delivery by acknowledging the group's time, patience, and attentiveness. You may also wish to refer back to the most significant point you made in the presentation.

Cautions

Impromptu presentations are challenging. The following cautions can help you to avoid the largest pitfalls of impromptu delivery.

Avoid rambling.   Rambling demonstrates the speaker's unpreparedness, so it is a particular problem in impromptu presentations. Be concise; once you have made a point and elaborated it, move on. Do not fish for additional examples or repeat yourself. In contrast to other styles of delivery, you should not even try to summarize what you have said — impromptu speeches are too short to warrant a summary.

Limit the number of points.   It is far better to say "more with less" than "less about more." In other words, give the audience more content while making fewer points (not more than three) rather than throwing out a large number of poorly developed points.

Stick to the topic.   Even though new ideas may come to mind as you speak, avoid the temptation to digress from the introduction and preview line you have already given. Doing so will confuse the audience and give the impression that you do not know what to say next.

Do not call attention to your lack of preparation.   Audiences quickly tire of apologetic speakers. Impromptu speaking is not an excuse not to try; it is an opportunity to demonstrate your skill. Your presentation will speak for itself. By calling attention to negatives, you may emphasize something that no one would have otherwise noticed.

Symposiums

A symposium is a collection of speeches that relate to a single topic. Without collaborating, three or more people prepare speeches on the topic and deliver them within set time limits. Following the speeches, the participants may discuss the topic among themselves, and if performing in front of a large audience, they may take questions from those present. The presentations in a symposium may be informative or persuasive in nature.

One factor that marks a symposium is that each speech is prepared individually. The speakers do not consult one another on their approaches to the topic. They do not adapt to or make references to one another. Even if speaker number two takes the same position and uses some of the same evidence as speaker number three, the third speaker does not alter her or his presentation. Nor do participants interact with one another while the symposium speeches are in progress. Each is a formal, individual presentation. To get a better sense of what a symposium is, let us look at a few potential symposium topics:

> *Question:* What are the prospects for expanding our business into international markets?
> *Speaker 1:* China
> *Speaker 2:* Great Britain
> *Speaker 3:* Brazil
> *Speaker 4:* Canada
> *Speaker 5:* Japan

> *Question:* What are the attitudes toward compensation of employees in our organization today?
> *Speaker 1:* Executive viewpoints
> *Speaker 2:* Part-time employees' viewpoints

Speaker 3: Salaried employees' viewpoints
Speaker 4: Hourly wage employees' viewpoints

Symposiums may also be held to inform subgroups in an organization or association, or to increase the sense of unity and cohesiveness between branches and the main headquarters of an organization. For example, the American Society for Training and Development has hosted symposiums as part of its national campaign, "Train America's Work Force." The symposiums include key community leaders and decision makers from four groups: business, government, labor, and education. Issues such as work force preparedness and economic competitiveness were explored from these perspectives.

The Nature of Symposiums

Symposiums are quite different from group meetings and panel discussions. These differences can be distinguished in purpose, consistency, decision-making style, and degree of formality.

Purpose. Panel discussions use debate and discussion to find a solution to a problem. Symposiums allow participants to voice different viewpoints about a question.

Consistency. Paricipants in a panel discussion frequently change topics and positions, and introduce new sides to the issue under discussion. In a symposium, participants speak on only one aspect or subtopic of the question.

Decision making. In a panel discussion, the group reaches a decision internally. Symposium groups do not make decisions. Any decision on the topic is arrived at by the audience after listening to the speakers.

Formality. Panel discussions are relatively informal, without an established speaking order or agreed-on procedures. Participants are frequently interrupted, and the speaking is discontinuous. Symposiums are governed by formal rules, such as time limits for each speaker and a predetermined speaking order. Each participant delivers a prepared, formal speech on a subtopic relevant to the general question.

Topic Selection and Consistency

Our focus is on the speaker as a participant in, rather than an organizer of, a symposium. The following guidelines will help you to select a topic appropriate to the symposium format.

◆ Is the topic worded as a question? If so, your presentation should serve to answer the question.

◆ Is the answer to the question uncertain? If so, consider that others are likely to present answers different from your own. How can you capture the interest and support of the audience?

◆ Is the question broad enough to provide a variety of subtopics? If so, which are you most expert on, interested in, or concerned about?

◆ Why is the question worth answering? What can you tell the audience that will make your presentation most relevant and meaningful to them?

◆ Does the question relate to the basic topic? Audiences are frustrated by presentations that are only loosely related because it is difficult to make comparisons among them.

◆ Is the question timely? Most successful symposium presentations discuss "what is" or "what will be" rather than "what was."

◆ Will the audience be interested in the question? This is a fundamental concern for any presentation, and no less so for one given in a symposium format.

Contrary to the assumption that an audience will not be interested in listening to a series of speakers talk, symposiums have the potential to capture audience members' attention because they are given the opportunity to compare and contrast different information and perspectives. Nevertheless, symposium speakers who present a subtopic or talk on an aspect of a question are only as interesting as the general topic itself. Speakers who touch on the topic through familiar language and experiences increase their bond with the audience.

Televised Speaking

In her work *Speak Like a Pro,* Margaret Bedrosian argued that probably the single biggest emerging challenge to business communicators today is that they will need on-camera skills within their careers. A wide range of applications, from video annual reports and video pamphlets, to video product demonstrations, video training sessions and video-enhanced speaking at conferences show the camera's pervasiveness. Sooner or later, the focus will be on you![1]

Our discussion focuses on formal presentations that are transferred from one source to another via televised airwaves. These could include speeches given in one room and piped to different locations on multiple television monitors; speeches that are presented live to large audiences and incorporate a big-screen monitor to aid the audience's view of the speaker; and speeches that are recorded on videocassette for playback on a monitor at a later time. Although we do not directly address interviews, debates, or panel discussions, these are televised on a regular basis and many of the principles we refer to here apply to those events.

Projection on the Big Screen

In modern businesses and professions, speeches are often given on the big screen. You may have attended conferences or conventions where this technique was used, especially for major or keynote presentations. (You may also have attended concerts or sporting events where the audience's view of the star was enhanced by big-screen technology!)

Rather than having the audience strain to see the speaker from a great distance, television cameras project the speaker's image onto a big screen that is raised for all to see. These screens are as high as sixteen to twenty-

Many organizations televise important speeches, such as annual earnings announcements or major developments in the industry. Here, a satellite uplink connects televised speakers at Tufts University and the University of Moscow.

four feet and enable audiences to focus on the speaker's facial expressions, gestures, and other aspects of delivery that would remain unseen in a conventional format.

The big screen technique enables audiences to feel much more comfortable with and captivated by the speaker. One reason for increased audience attentiveness is that the strain involved in simply seeing the speaker has been removed. There is no question that the audience is likely to respond more readily when it can see the speaker's face and expressions.

Of course, the big screen creates some difficulties for the speaker. Variables captured by the camera are micro in nature. Facial expressions such as raised eyebrows, smiles, frowns, or pauses with the mouth held slightly open are emphasized greatly. The screen reveals nervous tics as readily as it does friendly, conversational gestures, such as upward palms to signal openness or downward pointing to indicate concreteness.

At the same time, the speaker must restrict her or his body movement. In most cases, speeches delivered through the big screen medium are scripted and read from a *teleprompter* (a screen showing a large-type copy of the speech that can be seen by the speaker and not the audience). It is difficult, if not impossible, for a speaker to read a presentation from a teleprompter if he or she is moving around the stage. In addition, the speaker's microphone is generally placed on the podium and movement away from it causes her or his voice to fade out. A *lavaliere* microphone (which is attached to the speaker's clothing) can help to prevent the problem of fadeout.

The challenge for you as a speaker is to take advantage of these variables. Television has the potential to reveal your confidence, forcefulness, or emotion much more readily than does any other medium.

Practice

Many people are frightened by the prospect of making a televised presentation because they have never done so before! If you were told that your presentation would be broadcast, would you have some of these concerns?

◆ "I'll look funny."

◆ "I won't sound like myself on television."

◆ "My lips will quiver, and my voice will shake."

◆ "I don't want someone to be able to replay my speech."

◆ "Anything I wear will make me look fat."

If you suspect that you might think some of these things, you are not alone. These are natural feelings that cause apprehension. Remember that giving a speech in public is the behavior most feared by American adults. Having a presentation aired over television only heightens that apprehension, whether the speech is a live big screen presentation or a taped presentation that will be distributed for viewing by many people.

We cannot alleviate all of your concerns. Nor do we believe that you should be completely calm when delivering your presentation. As we have noted, some apprehension provides the adrenaline needed to keep you excited and energetic. Our goal is to help you to manage the additional apprehension caused by the televised medium.

Practice is the key to reducing anxiety. When you become accustomed to cameras running, bright lights shining in your face, and microphones clipped to your clothing, your level of apprehension will decrease. Only time and repetition of the experience will allow a televised presentation to seem like a somewhat natural behavior.

Nevertheless, there are ways to combat anxiety in your very first televised presentation. Watch yourself on tape with a critical but constructive eye. Do not say, "I look awful." Watch the tape and ask, "What actions can I take to improve my appearance during this presentation?" Are there some things that you are wearing, ways you are standing, and so forth, that could be changed?

Practice how you sound as well as how you look. If your microphone is on the podium, speak over the microphone rather than into it to avoid "popping" sounds that occur frequently in speech. If you are using a lavaliere microphone, avoid excessive rustling and fidgeting that will cause static or interference.

If possible, show your practice tape to someone else for his or her comments. This person does not have to be an expert to offer you a constructive opinion. If you do not have access to video equipment before the presentation, practice in front of a mirror or with a friend. Doing so can go a long way toward reducing your anxiety when you actually have to perform on camera.

Where Do You Look?

You look out at the studio and see the red light on one of the cameras, signaling that your presentation is being taped, broadcast, or both. Where should you look? Should you look directly at the camera? Should you look only at the camera whose red light indicates it is operating? Should you ignore the camera and focus on the audience (even if you cannot see it because of the camera lights shining in your eyes)? If an audience is not present in the room or studio, should you pretend that there is one and talk to it?

The answers to these questions are difficult to provide, because many variables can affect individual televised performances. We offer the follow-

FOCUS on *Corporate Communication*

AMERICAN RED CROSS

*T*he American Red Cross headquarters in Washington, D.C., is the focal point of the organization's activity in the United States. Its volunteers and staff support the efforts of 1.1 million chapter volunteers, help the federal government to abide by the Geneva Convention, develop and guide many of the programs of service available through the Red Cross, and participate in the international Red Cross movement, which includes the 149 national Red Cross and Red Crescent organizations that provide humanitarian relief throughout the world.

In the United States, the Red Cross has two major national responsibilities, which were granted to it in a congressional charter in 1889: to provide assistance in national disasters and to act as a medium of emergency communication between members of the armed forces and their families. During the 1990–1991 Gulf War, several hundred thousand such messages (relating to births, deaths, serious injury, or other critical situations) were transmitted. In addition, the Red Cross operates the nation's largest blood service through fifty-three regional centers; provides first aid, health, and safety education; and has begun a tissue services program to collect and distribute tissues such as bone and corneas (but not solid organs) for medical use.

The resources for most Red Cross services come ultimately from 2,600 local chapters, especially the largest 200 to 225 chapters that provide 85 percent of funds, blood donations, volunteers, and other needs. The organizational culture within the Red Cross reflects this grass-roots, volunteer base. Characterized by dedication, loyalty, a strong sense of the importance of the organization's work, and commitment to social ideals, many employees and volunteers view the Red Cross as a significant part of their lives and a way to give something of themselves back to the community and society. Communication within the organization is designed to support the local chapters as much as possible. An appreciation of the bottom-up nature and community focus is of vital importance to the national headquarters staff.

Because the needs of individuals and local chapters vary widely, the communications staff at national headquarters produces a broad range of media, each designed to serve a particular group's needs. For example, *Red Cross News* provides general organizational information to seventy thousand volunteers every two months. Nine thousand middle managers who need more detailed and frequent information receive an additional monthly newsletter, *Cue-In*. Still another publication, *Colleagues,* carries information,

ing general guidelines as a starting point for performing in some of the more common television setups.[2]

If you are speaking with a teleprompter that is located above or on the camera, you necessarily must look at that camera to read your manuscript. Getting the words right is your primary concern and should be emphasized over placement of eye contact.

strategies, and advice to people involved in recruiting blood donors. Many specialized materials are produced as well.

Several important trends in communication have taken shape in recent years as the relationship between the local chapters and national headquarters has become more interactive. An 800 number that offers to chapters — particularly smaller ones — daily recorded updates of important information has been installed. After listening to the update, callers from local chapters can also talk to a staff member in Washington if they wish to do so. The new voice mail system provides continuous information as well as the opportunity for two-way communication. The 800 number supplements a teletype system designed to receive and distribute bulletins two or three times per day among major Red Cross units.

Business television has also strengthened the national-local link. The Red Cross is not new to video — it has used television since 1973, dating back to the tenure of a former president of CBS as head of the organization. Business television, which has a two-way audio and one-way video capacity, has helped to improve interactive communication with the seventy-four chapters that have so far purchased downlinks. In the eight or nine business television programs produced each month, members of local chapter audiences have the opportunity to ask questions and make suggestions to the speaker during the live broadcast.

The advantages of this technology are substantial. In one case, the fifty-three directors of regional blood banks participated in a ninety-minute symposium with the national blood services director at a fraction of the cost he would have incurred by traveling to each center to do a separate presentation or by bringing all fifty-three directors to one location for a conference. More than any other group in the Red Cross, the blood service needs communication to be rapid, clear, and accurate because of the delicate and highly technical nature of its work and the existence of strict federal regulations on handling blood. Business television helps to provide such information quickly and uniformly to everyone who needs it.

In the future, the Red Cross is looking to technology to enhance communication not only with local chapters but with individual volunteers and donors through direct broadcast satellite (DBS) systems. DBS, which will reach people in their own homes through a relatively inexpensive twelve-inch satellite dish, offers the opportunity to expand communication with those the Red Cross is dedicated to serve — individual citizens and communities.

If teleprompters are located to the left and right of the podium, you can alternate eye contact between them (and the audience seated in front of you) without losing focus on your manuscript. The camera operator will follow your gaze as you alternate between the teleprompters.

If you are not using a teleprompter, your notes or speaker's outline should be prepared on small blue- or green-colored note cards to avoid causing camera glare or distracting the audience. If there is a live audience present, focus on the audience and let the cameras find you. Awkward changes in eye contact are likely to occur as you glance from one camera to another.

If there is not a live audience present, decide to whom you want to direct the presentation. Looking directly at the camera gives those who watch the tape on a monitor the impression that you are speaking directly to them. If you want to convey the impression that you are actually speaking to an audience and that viewers are "eavesdropping" on the presentation, speak to the room and let the camera find you.

Appearance

We want to conclude this section with a few remarks about how you can maximize your appearance in a televised presentation.[3] These are basics; we hope you take time to consider the particular needs of your own presentation.

Cosmetics.   A speaker's features often appear flat on television, and other distortion may occur as well. Cosmetics, especially eyeliner and blush, restore the natural dimensions of the face. (Do not, however, expect to change your on-camera appearance radically through make-up!) Powder can reduce glare and reflection produced by hot lights. If you are not skilled in applying powder, blush, or other cosmetics, have someone on hand to help you. Remember always to check yourself on a monitor to see how you look. The picture on the television monitor is the most accurate gauge of your appearance.

Clothing.   When you are choosing clothing for a televised presentation, consider the background against which you will be speaking. Be sure to find out from the director what the background is before you begin the session.

Dark clothing against a dark background or light clothing against a light background will cause problems for the studio engineers. In most cases, cool colors such as blue, gray, or pastels are preferable to black, and white should be avoided at all times because it causes camera glare. The guiding principle is to avoid major color contrasts within your outfit or against the background.

Patterns such as stripes, checks, or polka dots should be avoided because they blur on camera. Minimize or avoid wearing jewelry — it can cause glare and distract the audience from your presentation.

By following these general principles you can improve your appearance, self-confidence, and delivery on camera.

Ceremonial Speaking

Ceremonial speeches play a variety of roles in business because their function is to bring people together to recognize and celebrate achievement, tradition, and organizational values. They may also be used to lift employee morale or strengthen commitment to the organization. In this section, we discuss three common categories of ceremonial presentations: speeches to introduce another speaker, to accept an award or honor, and to entertain.

Speeches of Introduction

On most occasions, guest speakers who address business and professional groups are given formal introductions. These may be done by the president or chair of the company, the leader of the group to whom the presentation is being given, a master of ceremonies, or the person responsible for bringing the speaker to the group. An introduction should make the speaker feel genuinely welcome, and indicate that the group feels privileged to have him or her present and eagerly anticipates the talk. Although introductions are brief and not the main focus of the speaking event, several considerations merit attention in ensuring a successful introduction.

Research.   Information about the main speaker must be accurate and up to date. The introductory speaker can collect information by soliciting a résumé or a public relations "sell sheet" (a short personal biography) from the main speaker or his or her organization. Doing so ensures that the information presented by the introductory speaker is agreeable to the main speaker.

If you are handed information by a person who claims to "know the speaker well," it is important to verify the facts before beginning the introduction. Some speakers appreciate being asked if there is anything special that they would like said about them or a particular way that they would like to be introduced. You will be surprised at the number of detailed responses you receive to this request.

Brevity.   Introductions should be short. Long, laborious introductions may cause the audience to become restless and uninterested. Long-winded introductions can also embarrass the main speaker and cut into his or her speaking time. Always remember that the audience is present to hear the main speaker, not the introduction!

Organization.   An introduction can give the speaker's name first followed by her or his qualifications and accomplishments, or focus on achievements before identifying the speaker. The second approach is more dramatic than the first, but when the speaker's name is revealed, the audience members

"Before I introduce tonight's author, I thought perhaps
I'd read something of my own."

Drawing by Stevenson; © 1984 the New Yorker Magazine, Inc.

must be able to remember the qualifications and accomplishments they just heard for the approach to work well. The following list suggests possible items that might be included in an introduction:

◆ Title of current or past positions
◆ Academic degrees earned
◆ Honorary degrees earned
◆ Offices held in organizations
◆ Awards or honors given by organizations
◆ Places traveled
◆ Books or articles written
◆ Programs or panels participated in
◆ Personal achievements or interests (family, hobbies, skills, and so forth)

As you select the qualifications or accomplishments to include in the introduction, keep the audience in mind. Ask yourself, "What will this audience best identify with? What is meaningful to this group?"

Speeches to Accept an Honor or Award

We hope that you are called on at some time to speak following the presentation of an award or honor, whether it is for an individual accomplishment or on behalf of a group or organization you represent.

If the presentation is a surprise, you are likely to be overcome with emotion, joy, or astonishment. There is nothing wrong with allowing these emotions to come through your remarks, provided that they remain clear and concise. The information earlier in this chapter on impromptu delivery can be used to give an unexpected acceptance speech.

In cases in which you know that you will be presented with an award or gift, you have the opportunity to prepare your remarks in advance. Consider that effective speeches of acceptance usually include the following features:

◆ Your reaction (initial or present)

◆ What the award, honor, or gift means to you

◆ A brief history of who or what helped you to achieve the honor

◆ Sincere appreciation and gratitude

Acceptance speeches are generally better if they are kept short and to the point. Like other ceremonial speeches, they become tiring for the audience if they ramble or digress from the main point.

Speeches to Entertain

Most speeches to entertain are of the "after-dinner" variety — the audience is usually in a light, jovial mood in anticipation of having a good time after participating in a celebratory dinner or banquet. Nevertheless, speeches to entertain are not easy to give. All too often, we find students equating "entertainment" with "comedy." If you are not by nature a stand-up comic, it is better not to pretend to be one when you give one of these speeches. The audience is likely to see through your attempts and fail to respond. In the next sections, we offer some suggestions on how to proceed with an entertaining speech.

Keep the speech short.   Even if you are good at it, audiences quickly tire of laughing. Talking at length will spoil even the best presentation. Remember that at most dinners, the participants have been present for a number of hours. They have renewed acquaintances, met new people, conversed during dinner, and perhaps listened to previous speakers. They may well be ready to leave.

Keep the speech simple.   Tired, restless listeners do not want to work to follow the speaker and may be barely paying attention. The speaker should avoid complex stories with many characters and details and limit the topics covered to one or two.

Keep the speech tasteful.   We strongly advise deleting from the speech any material that could be considered offensive, despite social trends to the contrary. Off-color humor will undoubtedly offend more audience members than it will amuse.

Be willing to laugh at yourself.   One of the best subjects available for use during entertainment speeches is yourself! Audiences respect and admire speakers who can laugh at themselves. By selecting a story about yourself that the audience can readily identify with, you make yourself a part of the group.

Summary

The special presentational formats discussed in this chapter are quite common in business and professional organizations. You are very likely to be involved in one or more of these situations at some point in your career.

Impromptu speaking requires confidence and the ability to organize, rather than elaborate, main points. Preview lines let audience participants know what is coming and help them to remember it once it has been said. Impromptu speaking usually comprises "ballpark" figures, opinions, or examples rather than extensive hard data. Impromptu speakers should avoid rambling, excessive numbers of main points, unrelated points, and calling attention to the fact that they had no time to prepare.

Symposiums are collections of speeches on the same general topic. The speeches are prepared individually, and each presents a fully researched viewpoint on the topic. Symposiums do not involve decision making by the speakers, although the audience is free to draw conclusions after hearing all sides. A symposium includes set time limits and a prescribed order of speakers.

Televised speaking entails special preparation and adaptation to the broadcast medium. Big-screen presentations exaggerate facial expressions, gestures, and body movement. Competent speakers can take advantage of these factors to enhance their contact with and appeal to the audience. Understanding and practicing with broadcast technology can decrease anxiety and ensure a successful presentation.

There are several types of ceremonial speaking. Introductory speeches should be well researched, brief, and attuned to the audience's needs and interests. Introductory speakers should make the main speaker sincerely welcome. Acceptance speeches should include your reaction to the honor or award and its significance, recognition of others who helped you in the achievement, and sincere appreciation and gratitude. Speeches to entertain usually occur after a dinner or banquet. Speakers can laugh with the story and laugh at themselves to connect with the audience.

Discussion

1. When is impromptu speaking likely to occur? Describe the process of giving an impromptu speech. What are some things to avoid?

2. What is a symposium? What are the major considerations for the preparation for a symposium presentation? What are some topics that would work well with this format?

3. How are televised presentations used in business? Have you been involved with producing or presenting a televised performance? How did you prepare?

4. How does televising a presentation affect the content and delivery of the message? Discuss these issues from both the audience's and the speaker's perspective.

5. What are the different types of ceremonial speaking? Discuss preparation and delivery techniques for each.

Activities

1. Give a two-minute presentation in which you respond to a question asked by your instructor. Afterward, review the principles of impromptu speaking discussed in this chapter and assess your own performance.

2. Construct a symposium topic question, and write at least four subtopics for speakers.

3. In this chapter, we mentioned that speakers typically have apprehension about making a presentation that will be broadcast through a televised medium. Write at least five self-negative statements arising from this apprehension that are different from those in this chapter, and then counter each with an appropriate coping line.

4. Pretend your college or university has just named you "Student of the Year" and will honor you at a formal banquet. Give a brief acceptance address that follows the principles discussed in this chapter.

Notes

1. M. M. Bedrosian, *Speak Like a Pro in Business* (New York: Wiley, 1987).
2. For further reference on the topic of television production and televised speaking, the following sources are recommended: S. Hyde, *Television and Radio Announcing* 6th ed. (Boston: Houghton Mifflin, 1990); S. Bension, *Producer's Masterguide, 1990: The International Production Manual for Motion Pictures, Broadcast Television, Commercials, Cable, and Videotape Industries*, 10th ed. (New York: NY Production Manual, 1990); Hyatt Research Corporation Staff, *The Executive's Guide to Network Media* (Fairfax, Va.: DataTrends Publications, 1990).
3. S. Hyde, *Television and Radio Announcing*.

Diversity in the Workplace: The Relationship between Communication and Culture

*A*cross the United States — in school systems, universities, businesses, and government — a heated debate is taking place on the topics of multiculturalism, diversity, and affirmative action. These interrelated issues arise from the fundamental perception that equality of opportunity remains an elusive goal in both the business and academic spheres of American society. To understand the debate from the perspective of business communication, productivity, and employee satisfaction, it is helpful to know the roots of the policy known as *affirmative action*.

Americans traditionally have taken pride in their diversity and their acceptance of new peoples and cultures to the "melting pot" of mainstream society. In reality, however, the more diverse elements in the melting pot are forced either to try to melt down until they resemble the majority of the pot or to leave the pot altogether and all of the benefits and privileges that go with it. As a result, social and economic inequalities have developed along lines of race, gender, and ethnicity. Diversity has often been a handicap rather than an asset.

Affirmative action refers to government policies created in 1961 whose goals were to rectify the injustices and socio-economic inequalities that have accompanied diversity in our society. The policies specifically address the *accessibility* of educational and career opportunities to women and members of minority groups by giving preference to these individuals in matters of hiring and admission. The philosophy underlying affirmative action is that to compensate for the inequalities that have developed in this country over hundreds of years, preferential treatment should be given to members of disadvantaged groups. Achieving the long-term goal of a more just and equal society requires the use of inherently unequal measures in the short run.

As a student, you may have encountered a similar debate on the subject of a multicultural curriculum. On the surface, the issue appears to be relatively simple. Advocates of multiculturalism believe that achieving true tolerance and acceptance of different people requires an understanding of their lifestyle, values, and history, especially as learned through courses that emphasize these topics. But the decision to implement new courses of study has raised questions, such as "Will traditional knowledge and values be sacrificed in exchange for a multicultural curriculum?" "Will institutions relax their standards in the quest for multiculturalism?" "Will students begin to lack an understanding of their common American culture and heritage?"

As advocates on each side push for agendas rather than understanding, the constructive debate is reduced to labels, lists, and ultimately limitations for both the traditional studies and the multicultural programs. Ultimately, affirmative action and multiculturalism (because they look to correct the past rather than build for the future) cannot by themselves achieve the simultaneous equality *and* quality necessary for excellence.

While the problems of affirmative action are undergoing serious scrutiny, the more important question (according to R. Roosevelt Thomas) has been neglected: How can businesses adapt their communication styles and cultures to make the most of their diverse work forces? The major shortcoming of affirmative action is that its policies are aimed at tangibles, such as percentages, promotions, and titles, rather than intangibles, such as access to networks, ease of communication, or conflicts in communication styles. Weak communication skills — either underdeveloped or nonexistent — frequently result in the perception of diversity as a struggle between "us" and "them".

The communication breakdown poses several dangers. Because affirmative action involves emphasis on the interests of minority groups, an accompanying lack of communication further marginalizes them and sets them in opposition to the majority. The result is a sense of hostility between those who benefit from affirmative action and those who do not instead of a climate of mutual support and collaboration.

Viewing co-workers and managers in terms of "us" and "them" also tends to oversimplify and obscure many of the issues specific to individual people. Regardless of their ethnic backgrounds, employees' unique needs and individual characteristics mean that they respond differently to amounts and kinds of support. Affirmative action policies alone that do not successfully counteract the "us" versus "them" mentality cannot take these specifics into account.

The challenge for academics and businesspeople alike is to find an appropriate balance — based on strong and effective communication — before dissensions tear educational systems and workforce relations apart. In business, Thomas proposes, this can be accomplished through a strong commitment to the process of "managing diversity." Managing diversity includes affirmative action but is broader and more far-sighted in scope, because it focuses on the potential of individual employees rather than the fact of their ethnic or sexual status. Women and members of minority groups do not reach their potential by successfully conforming to a system but by being given the power to help shape the system through their distinct contributions.

Managing diversity includes reflecting honestly on opinions, behaviors, values and stereotypes regarding the people around us and communicating respect and openness rather than defensive attitudes toward "others." Communication skills are the key to addressing this challenge. As you read the following article, think about the role communication plays in successfully managing (and taking part in) a work force made up of many people from widely varied backgrounds.

The article and discussion questions are meant to serve only as a starting point for your own consideration of how these issues affect you now and later in your career. There are no "answers" to the questions raised by issues of diversity, and no set solutions to communication problems that can be applied to entire groups. Learning to think critically about how individual and group characteristics affect communication is the starting point for real progress.

FROM AFFIRMATIVE ACTION TO AFFIRMING DIVERSITY

by R. Roosevelt Thomas, Jr.

Sooner or later, affirmative action will die a natural death. Its achievements have been stupendous, but if we look at the premises that underlie it, we find assumptions and priorities that look increasingly shopworn. Thirty years ago, affirmative action was invented on the basis of these five appropriate premises:

1. Adult, white males make up something called the U.S. business mainstream.

2. The U.S. economic edifice is a solid, unchanging institution with more than enough space for everyone.

3. Women, blacks, immigrants, and other minorities should be allowed in as a matter of public policy and common decency.

4. Widespread racial, ethnic, and sexual prejudice keeps them out.

5. Legal and social coercion are necessary to bring about the change.

Today all five of these premises need revising. Over the past six years, I have tried to help some 15 companies learn how to achieve and manage diversity, and I have seen that the realities facing us are no longer the realities affirmative action was designed to fix.

To begin with, more than half the U.S. work force now consists of minorities, immigrants, and women, so white, native-born males, though undoubtedly still dominant, are themselves a statistical minority. In addition, white males will make up only 15% of the increase in the work force over the next ten years. The so-called mainstream is now almost as diverse as the society at large.

Second, while the edifice is still big enough for all, it no longer seems stable, massive, and invulnerable. In fact, American corporations are scrambling, doing their best to become more adaptable, to compete more successfully for markets and labor, foreign and domestic, and to attract all the talent they can find. (See the inserts for what a number of U.S. companies are doing to manage diversity.)

Third, women and minorities no longer need a boarding pass, they need an upgrade. The problem is not getting them in at the entry level; the problem is making better use of their potential at every level, especially in middle-management and leadership positions. This is no longer simply a question of common decency, it is a question of business survival.

Fourth, although prejudice is hardly dead, it

Out of the Numbers Game and into Decision Making

Like many other companies, Avon practiced affirmative action in the 1970s and was not pleased with the results. The company worked with employment agencies that specialized in finding qualified minority hires, and it cultivated contacts with black and minority organizations on college campuses. Avon wanted to see its customer base reflected in its work force, especially at the decision-making level. But while women moved up the corporate ladder fairly briskly — not so surprising in a company whose work force is mostly female — minorities did not. So in 1984, the company began to change its policies and practices.

"We really wanted to get out of the numbers game," says Marcia Worthing, the corporate vice president for human resources. "We felt it was more important to have five minority people tied into the decision-making process than ten who were just heads to count."

First, Avon initiated awareness training at all levels. "The key to recruiting, retaining, and promoting minorities is not the human resource department," says Worthing. "It's getting line management to buy into the idea. We had to do more than change behavior. We had to change attitudes."

Second, the company formed a Multicultural Participation Council that meets regularly to oversee the process of managing diversity. The group includes Avon's CEO and high-level employees from throughout the company.

Third, in conjunction with the American Institute for Managing Diversity, Avon developed a diversity training program. For several years, the company has sent racially and ethnically diverse groups of 25 managers at a time to Institute headquarters at Morehouse College in Atlanta, where they spend three weeks confronting their differnces and learning to hear and avail themselves of viewpoints they initially disagreed with. "We came away disciples of diversity," says one company executive.

Fourth, the company helped three minority groups — blacks, Hispanics, and Asians — form networks that crisscrossed the corporation in all 50 states. Each network elects its own leaders and has an adviser from senior management. In addition, the networks have representatives on the Multicultural Participation Council, where they serve as a conduit for employee views on diversity issues facing management.

has suffered some wounds that may eventually prove fatal. In the meantime, American businesses are now filled with progressive people — many of them minorities and women themselves — whose prejudices, where they still exist, are much too deeply suppressed to interfere with recruitment. The reason many companies are still wary of minorities and women *has much more to do with education and perceived qualifications than with color or gender.* Companies are worried about productivity and well aware that minorities and women represent a disproportionate share of the undertrained and undereducated.

Fifth, coercion is rarely needed at the recruitment stage. There are very few places in the United States today where you could dip a recruitment net and come up with nothing but white males. Getting hired is not the problem — women and blacks who are seen as having the necessary skills and energy can get *into* the work force relatively easily. It's later on that many of them plateau and lose their drive and quit or get fired. It's later on that their managers' inability to manage diversity hobbles them and the companies they work for.

In creating these changes, affirmative action had an essential role to play and played it very well. In many companies and communities it still plays that role. But affirmative action is an artificial, transitional intervention intended to give managers a chance to correct an imbalance, an injustice, a mistake. Once the numbers mistake has been corrected, I don't think affirmative action alone can cope with the remaining long-term task of creating a work setting geared to the upward mobility of *all* kinds of people, including white males. It is difficult for affirmative action to influence upward mobility even in the short run, primarily because it is perceived to conflict with the meritocracy we favor. For this reason, affirmative action is a red flag to every individual who feels unfairly passed over and a stigma for those who appear to be its beneficiaries.

Moreover, I doubt very much that individuals who reach top positions through affirmative action are effective models for younger members of their race or sex. What, after all, do they model? A black vice president who got her job through affirmative action is not necessarily a model of how to rise through the corporate meritocracy. She may be a model of how affirmative action can work for the people who find or put themselves in the right place at the right time.

If affirmative action in upward mobility meant that no person's competence and character would ever be overlooked or undervalued on account of race, sex, ethnicity, origins, or physical disability, then affirmative action would be the very thing we need to let every corporate talent find its niche. But what affirmative action means in practice is an unnatural focus on one group, and what it means too often to too many employees is that someone is playing fast and loose with standards in order to favor that group. Unless we are to compromise our standards, a thing no competitive company can even contemplate, upward mobility for minorities and women should always be a question of pure competence and character unmuddled by accidents of birth.

And that is precisely why we have to learn to manage diversity — to move beyond affirmative action, not to repudiate it. Some of what I have to say may strike some readers — mostly those with an ax to grind — as directed at the majority white males who hold most of the decision-making posts in our economy. But I am speaking to all managers, not just white males, and I certainly don't mean to suggest that white males somehow stand outside diversity. White males are as odd and as normal as anyone else.

The Affirmative Action Cycle

If you are managing diverse employees, you should ask yourself this question: Am I fully tapping the potential capacities of everyone in my department? If the answer is no, you should ask yourself this follow-up: Is this failure hampering my ability to meet performance standards? The answer to this question will undoubtedly be yes.

Think of corporate management for a moment as an engine burning pure gasoline. What's now going into the tank is no longer just gas, it has an increasing percentage of, let's say, methanol. In the beginning, the engine will still work pretty well, but by and by it will start to sputter, and eventually it will stall. Unless we rebuild the engine, it will no longer burn the fuel we're feeding it. As the work force grows more and more diverse at the intake level, the talent pool we have to draw on for supervision and management will also grow increasingly diverse. So the question is: Can we burn this fuel? Can we get maximum corporate power from the diverse work force we're now drawing into the system?

Affirmative action gets blamed for failing to do things it never could do. Affirmative action gets the new fuel into the tank, the new people through the front door. Something else will have to get them into the driver's seat. That something else consists of enabling people, in this case minorities and women, to perform to their potential. This is what we now call managing diversity. Not appreciating or leveraging diversity, not even necessarily understanding it. Just managing diversity in such a way as to get from a heterogeneous work force the same productivity, commitment, quality, and profit that we got from the old homogeneous work force.

The correct question today is not "How are we doing on race relations?" or "Are we promoting enough minority people and women?" but rather "Given the diverse work force I've got, am I getting the productivity, does it work as smoothly, is morale as high, as if every person in the company was the same sex and race and nationality?" Most answers will be, "Well, no, of course not!" But why shouldn't the answer be, "You bet!"?

When we ask how we're doing on race relations, we inadvertently put our finger on what's wrong with the question and with the attitude that underlies affirmative action. So long as racial and gender equality is something we grant to minorities and women, there will be no racial and gender equality. What we must do is create an environment where no one is advantaged or disadvantaged, an environment where "we" is everyone. What the traditional approach to diversity did was to create a cycle of crisis, action, relaxation, and disappointment that companies repeated over and over again without ever achieving more than the barest particle of what they were after.

Affirmative action pictures the work force as a pipeline and reasons as follows: "If we can fill the pipeline with *qualified* minorities and women, we can solve our upward mobility problem. Once recruited, they will perform in accordance with our promotional criteria and move naturally up our regular developmental ladder. In the past, where minorities and women have failed to progress, they were simply unable to meet our performance standards. Recruiting qualified people will enable us to avoid special programs and reverse discrimination."

This pipeline perspective generates a self-perpetuating, self-defeating, recruitment-oriented cycle with six stages:

1. *Problem Recognition.* The first time through the cycle, the problem takes this form — We need more minorities and women in the pipeline. In later iterations, the problem is more likely to be defined as a need to retain and promote minorities and women.

2. *Intervention.* Management puts the company into what we may call an Affirmative Action Recruitment Mode. During the first cycle, the goal is to recruit minorities and women. Later, when the cycle is repeated a second or third time and the challenge has shifted to retention, development, and promotion, the goal is to recruit *qualified* minorities and women.

"It Simply Makes Good Business Sense."

Corning characterizes its 1970s affirmative action program as a form of legal compliance. The law dictated affirmative action and morality required it, so the company did its best to hire minorities and women.

The ensuing cycle was classic: recruitment, confidence, disappointment, embarrassment, crisis, more recruitment. Talented women and blacks joined the company only to plateau or resign. Few reached upper management levels, and no one could say exactly why.

Then James R. Houghton took over as CEO in 1983 and made the diverse work force one of Corning's three top priorities, alongside Total Quality and a higher return on equity. His logic was twofold:

First of all, the company had higher attrition rates for minorities and women than for white males, which meant that investments in training and development were being wasted. Second, he believed that the Corning work force should more closely mirror the Corning customer base.

In order to break the cycle of recruitment and subsequent frustration, the company established two quality improvement teams headed by senior executives, one for black progress and one for women's progress. Mandatory awareness training was introduced for some 7,000 salaried employees — a day and a half for gender awareness, two-and-a-half days for racial awareness. One goal of the training is to identify unconscious company values that work against minorities and women. For example, a number of awareness groups reached the conclusion that working late had so much symbolic value that managers tended to look more at the quantity than at the quality of time spent on the job, with predictably negative effects on employees with dependent-care responsibilities.

The company also made an effort to improve communications by printing regular stories and articles about the diverse work force in its in-house newspaper and by publicizing employee success stories that emphasize diversity. It worked hard to identify and publicize promotion criteria. Career planning systems were introduced for all employees.

With regard to recruitment, Corning set up a nationwide scholarship program that provides renewable grants of $5,000 per year of college in exchange for a summer of paid work at some Corning installation. A majority of program participants have come to work for Corning full-time after graduation, and very few have left the company so far, though the program has been in place only four years.

The company also expanded its summer intern program, with an emphasis on minorities and women, and established formal recruiting contacts with campus groups like the Society of Women Engineers and the National Black MBA Association.

Corning sees its efforts to manage diversity not only as a social and moral issue but also as a question of efficiency and competitiveness. In the words of Mr. Houghton, "It simply makes good business sense."

Sometimes, managers indifferent or blind to possible accusations of reverse discrimination will institute special training, tracking, incentive, mentoring, or sponsoring programs for minorities and women.

3. *Great Expectations*. Large numbers of minorities and women have been recruited, and a select group has been promoted or recruited at a higher level to serve as highly visible role models for the newly recruited masses. The

---

Turning Social Pressures into Competitive Advantage

Like most other companies trying to respond to the federal legislation of the 1970s, Digital started off by focusing on numbers. By the early 1980s, however, company leaders could see it would take more than recruitment to make Digital the diverse workplace they wanted it to be. Equal Employment Opportunity (EEO) and affirmative action seemed too exclusive — too much "white males doing good deeds for minorities and women." The company wanted to move beyond these programs to the kind of environment where every employee could realize his or her potential, and Digital decided that meant an environment where individual differences were not tolerated but valued, even celebrated.

The resulting program and philosophy, called Valuing Differences, has two components:

First, the company helps people get in touch with their stereotypes and false assumptions through what Digital calls Core Groups. These voluntary groupings of eight to ten people work with company-trained facilitators whose job is to encourage discussion and self-development and in the company's words, "to keep people safe" as they struggle with their prejudices. Digital also runs a voluntary two-day training program called "Understanding the Dynamics of Diversity," which thousands of Digital employees have now taken.

Second, the company has named a number of senior managers to various Cultural Boards of Directors and Valuing Differences Boards of Directors. These bodies promote openness to individual differences, encourage younger managers committed to the goal of diversity, and sponsor frequent celebrations of racial, gender, and ethnic differences such as Hispanic Heritage Week and Black History Month.

In addition to the Valuing Differences program, the company preserved its EEO and affirmative action functions. Valuing Differences focuses on personal and group development, EEO on legal issues, and affirmative action on systemic change. According to Alan Zimmerle, head of the Valuing Differences program, EEO and Valuing Differences are like two circles that touch but don't overlap — the first representing the legal need for diversity, the second the corporate desire for diversity. Affirmative action is a third circle that overlaps the other two and holds them together with policies and procedures.

Together, these three circles can transform legal and social pressures into the competitive advantage of a more effective work force, higher morale, and the reputation of being a better place to work. As Zimmerle puts it, "Digital wants to be the employer of choice. We want our pick of the talent that's out there."

stage seems set for the natural progression of minorities and women up through the pipeline. Management leans back to enjoy the fruits of its labor.

4. *Frustration.* The anticipated natural progression fails to occur. Minorities and women see themselves plateauing prematurely. Management is upset (and embarrassed) by the failure of its affirmative action initiative and begins to resent the impatience of the new recruits and their unwillingness to give the company credit for trying to do the right thing. Depending on how high in the hierarchy they have plateaued, alienated minorities and women either leave the company or stagnate.

5. *Dormancy.* All remaining participants conspire tacitly to present a silent front to the outside world. Executives say nothing because they have no solutions. As for those women and minorities who stayed on, calling attention to affirmative action's failures might raise doubts about their qualifications. Do they deserve their jobs, or did they just happen to be in the right place at the right time of an affirmative action push? So no one complains, and if the company has a good public relations department, it may even wind up with a reputation as a good place for women and minorities to work.

If questioned publicly, management will say things like "Frankly, affirmative action is not currently an issue," or "Our numbers are okay," or "With respect to minority representation at the upper levels, management is aware of this remaining challenge."

In private and off the record, however, people say things like "Premature plateauing is a problem, and we don't know what to do," and "Our top people don't seem to be interested in finding a solution," and "There's plenty of racism and sexism around this place — whatever you may hear."

6. *Crisis.* Dormancy can continue indefinitely, but it is usually broken by a crisis of competitive pressure, governmental intervention, external pressure from a special interest group, or internal unrest. One company found that its pursuit of a Total Quality program was hampered by the alienation of minorities and women. Senior management at another corporation saw the growing importance of minorities in their customer base and decided they needed minority participation in their managerial ranks. In another case, growing expressions of discontent forced a break in the conspiracy of silence even after the company had received national recognition as a good place for minorities and women to work.

Whatever its cause, the crisis fosters a return to the Problem Recognition phase, and the cycle begins again. This time, management seeks to explain the shortcomings of the previous affirmative action push and usually concludes that the problem is recruitment. This assessment by a top executive is typical: "The managers I know are decent people. While they give priority to performance, I do not believe any of them deliberately block minorities or women who are qualified for promotion. On the contrary, I suspect they bend over backward to promote women and minorities who give some indication of being qualified.

"However, they believe we simply do not have the necessary talent within those groups, but because of the constant complaints they have heard about their deficiencies in affirmative action, they feel they face a no-win situation. If they do not promote, they are obstructionists. But if they promote people who are unqualified, they hurt performance and deny promotion to other employees unfairly. They can't win. The answer, in my mind, must be an ambitious new recruitment effort to bring in quality people."

And so the cycle repeats. Once again blacks, Hispanics, women, and immigrants are dropped into a previously homogeneous, all-white, all-Anglo, all-male, all native-born environment, and the burden of cultural change is placed on the newcomers. There will be new expectations and a new round of frustration, dormancy, crisis, and recruitment.

Ten Guidelines for Learning to Manage Diversity

The traditional American image of diversity has been assimilation: the melting pot, where ethnic and racial differences were standardized into a kind of American puree. Of course, the melting pot is only a metaphor. In real life, many ethnic and most racial groups retain their individuality and express it energetically. What we have is perhaps some kind of American mulligan stew; it is certainly no puree.

At the workplace, however, the melting pot has been more than a metaphor. Corporate success has demanded a good deal of conformity, and employees have voluntarily abandoned most of their ethnic distinctions at the company door.

Now those days are over. Today the melting pot is the wrong metaphor even in business, for three good reasons. First, if it ever was possible to melt down Scotsmen and Dutchmen and Frenchmen into an indistinguishable broth, you can't to the same with blacks, Asians, and women. Their differences don't melt so easily. Second, most people are no longer willing to be melted down, not even for eight hours a day — and it's a seller's market for skills. Third, the thrust of today's nonhierarchical, flexible, collaborative management requires a ten- or twentyfold increase in our tolerance for individuality.

So companies are faced with the problem of surviving in a fiercely competitive world with a work force that consists and will continue to consist of *unassimilated diversity*. And the engine will take a great deal of tinkering to burn that fuel.

What managers fear from diversity is a lowering of standards, a sense that "anything goes." Of course, standards must not suffer. In fact, competence counts more than ever. The goal is to manage diversity in such a way as to get from a diverse work force the same productivity we once got from a homogeneous work force, and to do it without artificial programs, standards — or barriers.

Managing diversity does not mean controlling or containing diversity, it means enabling every member of your work force to perform to his or her potential. It means getting from employees, first, everything we have a right to expect, and, second — if we do it well — everything they have to give. If the old homogeneous work force performed dependably at 80% of its capacity, then the first result means getting 80% from the new heterogeneous work force too. But the second result, the icing on the cake, the unexpected upside that diversity can perhaps give as a bonus, means 85% to 90% from everyone in the organization.

For the moment, however, let's concentrate on the basics of how to get satisfactory performance from the new diverse work force. There are few adequate models. So far, no large company I know of has succeeded in managing diversity to its own satisfaction. But any number have begun to try.

On the basis of their experience, here are my ten guidelines:

1. *Clarify Your Motivation.* A lot of executives are not sure why they should want to learn to manage diversity. Legal compliance seems like a good reason. So does community relations. Many executives believe they have a social and moral responsibility to employ minorities and women. Others want to placate an internal group or pacify an outside organization. None of these are bad reasons, but none of them are business reasons, and given the nature and scope of today's competitive challenges, I believe only business reasons will supply the necessary long-term motivation. In any case, it is the business reasons I want to focus on here.

In business terms, a diverse work force is not something your company ought to have; it's

Discovering Complexity and Value in P&G's Diversity

Because Procter & Gamble fills its upper level management positions only from within the company, it places a premium on recruiting the best available entry-level employees. Campus recruiting is pursued nationwide and year-round by line managers from all levels of the company. Among other things, the company has made a concerted — and successful — effort to find and hire talented minorities and women.

Finding first-rate hires is only one piece of the effort, however. There is still the challenge of moving diversity upward. As one top executive put, "We know that we can only succeed as a company if we have an environment that makes it easy for all of us, not just some of us, to work to our potential."

In May 1988, P&G formed a Corporate Diversity Strategy Task Force to clarify the concept of diversity, define its impotance for the company, and identify strategies for making progress toward successfully managing a diverse work force.

The task force, composed of men and women from every corner of the company, made two discoveries: First, diversity at P&G was far more complex than most people had supposed. In addition to race and gender, it included factors such as cultural heritage, personal background, and functional experience. Second, the company needed to expand its view of the value of differences.

The task force helped the company to see that learning to manage diversity would be a long-term process of organizational change. For example, P&G has offered voluntary diversity training at all levels since the 1970s, but the program has gradually broadened its emphasis on race and gender awareness to include the value of self-realization in a diverse environment. As retiring board chairman John Smale put it, "If we can tap the total contribution that everybody in our company has to offer, we will be better and more competitive in everything we do."

P&G is now conducting a thorough, continuing evaluation of all management programs to be sure that systems are working well for everyone. It has also carried out a corporate survey to get a better picture of the problems facing P&G employees who are balancing work and family responsibilities and to improve company programs in such areas as dependent care.

---

something your company does have, or soon will have. Learning to manage that diversity will make you more competitive.

2. *Clarify Your Vision.* When managers think about a diverse work force, what do they picture? Not publicly, but in the privacy of their minds?

One popular image is of minorities and women clustering on a relatively low plateau, with a few of them trickling up as they become assimilated into the prevailing culture. Of course, they enjoy good salaries and benefits, and most of them accept their status, appreciate the fact that they are doing better than they could do somewhere else, and are proud of the achievements of their race or sex. This is reactionary thinking, but it's a lot more common than you might suppose.

Another image is what we might call "heightened sensitivity." Members of the majority culture are sensitive to the demands of minorities and women for upward mobility and recognize the advantages of fully utilizing them. Minorities and women work at all levels of the corporation, but they are the recipients of generosity and know it. A few years of this second-class status drives most of them away and compromises the effectiveness of those that remain. Turnover is high.

Then there is the coexistence-compromise image. In the interests of corporate viability, white males agree to recognize minorities and women as equals. They bargain and negotiate their differences. But the win-lose aspect of the relationship preserves tensions, and the compromises reached are not always to the company's competitive advantage.

"Diversity and equal opportunity" is a big step up. It presupposes that the white male culture has given way to one that respects difference and individuality. The problem is that minorities and women will accept it readily as their operating image, but many white males, consciously or unconsciously, are likely to cling to a vision that leaves them in the driver's seat. A vision gap of this kind can be a difficulty.

In my view, the vision to hold in your own imagination and to try to communicate to all your managers and employees is an image of fully tapping the human resource potential of every member of the work force. This vision sidesteps the question of equality, ignores the tensions of coexistence, plays down the uncomfortable realities of difference, and focuses instead on individual enablement. It doesn't say, "Let *us* give *them* a chance." It assumes a diverse work force that includes us and them. It says, "Let's create an environment where everyone will do their best work."

Several years ago, an industrial plant in Atlanta with a highly diverse work force was threatened with closing unless productivity improved. To save their jobs, everyone put their shoulders to the wheel and achieved the results they needed to stay open. The senior operating manager was amazed.

For years he had seen minorities and women plateauing disproportionately at the lower levels of the organization, and he explained that fact away with two rationalizations. "They haven't been here that long," he told himself. And "This is the price we pay for being in compliance with the law."

When the threat of closure energized this whole group of people into a level of performance he had not imagined possible, he got one fleeting glimpse of people working up to their capacity. Once the crisis was over, everyone went back to the earlier status quo — white males driving and everyone else sitting back, looking on — but now there was a difference. Now, as he put it himself, he had been to the mountaintop. He knew that what he was getting from minorities and women was nowhere near what they were capable of giving. And he wanted it, crisis or no crisis, all the time.

3. *Expand Your Focus.* Managers usually see affirmative action and equal employment opportunity as centering on minorities and women, with very little to offer white males. The diversity I'm talking about includes not only race, gender, creed, and ethnicity but also age, background, education, function, and personality differences. *The objective is not to assimilate minorities and women into a dominant white male culture but to create a dominant heterogeneous culture.*

The culture that dominates the United States socially and politically is heterogeneous, and it works by giving its citizens the liberty to achieve their potential. Channeling that potential, once achieved, is an individual right but still a national concern. Something similar applies in the workplace, where the keys to success are individual ability and a corporate destination. Managing disparate talents to achieve common goals is what companies learned to do when they set their sights on, say,

The Daily Experience of Genuine Workplace Diversity

Chairman David T. Kearns believes that a firm and resolute commitment to affirmative action is the first and most important step to work force diversity. "Xerox is committed to affirmative action," he says. "It is a corporate value, a management priority, and a formal business objective."

Xerox began recruiting minorities and women systematically as far back as the mid-1960s, and it pioneered such concepts as pivotal jobs (described later). The company's approach emphasizes behavior expectations as opposed to formal consciousness-raising programs because, as one Xerox executive put it, "It's just not realistic to think that a day and a half of training will change a person's thinking after 30 or 40 years."

On the assumption that attitude changes will grow from the daily experience of genuine workplace diversity, the Xerox Balanced Work Force Strategy sets goals for the number of minorities and women in each division and at every level. (For example, the goal for the top 300 executive-level jobs in one large division is 35% women by 1995, compared with 15% today.) "You *must* have a laboratory to work in," says Ted Payne, head of Xerox's Office of Affirmative Action and Equal Opportunity.

Minority and women's employee support groups have grown up in more than a dozen locations with the company's encourage-

ment. But Xerox depends mainly on the three pieces of its balanced strategy to make diversity work.

First are the goals. Xerox sets recruitment and representation goals in accordance with federal guidelines and reviews them constantly to make sure they reflect work force demographics. Any company with a federal contract is required to make this effort. But Xerox then extends the guidelines by setting diversity goals for its upper level jobs and holding division and group managers accountable for reaching them.

The second piece is a focus on pivotal jobs, a policy Xerox adopted in the 1970s when it first noticed that minorities and women did not have the upward mobility the company wanted to see. By examining the backgrounds of top executives, Xerox was able to identify the key positions that all successful managers had held at lower levels and to set goals for getting minorities and women assigned to such jobs.

The third piece is an effort to concentrate managerial training not so much on managing diversity as on just plain managing people. What the company discovered when it began looking at managerial behavior toward minorities and women was that all too many managers didn't know enough about how to manage anyone, let alone people quite different from themselves.

Total Quality. The secrets of managing diversity are much the same.

4. *Audit Your Corporate Culture.* If the goal is not to assimilate diversity into the dominant culture but *rather to build a culture that can*

digest unassimilated diversity, then you had better start by figuring out what your present culture looks like. Since what we're talking about here is the body of unspoken and unexamined assumptions, values, and mythologies that make your world go round, this kind of cultural audit is impossible to conduct without outside help. It's a research activity, done mostly with in-depth interviews and a lot of listening at the water cooler.

The operative corporate assumptions you have to identify and deal with are often inherited from the company's founder. "If we treat everyone as a member of the family, we will be successful" is not uncommon. Nor is its corollary "Father Knows Best."

Another widespread assumption, probably absorbed from American culture in general, is that "cream will rise to the top." In most companies, what passes for cream rising to the top is actually cream being pulled or pushed to the top by an informal system of mentoring and sponsorship.

Corporate culture is a kind of tree. Its roots are asssumptions about the company and about the world. Its branches, leaves, and seeds are behavior. You can't change the leaves without changing the roots, and you can't grow peaches on an oak. Or rather, with the proper grafting, you *can* grow peaches on an oak, but they come out an awful lot like acorns — small and hard and not much fun to eat. So if you want to grow peaches, you have to make sure the tree's roots are peach friendly.

5. *Modify Your Assumptions.* The real problem with this corporate culture tree is that every time you go to make changes in the roots, you run into terrible opposition. Every culture, including corporate culture, has root guards that turn out in force every time you threaten a basic assumption.

Take the family assumption as an example. Viewing the corporation as a family suggests not only that father knows best; it also suggests that sons will inherit the business, that daughters should stick to doing the company dishes, and that if Uncle Deadwood doesn't perform, we'll put him in the chimney corner and feed him for another 30 years regardless. Each assumption has its consituency and its defenders.

If we say to Uncle Deadwood, "Yes, you did good work for 10 years, but years 11 and 12 look pretty bleak; we think it's time we helped you find another chimney," shock waves will travel through the company as every family-oriented employee draws a sword to defend the sacred concept of guaranteed jobs.

But you have to try. A corporation that wants to create an environment with no advantages or disadvantages for any group cannot allow the family assumption to remain in place. It must be labeled dishonest mythology.

Sometimes the dishonesties are more blatant. When I asked a white male middle manager how promotions were handled in his company, he said, "You need leadership capability, bottom-line results, the ability to work with people, and compassion." Then he paused and smiled. "That's what they say. But down the hall there's a guy we call Captain Kickass. He's ruthless, mean-spirited, and he steps on people. That's the behavior they really value. Forget what they say."

In additon to the obvious issue of hypocrisy, this example also raises a question of equal opportunity. When I asked this young middle manager if he thought minorities and women could meet the Captain Kickass standard, he said he thought they probably could. But the opposite argument can certainly be made. Whether we're talking about blacks in an environment that is predominantly white, whites in one predominantly black, or women in one predominantly male, *the majority culture will not readily condone such tactics from a member of a minority.* So the corporation with the unspoken kickass performance standard has at least one criterion that will hamper the upward mobility of minorities and women.

Another destructive assumption is the melting pot I referred to earlier. The organization I'm arguing for respects differences rather than seeking to smooth them out. It is multicultural rather than culture blind, which has an important consequence: When we no longer force people to "belong" to a common ethnicity or culture, then the organization's leaders must work all the harder to define belonging in terms of a set of values and a sense of purpose that transcend the interests, desires, and preferences of any one group.

6. *Modify Your Systems.* Thefirst purpose of examining and modifying assumptions is to modify systems. Promotion, mentoring, and sponsorship comprise one such system, and the unexamined cream-to-the-top assumption I mentioned earlier can tend to keep minorities and women from climbing the corporate ladder. After all, in many companies it is difficult to secure a promotion above a certain level without a personal advocate or sponsor. In the context of managing diversity, the question is not whether this system is maximally efficient but whether it works for all employees. Executives who only sponsor people like themselves are not making much of a contribution to the cause of getting the best from every employee.

Performance appraisal is another system where unexamined practices and patterns can have pernicious effects. For example, there are companies where official performance appraisals differ substantially from what is said informally, with the result that employees get their most accurate performance feedback through the grapevine. So if the grapevine is closed to minorities and women, they are left at a severe disadvantage. As one white manager observed, "If the blacks around here knew how they were really perceived, there would be a revolt." Maybe so. More important to your business, however, is the fact that without an accurate appraisal of performance, minority and women employees will find it difficult to correct or defend their alleged shortcomings.

7. *Modify Your Models.* The second purpose of modifying assumptions is to modify models of managerial and employee behavior. My own personal hobgoblin is one I call the Doer Model, often an outgrowth of the family assumption and of unchallenged paternalism. I have found the Doer Model alive and thriving in a dozen companies. It works like this:

Since father knows best, managers seek subordinates who will follow their lead and do as they do. If they can't find people exactly like themselves, they try to find people who aspire to be exactly like themselves. The goal is predictability and immediate responsiveness because the doer manager is not there to manage people but to do the business. In accounting departments, for example, doer managers do accounting, and subordinates are simply extensions of their hands and minds, sensitive to every signal and suggestion of managerial intent.

Doer managers take pride in this identity of purpose. "I wouldn't ask my people to do anything I wouldn't do myself," they say. "I roll up my sleeves and get in the trenches." Doer managers love to be in the trenches. It keeps them out of the line of fire.

But managers aren't supposed to be in the trenches, and accounting managers aren't supposed to do accounting. What they are supposed to do is create systems and a climate that allow accountants to do accounting, a climate that enables people to do what they've been charged to do. The right goal is doer subordinates, supported and empowered by managers who manage.

8. *Help Your People Pioneer.* Learning to manage diversity is a change process, and the managers involved are change agents. There is no single tried and tested "solution" to diversity and no fixed right way to manage it. Assuming the existence of a single or even a dominant barrier undervalues the importance of all the other barriers that face any company, including, potentially, prejudice, personality, community dynamics, culture, and the ups and downs of business itself.

While top executives articulate the new company policy and their commitment to it, middle managers — most or all of them still white males, remember — are placed in the tough position of having to cope with a forest of problems and simultaneouly develop the minorities and women who represent their own competiton for an increasingly limited number of promotions. What's more, every time they stumble they will themselves be labeled the major barriers to progress. These managers need help, they need a certain amount of sympathy, and, most of all, perhaps, they need to be told that they are pioneers and judged accordingly.

In one case, an ambitious young black woman was assigned to a white male manager, at his request, on the basis of her excellent company record. They looked forward to working together, and for the first three months, everything went well. But then their relationship began to deteriorate, and the harder they worked at patching it up, the worse it got. Both of them, along with their superiors, were surprised by the conflict and seemed puzzled as to its causes. Eventually, the black woman requested and obtained reassignment. But even though they escaped each other, both suffered a sense of failure severe enough to threaten their careers.

What could have been done to assist them? Well, empathy would not have hurt. But perspective would have been better yet. In their particular company and situation, these two people had placed themselves at the cutting edge of race and gender relations. They needed to know that mistakes at the cutting edge are different — and potentially more valuable — than mistakes elsewhere. Maybe they needed some kind of pioneer training. But at the very least they needed to be told that they were pioneers, that conflicts and failures came with the territory, and that they would be judged accordingly.

9. *Apply the Special Consideration Test.* I said earlier that affirmative action was an artificial, transitional, but necessary stage on the road to a truly diverse work force. Because of its artificial nature, affirmative action requires constant attention and drive to make it work.

The point of learning once and for all how to manage diversity is that all that energy can be focused somewhere else.

There is a simple test to help you spot the diversity programs that are going to eat up enormous quantities of time and effort. Surprisingly, perhaps, it is the same test you might use to identify the programs and policies that created your problem in the first place. The test consists of one question: Does this program, policy, or principle give special consideration to one group? Will it contribute to everyone's success, or will it only produce an advantage for blacks or whites or women or men? Is it designed for *them* as opposed to *us*? Whenever the answer is yes, you're not yet on the road to managing diversity.

This does not rule out the possibility of addressing issues that relate to a single group. It only underlines the importance of determining that the issue you're addressing does not relate to other groups as well. For example, management in one company noticed that blacks were not moving up in the organization. Before instituting a special program to bring them along, managers conducted interviews to see if they could find the reason for the impasse. What blacks themselves reported was a problem with the quality of supervision. Further interviews showed that other employees too — including white males — were concerned about the quality of supervision and felt that little was being done to foster professional development. Correcting the situation eliminated a problem that affected everyone. In this case, a solution that focused only on blacks would have been out of place.

Had the problem consisted of prejudice, on the other hand, or some other barrier to blacks or minorities alone, a solution based on affirmative action would have been perfectly appropriate.

10. *Continue Affirmative Action.* Let me come full circle. The ability to manage diversity is the ability to manage your company without

unnatural advantage or disadvantage for any member of your diverse work force. The fact remains that you must first have a work force that is diverse at every level, and if you don't, you're going to need affirmative action to get from here to there.

The reason you then want to move beyond affirmative action to managing diversity is because affirmative action fails to deal with the root causes of prejudice and inequality and does little to develop the full potential of every man and woman in the company. In a country seeking competitive advantage in a global economy, the goal of managing diversity is to develop our capacity to accept, incorporate, and empower the diverse human talents of the most diverse nation on earth. It's our reality. We need to make it our strength.

Discussion

1. How does "managing diversity" differ from the legal policies of affirmative action in terms of goals, methods, and implementation?

2. What communication-related factors might prevent women and members of minority groups from advancing in a company whose culture and internal communications reflect the habits or preferences of a traditional homogenous white male workforce? (Also consider the *opposite* situation.)

3. What economic issues (including, but not limited to, communication in business settings) face groups who have experienced discrimination in our society? What are positive and negative aspects of policies (such as affirmative action) that address groups rather than individual employees?

4. In what ways has the issue of diversity affected you personally or those close to you?

5. How does Thomas's approach to managing diversity relate leadership and management as discussed in Chapter 3? What similarities and differences, particularly in relation to communication, can you identify?

6. How might other relationships (such as co-worker or mentoring relationships) besides manager-employee interactions be changed or improved by more open communication among diverse groups of people?

Text Credits

Page 4: From *International Handbook of Corporate Communication* © 1989 by William V. Ruch with permission of McFarland & Company, Inc., Publishers, Jefferson, N.C.; **Pages 4, 5, 6:** Reprinted by permission of Fortune; **Pages 24–25:** Reprinted by permission of Best Western International, Inc.; **Pages 37–38:** From Edwin Locke, et al. "Goal Setting and Task Performance: 1969–1980," *Psychological Bulletin 90*, pp. 125–152 © 1981 by the American Psychological Association. Adapted by permission; **Pages 50–51:** Reprinted by permission of Pacific Bell; **Page 97:** From P. Kearney, T. Plax, V. Richmond, and J. McCroskey, "Power in the Classroom III: Teacher Communication Techniques and Messages," *Communication Education 34*, pp. 19–28 © 1985. Reprinted by permission of the Speech Communication Association and the authors; **Pages 84–85:** Reprinted by permission of United Negro College Fund; **Page 130:** Used by permission of *Communication Education* and the author; **Page 152:** © 1985 by Houghton Mifflin Company. Adapted and reprinted from *The American Heritage Dictionary*, Second College Edition; **Pages 160–161:** Reprinted by permission of Warner-Lambert Co.; **Pages 190–191:** Reprinted by permission of Hewlett-Packard; Reprinted by permission of *Harvard Business Review*. An excerpt from "The Case of the Complaining Customer," by D. Finkelman and T. Goland, *Harvard Business Review 68* (1990) © 1990 by the President and Fellows of Harvard College; all rights reserved; **Page 302:** Adapted from L. Moran and E. Musselwhite, "Self-Directed Workteams: A Lot More Than Just Teamwork" (Paper presented to the national conference of the American Society for Training and Development, Dallas, Texas, 1988. Reprinted by permission of Zenger Miller, Inc.; **Pages 351–352:** From D. A. Infante and A. S. Rancer, "A Conceptualization and Measure of Argumentativeness," *Journal of Personality Assessment* © 1982 in DeWine, Nicotera, and Parry, "Argumentativeness and Aggressiveness: The Flip Side of Gentle Persuasion," *Management Communication Quarterly 4* (1991). Reprinted by permission of Lawrence Erlbaum Associates; **Pages 392–393:** From J. F. Wilson, C. C. Arnold, and M. M. Wertheimer, *Public Speaking as a Liberal Art*, Sixth Edition © 1990. Reprinted by permission of Allyn and Bacon; **Pages 410–411:** From D. Burns, *The Feeling Good Handbook* © 1989. Reprinted by permission of William Morrow; **Page 464:** Reprinted by permission of the author. **Page 194:** Used by permission of *Business Quarterly*; **Page 204:** Adapted from R. S. Goyer, W. C. Redding, and J. T. Rickey, *Interviewing Principles and Techniques* © 1968 by William C. Brown Group. Reprinted by permission; **Page 223:** Reprinted with permission of The American Enterprise Institute for Public Policy Research; **Page 224:** Reprinted by permission of the author; **Page 280:** Moorhead, Gregory and Ricky W. Griffin, *Organizational Behavior*, Second Edition © 1989 by Houghton Mifflin Company. Used with permission; **Pages 288–289:** Reprinted by permission of Ben & Jerry's; **Page 405:** Excerpt from *Nonverbal Communi-*

Photo Credits